BRIDGING THE DIVIDE

A project of the European Centre for Conflict Prevention
in cooperation with
Panorama–The Palestinian Center for the Dissemination of
Democracy and Community Development and the
Harry S. Truman Research Institute for the Advancement of Peace,
Hebrew University of Jerusalem

Financially supported by
the United States Institute of Peace, Cordaid Netherlands,
and the Netherlands Ministry of Foreign Affairs

BRIDGING THE DIVIDE

Peacebuilding in the Israeli-Palestinian Conflict

edited by
Edy Kaufman, Walid Salem,
and Juliette Verhoeven

LYNNE
RIENNER
PUBLISHERS

BOULDER
LONDON

Published in the United States of America in 2006 by
Lynne Rienner Publishers, Inc.
1800 30th Street, Boulder, Colorado 80301
www.rienner.com

and in the United Kingdom by
Lynne Rienner Publishers, Inc.
3 Henrietta Street, Covent Garden, London WC2E 8LU

Library of Congress Cataloging-in-Publication Data
Bridging the divide : peacebuilding in the Israeli-Palestinian conflict / Edy Kaufman,
Walid Salem, and Juliette Verhoeven, editors
(Project of the European Centre for Conflict Prevention)
  Includes bibliographical references and index.
  ISBN-13: 978-1-58826-365-0 (hardcover: alk. paper)
  ISBN-10: 1-58826-365-7 (hardcover: alk. paper)
  ISBN-13: 978-1-58826-390-2 (pbk.: alk. paper)
  ISBN-10: 1-58826-390-8 (pbk.: alk. paper)
  1. Arab-Israeli conflict—1993—Peace. I. Kaufman, Edy. II. Salem, Walid.
III. Verhoeven, Juliette. IV. Title. V. Series.
DS119.76.B745 2006
956.9405'4—dc22

                                                  2006002388

British Cataloguing in Publication Data
A Cataloguing in Publication record for this book
is available from the British Library.

Printed and bound in the United States of America

The paper used in this publication meets the requirements
of the American National Standard for Permanence of
Paper for Printed Library Materials Z39.48-1992.

5 4 3 2 1

Contents

Part 2 Directory

Foreword

Naomi Chazan

The recent history of the century-old Palestinian-Israeli conflict has diverged from most other sustained disputes in one important respect: it has been accompanied by persistent examples of cooperation between the adversaries in an effort to promote a just solution that would enable both peoples to live in peace, safety, and prosperity. During the past two decades the extent and diversity of these attempts have increased significantly. Even today, when the spiral of violence—and with it human suffering, impoverishment, and despair—has escalated to dizzying heights, Palestinians and Israelis continue their common quest for a livable future in their troubled land. The current intifada, which commenced in 2000, like its first predecessor (1987–1993), possesses many of the characteristics of what can best be described as a "talking war."

The peace camp in Israel and Palestine has played a particularly important role during the past decade. Its coalescence in the early1990s laid the foundation for the Oslo process. Its rapid expansion opened the door for a variety of subsequent interactions between different sectors in the Palestinian and Israeli communities. When the ugly specter of violence resurfaced, the perseverance of a core group of activists committed to nonviolence, human dignity, and a just political settlement of the conflict has helped maintain a ray of hope in what has become a bleak and seemingly intractable situation. Despite the palpable weakening of peace activism in both societies, it is still abundantly clear that the reinforcement of peace work is crucial to any future agreement and to eventual reconciliation. This, then, is a history of initial probes, some success, consequent overconfidence, breakdown, and now tentative remobilization.

Peace organizations, however, do not operate in a social or political vacuum. The present Israeli-Palestinian impasse points not only to the breakdown of peace initiatives emanating from civil society, but also to the triumph, at least temporarily, of militant extremists among both Israelis and Palestinians. The extremists have succeeded, through the skillful employment of fears and threats, to silence the moderate majorities in the two communities and to dominate the political agenda. Even though so many more Palestinians and Israelis support a viable two-state solution today than in the past and overwhelming portions of the two publics yearn for a cessation of violence, most have succumbed to the tactical dictates of conflict advocated by the militants and their allies in decisionmaking positions.

The atmosphere of mistrust fomented by the militants has developed a dynamic of its own. Negative stereotypes of the other have been reinforced, fueling further discord. The vicious cycle of misrepresentation, skewed perceptions, and consequent mutual dehumanization has become an integral part of the conflict and a formidable barrier to its resolution.

Inevitably, the preeminence of extremists and their message has sown confusion in the ranks of the peace movement and accentuated the contradictions associated with its efforts in recent years. Ambiguity about the objectives of peace work, its aims, its methods, and its target audiences has set in. The time has come for Palestinians and Israelis to reassess, separately and jointly, past activities and to extract lessons that will be more effective in the future.

This book is a unique, and incredibly courageous, effort by Israeli and Palestinian peace scholars and practitioners to take a critical look at themselves and their activities, to expose and analyze their weaknesses, and to suggest ways to improve their efficacy and impact in the years ahead. Its concept is rooted in the fundamental values of equality, human dignity, power parity, mutual respect, and democratic pluralism. Its preparation scrupulously adheres to these precepts. Its chapters reflect an agonizing and genuine process of self-evaluation. Its conclusions are an example of the benefits that can be derived from a candid review of previous activities, conducted under the most difficult of circumstances. The book is in itself a tribute to the constructive potential of civil society peace work.

The task of breaking the cycle of violence and retribution is monumental and vital in every respect. The contributors to the book, in a reciprocal learning process, not only offer insights into past mistakes, but also present a series of practical suggestions to correct existing practices. The cumulative efforts of the editors and the authors, through their critical self-analysis, furnish a hopeful message. It is possible, through systematic strategic thinking, better use of resources, and enhanced motivation, to challenge pernicious perceptions, overcome domestic extremism, and proceed once again toward peace and reconciliation.

Foreword

Hanna Siniora

This book chronicles the valiant work of civil society in both the Palestinian and Israeli camps in their quest toward reconciliation. It is an essential work for our understanding of the uphill battle that the peace movement in Israel and Palestine faces and the hard work done to heal the wounds resulting from occupation and violence.

Those who spent their lives and careers in mending relations are in a way the unknown soldiers, unsung heroes whose good deeds are rarely praised, and who in our conflict are often accused of treason.

In both camps we have skeptics. On the Palestinian side there are those who have dedicated their energy to peacebuilding, mutual dialogue, and rapprochement. They are often accused of "normalization," and there have been attempts on their lives. Issam Sartawi is one of the better known in this group, but many have paid the ultimate price. In Israel, though, even among some who are left of center, there is still doubt of the existence of a Palestinian peace camp, which this book documents as alive and vibrant.

The past century has seen nothing but conflict and spilled blood. Yet, during the past four decades, a minority on both sides has worked relentlessly for peace. This book is a record of their relentless efforts to move forward to mutual recognition in a two-state solution.

I began this journey some thirty years ago, coached by a great person who even in this important book has been forgotten. The late Simha Flapan was my mentor as I sought to learn and understand the other side. Today his major work, *New Outlook,* is defunct, but should be treasured as a courageous voice that worked toward reconciliation.

From my many years as journalist and editor of the daily *Al-Fajr,* I recall meetings and conferences that dealt with Track II diplomacy and opened the door for mutual recognition and the Oslo process. The road that led to meetings in Stockholm under the auspices of Foreign Minister Sten Anderson of Sweden, the leadership of the Palestine Liberation Organization (PLO), and brave men and women from the North American Jewish community paved the way for the Arafat declaration at the United Nations, and also led to the recognition of the PLO by US Secretary of State George Schultz during the waning days of the Reagan administration. These official steps were paved and arranged by the hard work of the peace movement in Israel and Palestine.

Even in the troubled days of the first intifada and the current one, this work has never ceased. It is highly appreciated that the European Centre for Conflict Prevention is supporting the compilation of the tale of those who always believed that the destiny of both our peoples is to eventually live in peace.

Many more publications are needed to describe, analyze, and disseminate information on conflict prevention and peacebuilding activities in our region. This book is an important pioneering effort to illustrate the agony, the pitfalls, and the achievements that a few of us have experienced for a better future for the coming generation.

Schools in both Palestine and Israel should take note of this book. They should use it as part of their curricula to teach students that the battle for peace is more important than war, and that those who engage in peace are the real heroes.

Acknowledgments

This book is the outcome of a joint effort by the European Centre for Conflict Prevention, the Panorama Center for the Dissemination of Democracy and Community Development, and the Harry S. Truman Research Institute for the Advancement of Peace at the Hebrew University of Jerusalem. Numerous individuals and organizations in Israel and Palestine participated in the seminars we organized, provided their insights and support in shaping the book, offered feedback on earlier drafts, and contributed to the discussion on lessons learned from peacebuilding practice in Israel and Palestine. This led to enriched texts, and we are very grateful for the constructive inputs of the reviewers and thank the authors for their flexibility and willingness to revise their chapters.

The publication has been made possible through the strong dedication of many people, and we would like to extend our sincere thanks to all involved. We wish to express a special and deep debt of gratitude to the authors of the chapters, without whom there would not have been a book. Likewise, the book would not have been possible without the generous grants from several funding sources; we are grateful to the United States Institute of Peace, Cordaid Netherlands, and the Netherlands Ministry of Foreign Affairs for providing financial support.

We greatly appreciate the support of our colleagues at our respective organizations. In particular, we thank Dima Bazbaz and Michal Miller for their invaluable and constructive assistance. They were instrumental in organizing the meetings in Jerusalem, providing research assistance to the authors, and collecting information for the directory. We thank Lambrecht Wessels for his advice and feedback on the chapters. Marte Hellema and Dana Azouri provided valuable assistance in the final stages of publication. In particular, we are grateful to Lynne Rienner for her patience and trust in this project and to the team at Lynne Rienner Publishers for their flexibility.

While thankful for all the support we received, we assume full responsibility for the content.

—*The Editors*

Introduction

Edy Kaufman, Walid Salem, and Juliette Verhoeven

This book is part of the Searching for Peace Program, a project of the European Centre for Conflict Prevention (ECCP), which seeks to describe, analyze, and disseminate information on conflict prevention and peacebuilding activities in areas of violent conflict. The ECCP has published a series of regional studies, focusing on conflict in Africa, South and Central Asia, Asia Pacific, and Europe and Eurasia, and only recently selected Israel and Palestine as subjects for a case study focusing on a specific conflict. The Jerusalem office of the Palestinian Center for the Dissemination of Democracy and Community Development (Panorama) and the Truman Institute for the Advancement of Peace at Hebrew University were invited to act as partners for the project. Recognizing the existing record of joint Palestinian-Israeli activities and cooperative ventures, ECCP felt it was of extreme importance to ensure the incorporation of local expertise, knowledge, and initiative. As a result, ECCP enlisted its local partners in jointly designing the framework, goals, and objectives. Furthermore, the civil society organizations have taken the lead in executing the project. Although ECCP maintains overall administrative responsibility for the project, the three editors of this volume—representing the European, Israeli, and Palestinian partners—share equally their responsibility for its contents.

Here we wish to introduce the reader to the book's overall goals and specific objectives; provide a justification for its unique character; discuss methodological considerations that include the time framework, the participatory approach, research questions, and target audiences; and to preview the book's structure.

Overall Goals and Specific Objectives

The overall goals of the book are to promote effective peacebuilding and conflict prevention strategies, to highlight the important peacebuilding role (actual and potential) of nongovernmental organizations (NGOs), to fulfill a service function for the various players in the field of conflict prevention and peacebuilding, and to facilitate the exchange of knowledge and insights among the different local, regional, and international actors involved in this field.

The specific objectives of this book include (1) providing better insight regarding the role of NGOs in conflict prevention and peacebuilding by documenting and analyzing what NGOs have done, including a directory profiling such NGOs working in Israel and in Palestine: (2) promoting bottom-up peace processes with public participation; (3) identifying best practices and lessons learned in order to create a tool for generating discussion and awareness within and between the societies, and (4) formulating recommendations and strategies for future peacebuilding efforts. The book will also provide, for the first time, an in-depth compilation of information about civil-society peacebuilding initiatives in Israel and Palestine.

Justification

An in-depth case-study approach to peacebuilding is presumably useful, but any additional book on the Israeli-Palestinian case needs justification, given the extensive extant material. This book looks at the entire spectrum of peacebuilding in the Israel-Palestine region, treating the large number of projects as a living laboratory for different peacebuilding strategies.[1] As presented in the last chapter, the book examines the overall picture in terms of three levels of interaction in which civil-society organizations interact: horizontally, by reaching out to their peers (i.e., academics); downward, by affecting the public at large (e.g., peace education); and upward, influencing the decisionmakers (e.g., Track IIs).

The investment of the international community in Israel/Palestine, through funds and third-party intervention, commands the envy of many other "forgotten" conflicts. It is hard to pinpoint one reason explaining why the international community has spoiled Arabs and Jews with their care and attention. The range of possibilities includes the international (especially Western) community's sense of partial responsibility for the suffering of the two nations involved; the importance of the Holy Land for the three monotheistic religions traditionally ascribed to the patriarch Abraham; the active involvement of the Jewish diaspora and the Arab states; hope for discovering new strategies for solving the protracted communal and national conflict; or the sense that peace was once nearly achievable and that now people are tired and want to break the cycle of violence.

The purpose of this book, therefore, is to provide added value to the funds, time, and energy already dedicated to Israeli-Palestinian peacebuilding. The relationship between the two nations has reached its lowest point ever, and antagonism at both the government and societal level is very high.

While sustained civil-society efforts attempted to build bridges across the national divide, extremist groups on both sides—even without coordinating with each other—managed to derail the peace process. Consequently, it seems that peace dividends have not paid off in the short run, and the "peace camps" on both sides have shrunk and been weakened. One of the main concerns of this book is to assess the reasons why, in spite of the high level of investment and experimentation, the peace camps have been overrun by the violent reality. In other words, what went wrong is not only on the part of decisionmakers and government policies, but what went wrong rests, too, with civil-society peace strategies. The failure has often been attributed to the insufficient *quantity* of civil-society interactions, since more was needed to make a significant difference within the broader societies. However, this criticism fails to examine issues related to the *quality* of the process and explore mistakes and difficulties that transpired within specific activities.

To the best of our knowledge, while an existing body of literature explores the issues of the third sector and universities in Israel and Palestine, there is no concise overview of NGO peacebuilding efforts with a focus on prevention, resolution, and transformation. Similarly, there is no thorough analysis of lessons learned and best practices to guide future peacebuilding efforts. We are in need of new diagnostic tools to assist us in prognosis and in energizing a new and effective peace process. Hence, this book looks forward and attempts to contribute to the development of a bottom-up peace-with-justice formula leading to the end of occupation and the acceptance of the "other." We hope this book will help inspire new visions and strategies for civil-society organizations' work in the fields of peacebuilding, conflict resolution, human rights protection, and democratization in both societies and across the divide.

Time Parameters

The book's primary focus is of the past decade and a half of bilateral peace efforts, and it provides a brief historical background of peacebuilding efforts since the birth of Zionism in the 1870s. The new millennium has witnessed record highs and lows in the dynamics of the conflict. The cycle of peace culminated in the summer of 2000, when Palestinians and Israelis met at Camp David, Sharm Al Sheikh, and Tabah. From all accounts, the negotiators were on the verge of establishing a peace accord. However, the outbreak of the second *intifada* and the collapse of the peace process created a historic low point in the conflict, resulting in an uninterrupted cycle of violence targeting mostly noncombatants, innocent civilians, large numbers of whom are children.

There is a growing consensus that the current political leaderships are not able to build a stable peace and resolve the conflict between Israel and the Palestinian people. Therefore, it is of crucial importance to recognize, and engage with, Palestinian and Israeli civil societies for their positive contributions to peacemaking. The work of NGOs and other civic associations provides opportunities for building peace from the bottom up. Civil-society organizations also fill important advocacy and lobbying functions, striving to influence decisionmakers in terms of both current policies and the possibility of new ones.

We—editors and contributors—see this project as an equal partnership, and view co-authorship as a peacebuilding project in itself. For those of us in Jerusalem, at the epicenter of a violent conflict, it is not easy to write together. As partners, we challenge alternative narratives of the "other" with empathy and understanding while explaining our own narratives to the best of our abilities. The book is a participatory venture, built using a consultative process that includes authors meeting at the beginning and the end of the project, including a lessons-learned seminar that engages in criticism and self-reflection.

Target Audience

This book is aimed at all individuals and institutions working in the field of peacebuilding and conflict prevention. This includes local and international NGOs; government policymakers; development, humanitarian, and donor organizations; academics, think tanks, and research institutes; and media.

It is our wish that the book be translated into Arabic to achieve wide distribution throughout the Middle East, particularly in places where civil society is actively struggling for the shared values of human rights, democracy, and peace. We also plan to conduct seminars in Israel and Palestine focusing on how to use the recommendations of this book in further developing civil-society peacebuilding processes.

Methodology Considerations

The book's focus is the potential of Israeli and Palestinian civil society in peacebuilding and conflict prevention. In particular, we examine organizations that work, directly or indirectly, across the societal divide; promote humanistic values such as indivisible human rights, democracy, and peace; recognize the principle of self-determination for both nations; and actively promote a nonviolent resolution to the conflict.

Because Palestinian and Israeli societies are highly mobilized, it is difficult to come to a consensus on criteria for selecting the NGOs and grassroots organizations represented in this study. Indeed, our contributors have used various definitions for civil society, and have diverse concepts of what type of NGOs are involved in peace work. Broadly speaking, we interpret civil society as the entities acting in the public sphere between the individual and the state. Civil society consists of all citizens' participatory initiatives that are established and run independently from the state and that respect in their goals, structures, and democratic principles to be such actions as representation, accountability, and transparency.

More specifically, even within such parameters, it is a complicated task to establish strict criteria for selecting civil-society organizations that are to be included in the Directory. First, the context of such organizations differs between Israel and the Palestinian territories, which are still under occupation. Other variations arise from diverse cultural traditions and the inherent power asymmetries of power. Consequently, we as editors opted to use a "referee system" of peer evaluation, requesting the book's contributors to review the list of Israeli, Palestinian, and joint Israeli-Palestinian organizations we had drafted using the following criteria for selection:

- To be a functioning organization, overseen by a board or other accountable leadership
- To have activity records and financial reports audited by a legal auditor
- To be active for at least one year
- To be committed to the values of human rights, democratization, and peace

At the same time we make it clear that, as important as they may be, certain peace efforts may be peripheral to the scope of this book. For example, the book excludes trilateral efforts engaging Israelis and Palestinians in work overseas, diaspora-centered peace initiatives, and Arab-Jewish cooperative efforts in Israel that have no reference to Israeli-Palestinian peace in their mandate.

Research Questions

We asked contributors to examine many difficult and painful issues facing all those involved in civil-society peace work in their chapters. These questions include examining civil-society responsibility for the failure of the Oslo process, and examining organizational challenges such as fragmentation, lack of unity, and the reasons for coordination challenges. We also asked the authors to examine the difficulties posed by the asymmetry between the Israelis and Palestinians and its attendant problems, including stances toward "normalization" and differing conceptions of "just and lasting peace." Further, what does it take for Israelis who profess to support human rights, democracy, and peace to transform their "knowledge" of the suffering of the Palestinians into action ("acknowledgment")?

Other questions involved the extent to which civil-society groups were working to combat extremist tendencies in their respective societies and to condemn all forms of violence and hatred. We asked about the effectiveness of civil-society efforts in affecting their governments and to support the implementation of previous agreements. Further, we wanted honest evaluations of the authenticity of the peace work: was it business-driven more than aimed toward real peacebuilding? Was the agenda driven by international money or was it locally initiated? And, practically, we asked how Israeli-Palestinian cooperation can endure and transcend the psychological and material obstacles posed by restrictions on movement and lack of meeting places, from the separation wall, settlement expansion, closures, and the other procedures taken by the occupation.

The Participatory Approach

This book has been a consultative endeavor, with the editors actively including its contributors in developing the book's overall design. Further, the NGOs themselves were invited to discussions about the book's chapters and to provide material regarding their organizations' activities.

We selected contributing authors from the pool of scholar-activists and practitioners with academic backgrounds. Further, we selected authors with extensive experience working with NGOs that support such values as inalienable human rights, democracy, and peace. Consequently, they understand the possibilities and challenges of bottom-up peace processes and have recommendations regarding best practices.

To ensure a balanced, inclusive approach to the subject matter, a review seminar was organized where individual chapters were discussed with local experts, scholars, and practitioners from Israel and Palestine who agreed to serve as reviewers. This Advisory Meeting for Critique and Analysis, held March 12, 2003, in Jerusalem, brought together thirty participants who reviewed and discussed the chapters. For most of the chapters we found a Palestinian and an Israeli reviewer. The reviewers were asked to reflect on the degree of accuracy and balance found in the chapter, as well as to ensure sufficient background was provided for understanding the issue at hand. Reviewers were also asked to determine whether recommendations and lessons learned were presented with sufficient explanation regarding NGO successes and failures.

Structure of the Book

The book is divided into three main parts, each focusing on a certain aspect of Israeli-Palestinian civil-society relations in the past ten years. Concentration on the previous decade does not reflect our belief in the magic of round numbers, although a major war or outbreak of hostilities between Israelis and Palestinians has occurred once each decade. Rather, this last decade begins with the public peace process at the White House of September 11, 1993, and continues through the Oslo years to the outbreak of the ongoing intifada in September 2000. This most recent expression of the Israeli-Palestinian conflict has steadily increased in intensity, to the point of war, with most of its victims, tragically, civilian noncombatants.

The chapters in Part 1 emphasize peace work conducted in each society and between them. Particular emphasis will be on the promise of nonviolence, as evidenced in actual strategies and programs of action, as well as future activities. This part also examines and assesses why the Oslo Track II civil-society efforts lost access to the official Track I process after their contributions during the Oslo process. Civil society has proven its ability at contributing innovative and attainable solutions for nearly all issues in dispute (e.g., sharing the underground water to Jerusalem), yet its voice is seldom heard in the corridors of power. The last chapter in Part 1 draws together themes connecting the chapters, analyzing the problems and successes, and suggesting achievable strategies for overcoming the challenges.

Part 2 provides a list of organizations working in the field of peace and conflict prevention, with a particular emphasis on their goals and activities. It consists of fifty profiles, each highlighting a specific NGO, grassroots organization, or peace movement in Israel or Palestine. The editors recognize that this directory is not a comprehensive list of all such groups in Israel or Palestine, but rather a compilation based on the selection criteria outlined above. The aim of this directory is to include NGOs and other civil-society initiatives in a forum where they can share information regarding their aims, projects, and strategies. Rather than providing skeletal descriptions, such as those appearing in almanacs and yearbooks, we seek to provide the reader with substantive data demonstrating the range of goals and extent of cumulative work of peace-oriented NGOs in the Israeli-Palestinian context.

Note

1. These include activities to get people and youth in particular to learn how to live with the conflict, sustained dialogue groups, and problem-solving workshops searching for common ground on key political issues. These include furthering cooperation for peace and coexistence between professional groups, establishing long-term educational efforts, building tolerance and understanding of the other through the media, and fostering artistic and musical expressions of shared values.

PART 1

Reflections

I

Palestinian-Israeli Peacebuilding: A Historical Perspective

Walid Salem and Edy Kaufman

This book investigates current peacebuilding efforts by Palestinians and Israelis and analyzes prospects for the future. To understand the efforts and prospects, their development needs to be anchored in an overall historical context. Our task is to understand and explain the bottom-up process that provided legitimacy to both Palestinian and Israeli leadership to engage in negotiations, produce the Oslo agreement, and then fail to implement them.

Time periods themselves can provide different interpretations: for example, if we focus on Palestinians and Jews struggling over the Holy Land, then the conflict's dimension would be dominant in both authors' narratives. However, one could start from the encounter of Muslims and Jews close to fifteen centuries ago; then cooperation and cross-fertilization would predominate, at least in comparison with the relationship with other nations at that time. We do not want to idealize the distant past—the relationship was based on religious, linguistic, and cultural conditions—and indeed would focus on the origins of the dispute over this land we live in. What has been often called "the Middle East conflict" or "Israeli-Arab conflict" has been triggered by communal strife between Palestinians and Jews that was created after the Jewish immigration to Palestine. This was the case before and during the British rule (1917–1948), and this is the first period that we succinctly but systematically would like to address. After the termination of the Palestine Mandate, the establishment of the state of Israel in 1948 resulted in a regionalization of the hostilities, called officially by Israeli and Arab leaders, the Liberation War (*Al Naqba*). Since then, there has been a war about every decade: the 1956 Suez War; the Six-Day War of 1967, the 1973 Yom Kippur War, Operation Peace in the Lebanon War of 1982; and the Persian Gulf War of 1991. Our analysis covers this time period, but we can go further and claim that the conflict has been brought back to its original dimension: the protracted conflict between Palestinians and Israelis.

In this context, let us briefly recall the development of the Palestinian National Movement, the Palestinian Naqba of 1948, and the Jewish presence before the first waves of Zionist migration until the early nineteenth century. These events, together with the Zionist state formation period and through the British mandate in Palestine, will be our first point of reference. The second period covers 1948 through 1967, during which the Palestinian people, mostly living under Arab rule, were hardly in any contact with Israelis. After the Naqba of 1948, with the impossible Palestinian refugee situation, the Israelis were not willing to build relations with the Palestinians. The third period explores the intense interactions across the dividing Green Line starting after 1967 when Israel became the occupier of the majority of the Palestinian territories in the West Bank and Gaza. Finally, our survey arrives at the Oslo process and the October 1991 Madrid Middle East Regional Peace Conference—triggered largely by the search for a "new world order" in the aftermath of the Cold War and the two Gulf Wars. While peace was made among Israel, Egypt, and Jordan, and while Israel left Lebanon, we returned to confrontation and the core of the conflict has not been resolved.

Hopes for a peace agreement raised expectations in 1993, but were nearly totally shattered a decade later. Without covering the entire Israeli-Arab conflict, this chapter focuses on the basic Palestinian-Israeli track and the efforts taken with civil-society initiatives rather than those by any government.

While much has been written about the Israeli-Palestinian conflict from conflicting perspectives of the two sides, the aim of this chapter is different. It is an attempt to highlight the tenuous cooperation and dialogue between Jews and Arabs before the interaction evolved into an official Palestinian-Israeli negotiation process in 1993. This is not an attempt to magnify the peace forces that function over the years without state power, but just to map them within the wider picture. We will attempt to assess, in short, the impact of the cooperation and dialogue, leaving the detailed assessment to a later chapter on lessons learned.

Arab-Jewish Relations from the First Zionist Immigrations to the End of the British Mandate in Palestine

One would trace the record of peaceful relations between Arabs and Jews under the rule of the Ottoman Empire and in the provinces (vilayets) of Beirut, Hedjaz, and the District (sandjak) of Jerusalem, which was later to become Palestine under the British Mandate, preceded by the development of the Zionist and Arab national movements in the late nineteenth century. It should be indicated that as a rule the Jewish minorities, mostly in urban settings, were treated with respect, seldom persecuted, and often protected. On the individual and family level the few thousand Jews living in the ancient cities of Jerusalem, Tiberias, Jaffa, Hebron, and Safed, called the old Ishuv (in Hebrew, community, settlement) maintained, in general, friendly ties with their Arab neighbors and no record of bloody incident is found. Salim Tamari refers to three methodologies in this regard: While the Arab secular historian tends to create a portrait of exaggerated harmony between Arabs and Jews for the pre-1948 period (see the example, Aref al-Aref, al-Mufassal fi Tarikh al-Quds, Muhammad Adib Al Amiry, Jerusalem)—Zionist historiography often tends to suggest that the conflict is perennial and that Jews, at best, were accorded the status of a protected (dhimmi) community under Ottoman and other Islamic rules. Relations at the turn of the century between the two communities, collected from contemporary testimonials confirm neither version.[1]

In any event, the nature of this relationship started to change when the first Zionist immigrants began building new settlements, increasingly employing their own labor force. Furthermore, purchase of land from absentee landlords resulted in evicting a significant part of Palestinian peasantry from their land. The native Arab leadership viewed such undertakings with suspicion and was not ready to accept any nationalist claims from the newcomers. Yet some exceptional initiatives aimed to reach an understanding.

The outcome of World War I was a watershed for the Zionist movement. With the blessing of the British government, the Balfour Declaration provided the land for the rebirth of a Jewish national home (even though this implied that such policy could not be used against the native Palestinian population). Subsequent legitimacy was granted by the text of the mandate by the League of Nations. The British mandate in Palestine lasted three decades, ending only in 1948. Most of the official versions from both Jewish and Palestinian sources highlight the confrontations that took place in 1921, 1929, and 1936, which caused casualties on both sides. However Palestinian families rescued Jewish neighbors from life-threatening situations in Hebron, and there were friendly gestures by Jewish settlers toward Arabs when the pressure for leaving their lands was mounting in the wars of 1947 and 1948.

For the Palestinian side, the impact of World War I was the emergence of the Palestinian national movement, which began in a conference in Jerusalem in 1919. It called for the end of the mandate, cessation of Jewish emigration, and an end to the confiscation of Palestinian land. It was clear from the beginning that a deep conflict for survival had begun.

Even in the aftermath of World War I, when the Arab leadership of Sharif Hussein of Mecca was frustrated by the failure to fulfill territorial promises as understood in the correspondence with Henry McMahon, the British representative in Cairo, Hussein's son Faysal agreed on a draft with the Zionist leader Chaim Weizman in 1919 to a mutual recognition of their rule over Lebanon and Syria and Palestine, respectively.[2] This initiative was not implemented because the 1919 Paris Peace Conference granted the French, and not the Hashemite dynasty, rule over the territories.

There were some scattered contacts between Arab and Zionist leaders early in the twentieth century. As early as 1913 M. Hochberg, on behalf of the Zionist movement, went to Paris to engage in negotiations with the leaders of the first Arab Congress who were meeting to endorse the principle of decentralization of the Ottoman Empire.[3] In 1914 the establishment of a Jewish entity in Palestine was discussed with a delegation from the Decentralization Party, and Lebanese intellectuals met with Nahoum Sokolov in Beirut and were willing to consider his appeal with the condition that the inhabitants of an Arab village must not be deported.[4] Subsequently, in a meeting between the Syrian-Palestinian delegation and one Mr. Saphir, a general understanding between Arabs and Jews was considered on 7 and 8 September 1922, which stated that "Arabs and Jews shall devise the modus of a declaration to be made concerning the particular links of the Jews to Palestine. . . . While making clear the attachments of the Jews to Palestinians shall equally establish the rights of the Arabs inhabitants of the country."[5]

Formally speaking, one could identify Jewish and Palestinian political movements during the British mandate as what we now call nongovernmental organizations (NGOs). Since the British recognized both as official representatives, our task here is not to cover official contacts between the Jewish Agency and the Arab Higher Committee. The civil society organizations were begun in Palestine as active bodies in urban areas by 1849 with the formation of the Jerusalem Literature Society and followed by different NGOs. Some NGOs in the imperial Ottoman period were political (part of them being Arab nationalist organizations with Palestinian participation); others were cultural, charitable, or women's organizations (e.g., the Orphan Orthodox Women Society in Acre).

During the mandate period the capacity of the work of nascent civil organizations developed. Starting then, and extending into the 1930s, NGOs included youth clubs, student societies, charitable societies, trade unions, political societies, and women's societies.[6]

Such Zionist groups as Bil'uim (Lovers of Zion) had already started coming to the Holy Land in the 1870s and developed a network of self-help institutions known as the New Yishuv (New Community). These mainly agricultural settlements differentiated themselves from the Old Yishuv, with their few thousand non-nationalist (and mostly religious) Jews already living in harmony with the majority of Arab populations in such cities and towns as Jaffa, Safed, Hebron, Tiberias, and Jerusalem.

In any case, diplomatic contacts were conducted among individual rulers, with no other level of negotiation and peacebuilding taking place.

Except for the workers' societies, which worked on occasion with Jewish colleagues, while the other civic organizations concentrated their efforts against Jewish immigration to Palestine and land sales, and called for the independence of Palestine.[7] But such cooperation was more among the workers themselves than among the trade unions, which stayed separate except for four: the Railway and Post Trade Union, the General Workers Club in Haifa, the Sea Workers Trade Unions in Haifa, and the Bakery Workers Trade Unions in Haifa.[8] One can add the Society of the Government Employees, at that time the Palestine Civil Servant Association, which included both Jewish and Palestinian members.[9] Put differently, this period witnessed Jewish-Palestinian interaction in seven main fields:

- Daily neighborly interactions among Palestinian and Jewish residential locations
- Interactions in the joint municipalities, mainly in Haifa and Jerusalem
- Interaction among state employees
- Interaction through labor trade unions, and the joint strikes of Jewish and Palestinian workers (for instance, in Jaffa) where both were working together in the citrus cultivation sector
- Interaction through the mandate companies like the railway and the oil companies
- Dialogue between the different political movements (see below)
- Interaction through joint bodies, such as the Palestine Communist Party, which was against Zionism, but still called for Jewish-Palestinian labor unity, representing the joint organization of workers of Palestine, and had been initiated by the Hebrew Socialist Labor Party (launched in 1919 demanding the realization of the "Principles of Proletariat Zionism, calling for a right way toward a joint life with the other people living here").[10]

In 1943 the party divided, one part continued as the Palestinian Communist Party calling for Jewish-Arab cooperation, another became the National Liberation League working for Palestine's independence, and a third became the Educational Communist Union, which supported the "Jewish immigration and the right of Jews to establish a national home land."[11]

More specifically, among the Jews we might point out several other groups that were calling for dialogue and cooperation with the Palestinians:

- Hashomer Hatza'ir (in Hebrew, Youth Guard): Formed in 1911, it later evolved into a Marxist political party and associated, on the eve of the declaration of Israel's independence, with the Left Socialist Workers' Po'alei Tzion Party. Hashomer Hatza'ir called for a binational state for Arabs and Jews in Palestine,[12] and a joint organization for Jewish and Arab Workers.[13] It also set up the Jewish-Arabic Rapprochement and Cooperation Group in 1939,[14] and was the predecessor of MAPAM (United Workers Party). Together with the leading social-democratic Hapoel Hatsair (in Hebrew, Young Worker), later to become David Ben-Gurion's MAPAI (Eretz Israel Labour Party), and the Histadrut (Jewish General Labor Federation), it organized the workers along nationalist lines. The Histadrut decided that the trade unions for both nationalities must be organized separately but "coordinate with each other."[15] In 1927, the Histadrut established the National Union of Israel Land Workers as a coordinating body for the workers' unions in Palestine, while the Histadrut continued to support the "Hebrew work," which limited the work in the Jewish settlements to only Jews.[16]

Despite the uncooperative policies, the laborers worked jointly in the government, the army, big companies, and citrus cultivation. All in all, Ben-Gurion's call for the Jewish proletariat and Arab *fellahs* to rebel against the colonials and *effendis* was an empty statement; it may have described the ideological commitment rather than the political reality of that time. No class solidarity evolved, and even the Histadrut Zionist trade unions did not accept Arab members until 1959.

• The Canaanite Movement: Referred to originally as "Young Hebrews" their conception of "the land of our ancestors (Eretz Hakedem) was for Arabs and Jews in the lands stretching from the Euphrates to the Nile, with a non-Zionist perspective, and with the joint Semitic origin being stressed and the possibility of arriving at a cohabitation considered feasible. Small and romantic in its vision, it was led by figures as different as the protoFascist writer Yonatan Ratosh, who at best advocated a paternalist approach of "converting" the rest of the local ethnopolitical groups into the Hebrew civilization, and the prominent progressive journalist Uri Avneri, who, shortly before the 1947 partition plan, aimed to join the Sunni Palestinians into a bilingual and bicultural state and form the nucleus of a progressive "Semitic alliance that would establish a federal model throughout the Fertile Crescent, from the Euphrates River to the Suez Canal."[17] After 1948, driven by the philosophy of establishing in Israel a common land for Jews and Arabs, he established a short-lived Palestinian Liberation Movement.

• Brith Shalom (in Hebrew, Peace Covenant): Founded in 1925, it included such prominent professors at the Hebrew University as Karl Deutsch (who later immigrated to the United States) and its president, Judah Magnes. It advocated a solution based on a binational state. The Ihud group, led by Martin Buber, saw Arab and Jewish coexistence as part of a religious challenge to Brith Shalom. The Ihud group remained in existence after Israel's independence and published the magazine *NER* (in Hebrew: candle) which dealt with the plight of the Arab refugees, restrictions on Israeli Arabs, and the search for peace.[18]

- Kedma Mizraha: Founded in 1936, it was a continuation of Brith Shalom, called for a binational state and Arab-Jewish understanding, and was dissolved in 1933.[19] One of its leaders was David Yelin.

Among the Palestinians were prominent groups and individuals calling for cooperation and dialogue. Among them were the following:

- The National Party founded in 1923, by Aref Dajani, one of the notables of Jerusalem, and Shiekh Sulieman Taji Al-Farouqi of Jaffa, who was a judge and a poet. The party called for good relations between all the sects in Palestine.[20] Al-Farouqi wrote in his newspaper, *Al-Jam'eah Al-Islamiyyah,* on 16 March 1932: "We sympathize with the concern of every sect, and give our efforts and care to every sect the same way we give to the other sects without discrimination or destination."[21] This party also urged accepting whatever was presented by the [British] government.[22]

- The Farmers Party founded in the 1920s, called for cooperation with the government for farmers' welfare.[23] The founders of the party were Musa Hdieb and other government employees.[24]

- Village Cooperation Society also founded in the 1920s by Mahmoud Madi, As'ad Shuqieri, Ibrahim Najjar, and other village notables in Palestine. This society was close to the National Party, and As'ad Shuqieri, one of its founders, was also a member of the National Party.[25]

- The Islamic National Society founded in Jerusalem in 1918, wrote this in its founding document: "We accept the British Mandate in Palestine on the condition that the status of the Islamic majority will be taken into consideration, and also to work for understanding between all the groups . . . in Palestine, whatever their religions and denominations."[26]

- Al-Ahali Party was established by Abdellatif Salah in Nablus in 1925. One year earlier, Salah had held a party in Nablus for Norman Bentwich, one of the British Zionists civil servants in Palestine.[27]

In addition to these societies and parties, other Palestinian political groups were formed during the 1930s. The groups entered into negotiations and held meetings with the Jewish leadership in Palestine. Among others, these groups included the National Bloc Party led by Abdellatif Salah, founded in 1930, the Defense Party founded in 1934 by Raghib Nashhibi, the Reform Party founded by Hussein Al-Khalidi in 1935, the Arabic Palestinian Party founded by Jamal Al-Husseini in 1935, and the Independence Party founded by Awni Abdelhadi in 1932.

These parties chose nonviolent means to achieve Palestinian rights, and through that process they met several times with Jewish leaders.[28] Most important, these meetings generated the idea of cooperation and the establishment of a joint country with Jews as fellow citizens. Still important to note is that the network of Arab-Jewish relations during this period was not represented only through the political negotiations. Cooperation already existed in some communities, government, private enterprise, and in municipalities such as Haifa and Jerusalem.[29] In Jerusalem proper, Jewish and Arab members issued a joint statement in 1927 calling for "peace and assistance to the authorities for the preservation of security."[30] In Jerusalem the education department was administered by a British director assisted by 32 employees: 22 Muslims, 6 Christians, and 4 Jews.[31] In this regard Jerusalem was one of the outstanding mixed communities in Palestine. Uri Davis mentions several anecdotes of neighborly relationships between the Jewish and Palestinian neighborhoods.[32]

In 1929, the Palestinian position of accepting Jews according to their percentage in Palestine became clearer in the draft the Palestinians presented to John Philby, one of the leaders of the Labour Party in Britain. This included the proposal of a representative assembly, composed of Palestinians and Jews in proportion to the numbers of Palestinian residents, that would enact legislation and would approve the constitution, and the government was to be composed of Palestinian Arabs and Jews.[33] This stand became these representatives' official position in 1939 during London Conference, with the delegation accepting "the Jewish participation in the government in Palestine according to their percentage of the inhabitants."[34]

All in all, there were the British white papers of 1929 and 1939, as well as plans for the partition of Palestine submitted by Lord Peel in 1935 and the United Nations in 1947, which were rejected either by the Zionists or by the Palestinian leadership.

In retrospect, strong relations between the two communities did not develop. Overall, the new Ishuv in Palestine was focused on state building; it had a nearly complete set of institutions and an infrastructure autonomous from British rule, hence making the transition to independence a formal act only. The "Arab problem" was recognized but put aside either by the belief that a wall needed to be built before the neighbors would accept negotiating a Jewish state's existence (according to Vladimir Jabotinsky), or by accepting compromises such as partition plans (according to Chaim Weizman and Ben-Gurion) with little hope that the Palestinian side would reciprocate.[35] As a result, there were two contradictory scenarios for power sharing. One was the Zionist notion of equal power shared by the Palestinian majority and the Jewish minority, while the Palestinian scenario called for equal power sharing between the Palestinians and Israelis based on community size in the overall population. The 1936 Palestinian rebellion was triggered by popular feelings of being dispossessed of its of land and fading dreams of independence. After three years of fighting, the national Palestinian movement entered a period of disintegration that led finally to the 1948 Nakba.

All in all, the two Jewish and Palestinian positions were unbridgeable; therefore it was not possible to find a broadly acceptable peaceful solution to the conflict at that period.

From the Israeli War of Liberation, or the Palestinian Nakba, in 1948 to the Six-Day War in 1967

After the establishment of Israel and before 1967, many Palestinians were driven from their homes and moved into refugee camps in Jordan, Lebanon, and Syria. This outcome produced a deep and open wound, which added to the sense of dispossession and defeat and made potential peace negotiations difficult.

The 1948 war also strengthened the "Jordanian option" for Israel, namely that the partner for peace from the Israeli official perspective was the Jordanian Hashemite dynasty—already popular with the Zionist leadership since the 1930s—that had agreed with Israel to keep part of the territory while annexing the larger part of the West Bank (land promised to the Palestinians in the 1947 partition plan). Given the shock and despair of the Arab world, it would have been considered tantamount to an act of treason for any well-intentioned citizens in the region to come to the Israelis with a message of peace. The only place where cooperation did exist in these early years of the conflict was between the marginalized communist parties (small in Israel, illegal in the Arab world) that found mutual recognition feasible on a class rather than an ethnic level.

While some indirect and secret contacts with Egypt could have sparked potential agreements, the conventional wisdom in Israel was that there was no chance for peace. Civil society on both sides was not involved in dialogue. Overall, the Israeli leadership's assessment was that it was premature to expect the Arabs to agree to Israel's existence until it had built a strong state. Then its neighbors would have no choice but to accept it and then negotiate; dealing from a position of strength continued to be part of the prevailing ethos. In the eyes of moderate Israelis in the Labor Party leadership, such as Moshe Sharett, issues available to advance peace were a gesture of acceptance of the return of some of the Arab refugees displaced during the 1948 war and reducing the damage produced by the retaliatory policies of his political foe, Ben-Gurion.

The period before 1967 also witnessed several domestic Arab-Jewish rapprochement initiatives within Israel, with projects to fight against such restrictions as the military governing authority over Israel's Arab population of Israel until 1966. Among such initiatives was a movement led by Uri

Davies, questioning at this stage the intrinsic nature of the state (stress on its Jewish identity or "a state of all its citizens"). Most Israeli peace-oriented forces were focusing on Arab-Jewish "coexistence." The term "peacebuilding" did not apply, since both parties agreed that the main issue was not to come to an accord between two independent or sovereign entities, but to recognize the existence of each other as equals within one political unit.

Coexistence differs from peace in that groups willing to coexist have recognized the fundamental differences between sometimes conflicting needs. They are navigating a status in which the overriding need for survival has been internalized to mean that all parties share equally the right to exist. In this situation a partnership will emerge, perhaps not born out of romance but nevertheless functional.[36]

Palestinians elsewhere were not in control of their destiny until 1964, when the PLO was founded, to be followed by Fatah in 1965, which later became the main faction within the PLO as the representative organization for the people.[37] These institutions came up with their own strategies. The PLO's first covenant, passed in the first Palestine National Council in Jerusalem on 28 May 1964, called for the liberation of Palestine and the establishment of a Palestinian state that would include citizens living continuously in Palestine since 1947, effectively excluding the majority of the Jewish population that immigrated afterward. Yet, the liberation of Palestine was considered an introduction to peace.[38] At that time, armed struggle was seen as the only way to redress the injustice of the creation of Israel against the dislodged Palestinians. Ideologically and practically there was to be no legitimate dialogue with the Israeli enemy until 1973.

The few direct contacts between Israelis and Palestinians that took place were more anomalies than opportunities for negotiations, and had been promoted by third parties. Under the auspices of pro-Soviet front organizations such as the Budapest-based International Federation of Democratic Youth, sporadic festivals brought Israeli Arab and Jewish members of the left to meet their counterparts from the Arab world. The Prague-based International Union of Students provided for a while an umbrella for both the National Union of Israel Students (NUIS) and the General Union of Palestinian Students (GUPS), but the Israelis were expelled in 1965 at the insistence of the Palestinian organization, not willing to accept any longer the NUIS suggestion that there was room for both to represent their respective peoples. Zionism and Zionist movements were still to be considered as invaders who stole the Palestinian land, so they were not recognized as having the right to be represented. The Israeli secretariat of the Soviet-controlled World Peace Council, inaugurated in Paris in 1949, was kept by MAPAM even after the time that this Zionist left-wing party broke ranks with the Stalinists. But once again this was only a skeleton organization without any popular roots. The more frequent meetings of the international communist movement allowed the Israeli affiliate (MAKI) during the the years after 1948 to meet with the banned, and underground, counterparts from the Arab world. Eventually MAPAM split in 1965 along the ethnic dividing lines, and a second prevailingly Arab communist party, RAKAH, came into being in Israel and eventually took over with the virtual disappearance of the older Jewish faction.

Associated with the MAPAM, the *kibbutz* movement, and the above-mentioned Zionist youth movement Hashomer Hatsair, Givat Haviva was founded in 1949 to work toward peace, pluralism, tolerance, democracy, and justice. Its goal was to promote understanding with the Arab world, in particular with the Arab minority in Israel through peace education and dialogue.[39] Generally, the same circles sponsored a pluralistic magazine, *New Outlook,"* that under the Middle East expert and kibbutz member Simha Flapan reached intellectuals in the diaspora and Arab world, coming to a peak at a conference in Tel Aviv (this meeting was given the blessings of the late President Sadat of Egypt just before his historic visit to Jerusalem). In Italy, a series of Congrès Mediterranéen de la Culture were sponsored in 1958, 1960, and 1961 by the progressive mayor of Florence, Giorgio la Pira. Nahum Goldman, the perennial president of the World Jewish Congress, acted as a self-appointed messenger in the same years, furthering contacts with the influential and ruling circles in Morocco, Egypt, and Tunisia.[40] Habib Bourguiba, president of Tunisia, called upon the Arab states to recognize and negotiate with Israel.

At the revisionist, nationalist end of the Israeli political spectrum were small groups, ideologically related to the Canaanite movement, that interpret the doctrine of the "pact of minorities" as including all the groups in the ruling Arab Sunni elite, which were put in power by the Ottoman rulers to dominate the other peoples. One of the proponents was Vladimir Jabotinsky's son, Ari, a mathematician at the Technion in Haifa, and his long list of the Middle Eastern mosaic pieces included Kurds, Druzes, Copts, Maronites, Shi'ites, Samaritans, Ahmedians, Baha'is, old Eastern Christians such as Nestorians, Chaldeans, Greek Orthodox, Assyrians, and Armenians, and all Protestant denominations all estimated to constitute the majority of the region's population. Such an intellectually isolated position led a few members of the Herut Party (the main component of the current Likud ruling party) to support the internally displaced inhabitants from Ikrit and Biram, two Christian Arab villages within the border with Lebanon, to return to their villages, a promise that to date has not been implemented.

The last peace venture of this period was in 1966 with the risky flight to Egypt by Abie Nathan, an Indian-born Israeli fighter pilot. At first, it was feared that he had been shot down, but he landed safely in Port Said—where his request to meet President Nasser was not granted, and he was returned to Israel. Though not originally focusing on the Palestinians, Nathan sponsored the "Peace Ship" pirate radio station in 1973, broadcasting from Mediterranean waters. He became known as a champion of Palestinian-Israeli dialogue, and openly met with Yasser Arafat at a time when this was illegal in Israel, and spent several months in prison.

All in all the period of 1948 to 1967 witnessed different Israeli attempts to get Arab recognition of Israel, something that did not happen except for Tunisian President Habib Bourguiba's call for recognition of Israel in 1966 within the terms of a peace agreement.

The Israeli/Palestinian Encounter
from 1967 until the 1993 Oslo Accords

We can analyze the rapprochement of both civil societies through the development of two separate trends. On the one hand, Magnus Norell delineates the Israeli peace camp after 1967 in three phases. The first stage was right after the 1967 (Six-Day)War when there was a general connection to the idea of trading the occupied territories for peace. The second stage was from the 1973 (Yom Kippur)War until 1977 in which not much happened. Finally, the third phase was stimulated by President Anwar Sadat's visit to Jerusalem.[41] Let us first deal with the development of peace forces in each society separately.

Israel's occupation of Sinai, the West Bank, Gaza, and the Golan Heights as a result of the military victory in the war in 1967 produced a polarization of its Jewish population into two camps. In one, the nationalistic religious groups joined with secular organizations that called for the annexation of the Palestinian territories. The secular grouping called itself the Land of Israel Movement, or Eretz Israel Hashlema (in Hebrew, Entire Land of Israel). Even if triggered by the new territorial gains, it also "represented the revival of a traditional ideology never renounced by some groups within Israel that had now found both new relevance and unaccustomed supporters."[42] On the other hand, the Movement for Peace and Security could be seen as a counterforce, but it is clear that it would have developed even if the Land of Israel Movement had never been formed.[43] For the peace movement, the war of 1967 provided the opportunity to solve the problem of Israeli-Arab relations.[44]

Attitudes in favor of peace have been popularly identified in the Israeli context as "right" or "left," terms used elsewhere in the world to characterize the forces supporting more capitalist or working-class policies. The terms are, however, also correlated to a large extent with such main political groups in Israel. Yet, one could find within the kibbutz movement a trend toward annexing Palestinian land but many among Israeli industrialists and major entrepreneurs supported a meaningful compromise with the Palestinians. Likewise, in both the Labour and Likud parties, it was possible to find individuals approaching the territorial preferences and policies of the other.

Within the two camps there has been a silent majority of the Jewish population, undecided and willing to follow any current leadership on such crucial decisions.

Influenced by the "new left" trends, groupings of younger elements in, for example, such organizations as Siach (in Hebrew, dialogue) joined some of the leading figures, like Shulamit Aloni, Matti Peled, Liova Eliav, Me'ir Pail, Uri Avneri, and Ran Cohen in Ya'ad (later in Sheli, a Zionist left party) for the pro-Palestinian option.

As for academicians, some of the individual pronouncements had already appeared right after the Six-Day War, most prominently those of the historian Ya'akov Talmor and the religious scientist and philosopher Yeshiahu Leibowitz, who in different ways spoke out against the postwar occupation and the evil aspects of ruling another nation. And a group of important professors led by Yeoshua Arieli of Hebrew University created the Committee for Peace and Security, stressing the connection between the term "peace" and the issue "security" that has overwhelmingly bothered the moderate left, as concerns Israeli society in general. (One of our then active members, Dr. Gadi Yatsiv, was a leader in the 1969 national elections for the Movement for Peace, which failed, however, to garner the 1 percent threshold of votes for representation in the Knesset.

In general, though, the Labour Party's reluctance to take a clear stand on this issue brought to the fore the "doves" and "hawks" in the party's ranks. Prominent among the doves was Aryeh (Lova) Eliav, a long-serving member of parliament, secretary general of the Labour Party, regional development planner, educator, and rescuer of Jews during the diaspora. He wrote as early as 1970 that the Zionist struggle for the right to self-determination for Jews had succeeded. And he wondered how the Israelis could deny this right to others, to people who wish to see themselves as a nation? The Palestinian nation has had a history of its own, special memories of its own: wars, sacrifices, suffering, and heroes, not to mention poetry and literature. This explication was most important since the Israeli establishment ignored all this; for example, statements by the late Prime Minister Golda Meir, who mocked Eliav and called herself a Palestinian, denied the existence of the Palestinians as a distinct people.

More radically, only a few days after the 1967 war we witnessed the minuscule Israeli Socialist Movement (in Hebrew, Matzpen) and the Democratic Front for the Liberation of Palestine publish a joint statement calling for "Socialist Federal over national state [sic], where the Jews and the Arabs enjoy comprehensive civil rights, and cultural rights."[45] Meanwhile, the Israeli Communist Party, which continued its secret relationship with the Palestinian and Jordanian Communists, after 1970 started to reconsider its position on the Palestinian National Movement and the PLO, and in 1976 the eighteenth conference of the party recognized the PLO as a representative (and not the sole representative) of the Palestinian people.[46] This new Israeli Communist Party position was followed one year later by a decision made by the PLO executive committee to hold a meeting with that party.[47]

From a Palestinian perspective, the first stage of contacts was primarily based on the Jordanian option with the involvement of individuals connected to the Hashemite regime, mainly in the West Bank. This dialogue was to the detriment of some "independentists," that is, Palestinians in the occupied territories who were ready to use the momentum after the Six-Day War for a "two-state solution." The first PLO dialogues with Zionist Israelis in the West Bank began in the mid-1970s. Before then, the Israelis had mostly concentrated on meeting with independent personalities, as well as those loyal to King Hussein (such as Elias Frej, the mayor of Bethlehem), consequent to the preferred "Jordanian option." Some Palestinian academicians living in the United States and Europe also participated in joint meetings with Israelis sponsored by US and European organizations.

The second period began with the Palestinian National Council (PNC) of the PLO deciding in 1974 to accept the establishment of a Palestinian state in any territory that could be liberated from Israel. This position reflected the beginning of the change of the PLO position from establishing a secular, democratic state in all the historical land of Palestine. The political significance of this position (that was taken in the shadow of the Geneva conference at that time) was that it gave support to those Palestinians who had begun contacts with the Israelis after 1974 in the name of, for instance, Said Hamami, Isam Sartawi, and others, who were PLO representatives in different European countries. It is important to note that the PLO leadership tried to push the positions of the twelfth PNC session in 1974 to adopt the idea of negotiations with Israel, suggesting the decision to be in on the establishment of a Palestinian state in any part liberated, or after an Israeli withdrawal. The leadership was seeking a withdrawal that might come through negotiations, and when Arafat was not able to convince the other factions of this position, the resolution was passed in an indirect manner. Arafat approved PLO ambassadors in Europe and also some others in the West Bank and Gaza, such as Hanna Seniora and Fayez Abu Rahmeh, to hold meetings with their Israeli counterparts.

During the 1970s the Palestinian society in the West Bank and Gaza decided to either choose PLO peace activities (as did Hanna Seniora and Fayez Abu Rahmeh) or to work separately for democratization and human rights (see the following relevant chapters), while in the Palestinian diaspora, under the leadership of Arafat, the idea of political negotiations continued. After the meetings with the Israeli Communist Party, the PLO position began to move toward opening channels to the Israeli peace and democracy movement, becoming favorable during the decade that followed the thirteenth PNC meeting in Cairo, in 1977.[48] In the nineteenth session of the

PNC in Algeria in 1988, it was stated that the organization "appreciates the role and courage of the Israeli peace movement in their fight and uncovering of the fascist and racist and aggressive powers in Israel, and also for their support to the struggle of our people and the courageous intifada."[49]

By that time, however, Israeli politics had moved to a hard rightist position with a Likud-led coalition government with Yitzhak Shamir as prime minister. Given that Palestinians in their own diaspora and in the occupied territories considered the PLO as the "sole representative of the Palestinian people," dialogue at the official level was all but frozen, if ever it was even intended to be productive. Meanwhile many Israeli peace activists continued meeting with representatives of the PLO, but in an attempt to stop such activity, during the national unity government of Shimon Peres, in 1986 the Knesset passed an amendment to the Prevention of Terrorism Act of 1948. The government then had the ability to prevent meetings that the Likud viewed as undermining the status, and the very existence, of Israel.[50] Not only did the law not lead to the "absolute delegitimation of the PLO," but to a certain extent actually led to its gaining further acceptance. The amendment transformed the discussions held with the PLO from marginal political contacts to acts of civil disobedience. This made the discussions more prominent in the public mind and also led to lawyers, judges, and jurists to vocally support the right of the PLO to freedom of expression and the right to hold meetings.[51] The law was repealed only in January 1993 after the Labour government, led by the late Yitzhak Rabin, was elected and made a strategic decision to negotiate with the PLO.[52]

As already noted, policy developments in the PLO's position on negotiating peace were already a product of its gradual move from its Cairo PNC meeting in 1974, away from the position of liberating all Palestine to the idea of establishment of a Palestinian state only in one part of Palestine.[53] This position continued to develop until the PLO nineteenth PNC resolution of 1988 clearly supported the two-state solution. Jordan's King Hussein renounced any claims to the West Bank territories in 1988, and with the Gulf War of 1991 the new political realities fostered conditions for an official accord between the Palestinian people and Israel. Yet, since 1992, political stability of Israel has been disrupted with frequent early elections and five different prime ministers since the Oslo Accords.

Peacebuilding in Israel can therefore be seen as an oppositional activity and, in the best case, the formation of the peace camp.[54] From the Palestinian side peacebuilding was an activity that was approved from 1974 onward by the first leadership of the Palestinian people (i.e., the PLO), and many different Palestinians participated in peacebuilding activities either at the official PLO level or the NGO level with explicit or implicit approval from the PLO.

Indeed, a few independent-minded Palestinian academics entered into dialogue with the Rehovot group led by the prestigious Weizman Institute of

Science. Professors Michael Feldman, Shneor Lipson, and Ra'anan Weitz, among others, prepared a systematic analysis of the potential for peace looking forward to the year 2000, proposing a massive development program aimed at increasing the standard of living for the Palestinian population under Israeli control in the occupied territories, and addressing the refugee issue. Academics from Birzeit University, including Salim Tamari, Rita Giacaman, Khalill Mahshi, and Nabil Cassis, met several times in 1982 and 1983 with Israeli peers at the Weizman Institute. These meetings were confronted by a campaign from the PLO left-wing organizations, which then wrote several articles against that activity in the magazine *Al Ahd*.[55] The editor of the newspaper *El-Fajer,* Hanna Seniora, conducted joint endeavors from 1974 with Simha Flapan of the magazine *New Outlook*. He opened his newspaper's pages to Israeli and Palestinian activists to express their opinions on Israeli-Palestinian peace. In September 1978 *New Outlook* hosted an Israeli-Palestinian debate in East Jerusalem. The attendees were leading intellectuals and politicians representative of the mainstream of public opinion on both sides. The debate was recorded and it explored the conflict, past and present, and prospects for the future.[56] At the time of the first intifada, Ziad Abu Zayyad disseminated the weekly newspaper *Gesher* (in Hebrew, bridge), which carried an editorial, also published in Arabic, to show that the same language was used when addressing both audiences. While this publication eventually came to an end, its pioneering efforts resulted in the *Palestine-Israel Journal,* still in existence.

In the early 1980s joint tours were undertaken in the United States, such as those by Peace Now leader Col. Mordechai (Morele) Bar-On (ret.), along with Muhammed Milhem and Nafez Nazal. We can also mention Fayez Abu Rahmeh, a lawyer and one of the main PLO figures in Gaza, and Abu Zayyad, as leading the way in Jerusalem in the dialogue during this period.

The Israeli Peace Camp

While all the contacts and small groups incrementally added to the formation of a visible trend for peace in the Israeli society, the real takeoff to the peace movement was launched by Sadat's visit to Jerusalem and in supporting Prime Minister Begin's move toward acceptance of President Carter's Camp David compromise suggestions. The peace faction then became mostly dedicated to peace with the Palestinians and had a passing involvement in demanding a territorial compromise with Syria on the Golan Heights. By 1982, when aware of the hidden agenda of the war in Lebanon, the peace faction began criticizing it for not being a defensive war of "no choice" but a grand design led by Ariel Sharon to dictate political aims that eventually did not materialize (to chase the Palestinians out of "Fatehland," which was the area the PLO controlled in Lebanon). Syria was not going to accept such a large number of new refugees (who would eventually migrate to Jordan, thereby increasing the total number of Palestinians in that nation so that they would eventually become the Palestinian state on the east bank of the Jordan—and thus Israel would annex the west bank of the river).

While activities in relation to Lebanon characterized the peace camp as an antiwar movement opposing military control of the West Bank, the myth of "benign occupation" was shattered by economic deterioration and increasing human-rights violations (i.e., administrative detention and torture). After the outbreak of the first intifada in 1987, moving away from the passive *summud* (in Arabic, steadfastness) to active resistance to occupation, new "trends" in Israel's peace groups focused on the dramatic deterioration in human rights (e.g., collective punishment, many casualties among unarmed Palestinians civilians). Organizations such as B'Tselem (founded in 1989) came out against occupation rather than stressing how to reach peace immediately. As an Israeli human rights organization, B'Tselem acts primarily to change Israeli policy in the occupied territories and ensure that the Israeli government protects the human rights of the territories' residents and complies with its obligations under international law.[57]

Special mention should be made about gender, since women are a majority in the peace groups in Israel. Women's groups act not only in antiwar activities (e.g., Four Mothers—Lebanon, Parents Against Silence), but also in overall protest against the occupation (e.g., Women in Black), as human rights organizations (e.g., Machsom Watch), and as political coalitions, such as the Jerusalem link between Bat Shalom and the Jerusalem Center for Women (the latter a Palestinian women's organization; see Part 2, Directory).

The Israeli peace faction was more than Peace Now alone, which by far was the largest movement. Other groups added variation in color and shape. For many activists on the Israeli left, Peace Now did not satisfactorily speak against the occupation and expansionist military activity. Organizations such as Yesh Gvul and Israelis against Silence emerged as an answer to the more difficult questions of military service.[58]

The Palestinian Peace Movement

While the Israeli peace movement witnessed the formation of Peace Now and other such organizations, the Palestinian context was different because it witnessed the transformation of the mainstream political orientation to a peace movement. In this regard the Palestinian Communist Party (now the People Party) had been pacifist all throughout its history, while Fatah, as the main PLO organization, progressed toward supporting peace and negotiation starting in the mid-1970s. In the end this transformation led Fatah to be a major producer in the Oslo Accords with Israel in 1993. Other factions, such as FIDA the Popular Struggle Front, and other smaller organizations followed.

To this list must be added the different Palestinian NGOs that joined

Shalom Achshav (in Hebrew, Peace Now) is the largest grassroots movement in Israel's history. It was founded in March 1978 by 348 reserve commanders, officers, and combat soldiers of the Israel Defense Forces in response to the failing Egyptian-Israeli peace process. It began with a letter imploring Prime Minister Menachem Begin to find security through peace with its neighbors. The movement quickly gained unprecedented popularity, and achieved momentum shown by the record-breaking number of participants in its first major demonstration of approximately 40,000 people. A protest letter from a few respected members of the community became the voice of opposition in Israeli society. To maintain effectiveness Peace Now identified a few basic principles to rally around. Bar-On cites these ideas: (1) peace is the highest priority presently facing Israel and Zionism; (2) the security of Israel depends of peace, not on territories; (3) the Israeli government should reconcile with Egypt on the principle of "territories for peace" as determined by UN Resolution 242; (4) Israel should halt all settlements in the occupied territories because the settlements are an impediment to peace and push the Arabs away from the negotiating table; (5) Israel and Zionism cannot be based on the domination and suppression of another nation—such actions corrupt the occupier. During the protests in Tel Aviv over the massacres in Sabra and Shatila in Lebanon, the Peace Now demonstrations drew a crowd of 400,000 protesters (20 percent of the adult population). Among the crowd were twenty-five members of the Knesset (the total number of Knesset representatives is 120). While united *against* the occupation and the settlement activity, there was a crisis with supporters of the Jordanian option within the organization as slowly moving to a *pro*-Palestinian state orientation. Over the past twenty-five years, Peace Now has had its ups and downs in popular support and in attempting to influence public opinion and government policy.

the PLO factions in peace work during different periods, including, among others, those that focused on women, conflict resolution, human rights, and nonviolence (see the Directory). The majority of the NGOs were affiliated with the PLO mostly until the mid-1980s. Later some formal NGOs were founded, which handled peace activities in a professional way and were able to do advocacy and lobbying activities for the sake of peace with the Palestinian Authority.

At the time of the first intifada there was also a beginning of cooperation in furthering a nonviolent strategy toward self-determination and peace such as by the Palestine Center for Nonviolence and a small group of Israeli members of the Fellowship of Reconciliation together with few academics. But in the Middle East the few who called themselves pacifists (e.g., Mubarak Awad, the founder of the Center for Nonviolence) were promptly deported by the Shamir government. Most Israelis have not only performed military service but supported most wars of Israel as "just wars" or defensive wars of "no choice" until the 1982 Lebanon nightmare, when a first antiwar movement emerged.

In Jerusalem at this period, more people, such as Sari Nusseibeh and Faisal Hussieni, joined the peace movement and held several meetings with Moshe Amirav from the Likud Party in August and September 1987, and also met with Mayor Teddy Kollek of Jerusalem. This is the same Nusseibeh who publicly called—in case that the collective right of the Palestinians for self-determination was not respected—for Israel to grant full citizenship to the Palestinians in the occupied territories so that they could vote in national elections and eventually become a majority in the future.[59]

In retrospect, some PLO representatives in the mid-1970s outside the territories risked their lives by pioneering dialogue with Israelis, once the organization had moved away from the call for the total liberation of Palestine. Said Hamami,[60] Wa'el Z'eitar, Na'im Khader, and Isam Sartawi participated in meetings with Israelis in different European countries. All of these meetings were coordinated and supported by Yasser Arafat who told them to go ahead with these meetings, but small PLO extremist groups opposed such contacts, for instance Sabri Al-Baana (the Abu Nidal group), took responsibility for assassinating the four cited above with the claim that they were collaborators with the enemy. Others, such as Khaled Al-Hasan, the prominent member of the Central Committee of Al Fatah at that time, participated in the meetings but were not assassinated.[61] Their counterparts were well-known left-wing Israeli personalities.[62]

On the other hand, while most Palestinian universities have maintained over the years an official policy of no cooperation with any Israeli universities, different Palestinian academics from different universities joined peacebuilding activities with their Israeli counterparts as well as with the NGOs on both sides. Other academics chose only to speak to the Israeli anti-Zionist or post-Zionists academics, others chose to do their professional work, without having the headache of involving themselves in political work, and finally the last group boycotted the Israeli academics because of the latter's national or religious positions against normalization of relations. Almost the same differentiations between different Palestinian scholars in their relations with Israelis might be found among Israeli academics in relations with their Palestinian counterparts.

Yet, it is important to stress that within the context of empowerment during the first intifada, while stones and rubber bullets were being exchanged in the streets of Jerusalem, an active public dialogue was taking place at Mount Scopus and other places, showing the determination of a significant group of academics to call for the end of occupation and respect for the self-determination of both nations.

We need also to point out the significant role of third parties as conveners and facilitators of dialogues. For nearly two decades, Harvard Professor Herbert Kelman conducted programs where scholars from both sides of the conflict joined those who were interested in conflict resolution. Harvard's third-party status served as a positive environment in which protagonists could exchange views and express their beliefs in an uninhibited manner. While it is difficult to assess the efficacy of the Harvard group's efforts, they did have a personal impact as well as relevance to policy when some of the participants became Oslo Accords Track I negotiators. Among Palestinian academics abroad, the late Edward Said mentioned that his participation in the dialogue with Israelis began at Harvard in 1969.[63] Among the other Palestinian academics who participated in the meetings were Walid Khalidi, Hisham Sharabi, and Rashid Khalidi.[64]

A similar project aimed at co-publishing Israeli-Palestinian work was sponsored by the American Academy of Arts and Sciences. The final product was *The Transition in Palestinian-Israeli Relations: From Self-Rule to Independence.*[65] In a similar vein, perhaps, is the first comprehensive cooperative action ever undertaken by the two sides. By 1989, the Israeli-Palestinian Peace Research Project (IPPRP) undertaken by the Truman Institute of the Hebrew University and Faysal Husseini's Arab Studies Society of Jerusalem attempted to publish twenty-two papers on some of the thorniest issues of the conflict: territory and boundaries, security dimensions, Jerusalem, settlements, economic relations, water resources, Palestinians in Israel, democracy, and education for coexistence. Given such a breadth of controversial issues, when policymakers resolved to sit down to negotiate, much of the work may already have been done. Unfortunately, the impact of such efforts outside their limited academic spheres seemed to be contingent on political climates that persuade or dissuade policymakers to move in the direction of peace. Even these modest undertakings were negatively affected by the Gulf War of 1991, and Israelis were disenchanted with the official Palestinian support of Saddam Hussein.

But the 1991 call for a "new world order" brought about renewed efforts throughout the region. This was begun under the auspices of Search for Common Ground, a decade-long Track II project started to bring together former diplomats, high-ranking military officers, parliamentarians, journalists, and academics. This was a prelude to the formal October 1991 Middle East peace conference in Madrid. More Palestinian-Israeli cooperative efforts, discontinued temporarily during the Gulf War, were resumed. Soon the absence of progress in the formal Track I negotiations in Washington, D.C., was seen to be that the parties were still locked in their long-time attitudes of mutual hostility. It was then, particularly, that Track II conferences among scholars acted as a legitimating forum in which both sides could meet, thereby avoiding officially sanctioned restrictions. The guise of academic conferences protected the participants, and even drew considerable (albeit silent) official observation by both the PLO and the Israeli government.

Perhaps one of the most ambitious activities of academics was the attempt at co-authorship. Here, because both parties must agree to virtually every sentence written, the challenges are great. Such a process really forces both parties to discard personal attachment to issues in their search for the common ground that is somewhere in between. Such a pioneering effort was begun by Sari Nusseibeh and Mark Heller in their groundbreaking work *No Trumpets, No Drums*. The book tries to outline a set of "overall principles which we believe should guide Israeli and Palestinian negotiators."[66]

The crown jewel of Palestinian-Israeli academic cooperation clearly came through the talks sponsored in 1992–1993 by Norway's Institute for Applied Social Science (FAFO). Yair Hirschfeld of Haifa University and Ron Pundak, affiliated with Hebrew University, led the Israeli team against two high-ranking PLO officials, Ahmed Qurai (Abu Alaa) and Hassan Asfour. In this case, the impact of negotiations directly led to the Israeli-Palestinian Declaration of Principles, which was later to be known as the Oslo Accords. It was at this venue that the "Gaza-Jericho first" approach was put forth, and later ratified by the PLO and the Israeli government on the White House lawn in September 1993. Here the role of academics in bringing about peace was instrumental because they had capitalized on an environment that was ripe for peacemaking.

Among the things that made the Oslo talks unique were those that sprang from academically based thinking. In the past, negotiations had been conducted by initially putting forth outrageous demands, with hopes of meeting somewhere in the middle. At Oslo, both sides presented real demands that encompassed true limitations and anxieties. Furthermore, participants dedicated themselves to focusing on the present and future, rather than on the past.

Conclusions

It is in itself a challenge for both of us to reach a consensus about what we learn from the past in order to understand the present and even more for going toward the future. At this stage we can make the following observations.

- During all the periods of conflict between Palestinians and Israelis, there were always two trends: one that called for war and violence between the two sides, and one that called for peace and reconciliation. The difference between the periods before 1967 and after is that before 1967, and mainly before 1948, the positions of the peace movements in both societies were unbridgeable because of conflict over issues of power sharing. After 1967 the development of realistic areas in both societies began. In retrospect, there has been a world of difference between the weakness of peacebuilding at that time and what we see currently in the societies' peace and opposition–driven initiatives looking for grassroots popular support.
- All in all, peacebuilding in Israel can be seen as oppositional activity and confined to a "peace camp" or temporary coalitions. On the Palestinian side peacebuilding was scattered before being officially sanctioned by the PLO leadership. Such attitudes strongly influenced the Palestinian NGO activism, often seeking explicit or implicit approval.

- The fragmentation of the political left has been a source of weakness over time. While the radical fringes could reach out with understanding, it distanced them from the mainstream elements in both societies. In Israel, the common denominator was the willingness to trade territory for peace, but differed from the Arabs' goals and in the ways to act toward such goals. Overwhelmingly, and with the well-known exception of Peace Now, peace groups in Israel did not last for more than a few years. In Palestinian society, the left (mainly Marxist) is divided among those in favor of a two-state solution without normalization with Israel (e.g., the PFLP), those who might agree to normalization if certain conditions were provided (the DFLP, the People Party), and a third party that believes in dialogue to pave the way for peace and two-state solution (e.g., Fida, Popular Struggle Front, many who quit the PFLP and DFLP). Moreover the dialogue with Israel was made mainly by the Palestinian mainstream centrists (Fatah mainly) and not the left wing.
- There is peace work related more to the future, often sounding naive and unrealistic, rather than how to move from here to there. Emphasis was put more on the ends of the struggle rather than on the means to achieve the shared vision. In Israel, after the war with Lebanon in 1982, there have been antiwar groups, and on the Palestinian side the nonviolent groups started their struggle with the first intifada in 1988.
- There is a lack of unity in action among the Palestinians between human rights NGOs and peace NGOs dealing with "the other" as well as those who work for the same principles at home and do not interconnect their struggles. In Israel most NGOs do not address the peace issue, not connecting Israel's social and economic issues of injustice to the absence of peace or the policy of illegal settlements. And in contrast, the struggle for democratization and reform in Palestine has not been connected for many with the few NGOs that focus on the struggle for peace.
- The development of Arab-Israeli cooperation was mostly conducted according to the common political ideologies or affiliations (e.g., women, religious faith, social work, psychology, geographical location), across the national divide rather than working with a wide spectrum of opinion on the other side (e.g., not only the Communists working together, but FIDA Youth with Hashomir Hatza'ir Youth, FIDA with Meretz, Palestinian Falcons with Labour's Youth with Labour). While there is no reason not to use sector-determined peace efforts, action should not be confined only to these.
- Among academics, on the Palestinian side there has been a strong tendency to isolate those who work across the Israeli-Palestinian divide. With the Israelis, by contrast, only a minority was willing to

translate the "knowledge" about the asymmetry between occupier and occupied into "acknowledgment"—that is, to move from passive understanding into acting to minimize the suffering.[67]

- At times of greater need for joint action, the major peace forces of both sides have been unable to act as protagonists and have been very much influenced by the majorities rather than having any impact on them.

- Attempts at international peace work on the ground have been weak in the past. While a small international solidarity contingent is finding its way to the occupied territories (with great difficulty), there has not been enough coordination between the peace camps of both sides on how to maximize this potentially large source of activity for peace.

- Over the years the peace movement on both sides has been aging, while the young people have been leaning toward ever more intransigency. Youths have become increasingly responsible for violence as well as being represented a lot among its victims. This trend is worrying, and it calls for a reversal through special approaches to the youth generation. While the present situation may present mirror images, the real asymmetry shows that young Israelis who become extremists are incited by the religious and secular nationalists as well as by settler groups who want to "swallow" the Palestinians lands. On the Palestinian side, youths who increasingly choose violence are doing this in reaction to the occupation, in all its aspects.

- From a historical perspective, the real challenge to the peacebuilders has been the ability to reach out to the mainstreams of their societies and bring them to accept now what was acceptable earlier. Some such initiatives have been presented (e.g., the Clinton parameters, the Saudi Initiative of "1948 x 1967," the Geneva's Beilin-Abed Rabbo agreement, the Ayalon-Nusseibeh National Accord) and cover practically all issues at stake. In the past, such initiatives failed to become dominant government strategies. Better coordinated strategies within and between the peace camps and initiatives in both societies are needed.

Notes

1. Salim Tamari, *Jerusalem 1948. The Arab Neighborhood and Their Fate in the War* (Bethlehem, The Institute for Jerusalem Studies and Badil Resource Center, 1999).

2. The text of agreement between the two was signed on January 3, 1919. See Mahdi Abdul Hadi, "Documents on Palestine," Palestinian Academic Society for the Study of International Affairs (PASSIA), 1 (1997), 28, 29.

3. Neville Mandel, "Attempts for a Zionist-Arab Entente," *Middle Eastern Studies*, 1, 3 (April 1965).

4. "Documents on Palestine," p. 55.

5. Ibid.

6. Walid Salem, T*he Voluntary Community Organizations and the Palestinian Authority* (Ramallah: Social Economic Studies Forum, 1999).

7. Bolous Farah, *The Palestinian Labor Movement* (Al-Mashriq House, 1987).

8. Martin Buber and J. L. Manges, eds., *Towards Union in Palestine* (Jerusalem: Ihud Association, 1947), 79.

9. *The Palestinian Labor Movement,* 25.

10. Samih Samarah, *The Committee Works in Palestine* (in Arabic) (Acre: Al-Aswar, 1980), 23, 24.

11. Sabri Jiryis, *The History of Zionism* (Jerusalem, 1987), 98, 99.

12. Ibid., p. 188.

13. Ibid., p. 393.

14. Abdallah Abu-Nimer, *Mi'arri Felastin (Shiekh Sulieman Taji Al-Farouqi)* (Jerusalem: Al-Rislah, 1993).

15. *History of Zionism,* p. 189.

16. Rael Jean Isaac, *Israel Divided* (Baltimore: Johns Hopkins University Press, 1976), 79.

17. Mordechai Bar-On, *In Pursuit of Peace: A History of the Israeli Peace Movement* (Washington D.C.: United States Institute of Peace, 1996), 15.

18. Magnus Norell, "Democracy and Dissent: The Case of an Israeli Peace Movement—PEACE NOW," Stockholm Department of Political Science, 95. The influence of the covenant never really reached outside the academic circles—it disintegrated by itself, but with some of the leading members continuing to take part in other frameworks—but the ideological leanings of the Zionists made attempts to reconcile with the Arabs an important priority, according to Maher Asherif, in *Communism and The National Question in Palestine 1919–1948* (in Arabic) (Beirut: PLO Research Center, 1981, 20–30).

19. Ibid., p. 393.

20. Kamal Mohmoud Khalleh, *Palestine and the British Mandate (1922–1939)* (Beirut: PLO Research Center, 1982, 373). Al-Farouqi wrote in his newspaper, *Al-Jam'eah Al-Islamiyyah,* on 16 March 1932: "We sympathize with the concern of every sect, and give our efforts and care to every sect the same way we give to the other sects without discrimination or distinction."

21. *Palestine and the British Mandate,* 373.

22. Ibid., p. 377.

23. Naji Alloush, *Arab Resistance in Palestine* (Acre: Al-Aswar, 1979), p. 60.

24. Khillah, Ibid., pp. 197, 386, and 393.

25. Ibid., pp. 36 and 823.

26. Ibid., p. 380.

27. Khillah, Jeryis, and Alloush (Ibid.), mentioned a lot of examples in this regard.

28. *The History of Zionism,* p. 265.

29. See the story of Jerusalem municipality in Usama Halabi, *Arab Jerusalem Municipality* (Jerusalem, PASSIA, 1997) and of Haifa in *Towards Union in Palestine,* p. 66.

30. Muhammed Izzat Darwazeh, *About the Arab Modern Movement,* 3rd part, (Sidon: Al-Asriyyeh Library, 1951), p. 185

31. Aref Al-Aref, *Detailed History of Jerusalem* (Jerusalem: Al-Andalus Library, 1992), p. 447.

32. Uri Davis, *Crossing the Borders* (London: Books and Books, 1995). Communal relations between some Palestinian villages and the new kibbutz communes

and other Jewish agricultural settlements were often friendly and in a few cases remained as such until the present (i.e., kibbutz Metser and Kafr Messer).

33. Issam Sakhnini, *Palestine the State* (Acre: Al-Aswar, 1986), p. 11.

34. Ibid.

35. Avi Shlaim, *The Iron Wall Israel and the Arab World* (New York: W.W. Norton and Co., 2001).

36. Eugene Weiner, ed. "Coexistence Work: A New Profession," in T*he Handbook of Interethnic Coexistence* (New York: The Continuum Publishing Company, 1998), pp. 13–26.

37. Fatah's Central Committee in 1965 declared in Article 2 that the Palestine liberation movement is not struggling against the Jews as an ethnic and religious community. It is struggling against Israel as the expression of colonization based on a theocratic, racist, and expansionist system and of Zionism and colonization. As described in Article 5.5, the final objective of its struggle is the restoration of the independent democratic state of Palestine whose citizens will enjoy equal rights irrespective of their religion.

38. "Documents on Palestine," p. 203.

39. Givat Haviva, http://www.givathaviva.org/about_us.html, 2004.

40. Bar-On, Mordechai, *In Pursuit of Peace: A History of the Israeli Peace Movement* (Washington, D.C.: United States Institute of Peace, 1996), p. 19.

41. Democracy and Dissent," pp. 137–138.

42. Rael Jean Isaac, *Israel Divided: Ideological Politics in the Jewish State* (Baltimore: Johns Hopkin University Press, 1976), p. 45.

43. The "Peace and Security Movement" was launched a year after the June 1967 War in Tel Aviv by a prominent group of professors, among them Yehoshua Arieli on the formula of trading back the Occupied Territories for peace and recognition by the Arabs. Several years later, a group of retired high-ranking officers in the military, police, and security services, and diplomats set up an organization, still active, with the same name, but with the word "council" replacing "movement."

44. Ibid., p. 73.

45. Musa Budeiri and others critical views about the Israeli Peace Camp, and the Palestinian-Israeli dialogue, *Alternative Information Center,* 1994, p. 16.

46. Mahmoud Muhareb, *The Israeli Communist Party and the Palestinian Question, 1948–1981* (Jerusalem: 1989), pp. 133, 142.

47. The meeting was held in Prague in May 1977 and another one in 1980 in which Yasser Arafat participated personally. Mahmoud Abbas (Abu Mazen), *Why These Contacts?* Palestine publishing house, May 1990, p. 2.

48. The thirteenth session of the Palestinian National council in Cairo (March 1977), Resolution No. 14 confirmed "the importance of relationship and the coordination with the Jewish and democratic and progressive Jewish forces that are struggling inside the home land and outside against Zionism as a faith, and as a practice."

The sixtieth session of the Palestinian National Council in Algeria (February 1983) became more flexible when it decided to call "the executive committee of PLO to study the movement in this framework (the framework of the relations with the Jewish and Israel Peace movement), in the way that is 'suitable to the interests of Palestinian case and the Palestinian national struggle.'"

The Palestinian National council session number 18 in Algeria (April 1987) become more clear speaking about the development of the relationship with the Jewish Democratic movements that support the Palestinian people's struggle for return, self-determination, and the establishment of a Palestinian state, and also which recognize the PLO as a "sole and legitimate representative of the Palestinian people."

49. "Documents on Palestine," p. 225.

50. Keren, M. (2003), pp. 27–28.

51. Ibid., Keren notes that although most jurists did not support the discussions with the PLO, their concern for civil rights caused them to vocally oppose conviction of people holding dialogues with the PLO. It may be that in doing so they contributed in some degree to changing the perception of the PLO by decisionmakers from an organization with which dialog is considered treason to a strategic partner, (p. 30).

52. Ibid., pp. 27–31.

53. Already in the Cairo twelfth PNC of 1974 resolution 2 stated: "The liberation Organization will employ all means, and first and foremost armed struggle, to liberate Palestinian territory and to establish the independent combatant national authority for the people over every part of Palestinian territory that is liberated."

54. The term "peace camp" can be interpreted as a field with many tents, the biggest being Peace Now but many other smaller tents coming up and down with sectoral characteristics (religious, ethnic, professional, location), for further analysis see E. Kaufman, "The Intifadah and the Peace Camp in Israel," *Journal of Palestine Studies* (Vol. XVII, 4, summer 1988), pp. 66–80.

55. *Al-Ahd Magazine,* Vol. 41, May 16, 1985, pp. 12–13.

56. Simha Flapan, Ed. "When Enemies Dare to Talk: An Israeli-Palestinian Debate" (London: New Outlook, and Croom Helm Ltd., 1979).

57. B'Tselem, *http://www.btselem.org/* 2004.

58. Ibid., p. 68.

59. Sari Nusseibeh was then beaten by Birziet University students for such provocative ideas, pro-peace activities, and realistic statements.

60. Sai'd Hamami's support for an Israeli Palestinian peace was clear when he spoke in 1975 in the National Liberal Club in London suggesting the establishment of a Palestinian state in the areas that would be returned by Israel as a result of a peace settlement; open borders between the state of Israel and the Palestinian state, in order to "encourage" mutual cultural and economic activities; the granting of the right of Israeli Jews to live in Palestine in exchange for the right of an equivalent number of Palestinian Arabs to return to Israel; the withdrawal of Israel to the borders of June 4, 1967, as a part of the peace, in which both sides would freely express their opinions. And, the aspiration for the reunion of the country, based upon the agreement on both nations, eventually, perhaps not during our lifetime. "In the form of a federation, or any other form." Budieri and others, Ibid., p. 38.

61. Sartawi called early for two states solution, and the modification of PLO National charter, *Al-Ahd Magazine,* Vol. 31, Dec. 16, 1984, p. 811. Symbolically the only existent peace center in a Palestinian institution of higher learning, in Al Quds University, is named after him.

62. From the Israeli side the participants in the meetings with Hamami and Sartawi included Uri Avneri, Matti Peled, Meir Pa'il, Mordechai Bar-On, and others. Some of these meetings were sponsored by the "International Center for Peace in the Middle East" founded in Tel Aviv in 1982 under the leadership of Abba Eban.

63. Edward Said added that "PLO, knew in general about these meetings which were mostly taking place secretly." *Al-Ahd Magazine,* Vol. 41, Apr. 16, 1985, pp. 12–13.

64. For instance, Walid Khalidi, Hisham Sharabi, participated in a meeting with Salah Khalaf from Fatah Central Committee, and Israelis from the International Center for Peace in 1984 in Budapest.

65. This initiative also included a paper, "Negotiating the Non-Negotiable: Jerusalem in the Framework of an Israeli-Palestinian Settlement," by Naomi Chazan

of the Hebrew University and later a member of the Knesset, with consensual commentaries by two distinguished Palestinian U.S.-based professors, Rashid Khalidi and Fouad Moughrabi. This example demonstrates that no topic is beyond the boundaries of possible discussion or potential agreement.

66. Mark Heller and Mark and Sari Nusseibeh. Another example is a book written by five Arabs and five Jews: Kaufman, Edy, Abed, Shukri, and Robert Rothstein, eds., *Democracy, Peace, and the Israeli-Palestinian Conflict* (Boulder, Colo.: Lynne Rienner Publishers, 1993).

67. These obstacles were already laid out before the first intifada by the argumentation of Jonathan Kuttab and Edy Kaufman in "An Exchange on Dialogue," *Journal of Palestine Studies* XVII, 2 (Winter 1988), 84–109.

2

Civil Society and NGOs Building Peace in Israel

Tamar Hermann

In Israel issues of war and peacebuilding, as in most other countries, have traditionally been among the most protected issues in terms of the ability of individual citizens and civil organizations to have a say in policymaking. Not only have the government and the military elite seen themselves as most qualified, best informed, and fully authorized to take such decisions on their own, but the majority of the citizens have also regarded them as such, while viewing themselves as barely capable of participating in the process. This granting to politicians and generals full authority while belittling the citizens' role was based on the common wisdom about the extremely complex and critical nature of the issues at stake and citizens' lack of access to classified information.

In the past few decades, however, in Israel as in many other countries, this monopoly has been gradually eroded. Now the public's voice is not only somewhat better heard but is considered legitimate. This gradual yet substantial change has had much to do with the worldwide decrease in public confidence in state institutions and political establishments. Traditional power centers have been losing their hegemonic position. This process of relocating authority has been augmented by the public availability of huge amounts of data on almost every conceivable issue, including the most confidential aspects of states' foreign and security relations. These data can be retrieved and disseminated through the mass media and the internet so that social actors can skillfully compete with official institutions at least in shaping public opinion, though still to a much lesser degree in crafting national policies. Too often civil-society experts, researchers, and activists alike have a blind spot for grassroots activities that contravene their own political preferences, which in most cases are on the liberal end of the political spectrum. These analyses often try to portray unidimensional civil societies that are benign in terms of civil rights, human rights, or peacemaking, while ignoring the groups that promote discrimination or racism or that oppose resolution of ethnic or national conflicts. Such resolution could mean sacrificing national, material, or ideological values that are cherished more than peace. Thus the civil organizations are often regarded, even when evidence suggests otherwise, as the institutions responsible for the delicate task of direct peacebuilding and reconciliation. The prevalent view of a society as the antithesis of the supposedly belligerent and oppressive state goes hand in hand with the belief in the basically amicable, nonviolent nature of the person in the street. Thus the existence of individuals and grassroots groups that inflame conflicts, and take actions meant to force the authorities into aggressive measures against the other side, is too often ignored. This blind spot also has a pragmatic aspect; societal organizations often receive substantial international funds and equally generous investments of hope.

Yet, in the name of academic integrity, the entire spectrum of civil activities should be examined regardless of one's own political or moral preferences. Furthermore, in each sociopolitical context there is a need to identify the conditions—the political structure of opportunity—that either facilitate or impede civil-society activities as such. These conditions include the relative flexibility or rigidity of the institutionalized political system; the stability of the broad set of elite alignments that typically underpin a polity; the presence of allies within the elite circles; and the state's propensity for repression. In other words, better understanding the organizations that interest researchers requires investigating the full spectrum of conditions for civil activity, regardless of its specific context. This broad perspective is even more important for accurately analyzing the situation, let alone for making the astute political predictions needed to remove potential "peace spoilers."

The first question to be discussed in this chapter is to what extent, if at all, the Israeli NGOs were a factor in launching the Middle East peace process, and what their relative influence was during the Oslo process years (1993–2000). Next, I examine these NGOs' ideological and operative reactions to the Oslo process and the way it developed. I will also look at the various peace-related NGOs' interactions with the general public and with the political establishment. Finally, I consider how the collapse of the Oslo Accords affected the Israeli NGOs, and draw some conclusions about the role of civil societies thus far in the Israeli-Palestinian peacebuilding process.

Before turning to those questions, it will be helpful to survey citizen activism in Israel.

Citizen Activism in Israel: A Brief Overview

Citizen activism became an integral part of Israeli political life only in the 1970s. The first two decades of statehood (from 1948 to the late 1960s) were characterized by centralist and collectivist tendencies. Voluntary, or civil, political endeavors, either as social movements or NGOs, were seen as being against the state's interest and discouraged. Thus, in the country's formative era, voluntary activity, which had been extensive before the formal establishment of the state of Israel, declined considerably. Particularly in the 1950s, the Israeli government was preoccupied with establishing its authority and regarded such activities as a threat. Political parties were the only channel though which the public was expected to transmit its views and demands. Israel in that period can unequivocally be defined as a "party-state," and did not change much in this respect until the late 1960s. Furthermore, rising living standards, consumerism, and individualism toward the end of that decade, together with the fatigue after years of national mobilization and warfare, sustained the tendency to concentrate on the private rather than the public sphere. Therefore civil activity was meager.

By the end of the 1960s, the political structure of opportunity became a bit more favorable to extra-parliamentary activity, as certain developments led to the advent of a civil society. First of all, both the political system and the decisionmakers' authority had become solid. Second, the threat to national security declined significantly after the Six-Day War of 1967, greatly relieving anxiety and fostering tolerance for nonconformist attitudes and modes of activity. At the same time, new controversies emerged, mostly concerning the territories acquired in the war.

There were other changes that promoted civil activity. News reports about the civil rights movement in the United States, and about student revolts and antiwar campaigns in the West in general, exposed Israel to the possibility of direct citizen participation in "high politics." A growing nonconformity and search for alternative modes of political expression were also encouraged by the generational change that took place in Israel in the late 1960s. Young people just entering the political arena had been politically socialized in the Israeli milieu, but they had never experienced such collective traumas as the Holocaust or the bloody struggle for independence and they had a much greater sense of security and self-reliance than their parents' generation—as well as a readiness to criticize the authorities.

In the early 1970s these changes were not fully visible and grassroots initiatives such as the Israeli Black Panthers often failed to gain political influence; such developments fostered a deep transformation in Israeli political activity. The wave of soldiers' protest after the war in 1973, which sparked an open debate over the decisionmakers' competence, contributed much to legitimizing action outside of the Knesset and to breaking the taboo on openly criticizing the government's foreign and security policies. Indeed, in the early 1970s, Israel witnessed increasing civil discontent that challenged the state monopoly that used the ruling ethos of security. And so in the mid-1970s the largest right-wing[1] movement to this day, Gush Emunim (Bloc of the Faithful), was established, and in 1978 the largest peace movement to this day, Peace Now, appeared on the political stage. Numerous smaller civil bodies dealing with peace-related matters also emerged, becoming visible participants in the national security discourse. Citizens' political activity in this realm peaked during the Lebanon War (1982) and the first Palestinian intifada (1987–1990). Both left- and right-wing groups have engaged in intensive peace/war-related civil activities, the former advocating concessions to obtain an agreement with the Palestinians and the latter working to make the occupied territories an integral part of Israel. The 1991 Gulf War diminished both the Palestinian resistance and the Israeli activism, but also created new domestic, regional, and international environments that changed the rules of the game in terms of peacebuilding in the Middle East.

Israeli Civil-Society Organizations and Launching the Oslo Process

Labour's victory in the 1992 elections, albeit by a very slim margin, marked a turning point in Israel's formal attitude toward the peace talks that began with the Madrid conference in the fall of 1991. Participation in the conference was imposed on Yitzhak Shamir's Likud government by the US administration of George H. W. Bush, and the talks soon ran aground. The new government headed by Yitzhak Rabin declared its intention to pursue peace and a political breakthrough as its main goal, and a majority of the Israeli public approved. At the same time, Rabin's victory was no less due to his reputation as "Mr. Security." He was a former chief of staff of the IDF and defense minister during the first intifada, whose concern for Israel's security was paramount. In other words, although Israeli society had authorized Rabin to go ahead with the bilateral and unilateral talks within the Madrid framework (in which the Palestinians were not separately represented but were part of the Jordanian delegation), Israelis also expected him to safeguard the country's security.

So the signing of the Oslo Declaration of Principles (DOP) in August 1993 and of the formal agreement in Washington, D.C., in the following September was not a total surprise. Yet the government went further than originally expected by many Israelis who voted Labour, let alone those who voted for Likud and other right-wing parties. Public opinion, it should be emphasized, was not at all prepared for such a leap forward. This marked the first time any Israeli government had publicly acknowledged that the territorial and other compromises a political solution entailed, however painful, were justified for the nation's long-term interests. Given the background of the formal position of all former Israeli governments, Labour and Likud, which defined the Israeli–Arab conflict as a zero-sum activity and made illegitimate any Palestinian claim to the land and to an independent state, the Rabin government's declared acceptance of the costs of a political solution came as a shock.

How did the Israeli public actually react to this shift? I will first consider unorganized public opinion, that is, public perceptions as measured by polls, and then "organized" public opinion, as manifested by civil-society actors.

Israeli Public Opinion and the Oslo Challenge

As Figure 2.1 indicates, throughout the Rabin-Peres era Israeli Jewish public opinion was split almost equally between supporters and opponents of the Oslo process.[2] At the same time the wide, but never all-encompassing, support was undercut by the considerably lower level of belief that the process would succeed. Not once since the signing of the Oslo agreement did an absolute majority of Israeli Jews support it.[3]

As expected, support for the Oslo process has been much higher among the voters of the left-to-center parties (Labour and Meretz) than among the voters of the right-wing and religious parties (see Figure 2.2).[4]

As both figures show, public support for the Oslo process began to decline significantly not, as commonly believed, after the failed Camp David summit in the summer of 2000, but even a few months after Ehud Barak was elected as prime minister in May 1999. Apparently the ongoing deadlock in the political negotiations (along with the frequent Palestinian terror attacks against civilians both inside and outside the Green Line—the internationally recognized pre-1967 border between Israel and Jordan), which was not broken after the elections, disillusioned most Israeli Jews about the Oslo process and Palestinians well before the process was declared dead by the decisionmakers. Nevertheless, this erosion was clearly accelerated after Camp David, as Israel adopted the formal position—eagerly embraced by the public—that the negotiations had failed because Arafat had rejected Barak's highly conciliatory offer and refused to announce, in return, the end of the Israeli–Palestinian conflict. With the outbreak of the second Palestinian intifada in October 2000, Israeli support for the process reached an unprecedented low, and so has been limited since then to less than 30 percent of the Jewish population. Almost without exception, all remaining supporters identify themselves in surveys as being on the left. This, at the moment, seems to be the rather small pro-Oslo "hard core," and the reservoir of civil activities promoting peace plans based on similar principles.

At the same time, for quite a while those supporting the resumption of negotiations with the Palestinian Authority, though not within the Oslo framework, amount to at least 50 percent. This means that while the Oslo package is indeed a nonstarter, a political solution is still considered desirable. It also indicates that the government has not been so successful in persuading the public that "there is no one to talk to" on the Palestinian side. This, as will be maintained below, may be a significant achievement of the peace camp, which has insisted that the Palestinians collectively have not turned their backs on peace. Furthermore, today over 70 percent of Israel's Jews supports the two-state solution, with 65 to 70 percent supporting the evacuation of all Gaza settlements, and 50 percent favoring the evacuation

Figure 2.1 Support and Belief in the Oslo Process
(Monthly mean calculation for June 1994–December 2003)

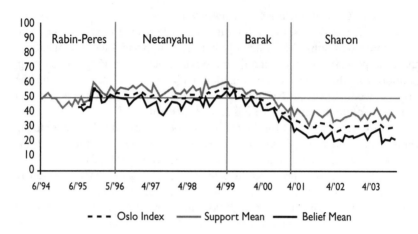

Figure 2.2 Oslo Index by Left–Right Voting
(Monthly Mean Calculations, June 1994–December 2003)

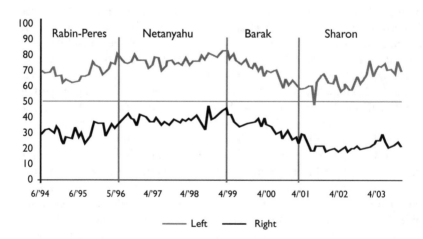

of West Bank settlements apart from the large blocs. These findings suggest that although Oslo per se is not popular, its basic postulates have indeed been absorbed.

Whom do Israelis consider the legitimate actors in the foreign and security realm, including peacebuilding, and what means do they see as legitimate in this context? As noted, Israel has had an establishment-oriented sociopolitical system, and still does, with civil actors perceived as marginal in general and even more so in foreign and security issues. The government is regarded as the main source of authority, other sources (including, for example, international law) as secondary or tertiary only. For example, in October 2003, 65 percent of the Jewish respondents in the Peace Index survey said about the Geneva Initiative that only the government should negotiate peace with the Palestinians and that any civil group conducting such negotiations undermines the government's authority. Only 28 percent thought it legitimate for NGOs to conduct such talks even though such talks clearly are not binding. A majority also thought that only the Israeli government can decide the route of the separation fence, and that the Green Line should not dictate this route.

As for the legitimate means available to civil actors, when asked several times since 1994 about the right of citizens dissatisfied with the government's handling of the peace process to protest against it, each time 80 to 85 percent acknowledged this right, but only if the means of protest are strictly legal. Around 10 to 15 percent also legitimized illegal but purely nonviolent civil activity such as refusal to pay taxes, and the constantly tiny remainder, around 5 percent, also sanctioned illegal, even violent acts of protest. A similar tendency to delegitimize any civil act that is not totally legal emerges in Israelis' overwhelming disapproval of conscientious objection, or of refusal to serve in the occupied territories. This opposition is not based on the fact that such refusal generally comes from the left, since a similar number opposed potential refusal by right-wing soldiers to evacuate settlements under orders. Around 75 percent saw as illegitimate both kinds of refusal in the various measurements, with at most 25 percent approving such refusal.

Civil-Society Organizations' Reactions to the Oslo Process

Civil Activities of the Right During the Oslo Period
Forces on the right saw the strategic shift represented by the process in Oslo as mistaken and extremely dangerous. The Oslo narrative adopted by the right-wing parties and groups reflected many reservations about the process, involving the security risk, the impairment of the Zionist endeavor, the religious transgression, and the ominous achievement of the leftist Labour-Meretz government. This narrative maintained that although peace

was desirable, the Oslo peace was a mirage. It attributed major blame for this ill-conceived step to the Labour decisionmakers. It could not be denied, however, that Rabin and his cabinet members were known for their patriotism and long experience in dealing with security matters. The right therefore needed another target to blame, and putting the onus on the left in general and the peace movement in particular made perfect tactical sense. Thus, the right attributed much more efficacy and influence to the peace camp than did Labour and most Israelis, including many peace activists.

Considering that the right wing ascribes ultimate religious and national importance to Jewish ownership of the entire land of Israel, and since 1967 had invested so much energy and resources in the settlement project, it was not surprising that when grasping the significance of the DOP, the right-wing parties and NGOs joined forces to stop the process and reverse the moves already taken. Effective civil opposition was not easy at this stage. The traditional, major NGO of this camp, Gush Emunim, had been hibernating for much of the late 1980s and early 1990s, with many of its prominent activists already absorbed into the state-sponsored administration of the settlements. Although this coopting had done much to advance the settlers' cause during the initial Likud era, it was now a significant obstacle to organizing right-wing protest against Labour's peace policy. Nevertheless, with the help of the right-wing parties and of wealthy Jewish supporters mostly from the United States and Australia, various smaller groups managed to organize large-scale anti-Oslo activities. Numerous ads against the government's and the prime minister's policies were also published in daily newspapers, and vicious pamphlets, some bearing a photomontage of Rabin dubbed "traitor" and dressed in a Nazi uniform, were distributed all over the country.

Typically, these right-wing activists were between the ages of 16 and 40, traditional or Orthodox in religious self-definition, and average or lower in education and income. They included both Mizrahi (Sephardi) and Ashkenazi Jews, with somewhat more men than women. The settlers and their supporters played a pivotal role in activities against Rabin's government, knowing that the process would eventually have entailed an extensive settlement evacuation. Right-wingers perceived immediate dangers both to their personal well-being and way of life and to national security.

Along with their massive anti-Oslo campaign, the settlers continued expanding the settlements, often without the government's permission. Admittedly the Israeli authorities, even when Labour was in power, have never taken real steps to prevent these civil initiatives, even when clearly unlawful. In other words, while the government talked peace with the Palestinians, these Israeli civilians took steps to create facts on the ground that would impede any peace plan. Furthermore, some new, small, radical right-wing groups appeared at that time, such as the women's group Women in

Green, whose members vigorously protested any move aimed at advancing the peace process. The most visible right-wing extra-parliamentary group at that time, however, was one called This Is Our Land (Zo Artzenu). Ironically invoking Martin Luther King as a model of civil disobedience, it protested the government's alleged betrayal both of vital security interests and of the religious value of land settlement. The group used such techniques of nonviolent resistance as blocking roads and burning tires, and was fairly successful in conveying its message. Its leader, Moshe Feiglin, was indicted for disrupting public order but eventually was almost fully acquitted on freedom-of-speech grounds.

Prominent figures of the Orthodox rabbinical establishment, which largely backed the settlers, strongly condemned the expected ceding of territories and, with the signing of a final status agreement, extensive settlement evacuation. A few rabbis even declared Rabin a transgressor deserving the death penalty according to *halacha* (Jewish law). As a direct or indirect result, on November 5, 1995, Rabin was murdered by Yigal Amir, a political activist of the religious radical right and a law student at the religious Bar-Ilan University. Apparently not dispatched by any specific civil group, but involved in many civil-society activities aimed at stopping the Oslo process, Amir took a step that, in retrospect, appears to have been successful in derailing the peace process. All of Israeli society was deeply shocked by the assassination, but there is evidence that in certain civil circles of the right and in various settlements people actually expressed satisfaction at Amir's deed. Indeed, less than a year later new elections were held and the winner was the head of the right-wing Likud Party, Binyamin Netanyahu.

In the ensuing years civil activities by the right decreased considerably in volume and visibility. To some extent, this reflected the prevalent sense in Israel and elsewhere that while Rabin's assassination was perhaps the handiwork of an individual, it basically was the bitter fruit of incitement against the peace process and its leaders by many on the right. In addition, there was much less motivation for such activities as the Likud-led government slowed the peace negotiations to a minimum, let alone withdrawing from the territories.

Civil Activities of the Left During the Oslo Period

From the late 1960s, and much more emphatically since the late 1970s, various groups on the Israeli left, often categorized as the peace camp or peace movement, have rejected the logic of power politics and promoted the notion of compromise and win-win solutions to the Middle East conflict. These groups greatly differ from each other in terms of their preferred tactics. Thus some focus on a humanitarian mission, while others prefer more political activities, but all have denounced military means of resolving conflict as more costly and less effective than political means. Unlike the Israeli mainstream in the pre-Oslo era, the peace groups recognized the Palestinians' right to self-determination and the Palestine Liberation Organization (PLO) as their legitimate representative. They also acknowledged that significant territorial concessions by Israel, however painful, are worthwhile in terms of the state's long-term security. In fact, apart from the Israeli Communist Party, which has always been widely suspected of siding with the Arabs and whose agenda has never received much attention, the peace movement was the first to promote the two-state solution, an idea that was widely deplored at the time.

Unlike most other peace movements around the world, neither pacifism nor religion (or religious dictums about war and peace) has ever been a significant part of the Israeli peace movement's ideology. Furthermore, the larger and more visible peace organizations, primarily Peace Now, have openly identified with the basic Zionist creed and have never embraced antimilitaristic positions. The notion of justified wars, or "no-choice" wars, was an integral part of most of these organizations' agendas, and most peace activists have done military reserve duty when called up, sometimes immediately before or after taking part in a peace demonstration. This, incidentally, is one of the main reasons Israeli Arabs have not joined the peace movement or participated in its activities, though politically speaking their views on resolving the conflict were fairly similar.

The Israeli Arabs who work for peace have preferred to do so in their own organizations, though for many years they were careful not to give the impression that they were siding with their Palestinian brethren. As we shall see, since the September 2000 events in which Israeli Arabs clashed violently with the police, Israeli Arabs have adopted a more negative stance toward the state. Another catalyst for their deeper involvement in peace-oriented, antigovernment initiatives was the emergence in recent years of non-Zionist or anti-Zionist peace groups, such as Ta'ayush, in which Jewish and Arab activists join forces. A further factor in Israeli Arab absence from most Israeli peace groups and NGOs through the early 2000s, even from the more radical ones such as Gush Shalom (Peace Bloc), was the implicit but real reluctance of the Jewish participants to further undermine their groups' public appeal by having Arabs on board, which might have put in question these groups' primary loyalty to the Israeli Jewish collective. Indeed, although Israeli peace organizations have often engaged in dialogue (along with occasional joint activities) with Palestinians from the occupied territories, even when such meetings were illegal, mostly they have looked inward and addressed the Israeli Jewish public and decisionmakers.

Israeli peace activists, whose number has declined from tens of thousands at certain peaks of activity to thousands or even fewer, have had a fairly homogeneous sociodemographic profile, considerably different from that of the right-wing activists. The peace activists were somewhat older, mostly in their thirties and forties, and today tend to be older still on average. With few exceptions they were of Ashkenazi descent, secular, urban, usually highly educated, and mostly of the middle class. They included a high proportion of women, which proved problematic, since many Israelis regard women, who usually have had no combat experience, as unqualified to deal with security issues. The average peace activist as an individual was then located in or near the Israeli sociopolitical center, with many of them holding prominent academic and other positions. Yet, because of their nonconformist views about the conflict, as a political collective actor the peace movement was relegated to the margins. The mainstream parties and groups, from Likud to Labour, tended to reject the peace movement's outlook—until suddenly, in 1993, almost all its principles were adopted by the Rabin government as it began the Oslo process (a process originally launched, it is worth recalling, by a group of Israelis acting as a Track II without official authority).

On the face of it, then, the strategic transformation entailed by the Oslo process was a great success for the peace movement, and indeed the movement in general, apart from some small radical groups, applauded the Labour government's steps from the beginning. Yet, almost immediately after the signing of the DOP, it became clear that the peace movement was being deflected and kept far from the negotiations. Moreover, in an apparently calculated attempt to dissociate the peace process from the peace movement, the Israeli decisionmakers refused to give the latter any credit for its past efforts and sometimes even scorned it in public. No member of the peace movement was ever invited to the signing ceremonies for the various agreements, nor were the movement's connections with Palestinians ever used, even at times when negotiations reached a dead end.

Nevertheless, as noted, the peace activists generally adopted the Oslo cause and did not claim credit for its basic underpinnings. Indeed, they continued to support the Labour government even when its stances, even at an early stage of the negotiations, were seen as too rigid by many peace activists. By the early 1990s, after years of arduous activism (and usually in contention with the mainstream), many of the activists were exhausted and decided to leave peacebuilding in the hands of the government. There were also doubts about the need for civil activism when the government was promoting the cause of peace. So in the first half of the 1990s the peace movement basically went into hibernation.

In retrospect, this proved costly to maintaining the movement's momentum and visibility. Although in later years it was sometimes able to bring thousands to public squares to protest actions counter to peace taken by the Netanyahu or Sharon governments, these were only sporadic events that were insufficient to reawaken the peace camp even when it was called for. The heavy engagement of certain peace groups in reconciliation work (e.g., dialogues, joint projects, visits) did not serve well enough for massing any peace protest when the time arrived. Ongoing projects such as the "settlement watch" operated by Peace Now, which was indeed very important in exposing the realities of continuous land expropriations and expansion of the settlements against the agreements signed with the Palestinians and the official declarations of the various Israeli governments, were equally ineffective.

Despite the decline in its vitality, certain structural and ideological developments in the Israeli peace movement since the first half of the 1990s deserve attention, since they shed light on its activities since the collapse of the Oslo Accords in the summer of 2000. The first is the institutionalization the movement has undergone: organizations that formerly were completely voluntary and grassroots based, including Peace Now, are now at least partly composed of paid personnel. With generous financial assistance from such external donors as the European Union and international foundations, which were interested in supporting the peace process from below, some peace groups managed to rent larger offices, open bank accounts, and register with the Israeli authorities to obtain tax benefits. Newly emerging organizations, such as the Israeli-Palestinian women's organization The Jerusalem Link (Bat Shalom, Daughter of Peace, was its Israeli component), often were not only supported by external donors but their structure and modes of action were strongly influenced by donor suggestions. Hence, from the start these NGOs functioned as fully institutionalized bodies, with formal procedures of leader selection and a clear organizational structure. Later even more institutionalized peace groups emerged that are by no means grassroots oriented. The best example is perhaps the Peres Center for Peace, established in September 1997 and then headed by Shimon Peres, the Israeli politician most associated with the Oslo process and the vision of a New Middle East. The center organizes various dialogue forums, raises enormous amounts of money for joint Israeli-Palestinian ventures and, for example, further encourages foreign (mainly European) interest in Middle East peace.

Another development, stemming from necessity, was the creation of various ad hoc coalitions that included peace and human rights groups. The aim was to counter the negative effects the smallness of these individual groups. Thus, the decrease in the number of activists and available resources led to enhanced cooperation between the surviving peace NGOs. Some coalitions were formed for a single event (for instance, a demonstration). Others were intended to be more lasting endeavors, such as the campaign against the "silent transfer" of Palestinian residents from Jerusalem (to maintain the city's Jewish majority), or the problem of indefinite administrative detention of Palestinians suspected of hostile acts or even views. Along with participating in these coalitions, the organizations maintained their distinctive goals and character. A typical, highly active coalition is the

Israeli Committee against the Demolition of Homes, which encompasses Bat Shalom, Rabbis for Human Rights, Peace Now, and the (Palestinian) Land Defense Committee. The coalition's sole purpose is to fight the Israeli policy of destroying houses built without permits by Palestinians on their own property in the occupied territories. So far the coalition has not been very successful in stopping these acts, but is highly successful in gaining media exposure of the injustice and hardship they inflict on Palestinians. One of the most active coalitions appears to be the Women's Peace Coalition, which brings together all the women's peace organizations, from the moderate to the radical, and has initiated some of the more impressive peace protests and activities in recent years.

Despite the relative weakness of the peace camp, the late 1990s saw at least one case in which it influenced the state's security policy. The Four Mothers Movement was launched in 1997 by four mothers of Israel Defense Force (IDF) soldiers serving in southern Lebanon, and was rapidly joined by many more mothers demanding that Israel withdraw its forces from there. This movement attracted much attention from the media, the public, and even the political establishment. When Prime Minister Barak decided on an Israeli withdrawal from this area, and implemented it in June 2000, it was widely attributed to the pressures exerted by this group and its growing circle of supporters. Besides this specific achievement, this movement has left a legacy of success that was much needed for the peace movement to keep functioning.

This was particularly important in the late 1990s. The prolonged stalemate in the negotiations, along with Israel's apparent reluctance to implement the interim agreements and the Palestinian Authority's inability or unwillingness to prevent terrorist attacks, discouraged many peace activists who opted for what the literature calls "internal exit," or leaving the public sphere for private concerns. Many hard-core activists reacted to the deteriorating situation by moving further to the left and becoming more radical in their criticism, particularly of the Israeli government, but sometimes of the Palestinian Authority. Still, the whole peace movement was taken aback by the breakdown of the Oslo process in July 2000 and the eruption of the second intifada in October.

The Collapse of the Oslo Process and Its Effects on Civil Society

The failure of the Camp David Summit, after which Prime Minister Barak proclaimed all previous Israeli offers null and void, could have just turned the wheel back to the pre-Oslo era. But the disillusionment with the other side and the frustration at the futility of the Oslo negotiations were much greater than ever in the past because they came after a period of such great hope. Thus, the second intifada and ensuing deterioration of Israeli-Palestinian relations into waves of mutual violence, in many respects unprecedented, have pushed public opinion away from the peace camp. However, subsequently some of this camp's ideas, mainly the preference for the two-state solution, have been widely embraced.

The civil organizations have reacted to this traumatic experience in various ways. On the right, particularly among the settlers in the occupied territories, it was taken as solid proof of the accuracy of their reading of the other side's negative intentions. The time, though, was not suitable for dwelling on "we told you so" recriminations. The many incidents of Palestinians shooting at Israeli cars in the territories and the killings of civilians in the settlements led to the emergence of Jewish civilian militia groups, which have been patrolling the roads in addition to the regular IDF patrols— but without supervision by the authorities. Settlers in these patrols have sometimes also entered Palestinian towns and villages to take revenge for Palestinian acts, often targeting innocent bystanders and destroying the property of Palestinians who had no involvement in attacks on Israelis. Some settler activists have uprooted Palestinian olive orchards to demonstrate domination over the land. They have also violently disrupted, by shooting and rioting, the olive harvests by neighboring Palestinian villagers. Indeed, Israeli peace activists have gone to these villages to express solidarity with the Palestinians and protect them from the extremist settlers' wrath. But in most cases the peace activists did not remain more than a day or two, so their gestures, however symbolically important, were less effective than those of the right-wing activists, who lived nearby and posed a constant threat to the Palestinians around them.

Another form of civil activism by the radical right has been carried out by the younger generation of settlers, Noar Ha'Gvaot (Youth of the Hills). These young Orthodox males, many of them born and raised in the "old" settlements, create new, illegal, miniature outposts of a few people each outside the large settlements, often next to Palestinian villages. These outposts are sometimes established in response to terrorist events, but cumulatively they have a strategic aim: to create a new geopolitical reality of Jewish presence all over the West Bank, so that drawing a border there between Jews and Palestinian will become impossible. The not too serious attempts to remove these outposts by the IDF and the police have met fierce resistance by these youths, who have been logistically and even more so ideologically supported by older leaders of settler communities.

By and large, at the time of this writing, the right's motivation for energetic civil initiatives against the government seems rather low, since present policies are still fairly consonant with this camp's goals. Indeed, the settler leaders have close relations with the government and there are even representatives of the settlers in the cabinet. However, with the introduction of Prime Minister Sharon's unilateral disengagement plan in early 2004, a plan that includes the removal of all Jewish settlements in the Gaza Strip and a few ones in the West Bank, the citizens' groups on the right have awakened again. In fact, their activists managed a rather impressive demonstration of effective grassroots activity to convince the majority of the Likud members who took part in the referendum on this issue to vote against the plan. The right-wing activists inflicted a major political defeat on "their" government, which was apparently not right-wing enough. However, Sharon did not stop this move and in a few weeks managed to garner the support of the majority in his cabinet for his plan, which was fully implemented in the summer of 2005.

For the peace camp, the collapse of negotiations and, much worse, the upsurge in Palestinian violence against Israeli civilians, the suicide bombings came as a severe blow. Their political rationale seemed to have been discredited, and many former activists "went home," turning their backs on the option of reconciliation with the Palestinians. External financial support has shrunk considerably as many liberal Jewish donors became disillusioned with the cause of peace. The post–September 11 international environment is also not conducive to peace negotiations with Arabs.

Needless to say, after the massive retaliation campaigns by the Israeli army, the situation is not amenable to Palestinian-Israeli dialogue, not only because travel between Israel and the occupied territories has become virtually impossible, but mainly because the Palestinian counterparts have turned against such contact. All the same, certain Israeli-Palestinian joint peace ventures have actually proved resistant to the deterioration and continued to operate. These are usually the most "institutionalized" projects, such as the *Palestine-Israel Journal,* well-established NGOs such as the Israeli/Palestinian Centre for Research and Information (IPCRI), and, perhaps most interestingly, the Bereaved Parents, in which Palestinian and Israeli parents who have lost children in the violence work together for peace.

Given the shift in public opinion, peace demonstrations, which used to be highly popular among the peace groups, have become nearly obsolete. The remaining core of peace activists has had to develop new ideological options and modes of action in response to the recent dismal circumstances. As in the late 1990s, the common ideological reaction has become radical. Criticism of the Israeli government has reached new levels, with some peace organizations even calling for international intervention in the conflict, an idea strongly opposed by the government. A third party, it is maintained, would play the role of facilitator, convener, agenda setter, mediator, coordinator, messenger, and conflict resolver when necessary. Most peace groups strongly oppose the separation fence (in reality a wall). One group of activists traveled to The Hague in February 2004, while an international tribune was deliberating the fence, to express their opposition jointly with Palestinians. Considering that Israel decided not to take part in the discussions and did not recognize the tribunal's authority to deal with the matter, this was indeed a nonconformist initiative by the peace activists. In addition, some small peace groups have relinquished the two-state solution and opted instead for the idea of binationalism (i.e., a single secular-democratic state for both peoples), which currently is strongly rejected by both the Israeli and Palestinian sides, each of which desires a nation-state of its own.

Another development is the emergence of the new civil initiatives for peace, mainly the People's Voice project of Ami Ayalon and Sari Nusseibeh and the Geneva Initiative. Both are based on the assumption that if a sufficiently strong joint wave of public support for resuming the political negotiations is generated, decisionmakers will not be able to ignore it. Also, a much publicized campaign winning the support of many thousands on each side will signal to the other side that despite the hostilities and killings, the "silent majority" of the people on both sides are still interested in peace. The question the organizers had to deal with in both cases was how to create a popular wave of support when the facts on the ground appear so antithetical to the cause of peace. The idea of the People's Voice leaders—Nusseibeh is a renowned academician and independent Palestinian political activist, Ayalon a former commander of the Israeli navy and former head of the General Security Service (Shin Bet)—was to present to the general public (not the "classical" audience in favor of peace) a short document outlining the features of a final status agreement. The initiative aimed to collect hundreds of thousands of signatures of Israelis and Palestinians, hopefully even a million or more. These signatures, collected, for example, through the internet, signing stations in public places, the telephone, and the mail, were to be presented to the authorized decisionmakers of both sides in the hope that this would impel them to renew the negotiations and eventually arrive at an agreement. Over six months after the formal launching of the signing campaign, around 375,000 signatures of Israelis and Palestinians have been collected. This initial list was presented to the president of Israel in a small ceremony. However, this specific event and the campaign in general have garnered almost no media attention and the collection of signatures is progressing slowly, so far not showing enough momentum to shake the political establishment or change the climate of opinion.

The Geneva Initiative is based on a document that is carefully constructed and much longer than the Ayalon-Nusseibeh document, providing elaborate detail in its version of a final status agreement (even though it remains vague on some critical issues, such as the Palestinian refugee right of return). From its inception, the Geneva Initiative has received wide attention both inside and outside Israel for several reasons: (1) it was attacked as subversive by Prime Minister Ariel Sharon shortly before its publication; (2) its Israeli proponents—including Yossi Beilin, a major figure of the Zionist left and former cabinet minister, as well as other Labour and conservative politicians—worked tirelessly in gaining the blessing of prominent world figures such as Nelson Mandela, Mikhail Gorbachev, Bill Clinton, and Kofi Annan; and (3) the Geneva Initiative was printed by the millions and mailed to every home in Israel, so that most Israelis, though finding it far too long (forty-seven pages) and complex to read, became aware of its existence. The reactions of the media and the politicians have been mixed: some have applauded the initiative as courageous and promising, others have denounced it as an unauthorized (if not downright unlawful) move that undermines the Israeli government's efforts to deal effectively with the Palestinians. The fact that the initiative has been financially supported by such external bodies as the Swiss and Japanese governments and by certain Israeli businessmen has harmed its image because its opponents have portrayed it as a vehicle promoting foreign interests inimical to that of Israel. At present, after a festive signing ceremony in Geneva in December 2003, the initiative seems to have slowed considerably and its political effectiveness is unclear.

A third petition-based initiative, One Voice, has joined the former two. Yet, unlike the People's Voice and the Geneva Initiative, it does not present its potential signers with a *fait accompli* formulated by organizers, but aims at letting the public decide on the final document by repeating cycles of signing and amendments of the preliminary platform, based on the principles of deliberative democracy. Some 40,000 signatures of Israelis and Palestinians were collected in the first two phases of the process.

Another recent development on the civil-society level, which seems more significant in the long run than the two grassroots initiatives, is the "refusenik" phenomenon. Since the outbreak of the second Palestinian intifada and Israel's reoccupation of the Palestinian areas, the number of Israelis on active military duty or in the reserves who have refused to serve in the occupied territories has increased dramatically—to over 600 since January 2002.[5] The refuseniks are not all made of the same cloth; a very small number demand exemption from all military service based on a pacifist creed. The larger group, however, many of whom act in the framework of the new Courage to Refuse NGO, are willing to serve elsewhere than the occupied territories. They include not only ordinary soldiers but also members of elite units, such as air force pilots and commandos. This, in addition to the activity of an antimilitarist group called New Profile, which calls for demilitarizing Israeli society, apparently marks a significant change in the Israeli national ethos that previously had idolized the army and military service. This new phenomenon has clearly disturbed the authorities to the extent that Chief of Staff Moshe Ya'alon declared in January 2004 that the weakest link in national defense was the Israeli public and its "lack of stamina." Israelis, he said in a press conference, are not prepared to fight for their goals and risk their lives, and since September 2000 there has been no agreement on what the fighting is about.

Much like the resumed activity of the citizens' groups on the right mentioned above, the Israeli peace movement has also at least partly awakened with the introduction of Sharon's disengagement plan. Thus shortly after the Likud referendum, in which this plan was voted against by the majority of party members who took part in this deliberative process, the peace movement organized a huge demonstration in Tel Aviv, in which the left expressed its support for Israel's withdrawal from Gaza and the evacuation of the settlements there. The activity has not stopped there and is expected to remain high in response to and in order to counter the activities of the settlers and their supporters if this plan is indeed going to be implemented in the upcoming months.

Conclusions

This chapter has considered the main types of Israeli civil activities and NGOs related to the peace process, both on the right and in the peace camp, from the early 1990s to the present. Although it would have been easier and more congenial to present only the civil activities for peace, it would have been misleading to exclude those civil groups and NGOs that do not favorably view resolving the conflict with the entailed price tag—and therefore work to derail the peace process. In other words, this chapter assumes that it is inaccurate to portray a totally peace-seeking civil society that is struggling against a war-mongering state or government. The facts do not support the assumption, very popular in certain circles, that granting power to the people ensures that peace will prevail.

What conclusions, then, emerge from this discussion in terms of the efficacy of civil society in peacebuilding? To start with, it seems that in a given period civil organizations as such, whether for or against peace, all face a similar political structure of opportunity, either benevolent or open or unreceptive. The government's readiness to allow organizations to act and not to oppress them matches the public's legitimization of political activities outside the establishment in the sacrosanct realm of security policy, the ability of such organizations to mobilize support within the political establishment, and, not least, their success in raising funds. Thus, though certain circumstances are more conducive to activities for peace and others to anti-peace-agreement activities, one can expect periods of upsurges or declines in all sorts of grassroots activities depending on the prevailing political-opportunity structure. In times of change requiring critical decisions, when a leader's self-confidence diminishes—for instance, the dramatic shift involving the first Gulf War, the Madrid Conference, and the Oslo Accords—civil activities are considerably more likely to gain momentum, and perhaps political visibility and effect, than in more ordinary times.

Somewhat paradoxically, we have also seen that confrontation with the state authorities invigorates civil movements, whereas greater harmony between the state's and the civil organizations' agenda deflates the efforts of the latter. Thus, when the Israeli government adopted the settlement project and the army reoccupied the territories so that in many respects the pre-Oslo conditions were restored, the motivation for right-wing civil activities declined considerably. The same happened for the left-wing groups when the Rabin government adopted major elements of the peace movement's agenda. The Geneva Initiative's greater success in attracting more attention than the Ayalon-Nusseibeh project also seems to sustain the above inference about the advantages for a civil initiative of confrontation with the political establishment. Whereas the latter initiative has not exhibited defiance and has gone almost unnoticed, the former has been attacked by a prime minister and other politicians, apparently contributing to its greater public exposure and, perhaps, political efficacy.

This brings us to what may be the most important question in the study of civil organizations: to what extent can they effectuate change in so-called high-politics such as peacemaking? Our case study suggests that they do not directly influence specific policies or decisions and their success or failure should not be evaluated on that basis, since generally this is not what civil-society organizations are good at. They are much better at laying the groundwork for cognitive changes and at introducing new options to the national repertoire. Thus, in retrospect, the tireless efforts of the various peace groups to change the perceptions of the Israeli public and its leaders of the advantages of a political solution to the Israeli-Palestinian conflict, or, on a smaller scale, of withdrawing from southern Lebanon, were much more effective than the specific protests against, for example, the demarcation of the separation fence or home demolitions.

At the same time, it appears that civil organizations that struggle to maintain the status quo, such as those that fought against the Oslo process, tend to be more successful in mobilization efforts than organizations that work to change the national modus operandi, such as the peace groups that advocate a shift in Israel's traditional self-image and perception of its external relations. Furthermore, civil organizations that relate to national values and norms and emphasize their patriotic nature have a much better chance of gaining public support in times of conflict—which almost always prevail in the Middle East—than organizations, like the peace groups, that advocate universal values and apply the same normative standards to their own collective and to that of the "enemy." Furthermore, at least in the Israeli context, financial and other kinds of assistance from international bodies seem problematic because they lead the public to question the patriotic nature of the recipient organizations.

It might be of interest here to refer briefly to the relations between Israeli citizen activity and global initiatives and campaigns. Unlike many American and European grassroots campaigns, the Israeli ones on both sides of the political map have been traditionally rather careful not to associate themselves strongly with "external" sister movements and campaigns. The reason for this was their empirically based sense that such association would stain their "patriotic" image and cast doubt on their ultimate loyalty to the Israeli-Jewish collective. Therefore, only small and radical fragments of the Israeli peace movement have joined forces with peace movements all over the world in their protest against the launching of the war on Iraq in 2003. Israeli movements on the right have not even faced such a real dilemma of staying local or going global. Their right-wing counterparts in Europe are often strongly anti-Israeli, or even anti-Semitic, so the cooperation issue was not a relevant one.

As for the operational side, it seems that the classic means used by civil organizations—demonstrations, distributing written materials, petition-signing campaigns, and the like—are of relatively transitory effect. However, prolonged projects involving a higher level of institutionalization, such as ongoing publications, service provision, sustained lobbying, and, for that matter, settlements, are not only better ways to transmit messages but also more effective in terms of binding activists to organizations and nourishing their loyalty to the cause in terms of creating a more serious image both among the public and the decisionmakers.

Notes

1. It should be noted that unlike in Europe, in Israel the left-right dichotomy refers not to differences in the two camps' socioeconomic agendas but mostly to their antithetical security outlooks. The left regards the Israeli–Arab conflict as solvable and hence advocates the land-for-peace formula; the right sees the conflict as a basically zero-sum game and thus opposes significant territorial concessions as too risky.

2. All survey findings are taken from the Peace Index survey project conducted by the Tami Steinmetz Center for Peace Research, Tel Aviv University. The data can be found at www.tau.ac.il under Peace Index.

3. Somewhat paradoxically, on average, the highest support and belief levels were registered during the Netanyahu era. This probably reflects the then-growing number of right-wing voters who expressed support for the process based on Netanyahu's affirmation of Israel's commitment to its obligations under the different Oslo documents it had signed.

4. The reason the very high levels of support for Oslo among the left-wing voters do not influence the results for the overall sample is their much lower and still declining percentage in the population. Israel's Jewish population is not split evenly between left and right, and the much larger group, on the right, which generally opposes the Oslo Accords, pushes the calculated mean down.

5. Although formal records in this regard are not available, the common estimation is that the total number of Israeli men who had refused to serve in the IDF in the years from 1948 to 2001 amounted to no more than 500.

3

Civil Society and NGOs Building Peace in Palestine

Manuel Hassassian

For over a century political and social interactions have overlapped, making it difficult to draw clear, sustainable lines between the two. Both "third-sector" and nongovernmental organization (NGO) concepts are limited in the sense that Palestinians have never had a sovereign or democratic government, and therefore can scarcely have organizations that exist outside such a body. Furthermore, the representative structure that Palestinians have developed, and collectively embodied in the Palestinian Liberation Organization (PLO), incorporates a blend of strong political fabric woven on a social-ideological loom. This means that in contrast to other organizations that have as their raison d'être the liberation of a given homeland, the PLO acts as an umbrella organization that both shoulders responsibility for the breadth of Palestinian political articulation and acts as the sole collective depository for the protection and sustenance of Palestinian nationalism and, very possibly, Palestinian national identity.

One can hardly begin to talk of the effect of peace and conflict resolution organizations (P/CROs) and their role in peacebuilding when for the most part, there are few peace conflict resolution organizations in Palestine, there is very little peacebuilding being done, and there is even less peacebuilding in the larger context that such activity could be a part of. In a sense then, one should not blind oneself with illusions of an imminent Palestinian-Israeli or Arab-Israeli peace initiative when such initiatives are virtually paralyzed.

So what really exists? What precisely is the role of organizations in the "peace process"? What are all these P/CROs within the Palestinian NGOs and what are they doing? The study discussed in this chapter was able to reveal many aspects that reflect the much larger foundations, weakness, and underpinnings of the peace process as a whole.

Essentially, one must become attuned to the fact that the peace process failed to solve any of the major, or even the minor, problems that fundamentally define the conflict. By design, the Oslo peace process was intended to solve the "real problems to the conflict much later on: those of land control, sovereignty, borders, refugees, Jerusalem, settlements, and water." The way things have proceeded, due in large part to consecutive Israeli governments, the Oslo Tracks I and II failed to reach this stage and quixotic hopes were abandoned in favor of more realistic assessments. What the Oslo process began was, therefore, nothing more than scratching the surface: the attempted agreement to resolve the conflict in a political, negotiated, and nonviolent manner, and above all stressing mutual recognition. With the momentum of political movement going in the opposite direction, one can begin to assess what these changes have meant for the supposed peace and conflict resolution sector, which was hardly allowed to develop.

Historical Overview of the Conflict

The PLO: The Palestinian National Movement

To understand the evolution of Palestinian politics in modern times, it is important to examine the Palestinian National Council's (PNC) resolutions, in particular those since the twelfth PNC. Since 1974 the Palestinians have moved steadily toward accommodation and compromise. By the eighteenth PNC, convened in Algiers in April 1987, most of the elements for an embrace of a peaceful strategy and the acceptance of a two-state solution based on UN resolutions were in place. PNC resolutions are considered the culmination of the PLO's dialogue and an "important barometer of the actual thinking of the Palestinian movement." Thus, once adopted they become a legitimizing instrument for politics pursued by the PLO leadership. This role is best illustrated by Yasser Arafat's reference to the nineteenth PNC as the basis for his statement in Geneva in December 1988.

By the nineteenth PNC of 1988, Palestinians endorsed the principles of political accommodation based on UN Security Council resolutions 242 and 338 with the objective of reaching a two-state solution.

However, the essential stakes in the Israeli–Palestinian conflict are the core systems by which nation-states and peoples define their existence, sovereignty, territory, and, above all, security. For Israel, a basic dilemma is the relationship of territory to security and survival, and the question of "secure boundaries" has run through its history as a modern state. Israel's acquisition of more territory after the 1967 war has put it into greater opposition to Palestinian claims and those concerning the territorial integrity of neighboring Arab states.

The Palestinians have been deprived of territory and denied status as a sovereign state, two important factors that mold their political identity. The Palestinian concept of how much territory is required for a viable sovereign state has changed over time. From an early claim, as establishing policy, to all of British mandate Palestine, the Palestinians today are settling for 22 percent of historic Palestine. The building of the security fence (the wall) by Israel is shattering even this aspiration.

The Palestinian people are currently in the middle of a long and hard-fought national struggle that has spanned the greater part of this century. In this struggle NGOs have played a protean role that has fluctuated with the political climate. Before the Zionist conquest of Palestine, NGOs were little more than small groups of city-based individuals who would come together out of mutual interest in a particular issue—women's associations, literary groups, and religious formations all have a history in Palestine that dates back to the 1920s. At that time, civil institutions were limited to the middle and upper classes, which constituted only about 20 percent of the entire Palestinian population. The remaining 80 percent of Palestinian society, peasantry, lived out on farmland in communities without any major form of formal organization. For similar reasons, the Palestinian nationalist movement existed in a nebulous state, varying across communities according to their political hardships, education levels, and material needs. The formation of Israel in 1948 had a shattering effect on all Palestinians, from the ruling elite to the poorest of peasants.

Members of the Palestinian community existed thereafter in diaspora, and the hardships that they endured, whether in refugee camps, their West Bank and Gaza towns, or the newly created Israel, had a profound impact on their political consciousness. This, in turn, directly affected the groups that expressed Palestinian political thought, including political organizations and NGOs.

This study focuses on the period after the first intifada, the Oslo process, and the second intifada. It is during these formative years and thereafter that the roots of modern Palestinian NGO formation can be traced. The PLO was formed and attempted to liberate Palestine with varying degrees of success and failure. The Israeli occupation severely restricted the potential activity of the West Bank and Gaza communities and limited their development, while at the same time encouraged people to leave. In the absence of a representative government, the communities of the Gaza Strip and West Bank began to focus their efforts internally, hoping to maintain and solidify a network of organizations that could respond to their needs. Slowly but surely a network of NGOs emerged that worked on a variety of issues and services.

Methodology of Research

To start, a clear definition of peace and conflict resolution organizations is required. In the Palestinian context it includes any voluntary non-governmental body or groups of individuals who conducted activity in the post-1967 period (the occupation) in the occupied territories and had as its agenda a nonviolent resolution of the conflict with an understanding of the human rights of the other side. Such groups therefore sought understanding, both inside Israel and abroad, of the social, political, historical, and cultural context of the Palestinian concern for justice, thereby finding partners who could be mobilized to end the source of Palestinian grievances.

This study examined several Palestinian P/CROs, including the Palestinian Center for Human Rights (PCHR), Children of Abraham, and the Committee for Dialogue of Peace Forces. Also examined were some joint Palestinian-Israeli P/CROs, such as the Alternative Information Center (AIC), Rapprochement Center, Beit Sahour, and Jerusalem Center for Women. The approach used included interviews with representatives from these organizations and reviews of organization literature and programs.

The efficacy of these organizations was investigated through two basic means: first, interviews with people of varying occupational and personal views; and, second, analysis of P/CROs in relation to the historical struggle between Palestine and Israel. All interviewees were asked to respond to questions based on personal knowledge of verifiable facts, as well as their own opinions and interpretations of certain trends or dynamics. Interviewees were selected from six major categories:

- Representatives from Palestinian P/CROs
- Representatives from the Palestinian Authority whose work in some way depended on a relationship between P/CROs and the Palestinian Authority
- International representatives who dealt with Palestinian P/CROs, largely in the funding domain but also on a sociopolitical level
- Representatives of the mass media
- Academics and intellectuals
- Political leaders (both formal and informal) who were identified with the conflict and who represented the various factions involved in the conflict.

Most of the Palestinian interviewees generally displayed common nationalistic sentiments, often revealing different individual ideologies.

The study also took into account changes in the conflict over time and how interviewees' perceptions of the past differed from those of the present. For purposes of the study, the signing of the Oslo Accords on September 13, 1993, was construed as the breakthrough, even though this was a controversial topic for our interviewees. Questions tended to focus on the P/CRO impact in terms of (1) influencing key events, developments, or negotiations that contributed to the relation of the conflict and in which the P/CRO sector played a role; (2) gaining recognition from the mass media, the parties to the conflict, and government officials, as well as forging links that helped to influence or generate political change; (3) defining the conflict and its resolution in new and different ways—that is, facilitating changes in public perception of the conflict and its resolution, including new ways to define or to describe the conflict, and promoting new strategies or activities for dealing with the conflict. During the conduct of the study the political situation looked very bleak. This reflected the helplessness and even anger witnessed during some of the interviews. Additionally, owing to political stagnation, interviewees clearly were also reevaluating the utility of the Palestinian Authority, the P/CRO sector's potential to mobilize any form of political activity or support from an exasperated Palestinian populace, the adequacy of remaining in political negotiations, and the need for some groups to remain in operation. Palestinian P/CROs only demonstrated quantifiable influence in the public opinion/cultural areas and perhaps the political and social processes after the signing of the Oslo Accords.

Palestinian NGOs in the Context of the National Struggle

Defining the limits and scope of Palestinian NGOs is a challenge. The confluence of political and social interaction within Palestinian society has overlapped to such an extent over the last century that it is difficult to clearly differentiate between the two. Moreover, the existence of Palestinian third-sector and NGOs has been limited, since Palestinians have never had a sovereign or democratic government and therefore cannot have organizations that exist outside of it. Thus, although Palestinian civil society always has existed in a nascent form, consistently shadowing the development of national consciousness, it has failed to take a leading role in the national struggle because no clear and discernable lines exist between nationalism and societal development.

One factor that has impeded the growth of this NGO sector is that the Palestinians have, broadly speaking, considered the development of a culture of peace as coexistence with the Zionist movement. This emanates in part from a failure of the education system that, instead of developing its own agenda, has adopted a political ideology that defies the Zionist movement. In addition, after arriving in the occupied territories, the Palestinian Authority failed to focus adequate attention on societal development, concentrating on politics rather than community development.

This has created a vacuum, often to the benefit of Islamist trends, where both the Palestinian population and the civil-society institutions have lacked guidance as to their role in the national struggle: they only understand that crossing certain lines elicits the Palestinian Authority's wrath.

It is evident that relations among the Palestinian Authority, civil society, and the Palestinian people are strained. One could infer that there is a struggle for power over which best represents the will of the people.

In addition, the present patriarchal structure of Palestinian society and its cultural resistance to Western-style institutions of democracy have affected the development of P/CROs and other civil-society institutions. Such organizations are considered suspect if they do not adequately reflect the history, culture, and traditions of Palestinian society.

For over forty years, Palestinians have existed under an extremely repressive occupation, with a strong need for national unity and steadfastness (*sumoud*). Economic repression, the high costs of political participation (including imprisonment, torture, and death), and the Israeli occupying forces' deliberate efforts to infiltrate, root out, and thwart any attempts at a national or collective unity—be it political, cultural, or social—have hindered the growth and power of Palestinian civil-society institutions.

Palestinian society has sustained an assault on its national, traditional, cultural, intellectual, societal, and political development, and this helps to explain the imbalance between Palestinian representational institutions and their Israeli counterparts. So, many politically conscious Palestinians have found it more appropriate to oppose the occupation through armed resistance rather than through participation in NGOs.

Albeit this situation is beginning to change, in part because armed resistance has failed to end occupation, NGOs at this point are not likely to be at the forefront of Palestinian resistance. NGOs must first prove that they can achieve clear and sustainable ends. Although they were somewhat effectual during the period of the first intifada, it is unclear whether they will continue to be attractive to Palestinians and effective in realizing Palestinian national interests in the period after the Oslo process.

Despite all of these factors, over the past thirty-seven years the Palestinians clearly have attempted to build civil-society institutions and organizations in the occupied territories. These include an array of political parties, municipal service organization, cooperatives, educational institutions, student senates, women's organizations, health-care associations, charitable organizations, trade unions, business associations, child-care facilities, religious groups (which encompass welfare and social service organizations), think tanks, professional unions and syndicates (e.g. lawyers' guilds and medical associations), and chambers of commerce.

These various groups and organizations have responded to the social needs of the Palestinians in the absence of any indigenous government and have enabled the people to survive under Israeli military occupation.

In addition, the formation of these civil-society organizations has bolstered the process of democratization in Palestine since many of them have laid the groundwork for grassroots training in pluralism and democratic behavior; serve as a counterpoise to the autocracy of the Palestinian Authority; and recognize that building peace with Israel is absolutely essential for a prosperous Palestinian society. Ideally, these diverse groups will come to form an infrastructure of civil and political institutions: a prelude to an independent Palestinian state.

In addition, other significant factors have developed in Palestinian society that are conducive to the growth of democratization and civil society. First, a tolerance for divergent opinions has evolved into an intrinsic value and tradition among Palestinians. This is particularly true within the political infrastructure of the PLO, where the existence of pluralism among its various factions is widely acknowledged. Today the mainstream respects and tolerates opposition forces from the political spectrum. Undoubtedly, such groups do act as a monitor of the Palestinian Authority's performance.

Another major factor is the development of a participatory political culture in which elections and popular consent are considered legitimate. A good example is the active political participation of women, which is an essential part of Palestinian civil society today and has a crucial impact on the establishment and consolidation of pluralist thinking and democratic rule.

It appears clear that the future of Palestinian civil society and its effect on the process of democratization is organic to the political development of the region.

A Description of the Palestinian NGO Sector

NGOs worldwide tend to reflect accurately the grassroot values that provide a framework for the political culture. This is because the NGOs are directly in touch with the people, so they do not represent the official establishment but rather the other side of the coin. This was evident in the results of our interviews.

During the interview with Dr. Mohammad Shtayeh, director general of the Palestinian Economic Council for Development and Reconstruction (PECDAR), he stated that among the many reasons why Palestinian NGOs are important to the Palestinian Authority, three in particular are prominent because NGOs contribute to social development, constitute a mechanism for reaching the poorest of the poor, and fill gaps where the government fails to do so. Also, the local NGO culture is political in nature; during the years of Israeli occupation, Palestinians had to exist under a colonial power that did not work for the benefit of the people in the occupied territories. So in cooperation with the PLO, a parallel structure was created, with the NGOs working on education, health, agriculture, land reclamation, and women's issues, and getting the Palestinian people organized formally to provide services especially in areas neglected by Israel.

All the NGOs involved in this study were established as a response to conditions created by the Israeli occupation, either to assist the survival of Palestinian society or to offer an avenue for both Palestinians and Israelis to come together. The NGOs perceive their work as part of the efforts to raise public awareness about the Palestinian point of view, especially about the eventual final status of the Palestinian territories.

Publicity directed at Israelis seeks to make them more familiar with Palestinian reality and to change the misconceptions about and negative images of Palestinians. At the same time, information aimed at Palestinians seeks to raise awareness about issues relevant to the development of civic society and women's rights and to promote positive training in general.

In certain instances research is used to provide answers about both societies; however, not all NGOs were involved in the research. Others were involved in advocacy that flowed from certain convictions, stances, and conclusions, not linked to research but to people's views that certain important messages ought to be communicated to the general public.

All NGOs subject to this study believe in the importance of bringing Palestinians and Israelis together. There are Palestinian NGOs working jointly with Israeli NGOs, just as one organization with two branches. Others work on their own while keeping strong ties with Israelis. The objective is the same, which is the achievement of a comprehensive peace based on an equitable solution to issues of the final status.

Training is also being offered, largely unrelated to coexistence issues but more focused internally on Palestinian societal development. The NGOs concentrate on raising awareness during the interim phase, and are preparing for another when Palestinians and Israelis could live equally side by side. During the Al Aqsa intifada's initial period, none of the NGOs seemed discouraged by the then deadlock in the peace process.

Currently, there are signs in both societies that the peace process is quickly losing credibility. NGOs should be prepared not only for an optimistic scenario, but also for, say, a drastic deterioration in the standard of living, when they will have to face an emergency. Their being at the grassroots, as well as their size and formal structures, make them extremely dynamic and therefore highly able to respond to people's needs in crises. Although NGOs were quick in responding to the new conditions created by the peace process, they are still slow in dealing with the faltering peace process.

As revealed by the interview with the Children of Abraham, there are many possibilities for future work: because there is still a high level of misunderstanding between the two peoples, work still needs to be done in rectifying each group's perceptions. That necessitates finding sources of support. This statement reflects the large difference between Palestinian NGOs in terms of the availability of funds or in terms of the degree of sophistication in their programs. Few NGOs seem able to generate enough money to carry out programs and activities, while others barely make ends meet.

Following are the areas in which data received from Palestinian NGOs can be categorized:

Establishment

All interviews revealed that the NGOs were established as attempts to overcome the various aspects of Israeli occupation. Establishment can be attributed to one of the following reasons:

- The NGO was established to prevent Israeli human rights violations.
- The NGO was established in response to the peace process.
- The NGO was established during the first intifada in response to calls for becoming self-reliant and for rebuilding Palestine.
- The NGO was established to raise awareness among the public on women's rights, democracy, or the functions of government, but none dealing with conflict resolution as a science and a topic for training.
- The NGO founders came from both the intellectual circles as well as from the grassroots.

Peace and Conflict Resolution Activities with Israeli NGOs

Interviews revealed that Palestinian NGOs conducting a minimal amount of activities with Israeli NGOs perceived such activism as normalization of relations prior to solving the outstanding issues. At the same time, other NGOs were completely comfortable with that kind of cooperation and they even used that as a tool for their defense of Palestinian human rights.

Relations with the Palestinian Authority

NGOs interviewed perceived their role in this regard as one of two ways:

- As complementary to the Palestinian Authority. NGOs in this category work in training courses for Palestinians to provide the authority with the needed personnel equipped with the managerial and competitive skills needed for a modern and efficient administration.
- As monitoring the Palestinian Authority. Work here focused on keeping track of the authority's adherence to human rights and democratic principles. The same NGOs that gained their experience while resisting the Israeli occupation were utilizing the acquired skills for monitoring the indigenous Palestinian Authority.

Relations with the International Community

Interviews revealed that some NGOs had developed extensive links with the international community as the major source of funding for the various studies, advocacy, and training projects.

Women's Issues

Community relations included activities on women's rights with the aim of raising awareness stemming from the belief in equality between the sexes. Accordingly, the NGOs included women as members on the governing boards and as staff members. The aim is to empower women and incorporate their advocacy into civic education, as well as forming training programs on gender and equality. The NGOs believed this type of activity to be a human rights issue.

Internal Structures

The interviewed NGOs did not provide clear details about their internal structures. While none of them had worked out a clear mechanism, in some cases the employees themselves selected members of their general assemblies.

Accordingly, based on the data made available from the interviews, most Palestinian NGOs were all established in response to the various pressures of the Israeli occupation and to assist the Palestinian society survive the dangerous situation.

The separate NGOs did not perceive relations with Israeli NGOs as an important component for resolving the conflict. Often, such ties were perceived as normalization of relations prior to Israel's meeting the prerequisites for peace. At the same time, however, Palestinian NGOs were already part of an extensive network of international relations.

Work of the NGOs was focused on either complementing the public policy and administration work of the Palestinian Authority or on monitoring the performance of and adherence to human rights. In the middle of political changes and during the interim phase, they viewed this type of work as their contribution to peacebuilding in the region.

As for internal structures, the NGOs were all supervised by general assemblies, with varying numbers of representatives, as governing bodies for the oversight of work conducted by the executive boards and the staff members. An internal chart governed each one of the interviewed NGOs.

Analyses of the Formation Categories

The formation of PNGOs can generally be divided into two different groups: those that were started before or during the first intifada and those that began after its ending, generally with the signing of the Oslo Accords. In the former category, organizations tended to be characterized by a sense of strong ideology and activism. Of course it is difficult to make generalizations about the assortment of organizations we studied, but it can be said that given the political realities, combined with the political affiliations of these groups (largely associated with the center-left orientation), these organizations sought to bring about change through working within the given confines of the Israeli occupation. Working within the system, pushing its limits, and getting Israelis to see what the daily lives of Palestinians entailed were large motivating factors. The organizations also tended to be spurred by two other elements: the activists' own personal experience with politics and their ability to see and find openings in communicating their experiences to an Israeli audience that was just waking up to the question of Palestinian nationalism.

Concerning the group of organizations that began after the Oslo process, it can be stated that they were a function of the political process, namely the Oslo Accords. This distinction is made to contrast with the former group of organizations that seem to be characterized by an inclination, no matter what the political climate, to fight for the right of Palestinians and have that message heard by a foreign audience. Because the organizations started after the Oslo process tend to be less self-activated, they are more subject to the political climate, for their activities and attraction vary considerably with the political temperature. Recent impasses on the peace process have severely lowered the level of activity of these organizations and subsequently any possible efficacy. The same, however, is not true of those organizations that began before the Oslo process, which continue their work despite the bitterness of the political climate.

Leadership Patterns

Again a distinction can be made between those organizations created before the Oslo process and those that came afterward. Those in the first category seem to be characterized by strong individual or group leadership motivated by a defined political agenda and vision. Those in the second category, though clearly having strong individual leaders of their own, seem unable to command any popular support for their cause. In effect, despite their well-intentioned efforts and leadership, their efforts seem ineffective in any broad or popular sense.

Decisionmaking

Generally speaking, most organizations studied tended to embody a strong sense of democratic appreciation and procedure. This should be noted especially since the range of participants, activists, and leaders occupied a range of educational, religious, and gender spheres. Organizations came to collective consensus through open discussion with their constituencies, generally voting on the final decision.

Funding

It is difficult to break down the issue of funding and to come to any general conclusions about the financial workings of each of the organizations studied. Several elements, however, can be pointed out. Some of the organizations (particularly those with NGO experience and a history of the organization itself that predated the Oslo process) have developed complex and varied donor bodies. In contrast, we also studied organizations that had very little, and sometimes no, official fund-raising capacities.

Of the organizations that saw the need to have very adequate funding, many expressed a strong sense of particularity and individuality. For instance, some refused to take money from government sources, especially from US government sources (e.g., USAID). Furthermore, these organizations refused to take money when conditions were attached. They mostly operated with the understanding that if a fund source was to give money to them, it must operate with the belief that the money would go to the preestablished goals of the organization, and not to any particular goal of the funding entity. Various European sources, particularly those associated with Christian organizations, were truly philanthropic.

Ideology

The topic of ideology is a complex one to analyze without going into the particulars of each organization. Nonetheless, certain elements can be seen throughout the ideologies of the organizations studied and how these pertain to the overall activity and effectuality of given organizations.

To begin with, such organizations that were motivated by a strong ideology tended to survive better and be more effective than those that depended more on the political process. For example, organizations that sought to communicate the issue of human rights do not need to be tied closely to any official political leadership to continue operating. This is true for an organization like the Alternative Information Center whose task is spinning a critical slant upon the political leadership, using the medium of organized modern media, a task that will never end. In contrast, those organizations that are more concerned with feelings and attitudes, that is, for instance, changing the opinions of Palestinians and Israelis about each other, largely seem unconstructive and more likely to fail the test of time. The stalling of the peace process has all but paralyzed the forces of moderation in both societies, and this has weakened the overall efficacy of such forces. The loyal and dedicated activists on both sides who come to things as joint-discussion groups, are unable to mobilize anyone outside their organizations. In this sense, the well-intentioned work becomes a case of preaching to the converted. Even an organization like the Rapprochement Center (historically enjoying success with joint discussion) has in recent years ignored the importance of popularizing these meetings, instead focusing its energy upon building internal strength within the Palestinian community rather than trying to build any bridges to the other side.

Ideology seems to be an important part in the success or failure of an organization. Furthermore, ideology that motivates the activists who espouse it seems to directly correlate with the stamina of the organization. In contrast, when activists are drawn to an organization through a vague interest or lukewarm appeal, their commitment to the organization seems far more ephemeral and subject to the tides of politics and popular opinion.

Participation

Of all the organizations we studied, only one was particular about its constituency: the Jerusalem Center for Women had only women participants.

Otherwise speaking, the range of participants covered the spectrum of age, socioeconomic class, education, religion, and nationality.

Organizations seemed to exhibit three different roles for their participants. First was the kind with a closed group of participants who did the majority of the work. Second was the type of organization led by a group of activists who hoped to create more activists. Third was the organization led by activists who sought only people at the popular level to engage in activities for a given event, without any necessary follow-up or consistency.

Exploration of Relationships

Following are some general remarks and conclusions that can be drawn from our findings. They represent an effort to raise questions about further relationships that may be traced in the dynamic struggle between organizations, the political reality, and the struggle of both sides to affect each other and popular opinion as a whole.

- A strong sense of ideology tended to create a well-funded foundation. Once the organization had proved itself and shown its ideology in an uncompromising fashion, fund sources would be attracted to the regularity and commitment of the organization.
- As previously mentioned, ideology seemed to have great effect on the stability, stamina, and longevity of an organization.
- Organizations based on political realities (e.g., the Oslo process) often were affected too much by the turbulence of the struggle, thus losing internal strength as well as the ability to change others.
- An open and dynamic decisionmaking process that was open to change throughout the organization's activities seemed to be healthy for participant involvement and interest.

Impact and Efficacy

When one tries to examine the efficacy of a specific organization, such a task implies a given, perhaps idealized, goal the organization sets for itself and invests its energy and resources in realizing. It then becomes the judge's task to measure the organization's results against the original intention. The parity or discrepancy of the two determines overall the effectiveness of the organization in achieving its preestablished goals.

With this as the essence of an inquiry into effectiveness, we would like to mention some impediments and particular flaws that exist both on a theoretical and specific level in relation to our research.

To begin with, how does one go about measuring effectiveness, whether on a movement or organizational level? Here we find it important to note that most organizations have more than one specialized agenda that they hope to achieve through their efforts. Therefore if one is to talk about a group, it must be considered on an individual basis, as must the effectiveness of each goal the organization hopes to achieve. Hence the effectiveness changes both from organization to organization (given their different goals) and inside each organization (given its own agenda).

Second, it is important to remind ourselves that, in the context of the Palestinian nationalist struggle, questions of effectiveness take on a different shading, especially in relation to our research. In this regard, one must ask whether we are to examine effectiveness in relation to the organizations' ability to effect change for purposes of peace and conflict resolution or whether they were effective in creating change for purposes of their own ideology. The point, quite simply, is that the two are not necessarily the same. This once again has to do with the ambiguities that arise among the nationalist struggle, the desire for a just peace, and the role NGOs have played as partners in such struggles. Evidently, of the organizations examined in this study, most, if not all, have a preestablished commitment to the national struggle before they have any commitment to what is commonly seen as the peace process.

Here we would like to stress that this does not mean they are in any way less committed to the concept of peace than those who work in P/CROs that are not nationalistically oriented. It merely means that they are committed to a different form of peace than the one presently being pursued. For instance, one of the leaders of a joint organization researched for this study openly supported the idea of Palestinians walking away from the current peace process. Observers may accuse him of being against the idea of peace, and in no position to be running a joint Palestinian-Israeli reconciliation organization. This leader instead chooses to defend his beliefs with a strict understanding that he favors a comprehensive, just solution to the plight of and injustices to the Palestinian people. In his view, the Oslo process did not offer any opportunity to realize this solution, and so there is no reason why he should espouse it.

Some of these ideas may seem foreign to the reader, but in fact are quite common to many Palestinians. After the Oslo Accords were signed, a gray area of uncertainty surfaced in the consciousness of many Palestinian thinkers and the masses alike. Its nature had to do with carving out and articulating a position that existed somewhere in between open support and open rejection of the peace agreements. Articulation of this sentiment has gained eloquence especially with the subsequent failures of Oslo, now more than ten years after its initial signing. Still, these ideas are somewhat antithetical to the Israeli peace camp activists who tend to perceive Oslo, despite its flaws, as a panacea to the problems of the conflict.

General Effectiveness of the Movements

All said, we can begin to make distinctions among the degrees of effectiveness we seek to evaluate. It is helpful for our purposes to differentiate in terms of common themes that various organizations seem to follow. We found it more helpful to consider the efficacy of the example of the human rights movement in the occupied territories rather than to talk of the specific efficacy of a certain human rights group. Under this idea of thematically grouping efficacy, we have come up with some general headings that will help along the task of determining effectiveness:

- Human rights
- Consciousness-raising activity outside the home territories
- Consciousness-raising activity at home

Furthermore, each of the above topics shall be addressed through division in context to their pre-Oslo and post-Oslo relevancies. It must also be noted that many of these topics are interrelated and it is therefore incorrect to think of them as precisely and discretely applicable. Efficacy after all is a matter of opinion that when placed in a historical context makes yesterday's victories looks like today's defeats.

The Human Rights Movement

Of the many organizations we examined, the issue of human rights was a popular and firm foundation upon which many organizations organized. Organizations of both national and joint constituencies engaged in the discourse of trying to popularize the issue of human rights. This alone is evidence that the issue of human rights is common ground for both communities to work toward a mutual end. There are many internal aims that organizations engaged in human rights work share in the hopes of effecting certain changes in the status quo.

Pre-Oslo years. Human rights organizations played a crucial role during the intifada in trying to publicize the human rights abuses of the Israeli government and army. Of the organizations examined, some showed remarkable sophistication and experience in data collection, defense of political prisoners, publication of data, and other activities. They became warehouses of important information on human rights abuses by the Israeli army for which many human rights activists (both Israeli and Palestinian) were forced to serve prison sentences in Israeli jails, often having their references and data confiscated. This was often correlated with a strong international media presence, which often revealed television images that backed up many of the startling figures that were produced on human rights work during the time. For example, both the Palestinian Center For Human Rights (PCHR, and its predecessor Gaza Center for Human Rights) and the Alternative Information Center (AIC) played strong roles in producing high quality information that was widely distributed to a large foreign audience. In this sense, their models were most certainly successful and adopted by a series of smaller organizations that arose in their wake. (Please note that these two are not the only two organizations that were able to produce change. Al-Haq, the notable West Bank human rights group, was often pointed to as a tireless and effective voice in its cause. We only mention PCHR and AIC because it was these two that were studied in depth.)

Yet with the nature of a human rights organization comes certain limitations. As Raji Sourani pointed out, one hopes that one's work would end the human rights violations committed, but this is clearly not a realistic hope. The most one can hope for in human rights work is that one's work will reduce the number of violations committed, and will make the abusing authorities think twice before they decide to commit a violation again. Sourani himself acknowledged, as head of PCHR, that if his organization was not there, the level of violations committed by the Israeli army and government against Palestinians would have been much higher and would furthermore have continued unimpeded by any other force as it was being conducted unmonitored. Here the efficacy of Palestinian human rights organizations is clearly evident, yet nonetheless, difficult to measure. One could always say that one could do more, yet in our observations it is not the organizations that should be held responsible for efficacy. Oftentimes the information on abuses of human rights violations is available, yet the voices who could or should listen to them is too often not there.

Post Oslo Human Rights Movement

Part of the reason why the agenda of human rights can become a platform between people of differing backgrounds to join efforts is that the issue is less a question of political discussion that changes with individual perspective but rather one that is more clearly defined. Simply put, there are fundamental and basic rules outlined in the Fourth Geneva Convention that define what constitutes violations of international rights. All who have signed this accord participate in acknowledging the necessity of protecting human rights as a state's responsibility.

After the signing of the Oslo agreement and the arrival of the Palestinian Authority into parts of the West Bank and Gaza, the issue of human rights became a subject of debate for organizations that had previously focused their efforts on Israeli army and governmental violations. With general uncompromised unity of the organizations studied, the few human rights organizations showed no reservations about publishing and criticizing the newly arrived authority. (Not surprisingly, all the organizations we studied that did work on human rights had ideological affiliations with the opposition wing, which openly defined the Oslo Accords.)

As with the case of the Israeli occupation, professing human rights often comes with a political price: that of imprisonment and harassment, only this time at the hands of the Palestinian Authority. Various notable human rights figures have butted heads with the Palestinian Authority and since have served prison terms. Human rights advocates found this reality deeply disheartening as it was precisely the same advocates who had publicized the atrocities committed by the occupying forces. To see the Authority adopt the oppressors ways and abuse the human rights of the very people they sought to help and defend was an expressed moral low that human rights workers were particularly demoralized by. At least this was the attitude before the inception of the second intifada.

According to one organization, human rights work is now divided between coverage of Israeli and Palestinian sectors—operating on an 80–20 percent respective cut. Most notable figures that were interviewed on the question of human rights felt that the Palestinian organizations in operation were of high quality that demonstrated good standards of moral decency. They praised the work they had done under the occupation and also after the arrival of the Authority. Even PLC members (elected government officials) had praise for their work.

Of the general criticisms the movement seems to face are several. Dr. Sari Nusseibeh made an astute comment that pointed out how human rights organizations tended to create an awareness of human rights on the elitist level. By this he meant that if for instance the Palestinian Authority decided to imprison the well-known human rights advocate Iyad Sarraj, it would cause an international stir and draw international criticism upon the Authority. This is possible because Iyad Sarraj is a popular figure who has made a name for himself both locally and internationally. But Dr. Nusseibeh seemed quite critical of the fact that there are much fewer people who are willing to speak out against the illegal imprisonment of a whole variety of political prisoners inside Israeli and Palestinian Authority prisons. It is for instance easy for either the Palestinian Authority or the Israeli authorities to arrest someone upon suspicion of being associated with the Islamic Resistance Movement (Hamas), even when there is no evidence against him, there is no warrant for his arrest, he is not given access to a lawyer, and he is tortured and placed as an "administrative detainee" for a renewable six-month cycle. There are far fewer people, both locally and internationally, who are willing to stand up for the rights of these individuals which are being violated with far greater frequency than any of the rights of the "big name" activists. In this sense, human rights consciousness, both locally and internationally, has failed.

Another criticism brought up was how far the definition of human rights was extended. In one sense, gross violations of human rights are media friendly: torture, death, and imprisonment. Yet the issue of human rights abuse is far more delicate a subject than simply making headlines or enjoying article space. Human rights far too infrequently are extended to coverage of the basic difficulties and injustices that many Palestinians live under. The Israeli closure of the occupied territories, for instance, is a clear example of human rights violations in that it is a form of collective punishment. Unfortunately, the topic has lost international interest (if in fact it ever really had any) despite the fact that it continues to exist daily, affecting the lives of Palestinians. There are other similar spheres that can be considered violations of human rights that neither the Palestinian Authority, the Israeli government, nor the international audience seems willing to address. This includes availability to adequate health and educational services, the banning of child labor, and the right to one's own water. Sadly, this dimension is often left out of the equation when talking of human rights since it is pushed to the sides by the larger, seemingly more "grotesque" forms of human rights abuse.

One final criticism, highly related to the issue of communication both locally and internationally, is that of the question of raising public Palestinian and Israeli awareness to human rights abuses. The reasoning behind this criticism lies in the fact that there are latent hypocrisies among the masses of both populations that seem willing to turn a blind eye to human rights abuses if it originates from the wrong ideological pole. The Palestinian population, for instance, has not demonstrated a popular consciousness of human rights abuses where they would collectively be able to challenge the abuses that are currently taking place. However, when a Palestinian is tortured to death in an Israeli prison, there are sure to be riots the following day. Some form of blind spot clearly exists in the campaign for human rights. So far it has only articulated itself to say, "we refuse to have our human rights abused (by the Israeli authorities[11])." It is not that the majority of Palestinians do not realize that the Authority abuses their rights: in fact they know only too well. An assortment of reasons leads to the majority of Palestinians keeping silent: the need to show national unity behind the Palestinian Authority and genuine fear from reprisal by the Authority with very few others who are willing to stand at one's side, all compounded with an overall ignorance of human rights awareness to begin with. These issues are more complicated and certainly raise more questions about how effective the human rights movement has been.

Consciousness Raising at the Foreign Level

By "consciousness raising" we mean the movement of various Palestinian and joint organizations to somehow tell the story of the Palestinians whether through reports of the abuse of their human rights, through the communication of their desire for peace, or through the communication and recognition of their history of injustice. Let it be forewarned (to the reader as well as to the organizations) that the communication movement is flawed in that the struggle to get other people outside of the Palestinians themselves to recognize the depth and scale of the Palestinian plight does not emerge from a unified voice. There are of course basic things which all Palestinians fight for: a recognition of historic and present injustice, an end to the occupation, an end to the building of settlements, and a return for the Palestinian refugees. Yet the question of where to take this history is something that has plagued both the role and efficacy of NGOs as well as the national struggle as a whole. What is meant by this is the simple fact that the question of communicating what to whom is a bifurcated topic that has so many branches; it weakens any collective effort on that front.

Pre-Oslo Communication

Of the NGOs researched that had a history that extended to years before the Oslo Agreements, all tended to portray a nostalgic longing for the years of the first intifada. This sentiment seems to emerge from several reasons that largely are rooted in the historical context and comparison of the present with the past. The years of the first intifada tend to bring back fond memories because for many of these organizations it was the years of their birth, the years when they experienced incredible growth and efficacy, the years when it was much easier to find people with similar ideological beliefs who would work tirelessly with them in achievement of that end. Indeed, the intifada witnessed remarkable achievements from activists of all stripes working toward a collective goal. It is important to note here that it was the unity of the goal—that of ending the Israeli occupation—which was able to bring so much collective energy together, and, in so doing, attract the attention of the international, and especially the Israeli, audience.

Determining the efficacy of the researched organizations is difficult for several reasons: organizations were fighting for the end to occupation, not for peace. Furthermore, the end of the first intifada had an impact into the process that eventually brought the Oslo accords: a victory in the eyes of some, a failure for others. Lastly of course, it is difficult to determine the efficacy as a whole as things seem to take on new light in historical perspective. For instance, one of the organizations studied conducted wide-scale forms of civil disobedience during the first intifada that attracted international attention, even once gaining an editorial in *The New York Times*. How does one go about assessing the efficacy of this organization at this particular time? Yes, it is true that the organization was able to attract international attention for the activities it was doing. Yes, people read about what was taking place and heard about things that they previously wouldn't have known about. Yes also, perhaps it would have made the international audience more inclined to favor the Palestinians in their struggle and bring some form of international pressure on Israel to end the occupation and end its inhuman and racist practices. In this sense the organization was extremely effective.

But there are also other ways to consider the organizations' efforts a failure. To begin with, the movement of mass civil disobedience (which activists were hoping to spread across the West Bank) did not spread outside the activist territory. Second, their activities did not stop the Israeli occupation. Third, their activities helped bring about the Oslo accords, something the international community was incredibly supportive of, yet something the activists themselves were incredibly against and considered a complete failure. Fourth, their activities and activists have largely demobilized themselves (in comparison with their former selves) while the Israeli occupation of their land still exists. When looked through this lens, the organizations' efforts were a complete failure.

This example aims to illustrate the relativity of the concept of efficacy as a whole, with special emphasis on its exclusivity in a Palestinian context. One gets the sense that Palestinian NGO efficacy in communicating the problems of the Palestinians to the outside world is limited. There seems to be a dedicated international audience that is mobilized and relatively networked throughout the world, and hence supports the Palestinian cause. Before Oslo, they demonstrated efficacy in changing international pubic awareness in favor of the Palestinians, and against the Israeli occupation. The Oslo process was seen by many as the fruit of their struggle.

Post-Oslo Communication

The Oslo Accords shattered the unity activists experienced and, along with it, the unity of the international alliances that had been created throughout the years of the first intifada. Much of this had to do with the unpopularity of openly rejecting the Oslo track when it was developed. Palestinian organizations that chose to stick to their principles and refuse the Oslo track often saw their international supporters criticize them, sometimes even taking away donations. Though their principled nature later would reward them once the "golden calf" of Oslo had been revealed, it was largely too late as the Palestinian Authority was quick to move in and claim to be representative of the Palestinian voice and struggle. NGOs were no longer the only voice that could speak for what was taking place on the ground. Furthermore, there was a certain tension created between NGOs and the Palestinian Authority as the shift and balance of power between the two communities took place—problems that included everything from financial competition, freedom of expression, and the right to get licenses. NGOs had acted as the service-oriented government under the Israeli occupation. Now the Palestinian National Authority claimed to deserve the right to take over that responsibility. Differences arose especially when the two differed in a political position. One constraint in the communication efficacy of NGOs is that of division and lack of a clear voice. Some NGOs tried to get their audiences to believe that nothing had changed and that the Oslo agreements and the

Palestinian National Authority have done nothing to change the realities of the occupation and the historical injustice of the Palestinians. Others accepted the Oslo agreements and fought for international lobbying on their behalf. But several very real fissures divided the NGOs as a group, some even internally splitting them. Were organizations supposed to support the Authority against the Israeli intransigence in Oslo? Or were they supposed to try to rally support against the Palestinian National Authority, seeing it as an incompetent and insufficient representation of Palestinian needs? Such divisions seriously divided and in ways neutralized joint organizations especially. Israeli peace activists did not know how to react when faced with these questions. As a whole, the lack of a clear consensus and a viable alternative caused the international community to adopt a confused stance of its own, tentatively supporting the Palestinian National Authority with cautious appraisal.

Israeli/Palestinian Joint Movement Toward Dialogue and Peace

The time of the first intifada witnessed creativity by activists in reaching out to the portions of the Israeli community that were peace oriented. The first intifada had become a phenomenon that neither the Israeli government nor people could ignore. The Israeli "peace camp" had its own desires for seeking to bring about a peaceful solution. Palestinian activists hoped to tap into this strength and have it help dissolve the Zionist propaganda of a "benign occupation." They also sought to take advantage of Israeli contacts and experience, as well as bring about a certain legitimacy to their work by showing the international community that they had no reservations about working with Israelis as long as they were treated as equal partners and worked toward collective goals of justice.

Once again, as in the case of the international communications movement, the "purity of cause" of the first intifada made things easier than they are today. Palestinians who saw the emergence of the Israeli peace forces, and activists who were willing to work for their cause, began to be able to make distinctions between Israelis as people and Israelis as oppressors dressed in army uniforms. Likewise, the inverse is probably true as Israelis came to see the Palestinians as a people who are fighting for their national rights, and not just a people who are predisposed to "killing Jews" or "the destruction of the state of Israel."

As a movement, however, the synthesis of joint organizations was ineffective in the Palestinian and Israeli communities in accomplishing one specific goal. Individual efforts in each community may have proven effective in limited ends: the Rapprochement Center of Beit Sahour, for instance, was initially able to mobilize the community in fighting occupation together with the support of some Israeli activist friends who publicized their events in the Israeli media. It is difficult to measure how Palestinian organizations were able to effect change in Israeli society, as our research did not study the Israel peace camp. One can say at least that Palestinians can recognize that there are two very different camps of people within Israeli society who have very different opinions with regard to the Palestinians and their rights to their lands.

Among Palestinians, NGOs were seen as effective in producing creative avenues of the national struggle, raising the sophistication of the fight from the streets and the rocks, to the pen and the opinions of men and women.

Post-Oslo Israeli-Palestinian Dialogue

As previously mentioned, the onslaught of the Oslo process divided the approach of the national struggle together with the movement of NGOs. Whereas most Israeli peace camps viewed Oslo as the fruit of their struggle, the Palestinian camps seemed less willing to adopt the hype that was so freely thrown at the agreements. Since their signing, an ossification of Palestinian discontentment has come about, vocalized through the NGOs (and their network formation, newly created in opposition to Palestinian Authority totalitarianism). Initially this was not the case. The international donor community seemed quite willing to support a whole new genre of organizations that popularized the ideas of coexistence and mutual acceptance. Though many were established the first two years after the signing of the Oslo agreements, many complain that there is little momentum from either community in support of these causes. Even the election of Netenyahu and Sharon, thoroughly detestable figures to all peace camps, still is not enough to forge an alliance and strong network of bridges in support of "peace." In this, Israeli peace activists and Palestinian populations together hate the above-mentioned Likud leaders individually, rather than collectively. On the Palestinian street, much of this is attributed to their abilities to rebolster old fears that this current Israeli leadership is a replica of the Zionist conquerors of Palestine. Palestinian NGOs have so far been unable, however, to take this energy and collective hatred and use it toward anything constructive. The Palestinian street is unsure of where to take its emotions: toward support of the Authority? Toward the NGOs? Toward the Israelis? The lack of consensus, the constipation of the "peace process," the fateful hopes that something positive may come about sometime, somewhere, all compounded with an overall exhaustion of the struggle, have caused the political demobilization of large sectors of Palestinian society. NGOs are therefore unable to make large inroads into Palestinian society, as the people are genuinely uninterested, fatigued, or imbued with a sense of futility regarding their efforts.

That the collective initiative of Palestinian society brought about Oslo, now considered a "rotten egg" of sorts on the Palestinian street, makes the idea of individual effort on the "Peace Process" front unreasonable. NGOs have so far been unable to make any serious dents in this sense of apathy and despair, as the larger powers seem to be making all the decisions irrespective of the people. This is altogether made worse by a feeling that the Palestinian National Authority is willing to personally challenge in one way or another, all those who seek to stray from the path they are treading.

The Second Intifada and the PNGOs

During the second intifada, the PNGOs continued to function but with greater limitations imposed on them directly or indirectly. Some PNGOs continued to perform their regular functions of advocacy or joint ventures, while others that are more ideologically oriented curbed their functions of advocacy and joint ventures under the pretext that such activities are considered normalization with the enemy, i.e., Israel, while the Palestinian people are under heavy oppression from the Israeli war machine.

Moreover, the question of funding became more problematic, for PNGOs (quite a few in number) started refusing funding provided by USAID because of the latter's imposition of conditions and stipulations concerning "terrorism" and support of "terrorist" organizations. However, the European Commission in its turn also encourages tripartite relations (European/Palestinian/Israeli), which makes it very difficult for the Palestinians to consent to because of the repercussions of Israeli policies vis-à-vis the Palestinians, and any acceptance of such cooperation is interpreted as "collaboration with the enemy." Let alone, the Palestinian Ministry of Higher Education set a clear/explicit policy on noncooperation with the Israeli Higher Learning Institutions and NGOs. Consequently, the low-level of cooperation and the high-intensity conflict reduce the functioning of the PNGOs in the areas of conflict management and peace building.

It is worth mentioning that several joint organizations totally froze their functions as a result of the second intifada and, to date, they are functioning separately with much less stamina and enthusiasm.

This state of being reduced tremendously the efforts of peace building and the overcoming of the psychological barriers that always impede the process of cooperation and mutual trust.

The lack of progress in real political engagement between the Palestinians and Israelis further exacerbates any kind of cooperation or normalization between both sides. Moreover, the socioeconomic malaise that the Palestinians are suffering from is an added factor toward frustration and opposition to any kind of normalization or cooperation with Israeli NGOs. Therefore, the current political stalemate, the dire economic conditions, the frustration in the peace process, and the dissatisfaction with the performance of the Palestinian National Authority, all compounded, had a great impact on the role of PNGOs; as a result, their functioning and performance regressed considerably.

It is important, however, to note that lately there were serious attempts by Israelis and Palestinians to establish common/joint political platforms to end the conflict and set short- and long-range strategies to deal with pending final status issues. Vivid examples are the Nusseibeh and Ayalon Initiative and Abed Rabo and Beilin Geneva Initiative. Both initiatives were received by Israelis and Palestinians with mixed feelings; however, one cannot but appreciate such attempts that are considered to be bold, creative, and innovative. Unfortunately, these initiatives are not sustainable because they lack support at both official levels in addition to shortage of further funding.

On the other hand, the civic institutions and organizations established and supported by the Islamic fundamentalists like Hamas, Islamic Jihad, and the Muslim Brotherhood—the Mother Organization—are considered to be a success story for they were able to fill the void by catering to the socioeconomic and political needs of the Palestinian communities. Definitely, their functions were not geared toward peace/conflict resolutions; however, they cannot be discarded because they fit the functional definition of civil society. In addition, they were able to sustain their presence to date with their continuous services rendered.

It is difficult to really assess the current state of being of the PNGOs without a field study, in addition to limitations of length imposed by the project.

Conclusions

Can one begin to talk about a "peace camp" that refers to Palestinians? Most certainly. Such a group is represented by a large component within the Palestinian Authority: the very same group of people who have for at least the past two decades sought a solution based on a political compromise solution with Israel. The Oslo process was the fruit of this long and hard struggle to get the world and Israel to acknowledge the existence of the Palestinian people with a national right to self-determination and the land of Palestine. Unfortunately, for reasons not entirely of their own, the political leaders failed to arrive at a political solution that meshed with the national aspirations of the Palestinian people. They failed to bring an end to the occupation, failed to stop the continual barrage of human rights abuses by Israel, failed to stop the theft of land and resources, and failed to bring a state, a democracy, or even sovereignty. Hardly any of the foregoing were brought to the Palestinian public so that their best interests and their natural rights would be protected or secured by an agreement with the Israeli state.

Our goal has been not to examine or speculate whys or hows of such a phenomenon, but to acknowledge and describe its existence and then tell of its effects on the third sector. Essentially one can say that the physical failure of the Oslo process had a corresponding psychological failure, which subsequently spilled over into the third sector. NGOs reacted by abandoning much of the work associated with promoting the peace process. The perception quickly grew that the peace process was nothing more than something that legitimized the Israeli occupation, Palestinian Authority corruption, and self-aggrandizement after political marginalization, and ultimately Israel's securing control over fundamental Palestinian rights, resources, and properties. The tribulations of the disappointments of the Oslo process were mirrored in the tribulations of those in the third sector, which fought to hold onto the will of the people. Their work continues, perhaps gaining political merit by predicting the collapse of the Oslo Accords; yet for reasons that are not entirely clear, the effectiveness of NGOs at the grassroots level is clearly less than it had been. Much of this probably has to do with an overall weakening politicization of the Palestinian public, which has grown tired of the struggle and has become disillusioned with the promise of the Oslo process and the Palestinian Authority.

Although the third sector fought to retain the support of the people, only those organizations whose work had principled outlooks based on a realistic view of the Palestinian predicament remained. These surviving NGOs continue to work for peace, and have perhaps gained some prestige by predicting that the Oslo process would fail. Given their current status, it seems unlikely that these P/CROs will be leading movements of popular mobilization either for or against the stagnation of the Oslo process.

It seems unlikely that Palestinians will continue to have faith in the Oslo process's bearing any fruit, largely due to the fact that the Palestinian public feels trapped by the Israeli occupation, Palestinian Authority inefficiency, abandonment by the rest of the world—and the rhetoric of political action as a whole.

Joint Organizations

The following section gives a brief description of the historical development of each organization included in the study.

• The Alternative Information Center (AIC)

Formation. Came together as a collection of concerned leftists in 1984 hoping to create a new, alternative media to the existent "power serving" media. They hoped to take advantage of a burgeoning peace movement (and suspicion of government) in Israel that arose after the Israeli invasion of Lebanon in 1982.

Joint Organizations (con't.)

Leadership patterns. Led by an executive committee of joint activists and founders, who in turn create working groups of activists that carry out several functions including publishing a monthly magazine, performing field work, and collecting data on individual projects such as prisoner rights, refugee and residency issues, and the status of Jerusalem.

Decisionmaking. Direction of the organization is in the hands of the executive committee, though considerable freedom is given to activists on the individual projects the organization undertakes.

Funding. Financing comes from a wide assortment of loyal donor foundations and organizations. Generally government funds are not accepted, although they might be considered from purely neutral countries. Funds are never accepted on a contingent basis and never depend upon an individual source. A.I.C also receives funds from the services that it provides and the publications it sells.

Ideology. Anti-Zionist leftist, seeking a bipartisan solution in some form, secular democratic. Preach criticism of organized leaderships and organized information communication system.

Participation. Largely limited to the activists who work there, and not interested in personally leading the struggle, but in providing the necessary information to get people to think more critically. Around twenty activists in the two offices (Bethlehem, Jerusalem).

• *Palestinian Center for Rapprochement Between People*

Formation. Formed during the first intifada, directly out of the impetus of Beit Sahour to try to exploit the aims of the first intifada and take its message to the Israeli audience.

Leadership patterns. Officially under the umbrella of the Mennonite Central Committee (though it has no jurisdiction over any decisions). There are individual leaders in each age group among the adults and the university and high school constituency.

Decisionmaking. Overall carried out by the board of trustees, which then takes the decision to the various group leaderships. Ghassan Andoni acts as managing director.

Funding. From an assortment of organizations, largely European and Church money. Avoids government money, and never takes funds with restrictions.

Ideology. To create and support a group of activists who in turn become self-propelled in the cause of a just solution. Contact with Israelis in order to expose them to Palestinian problems and to forge allies.

Joint Organizations (con't.)

Participation. Very community oriented. Conducted large community-based campaigns during the first intifada. Involves all groups of people, including men and women and young and old. Recent focus on building internal Palestinian strength rather than communication with the "other" side.

• *Jerusalem Center For Women*

Formation. Created in 1985 by the joint impetus of Israeli and Palestinian women (largely of the civil-society class) to raise awareness of one another and to support principles of peace and coexistence.

Leadership patterns. Board of trustees that directs the administrative board, led by a director general.

Decisionmaking. Majority rule of all the members.

Funding. Largely funded through the European Union as well as individual European organizations.

Ideology. To recognize the right of self-determination of both peoples with Jerusalem accessible to all and that a just solution be implemented to the conflict by virtue of the Oslo Accords and UN resolutions.

Participation. In general, highly educated women from political and academic circles.

National (Palestinian) Organizations

• *Palestinian Center For Human Rights (PCHR)*

Formation. Created in 1995 after the dissolution of a previous human rights organization that collapsed, founder Raji Sourani emerged to create PCHR to help defend Palestinians in Israeli courts and report on the Israeli abuses of human rights. Later he would report on similar abuses conducted by the Palestinian Authority.

Leadership Patterns. Led by Raji Sourani, who has beneath him four major Palestinian lawyers who conduct the bulk of the work and coordinate the individual projects and data collection (that is, interviews of victims, family members).

Decisionmaking. Weekly meetings of staff members, democratically decides any particular changes. Ideology and function is clearly established, so little changes take place.

Funding. A wide range of international donors, private and public, mostly European.

National (Palestinian) Organizations (con't.)

Ideology. To defend the rights of Palestinian prisoners and to expose the abuses of their rights by their jailers, both Israeli and Palestinian.

Participation. Eighteen lawyers and activists.

• Palestinian Peace Organization–Children of Abraham

Formation. Established in the euphoria of Oslo, the group sought to popularize the themes of peaceful coexistence among Palestinians and encourage similar forces among Israeli society.

Leadership patterns. Through the administrative committee, which coordinates the logistics of meetings.

Decisionmaking. Direction of organization is taken by members putting forth suggestions and collectively voting on whether to embrace them.

Funding. No international funding, although the organization does receive small funds from local donations and fundraisers. No attempt to organize a funding campaign.

Ideology. To promote and create a just peace for all the "Children of Abraham."

Participation. All Palestinian. Consists of local activists who join together pending the political situation to work collectively in reaction to the status quo (for example, to hold a demonstration, write a collective letter).

• Palestinian Council for Dialogue with Peace Forces

Formation. Initially formed in 1992 under a different name, the organization evolved to the present status in 1996 in an effort to better understand the Israeli side and promote peace among Palestinians.

Leadership patterns. Twenty-five founding fathers.

Decisionmaking. Strategic decisions conducted by the general assembly, which in turn implement agreed-upon programs.

Funding. Does not seek funds and never has. Donations are occasionally collected from activists themselves.

Ideology. To forge links with like-minded individuals and collectively break down the barriers that impede the peace process. It hopes to explain to Israelis how Palestinians are suffering daily by Israeli practices and policies.

Participation. Palestinian veterans of the Israeli jail system, largely of the center/left politically.

4

Israeli-Palestinian Joint Activities: Problematic Endeavor, but Necessary Challenge

Mohammed Dajani and Gershon Baskin

From the early days of the first Palestinian intifada in November 1987, more and more mainstream Palestinians and Israelis began to engage in joint activities mostly aimed at creating a formal peace process between Israelis and the Palestinians. The main aim of these meetings was dialogue. Until that time very few Israelis and Palestinians had actually ever spoken directly with each other. During the period before the Oslo Accords of 1993, most of these joint activities fit into the category of Track II meetings. Most of the meetings involved Israelis and Palestinians from the occupied territories. Some of these Track II meetings were held abroad and included Palestinians from the PLO.[1]

Following the signing of the Oslo Declaration of Principles in September 1993, international focus on joint Israeli-Palestinian activities increased. International donors began to express an interest in joint activities, with the European Union taking the lead. Hundreds of new initiatives for creating joint activities followed the signing of the Oslo agreement and the 1994 creation of the Palestinian Authority.

In seeking peace, we are talking about eradicating a history of more than one hundred years of hostility, conflict, and enmity. This is a tremendous task that many have described as an impossible mission.

It is very disheartening to see joint activities wither away in times of crisis and conflict. Before the second intifada prior to September 28, 2000, there were hundreds of peace joint activities. Though joint activities began to be jeopardized long before the outbreak of the intifada, those engaged in joint activities were aware of the detrimental process that was starting to take place. Thus when at the outset of the intifada most of the joint activities closed shop, it became very difficult to get people from both sides back on the peace track to work together. For that reason, it is very important to look back and study what went wrong, what went right, and where do we go from here. What role would joint activities play in bringing two old enemies together?

Joint Activities: A Working Definition

To begin, we need to define a common understanding of what joint activities mean to each individual or organization. It seems that all have their own concept of what a peace joint activity should be. To come up with any type of overall strategy, we need first an understanding of what is meant by joint activities projects. What is their purpose? What do we want to achieve?

Generally speaking, joint activities are defined in terms of Israeli-Palestinian partnership as aiming at promoting peace, goodwill, and understanding between the Israeli and Palestinian peoples. By bringing together ordinary Israelis and Palestinians for dialogue and cooperative ventures, joint activities should ideally create the relational infrastructure necessary to advance and increase support for *a* peace process to be negotiated at the political level. This working definition does indeed include the expectation of one's becoming a peace activist.

Motivations for Participating in Joint Activities

Palestinian-Israeli Motivations

One Israeli or Palestinian motivation for participating in joint activities is to convince the other party of the justice of one's own cause or that a particular political agreement is beneficial. Another motivation is a curiosity to get to know the other side from close distance, to understand better the other side's attitudes toward resolving the conflict and the other side's society in general. (People have a natural sense of curiosity, and they are interested in learning about something that seems so foreign, at times threatening.)

Another possible motivation is the intention of not a few on each side to become "professionalized" in the field of peacemaking, in many cases dedicating themselves full or part time to work with each other as a way of life. Personal benefit (professional growth, becoming part of world networks) becomes a motivation to many of the peace activists (often referred to as "the usual suspects"). Similar to Israelis involved in joint activities, for most Palestinians the primary motivations for involvement are meant to contribute to ending the conflict and building peace. The major challenge for the joint activities is that many people on both sides come to teach rather than to learn.

Israeli Motivations

For Israelis involved in joint activities it is clear that the primary motivations for involvement are aimed at contributing to building peace. In research project after research project, empirical data have shown that Israelis—

individuals and institutions—testify that they are strongly driven by a sense that by organizing and by participating in joint activities with Palestinians they are making a real contribution to peace. This contribution is defined in several ways:

- There are Israelis who are deeply politically motivated and assert that peacemaking and peacebuilding must be both a top-down process of governments negotiating and reaching peace agreements and as a bottom-up process involving normal citizens in building support for peace from the grassroots.
- There are Israelis involved in Track II–type activities who believe that in Israel, as an open and rather small society, it is relatively easy to reach decisionmakers and influence them by providing well-thought-out policy analyses and proposals.
- There are also many Israelis motivated by a keen sense of good intentions and a sense that they are doing the right thing that lead them to take part in joint activities.
- There are some Israelis who believe that in a situation of extreme violence this should demonstrate, primarily to Palestinians, that there are "humanistic" Israelis who do not wish to subjugate them, humiliate them, or do them harm.
- There are also Israelis motivated by a sense that they must convince other Israelis that there are good Palestinians who are interested in peace, "just like us."
- Joint meetings can also be seen as a means for coping with a subjective lack of control. Israelis who feel that they have no understanding of the Palestinians, and fear them or the potential danger, may come to be relaxed enough to address the Palestinians directly.
- Participation provides a mechanism to cope with Israeli feelings of guilt stemming from the occupation or other perceived injustices inflicted on the Palestinian people by the Israeli state. To deal with the complexity of issues arising from the establishment of the state, from 1967 on, there are those Israelis who cope with this by engaging in direct dialogue with the other side, in learning, recognizing, and trying to find ways to fix the wrongdoings.

Palestinian Motivations

Palestinian motivations are usually quite different. They wish to show the Israelis that Israel is at fault, the occupation is wrong, and the only solution is to end the occupation and create a Palestinian state. In this context Palestinians wish to demonstrate their suffering at the hands of the Israelis and demand an apology for their perceived sufferings. Story telling and sharing the Palestinian narrative is an essential part of the Palestinian motives for participating in the joint activities. The Palestinian motivation is usually much more politically driven than that of the Israelis.

The wide gaps between the two peoples' motivations for participation creates, from the outset, a dilemma for the organizers in setting the goals and meeting the extremely varied expectations of the participants. One of the largest of the gaps is in the capacity to endure the existing situation. For the most part, Israelis engaged in the dialogue may feel a pressing need for a better solution, but for the most part they are not personally affected as the status quo persists. The Palestinians arrive with a feeling that the current situation is the worst possible, and they are searching for an immediate change. It could very well be that the Israelis and Palestinians working on a joint activity are in search of a changed political reality, and it could be that on both sides their personal lives have been affected by the situation. But, for the most part, the Palestinians feel more of a personal sense of concrete urgency about political changes, while the Israelis have the liberty to address things from a more theoretical moral stand.

Goals, Objectives, and Strategies

The goals of joint Israeli-Palestinian peace projects are these:

- To encourage open yet friendly discussion as a means for addressing controversial ideas
- To allow exposure to both cultures and thus strengthen cultural awareness and better understanding of where the other comes from, why he views things the way he does, and what his priorities are
- To advance, in Track II–type activities, ideas and proposals for resolving specific conflicting issues

These kinds of activities aim to influence official negotiations and the formal relations between the two governments.

For peace to be comprehensive, it is crucial that the audience of joint activities include a wide range of ages, fields, and sectors in society. The target group could be divided into four age categories: children (age 6–14); youths (15–18); young adults (19–25); mature professionals (26–60).

The whole idea of joint activities is to build an "army" of peace activists who would be in the forefront in times of conflict—and continued conflict should be expected, since it is not realistic to put an end to decades of hatred, bigotry, bitterness, and hostility in a few years. Both peoples do not know much about each other, and a part of joint activities is to get to know more about the other, socially and culturally. For instance, when Palestinians invite Israelis to their homes and cook for them their favorite national traditional dish, *mansaf,* a combination of rice, yoghurt, and meat, they get offended when Israelis do not share with them their food (many Jews do not eat milk and meat together for religious reasons). Joint activities are about understanding why.

Typology of Joint Israeli-Palestinian Activities and Classifications

Who are the participants and target audience of joint peacebuilding activities? Joint activities failed to target a wide spectrum of people on both sides. They targeted professionals of the upper class who were well to do, spoke good English, and were apolitical. They almost never targeted the poor, the refugees, and the underprivileged. Joint activities between Israelis and Palestinians that took place in the previous decade can be put into the following distinct categories:

- *Track II Activities Mainly Aimed at Brainstorming*
  These cover ideas for formal agreements between the two sides and for closing the gaps in positions between the two. Sometimes these activities include officials from both sides (usually more officials from the Palestinian side than the Israeli). At times, these officials have had direct access to decisionmakers, and at other times the participants are quite separate from official negotiators.
- *Women's and Shared-Identity Issues*
  Activities typically incorporate projects that address the distinctive needs of constituents on both sides with a shared identity. Activity is focused on shared identity that cuts across the cleavage between Israelis and Palestinians, and can be a potent and resilient form of peacebuilding. Other forms of joint activities organized around a shared identity include groups of religious leaders, and even one group of bereaved parents from both sides.
- *Professional Meetings*
  These are for bringing together professional people from the same areas of expertise to discuss professional issues not directly related to the peace process or to peacemaking and -building. The most common of these include professionals from the health profession (e.g., doctors, nurses, hospital administrators) and those in the education field. There has also been significant participation in this category by people in social work, tourism, archeology, and law.
- *Professional Training*
  These activities, in general, are concerned with skills, knowledge, and technology transfer and the transfer of know-how. While those managerial and financial training seminars were facilitated by both Israeli and Palestinian experts, almost always technology training workshops

were conducted by the Israeli or foreign partners. The training has covered agriculture, business management, and computers and other high-technology fields.

- *Formal Education Activities*
These activities usually involve schools with teachers and students. They ranged from one-time activities to long-term multiyear efforts of creating peace education on both sides. These activities also have involved curriculum development, student-teacher interaction, and formal and informal education frameworks.

   The formal education system was not first seen as a strategic actor in implementing the Oslo Accords. Although some activities were aimed at teachers and students, the overall structure outlines the roles to be assumed and monitored in the areas of security, borders, economics, and even agriculture. The obvious need for the education system to reorganize itself in light of the new reality and in terms of teacher training, community outreach, and curriculum development was barely noted and was only addressed in vague and negative terms—such as incitement to resistance action. If the formal education systems are to assume their roles, they should also have a mandate within the context of the political accords and the subsequent follow-up.

- *Cultural Activities*
These vary in populations participating and in their scope. Some bring people of the two cultures together to be exposed to each other's culture as well as to the different historical narratives and ideologies, and sometimes to "create" together some form of cultural expression.

- *Capacity Building, Institution Building, and Service Provision*
These activities are aimed primarily at empowering the Palestinian side in skills and knowledge to help cope with institution building and the running of public affairs. Some of the joint training was aimed at enriching NGO skills, including facilitation of conflict transformation workshops, merging human rights into the peace agenda, working for women's rights, and nonviolent action.

- *Environmental Cooperation*
Activities often included other regional partners, mostly from Jordan but sometimes from Egypt. They have focused on such cross-boundary issues as water conservation and water pollution, sewage, the Dead Sea, and pest control, among others.

- *Grassroots Dialogue Groups*
These are organized by individuals or groups, often as a result of personal motivation. Such activities are usually not funded nor organized by institutions or NGOs, and are also not documented in any formal way.

- *Political Struggle, Solidarity Groups, and Advocacy Groups*
  Groups have as their objectives in this field expressions of sympathy,
  empathy, and advocacy on the part of one group for the other. This
  type of joint activity may or may not take the form of the provision
  of goods or services, but rather, symbolic demonstrations of support
  or political protest. What distinguishes this category from the others
  is that it does not always necessitate interface between the two peoples. It is important to note here that there is an asymmetry in how
  both peoples react to this matter, the powerful side, Israel being more
  concerned with the suffering of the oppressed than vice versa. While
  Israeli streets witnessed many demonstrations in solidarity with peace,
  on the Palestinian side there were virtually none.
- *Religious Dialogue*
  These are organized to have an open dialogue among the three faiths:
  Judaism, Christianity, and Islam. The aim is to bring together leading
  religious figures to discuss issues that separate and those that unite
  the three communities in order to promote peace and coexistence
  among the three communities.

Joint Activities: Challenges, Obstacles, and Difficulties

Why did peace NGOs and activists disappear when the storm of the intifada
erupted? Obstacles, challenges, and difficulties that made this happen may
be summarized as follows.

Oslo Peace Process

Joint Israeli-Palestinian peace activities have experienced wide criticism
over the past years by protagonists and antagonists alike. The Oslo Peace
Process was a "top-down" strategy for achieving peace between the two
people in conflict, the Israelis and the Palestinians. The strategy was based
on the assumption that signing political agreements by the government of
Israel and the PLO would change the realities on the ground and the peoples of both sides would eventually join the peace parade. Thus there was
no policy for the encouragement of building and maintaining the peace
through offering official support to the civil society to actively get involved
in joint activities. Continuing occupation and the continuing increase of settlements eroded trust on the Palestinian side. The failure of Camp David
and peaceful negotiations at bringing the Palestinians a viable Palestinian
state played a central role sparking the Al-Aqsa intifada of September 2000
thereby demolishing the fragile yet extensive web of joint activities that
had gradually been formed on a voluntary basis after the Oslo Accords.
Before the intifada, a dramatic proliferation of joint projects was in evidence, but these activities appear to have ground to a halt, particularly in
the aftermath of escalating hostilities between the two sides.

Absence of Comprehensive Strategy

Despite the importance of the need to have a comprehensive joint-activities strategy, the unanswered questions remain. Can it be done? How? Why? Who should do it? What are the necessary logistics?

So far, there is no coherent, comprehensive strategy for joint activities, no shared knowledge of what should be done, no clear target audiences, no specific kinds of activities to be undertaken, no shared vision of how to reach people and change their attitudes toward peace.

What exists at present is a salad with no chef. You get funding from donors for a joint project. You get involved in the implementation of a project. But maybe somebody else has already done that work or is still doing it. How does your work relate to theirs? Who is looking out for the overall picture? There is no party in charge, a committee that could ensure that joint activities are organized within a shared strategy or shared strategies with agreed objectives.

As the violence of the Al-Aqsa intifada increased, Palestinians and Israelis held to their two conflicting narratives. Therefore they did not agree on basic points of departure from which they could contextualize the political, economic, and social circumstances of the violence and deteriorating relations between the two societies.

Environment

Most Israelis are proud of themselves when they participate in joint activities. They wish to let it be known to their family, friends, and communities that they are participants. Their participation provides them with a sense of being at the forefront—almost in the avant-garde.

On the other side, due to Palestinian perception that the Israelis are to be blamed for the demise of the peace process, joint activities with Israelis became very unpopular in Palestine. Palestinian participants are criticized for their participation in joint activities; at times they are stigmatized for working with the "enemy," whose transgressions against the Palestinian people have not subsided. In times of conflict and crisis, those participating in joint activities are worried that if the public finds out that they were meeting Israelis, they would be ostracized or worse, particularly since they received mixed signals for participation—red and green lights for the same activity.

The Al-Aqsa intifada made both peoples very skeptical about the chances of peace and such concepts as peace or normalization, which started to have negative connotations in both societies. Even those who had worked with and benefited from joint peace projects, and who had received money to conduct such activities, began saying, "Are you kidding? Are you serious? You're talking about joint peace activities? Where is the peace? We are now in a conflict. This is war. We should not be talking to the other.

We should not even be thinking in terms of peace." This suggests that in fact no solid base had been established for real peace in the Palestinian–Israeli conflict.

Funding

Although the Oslo II agreement included an annex calling for the institution of people-to-people projects as a means of strengthening peace between the two peoples, during the seven years that followed the Oslo Accords between September 1993 until September 2000, an estimated $26 million was allocated for funding such people-to-people projects mainly through NGOs and civil-society institutions in Israel and Palestine.

Institutional Capacity

The Palestinian and Israeli NGOs and personalities in the aftermath of the Oslo declaration were faced with a sudden demand to meet the supply of requests for partnerships. While initially both the Palestinian and Israeli NGO community and leading public personalities usually viewed the need for joint activities favorably, they were often overwhelmed by the vast numbers of requests for partnerships. These leaders simply were not always in a position to match the requests with the necessary organizational and institutional capacities due to both shortage of funds and lack of experience. Often, the international donors and the Israeli initiators did not exhibit sufficient understanding of the sensitivities and requirements of implementing truly joint activities based on equal partnerships.

There is a clear disparity in power and abilities between Israeli and Palestinian NGOs. While both Israeli and Palestinian NGOs can be asked to do their best possible work, their abilities, capabilities, resources, and opportunities differ greatly. In practice this has very often meant that the projects were initiated by the Israeli organizations, the proposals written by them, the implementation managed by them, and the funds controlled by them. Needless to say, this was extremely problematic in developing partnerships. Many Palestinian institutions and individuals noted that many of the joint activities were beginning to resemble already well-established models of asymmetry between Israelis and Palestinians.

Palestinians in civil society have limited experience in fund raising and joint-project implementation. Israelis on the other hand, have long experience with it because they are very much part of the European and American culture. Israel is a country that has thrived by attracting donations, and has a long history of knowing how to address donors. Palestinian society is new, and the objective of its NGOs and of civil society up until 1993 was how to survive under occupation and how to confront it.

Then there was the Oslo agreement, and Palestinian civil society shifted from confrontation to coexistence and the concept of marketing peace.

There was virtually no transition period. The Palestinian society moved from one extreme to another: there was little if no psychological preparation; there was almost no mental readiness. It was just like shifting from forward to reverse, or the other way around. There was a change of direction that could take time to adjust to. At the outbreak of the second intifada in September 2000, the shift from peacemaking to war and conflict was even more abrupt. With the high numbers of casualties on the Palestinian side from the very early days of the uprising, many Palestinians involved in joint activities expected to see their Israeli counterparts taking to the street and rally against those in the Israeli establishment who were drumming up public support against the Palestinians and their leadership. The anger that took hold in Palestinian society immediately created an almost total loss of any legitimacy to talking or working with Israelis. Likewise in Israel, a strong sense of betrayal took hold of many Israelis, even those involved in joint activities, thinking that Palestinians had rejected Israel's "generous" offers for peace and then responded with attacks and violence. With the emergence of two completely different narratives of the breakdown of the peace process, not only did communication cease at the upper political levels, but for many of those Israelis and Palestinians involved in joint activities communication also abruptly ended.

In addition, fragmentation among NGOs and competition for resources led to a lack of cooperation and sharing knowledge, though a problem on both sides but in one more than the other.

Public Legitimacy
Many Israelis and Palestinians as well as many donors have a sense that joint Israeli-Palestinian activities are not "taken seriously" by the officials on either side. The governments of Israel and the Palestinian Authority contributed very little of their own resources (although it could be said that the US government deducted the Wye River Grant funds from the US bilateral grant of $400 million to the authority following the signing of the Wye River memorandum). Even those officials appointed by the two governments to coordinate joint activities within the framework of the official People-to-People Secretariat chaired by the Norwegians were not empowered by their governments to allocate any resources to this work. There were no official government statements in support of joint activities and almost no thought by officials on how to make this an integral part of the peace process and of peacemaking.

Logistics
The current violence, the restrictions on movement, and the inability to conduct meetings on a regular basis created great difficulties in implementing Israeli-Palestinian joint-activity projects at this time. Nonetheless, programs

and activities have been held successfully since the turn of the century. There are great obstacles in the way of conducting this work, but possibilities do still exist. The main logistics obstacle is centered around the inability of Palestinians to move freely within the Palestinian territories and into Israel as well as the law and the potential dangers to Israelis that prevent them from entering the territories. There is a complex process of applying for permits for Palestinians and getting the permits issued. Even once permits are issued, there are chances that due to closings the permits will be canceled without prior notice. With permits in hand, Palestinians may encounter many checkpoints where the soldiers can arbitrarily decide who can pass. Traveling even short distances from Ramallah to Jerusalem or to Tel Aviv can end up taking hours.

With the extremely volatile situation, such events as Israeli targeted killings or suicide bombings, will usually prevent planned activities from taking place.

Target Groups

Part of the problem of limited impact of these activities is that joint activities did not identify clearly the target groups they wanted to most affect, which are at the grassroots. A large majority of projects targeted the converted elites, hoping that these would affect and influence the wider societies. Issues that hamper spreading joint activities to the grassroots are complex. First is the language barrier. When participants are chosen, many times organizers try to find participants who speak English because that is the common language for joint activities. This immediately implies that organizers are looking for people best able to represent their class, society, country, or national cause. But when only English speakers are included in the programs, we lose great opportunities to reach the masses. It is important to include activities to teach children the other people's language, thereby preparing them to participate in the future in discussing peace issues. Eventually this will lead to each side better understanding the other.

Second, there are objective problems in reaching those at the grassroots. For instance, most joint activities within the education system have had to rely on private schools in Palestine. Public schools were not accessible for joint programs because the Palestinian Ministry of Education has, until now, prevented such activities in the schools under its jurisdiction.

Planners of activities mainly for youth should be conscious of the need for concentric circles linking youths with educators, and even parents. If these youths go back to their schools after a joint activity and encounter teachers who frown on peace or normalization—both of which have become words with negative connotations—or on trying to understand the other, that will have a negative impact on the goal of the activity and result in a major drawback to the process of understanding between the two peoples. At the same time, it is important to include the parents who have influence on their children by either encouraging or discouraging joint activities when they go home. Without a doubt, it is very important to keep talking to the converted because, very often, those thought to be converted actually knew very little about the other side. This became very clear when the intifada broke out and people in the peace camp on both sides, who were assumed to be totally converted, turned their back on the peace process. They felt that something had definitely gone wrong and they did not trust the other side anymore. Certainly this happened to people who may have met many Palestinians or Israelis in the past, but still never really understood the fundamentals of what the conflict is all about. They participated in, say, a hummus breakfast, where they found out that the other side did not have horns or tails and that they were pleasant people, but still often did not have the chance to engage in a real, honest discussion about the wounds, the pains, the fears, the worries, the narratives, and the traumas felt by the other side. So it remains important to continue to reach out to the converted to strengthen their beliefs, knowledge, and understanding. It is important also to design the strategies for reaching beyond these people.

Sustainability

One of the problems of joint activities was that many of them were of a one-shot, short-term nature. It is important to recognize that peacebuilding is a long-term endeavor and so joint-activities programs should also be. Short-term programs do not have the same lasting effect.

In general, most of these projects or activities had no long-term sustainability built into them. This is not how you build peace relationships, whether between people across a conflict line or whether between them after a peace accord is signed. It takes lots of work and time to build the relationships. It is a process, not a one-time shot. When one thinks strategy, process is the most important aspect. We need to think about how to build sustainable relationships over time.

Language Barriers

It is important for people to be understood. This might mean that the activities can take place in English or another neutral language, or it might mean that Hebrew and Arabic could be spoken so both peoples can speak freely and say what they have to say the way they feel comfortable saying it. But this requires efficient and qualified translators, a factor that significantly increases costs.

Media Attention and Public Exposure

The differences in goals and motivations heighten the dilemmas regarding public exposure of the activities of the program. Previous studies on the impact of people-to-people activities show that most joint activities had limited impact beyond the participants themselves due to the activities' lack of public exposure. This lack of exposure emanated from both the various organizers' decisions to conduct the activities under a media blackout and from the lack of interest on the part of the media in publicizing positive news or peace news, while at the same time jumping at conflict news.

If contacts to assemble a group to participate in a joint activity became known, more often than not the events were cancelled because many Palestinians put pressure on their fellow citizens not to participate, with some citizens being threatened. At various times over the past years, official boycotts of joint activities were organized by Palestinian organizations, political movements, and even Palestinian Authority officials. The Palestinian universities (with the exception of Al-Quds), as well as the Palestinian NGO network, adopted an official policy of boycotting joint activities, and the Palestinian NGO network even expelled one of its member organizations for continuing to engage in such activities. As a result, publicity and media attention shied away from them. Palestinian peace activists voicing their opinions did not publicize the fact that this negative stance reflects the views of a vocal minority opposing such activities and that it is not necessarily a reflection of the views of a majority of Palestinians. Nonetheless, it is essential to recognize that this is the situation and that organizers proceed with extreme caution.

Israelis, on the other hand, wish to attract as much media attention as possible. Israelis wish to show their public that there are Palestinians, like themselves, who are interested in making peace. They wish to spread the word and to have a wider impact. They are often very discouraged when Palestinians refuse to publicize this fact and when they prevent distribution of joint statements and declarations to the press. Even though organizers sometimes publish the proceedings of the joint meetings, only limited editions are printed.

Each side comes to these activities with different goals. Not many on either side have the courage to go against the stream in their own societies, though Israelis exercise more their freedom to do so than Palestinians, and it is almost always that the organizers and participants will agree to adopt the Palestinian position—mainly in the name of safety for the Palestinian participants. This must be recognized as a significant limiting factor on the ability to inform the public, spreading the word, and having a wider impact beyond the participants themselves.

Normalization Label

There is no doubt that the media on both sides of the conflict not only failed to give their full support to the peace process, but actually focused on conflict issues that incited a further drift from peace to conflict. Much of the joint activities were done without any media publicity, and joint meetings were held in closed rooms. Peace activists stayed away from the media for fear that the media would expose them to criticism from radical groups on their own side. On the Palestinian side, "normalization" carried a negative connotation, while on the Israeli side, the word *shalom* had a hollow sound.

Israelis participating in joint activities desire to normalize relations with the Palestinian participants. This has been the goal of the Zionist movement and of Israel from the beginning of their inception. Israel wants to be accepted in the region as a normal state with normalized relations with all other states in the region. The desire for normalization emanates from the belief that peace and peacemaking should be based on mutual acceptance and recognition. But a blacklist was published on the internet that included names of those Israelis who participate in joint activities with Palestinians, along with the Israelis' addresses. These peace activists were described as Jews who were self-hating, Jews who threatened the existence of the state of Israel by their collaboration with the enemies of Israel.

On the other hand, Palestinian desire for normalization is preconditioned on their call for justice. Thus, normalization in Palestinian political oratory under the conditions of continued occupation has a negative connotation. Normalization, according to Palestinian officials, is a bargaining chip that should not be handed over until the occupation is terminated and a Palestinian state is established. Thus normalization for most Palestinians is viewed as a prize that should be given to Israel only once the conflict has reached an end. For Palestinian Authority officials and hard-liners normalization during continued conflict and occupation is a form of treason. Those Palestinians who participate in joint activities with Israelis are often portrayed as collaborators. A book published in Arabic, *Intellectuals in the Service of the Other,* named many of the leaders, personalities, and organizations participating in joint activities. The book's subtitle is *The Communiqué of the 55 as a Model,* in reference to a declaration published in the local press by fifty-five prominent Palestinian intellectuals, authors, and academicians denouncing suicide bombings and the militarization of the intifada.[2] This highlights the extent to which Palestinians participating in joint activities are on the defensive within their own society. Thus Palestinian peace activists prefer to describe what they are doing as "dialogue"—aimed at convincing the Israelis about Palestinian justice, or to show them the error of their ways, or the evils of occupation, and so on.

Joint Activities: Measuring Impact—A Complex Endeavor

Public opinion polls in Israel and Palestine over the past years have indicated that only half a percent of either Israelis or Palestinians have met people from the other side as a result of peace-oriented, that is, joint activities.

How can more people be reached? How may a process be developed that will involve a critical mass of people in positive interactions?

The issue of impact is extremely elusive, analytically speaking. Indeed, impact means different things to different people. From an operational perspective, the question is raised of how one measures impact.

When planning for joint activities it is important to keep in mind the impact issue. Joint activities should be aimed to have a wider effect on society beyond the participants themselves. Therefore it is necessary to place the challenge of confronting issues of impact in the planning stages of these activities. The following questions could be asked when seeking to assess impact:

- Did participants learn anything positive about the other?
- Are participants more aware of the problems and fears of the other?
- Did they get a personal stake in the success of the peace process?
- Do the participants feel that by participating they are being loyal to their own national cause and directly responding to the needs of their own communities?
- Are they going to return for more dialogue?
- Are they willing and committed to enlisting others in dialogue activities?
- Are they willing to speak out for peace and coexistence in their own societies?
- When confronted with the realities and social pressures of war, does their commitment withstand the test?
- Were they honest and frank with each other?
- Did organizational coordination work smoothly?
- How does the project contend with internal controversy?
- To what extent do participants feel that they are learning from one another?

Other factors to examine include the following:

- Number of people actively involved in the more nuts and bolts of working together
- Length of time that the activity takes place
- Organizational commitment to the activity
- Desire/willingness of participants to come back for a second round
- Feelings of participants on their way back compared to their feelings on their way to the meeting

Questions Concerning Impact
The limited impact of the joint activities thus far emanates from a multitude of factors which include the following:

- Lack of public legitimacy
- Severe limitations of funding
- Inability to develop long-term programs with built-in continuation
- Too much focus on elite groups from both sides and not enough outreach to grassroots populations
- Little or no inclusion of built-in multipliers, that is, creating ambassadors or agents of change to carry on processes beyond the joint programs
- Ineffective strategies for addressing, involving, and utilizing the media in the programs

Joint Activities: Lessons Learned and Best Practices

What Types of Joint Activities?

It is extremely difficult to provide clear guidelines regarding a prioritization of the kind of joint activities that should be most encouraged and supported. However, there are criteria that might help in determining emphasis in terms of what kind of activities should be supported at the current time. These criteria include the following:

- The extent to which the activity will involve and develop real Israeli-Palestinian cooperation, working together and building long-term relationships and partnerships
- The extent to which the activity will reach out beyond those who participate directly in the activity either through multipliers or through the media
- The extent to which the activity is conceived of as a continual longer-term endeavor and not a one-time event
- The extent to which the activity either produces wider public legitimacy for joint activities or has wider public legitimacy built into its conception
- The extent to which the activity has a thought-out and articulated coherent strategy for positively influencing attitudes of Israelis and Palestinians toward peacemaking and peacebuilding
- The extent to which the activity reaches out to new populations that have not previously participated in joint activities
- The extent to which the organizers of the activity work in a real and equitable partnership
- The extent to which objectives are responsive to volatile political circumstances and developments

Joint Activities: Strategies

If it is agreed that it is necessary to have a comprehensive strategy or comprehensive strategies for joint activities, the question is what should those strategies be to have maximum impact? Coherent, comprehensive strategies for joint activities ought to show clearly what should be done, who are the target audiences, which kinds of activities should be undertaken, what are the goals to be achieved, and how do we determine whether or not they have been achieved.

Projects as a long-term investment. Changing attitudes is a long-term endeavor. Working over a long time with the same people strengthens the abilities of those people to become agents of change within their own communities. Many of those people who have remained dedicated to peace over the past years of violence are those who have taken part in joint activities over an extended period. It is recommended that donors and NGOs consider these long-term strategies in their planning and implementation.

Projects addressing specific societal needs and exploring how the cooperation or dialogue responds to these needs. The need for "peace" is often broad and is a long-term process. It is difficult for the participants to evaluate exactly what they have managed to achieve. Responding to a specific need, without ignoring the Palestinian-Israeli context, yet showing the benefit in cooperation, help create measurable short-term achievements that contribute to long-term sustainability.

Projects having good partnership. What are the key lessons we have learned that would facilitate better joint activities? One is that the chances of success of joint projects are increased when there is a good partnership between the two groups conducting the activity.

Projects with multiplier aspects. It is desirable for joint activities to include multiplier aspects built into the work. Models for expanding the work beyond the immediate participants ought to be considered as a vital element for having broader impact in the two societies.

Reaching out to grassroots groups: Learning each other's language. Due to language barriers, more often than not, the participants of joint activities represent elite groups from both sides. It is recommended that these participants be included in discussions of how to effectively bring the messages and the work of the joint activities to broader cross-sections of both communities. While the use of translators can be cumbersome and expensive, it is nonetheless thought valuable in considering the need to involve other than elite groups in joint activities. It is also believed that the protagonists of these activities should advance the possibilities for Israelis and Palestinians to learn each other's language.

Joint work not existing in a vacuum. Work between professional groups is important; however, it is recommended that this work be connected in various ways to the Israeli-Palestinian context. Assumptions should not be made that meetings between people sharing a profession will have a positive impact on the relations of the two sides without also considering the need to address the broader questions concerning the Israeli-Palestinian relationship. This is at times somewhat problematic because in many cases the mutual professional work is carried out by organizations that are not chartered to address political issues. Therefore, it might be possible to link these activities with organizations that do deal specifically with the more political aspects of the joint work. There is debate on the importance of addressing the politics of the conflict within the framework of mutually professional meetings and whether or not this is possible or even recommended. There is, however, broad agreement that within the context of professional meetings that the human side of the encounter—who they are, where they come from, what their lives are like, and how their lives are influenced by the conflict—should be built into the planning and not be left to chance dialogue.

Using the media to create public awareness about joint activities. It is essential to develop a way for the joint activities to open themselves up to the media. Planning for these activities should include a plan for creating public awareness about the activities themselves with the aim of informing the wider public and rebuilding confidence in the possibilities of real peace. The public ought to be made to understand that there are partners on the other side.

Wider public need to be engaged in and made aware of joint activities. While it is understood that certain Track II types of activities must be conducted discreetly and out of the light of the media, the Israeli and Palestinian public should be able to engage in debates about the issues being discussed. Greater public awareness and debate is important regarding the possibilities for reaching agreements, and it is recommended that knowledge of the parameters of those potential agreements be shared with the wider public on both sides.

Official commitment. In any and all future agreements both governments should sign an agreement stating their commitments to joint Israeli-Palestinian activities. In all new agreements the parties should spell out their obligations, financial and otherwise, and specific benchmarks of implementation should be explicit.

Providing legitimacy. It would be greatly beneficial if leaders and politicians would provide legitimacy for joint Israeli-Palestinian activities to be effective and acceptable. There should be a concerted effort on the part of the NGOs involved in these activities, as well as the donors, to lobby for positive public statements by Israeli and Palestinian officials in support of people-to-people activities. These public statements may not be offered automatically and therefore, when and where needed, should be encouraged and publicized. Donors should also speak to the political leaders on both sides to encourage the public support of the political levels on both sides. This should be done regardless of the state of formal peace processes or even the lack of them.

Coordination, cooperation, and transparency. Many Israeli and Palestinian institutions involved in joint activities have spoken about the need to increase coordination, cooperation, and transparency at all levels of joint-activity work. These organizations have voiced the opinion that little real cooperation exists between many of these NGOs. Furthermore many NGOs have spoken about a sense that due to finance constraints, many perceive the field as much more competitive than cooperative. Many also express a sense that there is little cooperation and coordination among the various donors and that donor financing is not used effectively as a result.

Forums for multilevel coordination and cooperation of joint activities are necessary. These should include coordination by the NGOs engaged, both in binational meetings as well as at home; coordination and open communication between the NGOs and relevant government officials from both sides and among the NGOs and the donors—as well as among the donors themselves.

Palestinian NGOs should establish a forum for coordination of joint activities; Israelis should continue theirs. The Israeli NGOs should continue to convene periodic meetings for the Israeli participation in the dialogue and joint-activity NGOs, and the Palestinian NGOs should establish a similar forum for convening periodic meetings of the Palestinian NGOs involved in joint activities. These separate meetings are useful for creating internal support for the organizations involved in these activities, for raising issues of mutual concern, and in confronting challenges that the organizations are facing. At least one of the donors should take responsibility for providing support for the convening of these meetings, while the NGOs should take responsibility for ensuring that the meetings are held.

Support and cooperation mechanisms. For the purposes of support and cooperation it is important to address the different tasks that exist within this field. No doubt, there should be a separate support mechanism for the different tasks, such as program directors, field coordinators, primary participants, and secondary participants. These distinctions may ensure more openness among the participants and may prove to be more valuable in the long run.

Annual meetings. At least one annual several-day conference of all joint-activity players should be convened. At least once a year a meeting of Israeli and Palestinian joint-activity NGO leaders and donors should be organized to brainstorm and coordinate their activities and plans. This meeting should be used to review progress, to discuss planning and strategies, and to work out and work on emerging problems and challenges. Perhaps this could be undertaken by the country holding the presidency of the European Union at the time. Participants must include the representatives of the primary donors to joint activities and the main Israeli and Palestinian NGOs. Official representatives of the governments of Israel and Palestine should also attend.

More emphasis on work at home. Meetings inside a nation that address peacemaking and peacebuilding can also be held within the framework of joint activities. There seems to be a great need and desire to include such national elements of this work and seems completely legitimate at this time.

Partnering and partnerships. After September 2000, many of the cooperative projects of Israeli and Palestinian NGOs working on joint activities ceased. There was a deep sense of disappointment on both sides regarding the political responses and reactions from the partners. There was also a general question raised, following the breakdown of the peace process, about the motives and attitudes of people who had been working together for peace. Many accusations were made across the conflict lines by people who shortly before had been partners in joint activities. A group of some Palestinian NGOs called for a boycott of joint activities, branding some of the Israeli NGOs specifically as being "worthy" of the boycott. There was a general breakdown of many partnerships, and it seemed that joint activities had completely come to an end.

In reality, a number of organizations and activities continued despite the new situation. Some of those organizations and activities have even grown during the past two years. The subject of partnering and partnerships was raised by almost all the participants in this study. The following are the main lessons and recommendations raised:

Needed: True Sense of Parity and Equality for Successful Partnership

The activities and organizations that have continued and sustained themselves over the past few years tend to be those with the highest levels of joint work and true partnerships. The issue of partnerships across the conflict line should not be underestimated. This requires a high level of coordination and building understanding at the institutional level. Transparency between the partners is essential. Developing a true sense of parity and equality at all levels of working together are the guidelines for sustainability.

Establishing terms of partnership from the outset. Partners should develop a plan for how they will work together and how decisions will be made. It is advisable for partners to write and sign memorandums of understanding between them as part of the submission of the project proposal for funding. The use of the funds and the means of allocating the funds should be clear and written down before the outset of work on the project. It was in this area that many conflicts developed between partners.

Complete parity in funding is not always a possibility. Funding between the partners does not necessarily have to be equal. There are situations in which one of the organizations (usually on the Palestinian side) will have greater needs for capacity development, equipment, or other needs. It should be seen as possible for one side to receive a larger share of the available funds based upon agreements between the partners and with the donors.

Need for efforts to include all voices in public debate over peacemaking. Without high-level public support during the critical phase of political transition, and without including all political sectors, even the most extreme, in the public discussion, it is mere romanticism to think that a group of high-minded individuals, with a minimum of financial and government backing, can be an effective partner with or catalyst for any peace agreement. There has to be a concerted effort to be inclusive, to make peacebuilding a national priority, not a privileged game for the initiates. It is recommended that the initiators of joint activities consider how to expand the scope of the participants in the programs so as to include those who are not automatically supportive of the same general political goals and strategies.

Issues Concerning Donors

More funding for long-term and continuing programs. Donors should examine the possibilities for allocating funds for joint activities for multiyear, continuing, and current programs. Recognizing that this is sometimes difficult due to budgetary restrictions at home, efforts should be made by donors to convince their governments of the real needs enabling long-term planning and implementation of programs that require time and continual efforts to ensure the success of having impact and changing attitudes.

More attention to constraints and difficulties imposed by joint structures. Donors should be made more aware of the difficulties of implementing programs by Israeli and Palestinian NGOs trying to cooperate under very adverse circumstances. Donors should make allowances for the extra costs involved in having a joint structure of people from both sides to run the programs—an issue that involves additional funds.

Additional funding to allow for programs held abroad. Donors should be willing to make allowances for programs being implemented outside Israel and Palestine. There are great difficulties involved in holding Israeli-Palestinian meetings in Israel and Palestine at this time. This also involves additional funding.

Creating a sense of parity in contracts and funding. Donors can help in the partnering process by developing mechanisms for joint contracts among the organizations and means for funding both sides of the project (rather than transferring the funds to only one partner). An alternative is a single contract cosigned by both partners.

Lobbying the Palestinian Authority and Israeli governments. Donors should put pressure on both governments whenever necessary to aid in promoting joint meetings, for instance, in lobbying the Palestinian Authority to encourage and facilitate participation in joint meetings, as well as prompting the Israeli government to provide permits for Palestinian participants, a process that is still much too cumbersome and arbitrary. In the current difficult situation, the possibilities for joint meetings of Israelis and Palestinians are extremely limited. Many of these meetings must be held abroad. But the security requirements have made it increasingly difficult for travel. Such issues must be dealt with in a coordinated and concerted effort by all concerned in order to ameliorate bureaucratic constraints and to enable more people to participate.

Conclusions

A naive assumption about joint activities was that if Israelis and Palestinians were brought together, they would like each other, go home, and be friends thereafter. The fruits of peace would grow. But it turned out that this was not necessarily the case. People meet, perhaps they may like each other, but perhaps not.

At least joint activities give Palestinians and Israelis an opportunity to meet and get to know each other as human beings, say, as doctors, engineers, or professionals, rather than only as soldiers at checkpoints or people with whom they have to deal in conflict.

The deeper understanding of the other's religion, history, culture, civilization, and political institutions will help all to look for more mutual appreciation that reaffirms commitment to the ideals of peace and democracy and the pursuit of mutual interests and cooperation.

This is needed especially after the damage to relations caused by the failure of the Camp David summit in July 2000 and the launching of the Al-Aqsa intifada in September 2000.

The context ought to complement, enrich, and bring closeness rather than intimidate and demonize either side. Such a context should contain positive aspects in the Israeli-Palestinian experience such as economic co-operation, social acceptance, political accommodation, and the ways that both peoples can benefit from the experience of the other in all ways.

It is important and healthy that we keep our cross-border friendships and professional contacts. But in the present violent reality, it would be hubristic in the extreme to think that the same small groups of Israelis and Palestinians, a few thousand at most on either side, are sufficient and acceptable as leadership in bringing about or sustaining change. Nonetheless, it is very important to encourage Israeli-Palestinian joint activities at this time to cement the infrastructure of joint programs for future expansion and as a means of keeping alive the message that there "are people on the other side to talk with."

The current lack of leadership on both sides affects the potential for civil society contribution and the need to share more the grief of those on the other side, often at times when the issue of violence brings extreme suffering that affects the moods and motivations of those involved in peace work. Settlers from Israel and Islamic fundamentalists seem to have a dominant strategy and, even if they do not coordinate their activities, they definitely feed off each other.

The joint peace activities are reactive rather than active, and unfortunately they are weaker than ever at times when there are most needed.

Notes

1. Until 1993, Israeli law prohibited meetings with members of the PLO, so such meetings were organized by third parties and usually held under academic auspices and thus avoided media coverage.

2. Dr. Adel Samara, *Intellectuals in the Service of the Other, The Communiqué of the 55 as a Model* (Ramallah: Al-Mashreq Center, 2003). Actually, the communiqué of the subtitle was followed the next day by another list of names in support of the same cause, and this would have continued if strong pressures were not exerted to stop it. The book voices the thinking and rhetoric of the 1950s. In one of its outbursts, the author asks rhetorically: "Isn't the United States the financier for women's organizations that operate in the Occupied Territories as NGOs, such as the organizations of Violence Against Women, noting that the United States is preparing itself again to slaughter the Arab people of Iraq and half of them are females!" Another publication by the same author carried the title *NGOs or Bases of the Other?* (Ramallah: Al-Mashreq Center, 2003).

5

Israeli-Palestinian Track II Diplomacy

Menachem Klein and Riad Malki

This chapter was written separately by Menachem Klein and Riad Malki. Klein's part focuses on the theoretical background of the Oslo Accords' Track II diplomacy, classifying and defining this growing tool of unofficial negotiations, and widely used in the Israeli–Palestinian context. Klein also provides us with a comparative perspective as well as with a brief analysis of Track II on the disputes over Jerusalem.[1] The second part, Malki's provides a variety of issues relevant to the Israeli-Palestinian Track II issues and focuses on specific examples. Due to space limitations, we cannot cover the full picture of such channels that perhaps make the Israeli and Palestinian cases the richest in Track I, both in quantity and quality, as analyzed in a recent book by Hussein Agha and associates.[2] In a recent conference at Tel Aviv University on Track IIs in which several of the contributors of this book have participated, the potential of such avenues was explored. The original concept of an alternative channel to official diplomacy has now been widened so that it includes citizen's diplomacy (or societal track IIs). Hence a first conceptual categorization may be useful for a better understanding of the scope that now includes concepts such as multitrack diplomacy, citizens' diplomacy,[3] or societal Track II.

Background to Track II Diplomacy and the Israeli-Palestinian Case Study on Jerusalem (by Menachem Klein)

Track II: Definitions and Types
Track II is different from secret negotiation and back-channel talks. While secret negotiations and the back channel are "secret official negotiations between the contending parties that take place in parallel with front-channel negotiations or replace them," Track II is not an official negotiation.[4] First,

the very existence of Track II as a form of negotiation and its outcome are deniable by government officials. Second, Track II negotiators are unauthorized, whereas invisible negotiation is managed on behalf of the statesmen. Oslo talks illustrate these differences. They began in January 1993 as a classical Track II negotiation between two Israeli academics and two PLO senior members acting in their private capacity to help the official talks in Washington, but soon this Track II came to be a secret negotiation and a back channel. The two Israeli academics were authorized by their leaders to negotiate, alongside two official envoys, with their Palestinian counterparts acting formally as PLO negotiators.

Track II had many variations and modes of operation. It could be categorized by means of participants, aims, success in influencing target audiences and achieving the track's main goals, timing, political context, and relation to official talks and power holders. Track II could be run by retired diplomats and civil servants, as well as by people-to-people activists with no previous official position, or volunteer advisers, or academic experts with access to decisionmakers.

The aims of Track II were varied as well. Track II could be geared toward influencing a small group of negotiators and bureaucrats by offering them strategies of negotiation and understandings, providing the decisionmakers substantive input, and setting the prenegotiation stage for the benefit of the later formal discussion. Track II could also seek to shape public opinion and expose the public to creative ideas and new approaches, as well as to change the contentious discourse within and between each side. The Geneva agreement of October 2003 is the best expression of Track II. Track II participants could be either optimistic or pessimistic about their ability to influence decisionmakers; in either case they aimed to define concretely the issues at stake and to conceptualize in terms of cognitive and social psychology the different perceptions of self, the other side, and the conflict. As such, Track II participants were to act as agents of change. Nevertheless, no special timing was involved in Track II activity, nor was it a necessary introduction to the official negotiations. It could operate in the absence of official negotiation or parallel to it, and parallel to secret backchannel talks as well.[5]

Using the well-known concepts of peacebuilding, peacemaking, and peacekeeping, Benjamin Gidron, Stanley Katz, and Yeheskel Hasenfeld preferred to put Track II activities into the categories of peacebuilding and peacemaking.[6] Track II contributes to those two categories by developing bridges between rival communities and offering their interested members a chance to interact and develop effective means of communication—a prerequisite for any successful negotiation. These means include the creation of common language, joint technical terms, and shared cultural symbols, as well as interpersonal skills, mutual respect, and trust. The use of these tools helps to create a perception of common ground and parity in status between unequal sides. The authors classify Track II organizations not only in terms of their aims but also according to their structure and type of activity: service delivery (e.g., social, legal, and educational services); advocacy (exerting political pressure with the aim of changing political policy from confrontation to negotiation); dialogue (face-to-face dialogues and work on joint projects with the other side); and consciousness raising (educating the public about the conflict's high cost and its possible peaceful resolutions).[7]

Daniel Lieberfeld is more specific. He defines a Track II meeting as one being held between participants who belong to adversarial groups that discuss specific political programs for action without forming a secret channel of talks between officials. No participant tries to bypass the official representative of the other side. Track II thus aims "to further conflict resolution by improving understanding and relationships between groups, by humanizing adversary groups through face to face meetings, and by preparing the ground for official negotiations by exploring in an unofficial and informal setting and without commitment underlying issues and possible solutions."[8]

Lieberfeld argues that Track II has only a long-term impact. In the short run, a public debate on Track II by an open society with a well-functioning communications system can contribute to political polarization by pushing the mainstream out to the extreme. Unless shown differently, in such a case the decisionmakers have an incentive for status quo negotiations to preserve their political power base. Shifts in electoral politics can result when politicians with Track II experience gain popularity among moderates with arguments that a conflict is resolvable at a lower cost than its continuation. In this case, Track II can strengthen negotiation-oriented leaders within their organizations, as happened in South Africa, and become an agent of change.

Track II does not always serve the decisionmaker's opposite interest, as Nadim Rouhana argues. He suggests that Track II enables the decisionmaker to have a better sense of negotiation possibilities and thus smoothes the way. It can serve in the prenegotiation stage to find options of understanding, gain familiarity with others' points of view, and clarify and probably redefine the vague goals of the decisionmaker and negotiating partners. Two other means that Track II may provide the decisionmaker are gathering information about the other side and exploring optional divisions. Moreover, through public Track II meetings the decisionmaker can measure possible shifts in public and elite opinion, calculate his or her political risks and rewards, and lead the concerned constituency toward accepting the negotiation and the needed concessions.[9] Like many Track II activists and scholars, Herbert Kelman tried to find criteria for successful influence by Track II in changing the political systems and values involved. According to Kelman, Track II is successful insofar as it contributes to changes in the political culture on each side in ways that make the parties more receptive to negotiation. Such outcomes include "the emergence of a sense of possibility"; "belief that at least some elements on the other side are interested in a peaceful solution"; "greater awareness of the other's perspective"; "initiation of mutually reassuring actions"; "a shared vision of a desirable future"; "exploration of ideas for the overall shape of a solution to the conflict"; "exploration of ideas for moving the negotiations forward"; and "developing 'cadres' with direct experience in communication with the other side."[10]

Professor Kelman is not only a Track II theoretician but a practitioner as well. He developed the working group model at Harvard University and experimented with it in an unofficial third-party effort to promote resolution of the Israeli-Palestinian conflict in Track II meetings based on interactive problem solving.[11] Kelman's method is to bring together politically engaged and highly influential Palestinians and Israelis for private, confidential discussions facilitated by a panel of social scientists who are knowledgeable about international and intercommunal conflict, group processes, and the Middle East. These discussions take place in intensive workshops designed to enable the parties to explore each other's perspective and understand each other's concerns, needs, fears, priorities, and constraints. On the basis of the resulting analysis, participants are encouraged to engage in a process of creative, joint problem solving to generate new ideas, which are responsive to both sets of needs and fears, to resolve their conflicts. The ultimate goal is to transfer the insights and ideas gained from these interactions into the public debate and the decisionmaking processes in the two communities.[12] In another project, also at Harvard, such meetings brought about some consensus on how to structure the negotiations and accepted main points on subjects relevant to a future Palestinian state, the Palestinian refugees, and Jerusalem.[13]

The distinction between a "hard" and "soft" Track II is introduced by Hussein Agha and associates: Soft Track II is aimed at the exchange of views, perception, and information between the sides involved and improvement of their mutual understanding. Hard Track II, on the other hand, is more politically oriented. It is not only about achieving better knowledge of the other side, but helping to negotiate with it, and if possible even achieving a breakthrough that will help to conclude a political settlement between the sides.

Agha et al. suggest that learning lessons from the Middle East Track II cases on sponsorship, procedure, participation, methods, substance, secrecy and leakage, formality, the right environment, moving form Track II to official talks, and measuring success and failure. On procedure they emphasize the importance of informality; the need to avoid contentious issues at the outset; allowing ideological exchange; devising rules of engagements; setting an agreement on timetables, frequency and places of meeting; and reaching an understanding on conditions of confidentiality and release of information. On participants they recommend selecting the best qualified experts available, who are risk takers, good deal makers, and problem solvers, and who share a common language and outlook. The participants should be selected according to the nature of the track either by the negotiating sides or by the sponsor. No less important is to work with a small core group of participants that creates its own modus operandi, group interest, and group dynamic. Track II organizers must deal constantly with the dilemma of whether to include hardliners, who more truly represent the societies involved in the conflict, or to limit it to moderates who have a better chance of reaching an understanding. While it is preferred that Track II leaders should maintain an open channel to their respective leaders, they also must keep a distance from the political echelons in order to keep thinking freely and to understand the other side's limits.

On method and substance, Agha et al. find it important for Track II to work on solutions, but not on too comprehensive ones that often turn out to be more elusive than real.

Track II participants should refrain from dealing with daily crisis management. Instead it is better for them to choose the right and ready context to work on a goal. In most cases the whole exercise should be kept secret to achieve positive results. However, the Middle East experience shows that ideas raised and texts composed in Track II run the risk of rejection by public opinion or by decisionmakers who feel belittled in being denied information about the exercise. Therefore careful attention should be taken to inform potential troublemakers and to sell the track's main ideas. Secrecy provokes abusing and deliberately misrepresenting Track II outcomes by certain individuals and groups. Maintaining control over the process and mutual trust cannot prevent manipulation but can help to reduce its chances for misrepresentation and leaks. Leaks, however, do not necessarily produce negative results. They can serve the overall aims by demystifying the track and protecting it, or protecting similar Track IIs by moving public attention to only a certain one. Since almost nothing remains secret in Middle East politics it is strongly suggested for Track II practitioners to conclude how to face a negative leak and the ways to reduce its destructive results.

Finally, according to Agha et al., there are some criteria to measure the success of Track II besides the obvious one of endorsing a Track II product partly or completely by Track I. It can be measured by the extent to which the track fulfilled its stated purpose by checking the impact on other Track II agendas and outcomes. When the sides face major physical or psychological obstacles to getting together, the very existence of a Track II can be seen as a success. The above-mentioned authors suggest the following criteria for establishing the success or failure of Track II talks. These range from the readiness to sit together, after building a joint frame of reference, to achieving agreement or understanding, establishing informal contacts and political networking, and bringing new and positive ideas to each of the involved constituencies.

A Comparative Perspective: Case Studies of Track II
in South Africa, Northern Ireland, and Israel/Palestine

The main conclusion of Gidron, Katz, and Hasenfeld on peace and conflict resolution organizations in South Africa, Northern Ireland, and Israel/Palestine is that they were most successful in institutionalizing their values for peace in public discourse.[14]

Utilizing the media, these organizations brought about changes in the public perception of the conflict, redefined it, and introduced new ways for proceeding toward peace. Track II groups also suggested new types of relationships between the parties, linked their idea of peace to other moral values such as human rights or democracy, and developed a new set of public activities to promote peace and understanding. The organizations were less successful in bringing about changes in the structure of their respective political systems. However, they had almost no impact on key events or major developments in the peace and conflict resolution process.[15]

In his comparative research on the involvement of conflict resolution organizations in Track II activity and its influence in South Africa, Israel/Palestine, and Northern Ireland, Feargal Cochrane reached several interesting conclusions.[16] First, political compromises that were made in the official negotiations between members of the elites did not penetrate down to the popular levels. Still, these organizations built a consensus that filtered up to the Track I level and made a positive contribution to the political process. Second, the focus, roles, and impacts of these organizations depend on their respective political context. Understanding and defining such terms as "peace process" depend on the specific political context. In the Israeli-Palestinian case the research found that most of the activists are well-educated, middle-class Israelis concentrating on consciousness raising. As in South Africa, the peace groups in Israel possess ideological cohesiveness and are funded largely by international donors. And unlike Northern Ireland, in the Israeli-Palestinian case there is much less cross-community activity within the peace sector. Although Israel and the Palestinians signed political agreements, the relationship between them, far from being substantively transformed, was made worse. Extremists on both sides reacted violently to the political agreements, heightening mistrust, hostility, and antagonism between the communities. Nevertheless, the peace movements in Israel had an important impact on the political process by changing the way in which both sides view their self-interest, from a zero-sum game to a positive-sum equation based on the formula of land for peace.

Within the Palestinian sector, peace and NGO organizations are much smaller than in any of the other cases studied and concentrate on delivering services rather than promoting the values of reconciliation. Most believe in justice before peace and are committed to the national struggle in the same way that the South African groups were. According to Cochrane, if the Palestinian peace and conflict-resolution organizations have had any impact it is at the level of providing support to their beleaguered communities rather than in transforming conflict relations between Palestinians and Israelis.

The Role of Track II in Connection with the Israeli-Palestinian Final-Status Talks

I would like to share with the readers some illustrations of Track II, based on personal knowledge as well as formal analysis.

1948 refugees. The issue of the 1948 Palestinian refugees is highly sensitive and challenging. It touches both the most delicate nerves of the Israeli-Palestinian conflict and the formative myth of each of the two nations. Discussions over the Palestinian refugee issue commenced upon the conclusion of the 1948 war, though the main drive for it started in the late 1980s with the establishment of Israeli-Palestinian unofficial contacts. To this present day, the 1948 refugees issue has received much attention in many informal Israeli-Palestinian interactions. These happened mostly in Track II meetings, with their various formats: professional academic forums; discussions that were meant to prepare for the official negotiations and to release the Track I talks from any deadlocks; as well as talks made by official personnel yet in their private capacity.[17] Besides extensive discussions about compensation, Track II on 1948 Palestinian refugees introduced the following differentiation between permitted modes of return to those which are forbidden.

1. The right of return in principle to return in actual practice.
2. Return and family unification: in the range between a semantic change made by titling the return "family reunification" to that of limiting the return to this title-specific content and persisting in it in the phases of enactment.
3. The right of return as an unfulfilled principle on the one hand and compensation on the other (i.e., financial, territorial and symbolic optional Israeli compensations, including an official apology for the wrongs during the war).
4. Distinction between return to Israeli territories and return to Palestinian sovereign land.
5. A distinction between the individual argument on realizing the right of return to an area under Israeli sovereignty from the immigration process that rules the practical arrangements of changing the refugee's permanent place of residency. These arrangements provide Israel the authority not to let the refugee in, while according to the right of return Israel is imposed to absorb him/her.

These optional distinctions do not necessarily exclude one another. Mostly attempts have been made to introduce several of them simultaneously in order to maximize the compensation to Palestine for not permitting all the refugees to exercise their right to return. Unfortunately, the impact of these Track II models in public debate and in official talks was limited. The dispute in principle over the refugee issue was sharp in all the official talks, and the debate was dominated by discussion of national rights rather than oriented toward problem solving and pragmatic solutions.

Jerusalem. Since 1994 more than thirty Israeli and Palestinian groups have discussed the parameters of a permanent status agreement in Jerusalem.[18] The contacts between the two sides have created a common professional discourse and a program based on more or less agreed-upon data. In some cases the participants stopped at that point, though they sometimes went beyond it in an attempt to find a political structure that would encompass and give direction to the points on which the experts reached consensus. Some of the groups dealt with the city and the metropolitan region only, while others included Jerusalem in a wider framework and addressed all the issues of a permanent status agreement.

As far as is known, most of the groups met under Western European auspices, sometimes under the sponsorship of government institutions and sometimes at the initiative of NGOs. A Palestinian participant in many Track II meetings summed them up this way: "The Dutch and Swedish track sponsored issues related to planning, zoning and infrastructure for the whole city in times of peace, while the British track focused more on the political dimension of the conflict in Jerusalem. The Spanish track sponsored the religious dimension of the Holy City, and the Greek track focused on the discussion of general issues in preparations of the final talks."[19] The United States government was influenced by the Israeli taboo that forbade any discussion of the future of Jerusalem. Washington did not initiate informal channels for talks on a subject that could have impinged on internal US politics through the domestic Jewish vote and lobbies.

There were only *three cases* in which the participants in the informal channels went public, announced their position, and submitted their paper to the heads of the relevant states. In January 2000, a joint statement on the principles that were to guide the negotiations on Jerusalem was published following discussions held under the auspices of the University of Oklahoma and the Rockefeller Foundation. In 2003, the Ayalon Nusseibeh document on the final-status principles was published and in October 2003 the Geneva agreement was signed.

It would be difficult to exaggerate the importance of the informal channels and their contribution to the negotiations. They prepared the professional and political infrastructure and created a common language between the two sides. Through them, several breakthroughs were made and creative ideas formulated that were later brought to the negotiating table. These ideas included new concepts of sovereignty—suspended, joint, and divine; a common economic regime for Jerusalem and Al-Quds; territorial exchange by mutual agreement; a Jewish-Muslim-Christian religious council that would coordinate management of the holy places; cooperation between the Israeli and Palestinian police and the creation of a joint police force for the seam zone between East and West Jerusalem; and the concept of the sacred basin.[20]

However, these back channels had their shortcomings. They were conducted almost exclusively between professionals, and insufficient effort was made to bring together community leaders representing the two peoples who would have to live side by side under the terms of a peace accord. Second, government officials and bureaucrats rarely participated. (True, a few highly placed decisionmakers on each side were briefed about the issues discussed, but they were content to remain outside Track II meetings.) Their attitudes to the back channels varied. Some of them underestimated the potential of Track II talks for creating understanding, let alone an acceptable agreement; others were apathetic, and some used the back channels to float experimental balloons without incurring political costs.

Thus when the official track was about to commence, and as it proceeded, mutual dependence produced relationships between officials and professionals. The taboo that prevented government officials from adequately preparing their brief for negotiations over Jerusalem forced them to open their minds to understandings reached and ideas exchanged in the Track II talks over the capital city. For their part, the Track II professionals were eager to inject their insights, ideas, and proposals (whether fully thought out or half-baked) into the official talks. On both the Israeli and Palestinian sides, however, official-professional dialogue was shaped by the decisionmakers' selectivity, preferences, and limited attention span. All officials chose the professional voice they would listen to and placed time limits on professional involvement. The outsider professional was called in either intermittently or when the talks faced a deadlock and a serious crisis. The leaders also decided which government level the professionals would meet with and were able to limit access to senior decisionmakers and to the official negotiating team. The officials' decision about which professionals to heed did not depend solely on the professionals' skills and expertise. The officials tended to prefer mainstream, level-headed voices, as well as people that the political leader sensed were loyal to him, to his negotiating goals, or to his administration. Former civil servants and experts who maintained open channels with the administration also had a great advantage. Furthermore, the decisionmakers' selection was influenced by "packaging" considerations. A professional's influence increased to the extent that his ideas were consistent with other components of the deal the political leader had prepared or already offered. Finally, in choosing his negotiating strategy and tactics, the leader's approach was shaped also by political and public relations considerations. The decisionmaker did not share these considerations with the ex-establishment professionals, confiding only in his own close and loyal assistants.

Consequently, ideas created or understandings reached in Track II were rarely adopted by the official negotiators in their original form. They were either rejected outright or revised or placed in a different context. It goes without saying that they were presented in a style very different from that used by the Track II professionals, which had smoothed their acceptance by the opposing side on Track II. This is neither to say that a decisionmaker went beyond his authority and responsibility, nor to conclude that the Israeli-Palestinian case is unique—quite the opposite. However, comparing the above-mentioned creative ideas and understandings produced in Track II with the positions taken by the decisionmakers during the official talks can help us understand the parameters that shaped the official talks and limited the influence of Track II.

Track II Diplomacy
(by Riad Malki)
The idea of the Track II diplomacy was presented only as a result of the 1967 Six-Day War, and after the Israeli occupation of the West Bank, including East Jerusalem and the Gaza Strip. Without such occupation, it could have been impossible to think about Track II at all. Dissolving existing borders between Israel and the Palestinian occupied territories and the initiation of movement of goods and people across the old borders have prompted the creation of a new reality. This later led to the creation and development of the Track II diplomacy to facilitate the contact and dialogue between the two sides that had been in conflict since 1948.

Isolated efforts to establish political contacts with Israel were initiated immediately after the end of the 1967 war, mainly by Palestinian Communists who contacted their comrades on the Israeli side, and right-wing Palestinian politicians started to survey possible contacts with their Israeli counterparts (and through the Israeli military commanders in the occupied territories). These people were encouraged by the Israeli officials to pursue some of the preliminary contacts, at least for the sake of knowledge and understanding. Such a channel was always limited in participation due to the few individuals who gambled at that time to initiate such contacts, either as exploratory meetings to assess the Israeli positions or to go deeper in uncovering potentials for national reconciliation and peace agreements. During those years the general and national mood did not help such initiatives, and people who were involved were either scared to continue such contacts or were isolated in their approach and not supported publicly. Nevertheless, others did opt for opening channels of dialogue on a smaller scale, but systematic and organized with a clear objective. The move was categorized as an initiative rather than a process because it lacked continuity, the permanent commitment by the people involved, and the mechanism behind it. Despite the fact that at a later stage there were some things in common between the promoters of such an approach among the Palestinian side, it did not gather any momentum or the backing of the population or the political elite. The same conditions remained unchanged for a decade with fewer people committing themselves to this path, and it is possible to say that Track II did not exist prior to the first unofficial PLO-Israeli meetings in the second half of the 1970s.

In summary, one could define the whole issue of Track II in the following way:

1. Track II is a direct result of the Israeli occupation of the West Bank and Gaza Strip.
2. The pioneers in introducing Track II activity were mostly from East Jerusalem.
3. It took some time for such activities to become a reality in Palestinian life. It did not start immediately with the beginning of occupation except in a few cases, and first efforts were not serious at all but spontaneous and unplanned.
4. The initiative was categorized as a selective initiative and not considered a process.
5. The nature of the activities was secret.
6. The reaction of people at large was negative, and in most instances publicly condemned.

Track II Characteristics

For the sake of knowledge it is worth defining the basic elements of Track II in terms of major aspects to illustrate the real characteristics of the specific track of public diplomacy beyond the norms of official approval and official constraints (see Table 5.1).

Historical Background

In retrospect, one has to look at the numerous initiatives and activities for the promotion of peace and in breaking the stereotypes about each other. One has to differentiate between the activities of ordinary citizens for peace and without any government connection to such initiatives, and between officially initiated actions by PLO officials according to a plan to proceed with such contacts. In the first case, many such initiatives are not documented. There is no accumulation of knowledge of achievements or conclusions. But in the other,

Table 5.1 Basic Elements of Track II

People Involved: Government, nongovernment, individuals, groups with special interest

Topics: All topics without any limitation or exclusion

Objectives: To play a role in peace promotion, to be useful and active, to be a catalyst and a bridge, to use existing connections, to respond to needs and invitation, to act as a mediator or a messenger, to put an end to human suffering, to reconcile with the enemy, to normalize relations and to turn enemies into nonenemies, to change people's perception versus the other side, to serve personal interests, to develop different pressure groups, to transform society, to improve professional cooperation, to improve living conditions, and so on.

Mechanism Used: One-time meetings, series of meetings

Geographical locations: Basically East Jerusalem, with participation from West Bank cities, in particular Bethlehem, Ramallah, Nablus, and Hebron

Personal background: Christians and businessmen

Outcome: Documents, statements, or nothing

Documentation: Nonexistence except in personal notes, if published

officially sanctioned situation there was always a clear objective in such activity, with clear short-term and long-term limits.

Table 5.2 illustrates the two approaches.

The Short Term Versus the Long Term

As noted, there are notable differences between the two approaches in Track II, between the approaches serving solely the official efforts associated with Track I and between the efforts made by different players in Palestinian civil society and others to bring together members of both societies to discuss specific issues of mutual concern in developing confidence and trust. This includes members of the Palestinian Authority. The aim and objectives of the latter group in Palestinian civil society is for the long term, despite its de facto short-term influence and its limited impact on the society. The least influence on society's life will produce limited attention and support by the different segments of the same society. On the other hand, while the activity and scope of events associated with the first group of Track II (serving the official negotiations) is limited in duration and discrete in action, the immediate impact is enormous and could influence the total outcome of negotiations and affect the historic and future expectations of the society at large.

Palestinian Official Approach to Track II Contacts

The Palestinian National Council in its 13th session, in the second half of March 1977, adopted for the first time a positive resolution referring to the importance of relations and coordination with democratic Jewish forces inside and outside occupied Palestine. The same resolution was reinforced

Table 5.2 Comparative Approaches

Comparative element	Unofficial approach	Official approach
Who is behind it?	Individuals or groups with a clear interest in promoting peace and ending hostilities	PLO leadership
Any connection to official policies and resolutions?	Not necessary; there could be cases where individuals decided to initiate contacts for the sake of doing something, but linked up with the PLO later; there could be cases with individuals asked to follow official instructions	Initial intentions and contacts not officially legitimized and approved, but when resolutions were adopted by Palestian national Council, then contacts became officially supported
Any limitation or selection of who should be the other side?	No specific criteria used, but initiatives targeting groups or individuals with similar characteristics or professional backgrounds	Selection intended to reach out to politicians (members of political parties and Knesset), close associates with people in authority, community leaders, intellectuals, and religious leaders
Any accumulation of results or building up on achievement of initial activities?	Not the case in most of the activities; no connection between one activity and the other; lack of communication at the level of participants or initiators	From the beginning the intention always to build on contacts, to proceed with results to serve the official objective
Role of participants?	Unofficial connections served as the bridge for official communication; were used as contact agents and go-betweens when official channels did not exist	Official side recruited civilians to carry out the mission; the tasks were coordinated fully with the officials, and civilians were not independent at all in their actions or missions
Were the activities secret or publicly known?	Some low-profile activities maintained for the sake of secrecy and confidentiality, while others were leaked and became known to the public	Most actions meant to stay secret
Any sign of interest from the public or the media?	In general, low interest shown, but depending on the period in which such meetings took place; most often, anti-normalization movements and factions behind most of the verbal attacks and condemnations	High level of interest from media, political parties, and governments; any leak of meeting could mean its collapse and embarrassment if not considered politically a risk for people behind it
Availability of information or any reference to publication?	No documentation whatsoever for this aspect of contacts; efforts lost for lack of collection and documentation; no agency or initiative to collect such efforts and document them for lessons learned or achievements made	Every effort, regardless of its outcome or importance, completely approved and documented for lessons to be learned and knowledge for leadership

again in the 15th Fatah session in April 1981, in the 16th in 1982, the 18th and the 19th in November 1988, and finally in the 5th Fatah conference in August 1989. Since then the contacts with the Israeli peace movement became legal according to PNC resolutions.

The Stockholm meeting in November 21, 1988, was considered a turning point in the Jewish-American relations with the Palestinians in general and the PLO in particular.

Track II Serving the Official Track

On July 4, 1987, at the house of Moshe Amirav, the Likud central committee member, were two Palestinians, Sari Nusseibeh and Salah Zahalka. The discussion was to look for the best solution to the Palestinian problem. Regardless of what was said, this meeting was considered another turning point in Israeli-Palestinian relations and history. Within a week another meeting was organized in Nusseibeh's house on the outskirts of Jerusalem, and this time Faisal Husseini attended the meeting. Both Husseini and Amirav reached the understanding that historic rights belong to history, and historic dreams are just dreams. The inclusion of Husseini in the second meeting openly reflected PLO participation in the official process. Thus, it was clear what role Track II could play in serving the basic interests of the official track, and could provide the necessary elements and a proper mechanism for contemplating the different options for an outcome to the conflict.

Track II Description

Basic differentiations. When discussing Track II, one needs to explain the difference between serious work helping Track I and between Track II activity to promote people-to-people cooperation and rapprochement. There has been much confusion in describing both activities and interplay between them, since both belong theoretically to Track II. This study has intended to give attention to both tracks without eliminating the overall picture, but always favoring the kind of activity that would help negotiations at the official level.

Track II Versus Political Realities

Track II activities are influenced by political reality and by realities on the ground. Track II implies joint work between Palestinian and Israeli individuals or groups in pursuing a specific objective or a series of objectives directly related from the two parties' points of view. From a thorough observation of the pace of Track II activities over a year, it is clear that Track II was directly influenced by political realities on either side. The beginning of the Oslo process was considered the opening for Track II initiatives by different and new people over different and new issues. The new ideas reached their peak between 1998 and 1999, and stopped in 2000 in expectation of the outcome of the Camp David talks. The collapse of the talks and the visit by Ariel Sharon to the Aqsa Mosque in Jerusalem provoked another round of hostilities associated with the Aqsa intifada. The collapse of the Camp David talks was considered the turning point, and end, of Track II activities. If we compare Track II between the first intifada and the second, it is clear that the level of activity in the first stage was superior in many ways to the level of Track II activity during the second. In other words, one could say that the Track II activity during the first intifada is the foundation for what followed in terms of a serious opening up of peace initiatives and political negotiations.

Political Reality
The top of the curve shown in Figure 5.2 shows the time span associated with signing the Oslo Accords as well as the time immediately before it and the longer time afterward. The "golden period," as it was called, described the period of opportunity for developing contacts and extending cooperation, not only at the Track II level, but also at other levels. The low points correspond to the first and second intifadas, which were times of increased security risks and instability during the political talks and negotiations.

Track II and Types of Cooperation

Professional cooperation, including professional training and capacity building. Palestinians could learn and benefit from the advanced Israeli experience in certain areas or fields of expertise, especially health, agriculture, water, and planning. Different professional groups had been directly engaged in certain cooperative projects, even during the most difficult times of conflict. Such projects were not interrupted by deterioration of the security conditions, but were treated separately and in their own atmosphere. The Israelis who were behind such projects stressed the importance for Palestine that such projects should continue, and evidently that was what happened. The good contacts that they developed over the years and the human and developmental dimension of such projects were strong enough to win official approval on both sides for their continuation.

People-to-people projects. Such projects were affected dramatically by the existing security conditions, and resulted in the huge reduction of the total number of projects classified as part of such projects. It is worth mentioning here that this specific experience was evaluated the most extensively by both sides and by donors. This element received the strongest criticism by the

Figure 5.1 Levels of Track II Activity

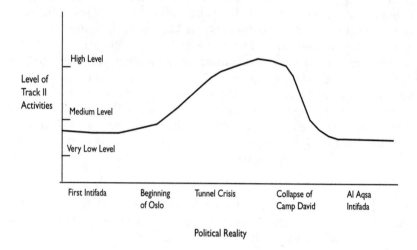

Figure 5.2 Track II Activities

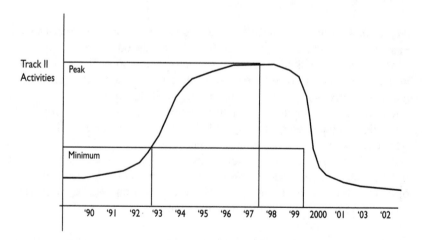

public at large and political parties in particular. Regardless of the strong attack on the people-to-people projects, they were able to survive the criticism and continue with a minimum level of projects and NGOs. The NGOs from both sides that decided to continue despite strong criticism opted for discreet action in the implementation phase of their projects instead of any previously publicized.

Nonessential cooperation. Track II has its own attraction and incentives. Some people looked at the Track II as a form of expressing their interests, for developing additional agendas, for political purposes because of frustration on other fronts, for financial purposes, and for employment, while others maintained their belief that such opportunities presented by Track II are intended to reduce the gap between the two sides and bring the prospects of peace closer. The Palestinians had witnessed, though, a sort of Track II activity reflecting the different interests of the people behind the activity. It had not been necessary that the activity represented either a Palestinian or Israeli priority or a donor interest. Since no serious effort was put into this activity, at least on the Palestinian side, this activity was the first to disappear because of the deterioration of the security situation and as a direct result of strong public criticism. Most of the earlier activity was driven by Israelis or was donor initiated; the Palestinian role was limited to a basic requirement of having a Palestinian partner in the project, without needing the partner to participate in the development of the idea or the project or to take any responsibility in their implementation and financial management. The outcome of such activity was a total halt to everything.

Visits and exchange programs. Some kind of cooperation was needed for maintaining visits between families, as a reflection of normalization, trust, and cooperation, and as a sign that hostilities resulting from the occupation were being transformed into a more humane aspect of family visits. Most donors have stressed the need to create such projects, in particular the need to work more with the younger generations and to influence their minds, especially among the Palestinians. Incentives were presented to such projects and found the necessary cooperation from the Israeli side. However, despite the facilities offered for such projects, the total number of projects presented for visits and exchanges was minimal compared to the total number of projects dealing with other issues. Such projects were completely reduced and even stopped when there were verbal or written attacks in schools, mosques, and political parties. Even at the height of such projects, the participants were limited to a narrow segment of Palestinian society, mostly associated with private schools, affluent families, and some religious groups.

Track II Versus Official Reaction

The reaction of the Palestinian Authority to this track, in terms of its importance, contribution, participants, timing, and topics, varied according to the
official interlocutor. There was no agreed-upon official assessment of Track
II. A person in the authority could always be found who could easily
endorse any project related to this track.

It is worth mentioning here that tracks I and II were not mutually exclusive, and always allowed for space to develop other options. It might be
said that Track II was initiated before even Track I was built and ready to
move. Still, everyone believes that the fundamental idea behind Track II is
to provide the necessary support to Track I, to pave the way for Track I to
move, and develop the conditions to succeed.

Observers have witnessed some fluctuation in the position of official
criticism, and the fluctuation stems from the notion that Track II might
endanger the role Track I could and should play. There had been a demand
that Track II should cease to exist as long as Track I was moving ahead with
its certain achievements: any duplication through the presence of Track II
dealing with similar topics of discussion might jeopardize the importance and
the role of Track I. Such pressure was never completely effective or able to
stop or delay all the Track II activities. On the other hand, there was clear
acknowledgment by the political leadership of the importance of Track II
when Track I was comatose or halted by political and security complications.
It was then that Track II again gained importance and was considered the
only active type of track, thus temporarily replacing the official Track I negotiations; people known to be active in Track II were asked to provide help to
officials during crises. Officials on both sides of the conflict were aware of
such advantages and availed themselves of Track II during critical times,
even replacing the official track. Government officials have gone even further
in their recognition of the role Track II plays and could act by requesting the
addition of some Track II higher-ups to work next to government officials in
order to benefit from the services and the venue Track II offers, without
endangering any official positions or being criticized publicly.

The basic criticism of Track II by objectors within officialdom has to
do with the lack of control mechanisms. The political leadership's lack of
complete knowledge and authority over the existing tracks, and the sometimes irresponsible attitudes or behavior of some of those active in the tracks
in terms of the topics they dealt with or the positions they offered that devi-
ated from official positions, endangered Track I negotiations.

Track II Versus Different Players

When writing about the different players in Track II, one needs to explain
that while there were groups of Palestinians ready to join, other groups were

completely against joining such activities. The criteria used by the opponents had to do with their fear that the general public was not supportive, and that such activities might be considered as normalization or leading to a process of normalization. The normalization threat has prevented the inclusion of many important segments of the Palestinian society, and prevented the direct benefit of their knowledge and expertise in Track II. The self-exclusion of important segments of the society, in particular most university professors, trade unionists, professional associations, intellectuals, journalists and other writers, and sectarians, among others, has deprived Track II of the added value of their contributions and knowledge. On the Israeli side such exclusions did not happen; to the contrary, there was a clear involvement of individuals coming from the corresponding Israeli groups, thus enriching the Israeli participation and strengthening its role in the Track II negotiations.

Qualification level of Palestinian participants. The self-exclusion of many important segments of the Palestinian population has promoted a serious lowering in the quality of Palestinian participants and resulted in the introduction of less qualified individuals.

Lack of prior knowledge or preparation. The immediate introduction of Track II onto the Palestinian scene and its forceful presence in the Israeli–Palestinian conflict developed a need to bring Palestinian participants into the exercise without their having time enough to go through training or preparation.

Lack of quality control and inspection. Track II is an unofficial track, government officials were taking positions regarding the nature of the second track, and officials in Track I even tried to sabotage Track II and the idea behind it. But there was not, and still is not, a proper, self-imposed mechanism among Track II activists and promoters to monitor performance, measure results, and evaluate actions and corrections in the direction of improving performance and securing a minimal level of results.

Serious lack of knowledge of official negotiating positions or fall-back positions. Some of the Palestinian participants lack the basic political background and knowledge of negotiating skills and basic information of their official negotiating positions. The lack of knowledge endangers the consistency of the official positions and official track, especially if those on the Israeli side discover the discrepancies between the two tracks and the weakness of the second in contrast to the first. This should encourage and even focus on, the need to develop and emphasize the role of Track II instead of the importance and role of Track I.

Sending officials to Track II occasions. It was very difficult sometimes for Track II promoters and even for officials in charge of negotiations to differentiate between tracks I and II. For some of them, the difference was in the names and the styles and not in the content. Sometimes because of ego and sometimes for serious reasons, officials in charge of negotiations felt the need to send official representation to some Track II meetings. This was to enhance the negotiations, control the kind of concessions offered, and enforce maintaining an official position, or have a presence in Track II processes in accordance with a donor's demand for official endorsement. On the other hand, it is clear that some senior official negotiators decided on their own to take part in the Track II activities without official approval—or by providing only partial information on the exercise, and thus obtaining official approval. Some of the official negotiators attending such activities and meetings received honoraria for their attendance directly from the organizers of Track II, without reporting anything about the associated earnings.

Lack of knowledge accumulation and results benefiting at the official level. Since there is no coordination at the Track II level between all participants and organizers, there is no institutional knowledge or available documentation. The absence of a data bank to record all activities as a reference for future needs has minimized the importance and the contribution of the track despite its serious additions to the official negotiations. The lack of any coordinating body to let people know what all are doing in the field of Track II, and how to benefit from the available results and achieved agreements, is an undermining factor in search for complementary elements between the two tracks.

Undermining the official track (Track I) through official participation and concessions. Whenever the official participants discuss the issues raised in Track II, and not in Track I, despite the fact that such knowledge is accepted by all participants in both tracks, the moment any official (i.e., Track I) participant offers any concession to the Israeli side and retreats from an officially announced position, the official position loses its protection and the concession offered by such an official, even in his personal and unofficial capacity, will be known in official Israeli negotiating circles. The Israelis, of course, will use and stress it whenever the official negotiating track is convened, taking advantage of any concession in promoting their side in official negotiations.

Palestinian participants chosen by Israelis. At the start of the people-to-people activities, and because the initiatives for such projects came from the Israelis, the Israelis opted to identify their own Palestinian partners and chose them according to Israeli standards and expectations and not according to adherence to the official Palestinian positions. This resulted in the promotion of new Palestinian people-to-people participants according to Israeli criteria and selection, imposed on the Palestinian population and Palestinian Authority as their own representatives. Most selected in this way were qualified only by Israeli criteria. All this was later corrected, after the damage it inflicted on the Palestinian position, making the general Palestinian public extremely suspicious about such joint "normalization" activities.

Track II Versus Achievements

In general, one could simply say that the total achievements of Track II went beyond expectations and contributed enormously to the development and promotion of the official track. Regardless of some of the setbacks from the less thought-out people-to-people activities, if one studies the direct and indirect contributions by Track II (that is, serving the official track), then the only conclusion is positive confirmation for Track II's role in serving and facilitating Track I.

Conclusions

- Track II is connected to the political development, and its pace does reflect the political mood.
- Track II gets its importance from either the failure of the official negotiations or from its limitations.
- Track II requires minimal conditions for its promotion. The lack of the necessary items will prevent its promotion, while the presence of the required items will accelerate such promotion.
- Track II is not expected to become a popular act, with any ability of attraction.
- Track II lacks clear official support and backing. Different signals and indicators were sent by different Palestinian decisionmakers in respect of the real Palestinian Authority position's view of the unofficial track.
- Track II is and has been seen as a catalyst track, a support mechanism, promoter of ideas, and a facilitator to the official track. It lacks an independent concept or consensus objective. It was never considered or developed as a process.
- Track II gets its importance at the expense of the decrease in the importance of the official track, or the latter's inability to perform.

Recommendations

- Collect, review, and study all work done by Track II over the years.
- Draw conclusions from collective study and analysis.

- Arrange study days for the people and organizations working on or involved in Track II, to come up with lessons learned, conclusions, and recommendations for future work.
- Establish a coordinating Track II committee among the participants to represent the relevant organizations to coordinate their work and to set up mechanisms and agree on future plans.
- Publicly introduce a set of well-known, creditable names associated with Track II to facilitate the public acceptance and to increase public support.
- Define Track II strategy, focusing either on specific issues and areas of work or opening it up without limitations and even expanding activities.
- Establish working communications and permanent contact with the Palestinian Authority for reviewing action, improving performance, and coordinating measures among the authority and NGOs regarding Track II.
- To publish and distribute reviews and conclusions, and to highlight actions and results through articles, meetings, and publications. To eliminate any secret activities associated with Track II; instead concepts like openness and transparency should become the leading Track II elements.
- Achieve a working standard among Track II practitioners and agree on a set of standards to be followed and acknowledged by the different civil-society organizations and NGOs. This should include improving the preparatory level and background knowledge, setting up quality control and inspection, developing smooth and comprehensive dissemination processes, and maintaining the knowledge accumulation process.
- Set up a Track II observation and resource center that can issue periodical reports about professional performance of Track II practitioners and identify recommendations to be adhered to by such activists.
- Adopt a series of meetings with the public as part of public diplomacy to create the necessary awareness among the people, political parties, and influential public figures.
- Get clear public statements from high-level decisionmakers and officials acknowledging the role, importance, and the continual need for Track II, in coordination with and complementary to the official track.
- Use the media to normalize the action among the general populace, and even as far as considering its own media outlets.

Notes

1. Menachem Klein's research on Track II is planned to be complemented in 2006 by his analysis of the impact of Track II on the official talks, under the auspices and support of the United States Institute for Peace.

2. Hussein Agah et al. *Track II Diplomacy—Lessons from the Middle East* (Cambridge, MIT Press, 2003).

3. For a recent book covering the wider scope see John Davies and Edward (Edy) Kaufman, eds., *Second Track/Citizens Diplomacy: Concepts and Techniques of Conflict Transformation* (Lanham, MD: Rowman & Littlefield, 2003).

4. Anthony Wanis-St. John, *Back Channel Diplomacy—The Strategic Use of Multiple Channels of Negotiation in Middle East Peacemaking* (Boston: Fletcher School of Law and Diplomacy, Tufts University, 2001), p. 12.

5. Ibid., 12–15; Gennady I. Chufrin and Harold H. Saunders, "A Public Peace Process," *Negotiation Journal* 9, 2 (1993): 155–178; Harold Saunders, "Possibilities and Change: Another Way to Consider Unofficial Third Party Intervention," *Negotiation Journal* 11, 3 (1995): 271–276. For additional references see the Bibliography.

6. Benjamin Gidron, Stanley N. Katz, and Yeheskel Hasenfeld, eds. "Introduction, Theoretical Approach and Methodology," *Mobilizing for Peace: Conflict Resolution in Northern Ireland, Israel/Palestine and South Africa* (Oxford: Oxford University Press, 2002), pp. 8–9.

7. Ibid., p. 25.

8. Daniel Lieberfeld, "Evaluating the Contribution of Track II Diplomacy to Conflict Termination in South Africa 1984–90," *Journal of Peace Research* 39, 3 (May 2002): 356.

9. Nadim Rouhana, "Unofficial Third Party Intervention in International Conflict: Between Legitimacy and Disarray," *Negotiation Journal* 11, 3 (1995): 255–271; Nadim Rouhana, "Interactive Conflict Resolution: Theoretical and Methodological Issues in Conducting Research and Evaluation," in Paul Stern, Alexander George, and Daniel Druckman, eds., *International Conflict Resolution: Techniques and Evaluation* (Washington, D.C., National Academy Press, 2000), pp. 294–337.

10. Herbert C. Kelman, "The Contributions of Non-Governmental Organizations to the Resolution of Ethno-national Conflicts: An Approach to Evaluation" (Paper presented at the Carnegie Corporation Conference on the Role of International NGOs in Ethnic and Nationalist Conflicts, New York, November 1996), 12–13; Lieberfeld, ibid., p. 370.

11. Herbert C. Kelman, "Interactive Problem Solving: An Approach to Conflict Resolution and its Application in the Middle East," *PS: Political Science and Politics* 31, (1998): 190–198.

12. Moshe Maoz et al., "The Future Israeli-Palestinian Relations," *Middle East Policy*, 7, 2 (February 2000): 3.

13. Naomi Chazan, "Negotiating the Non-Negotiable: Jerusalem in the Framework of an Israeli-Palestinian Settlement," *Occasional Papers of the American Academy of Arts and Sciences*, 7 (March 1991).

14. Gidron et al., *Mobilizing for Peace*.

One of the most difficult aspects of peace-making is the need to replace the arsenal of cultural tools (e.g., language, images, and symbols), that the contesting parties have institutionalized over time to define their opponents. These tools often are connected to events that are rooted in the historical ethos of each opponent's collective identity . . . because of the manner in which they frame the opponents and define the conflict, these tools become major impediments to the peace-making or conflict-resolution process . . . one of Peace and Conflict Resolution Organizations' major contributions is providing alternative cultural tools that redefine both the contesting parties and the nature of the conflict in a manner that enables dialogue and negotiation,

15. Ibid., pp. 205–234.

16. Feargal Cochrane, "Beyond the Political Elites: A Comparative Analysis of the Roles and Impacts of Community-Based NGOs in Conflict Resolution Activity," *Civil Wars,* 3, 2 (Summer 2000): 1–22.

17. Based on Menachem Klein, "The Palestinian 1948 Refugees—Models of Allowed and Refused Return," presented in an Exeter University international workshop on the comparative study of refugee return programs with reference to the Palestinian context, titled as "Transferring Best Practice," June 2004.

18. Based on Menachem Klein, *The Jerusalem Problem: The Struggle for Permanent Status* (Gainesville: University of Florida Press, 2003), pp. 23–32.

19. Issa Kassisiyyeh, "Second Track Negotiations: The Jerusalem File," *Jerusalem Quarterly* 15, (2002) *www.jqf-jerusalem.org.*

20. Ibid. and Michael Hassassian, "Final Status Negotiations on Jerusalem: An Inside Look" (presentation at PASSIA, March 13, 2001), http://www.passia.org.

6

Nonviolent Action in Israel and Palestine: A Growing Force

Mohammed Abu-Nimer

Methods of nonviolent action are as old as violence. Every culture and religion has developed a set of stories and beliefs that underscores the moral superiority of nonviolence over violence.[1] Of course, each culture also has its own ways of defining, and conditions for, justifying violence. For the purpose of this chapter the following working definition is adopted:

> *Nonviolence* is a set of attitudes, actions, or behaviors intended to persuade the other side to change their opinions, perceptions, and actions. Nonviolent methods use peaceful means to achieve peaceful outcomes. Nonviolence means that actors do not violently retaliate against the actions of their opponent. Instead, they absorb anger and damage while sending a steadfast message of patience and an insistence on overcoming injustice.[2]

In addition to the assumptions of moral superiority and individual and collective responsibility, the major features of nonviolent action include the following:

- "It is nonaggressive physically, but dynamically aggressive (i.e., assertive) spiritually."
- "It does not seek to humiliate, but to persuade the opponent to change and thereby reconstruct the 'beloved communities' through a new understanding and awareness of moral shame."
- "It is directed against forces of evil rather than against persons caught in those forces."
- Nonviolence seeks to avoid not only "external physical violence but also internal violence of spirit." Nonviolence is "based on the conviction that the universe is on the side of justice."[3]

Nonviolent resistance is successful only where there is sufficient preparation for it. A group has to be ready to engage in such resistance, particularly by actively establishing the conditions necessary for effective mass nonviolent resistance. After World War II scholars began systematically exploring conditions for effective resistance. For example, Mulford Sibley identified four major conditions for successful strategic nonviolence against invaders: (1) no service or supplies to be furnished to invaders; (2) no orders to be obeyed except those of the constitutional civil authorities; (3) no insult or injury to be offered to the invader; and (4) all public officials pledge to die rather than surrender. Such an approach is in accordance with Gandhi's distinction of passive nonviolence, between "nonviolence of the weak" and "nonviolence of the strong or brave" as an effective force for transformation. It is also derived from the distinction between the notion of "unviolence," where violence is not possible, and nonviolence, which involves a voluntary decision or commitment. These distinctions affect the opponent in different ways. Suffering is generally accepted as an inescapable component of successful resistance. "Not to be confused with passive suffering or nonresistance, nonviolent action involves suffering in resistance, in noncooperation, or disobedience."[4] It is the suffering generated by nonviolent campaigns that often stimulates a sense of injustice in third parties, and not from the opponent, as might be expected.

Another important feature of effective nonviolent campaigns involves separating the person from the system or problem, or separating the evildoer from the evil deeds. If the nonviolent resister targets the deeds and system and not the people who perform or operate them, the conflict becomes depersonalized, and allows a sense of trust to emerge in the opponent, while keeping attention relentlessly focused on the sources of injustice.

Activists and leaders of nonviolent campaigns have intensely debated the many alternative ways and strategies of applying the above principles and features to situations of conflict. Contextual conditions (e.g., cultural, religious, social, political) determine the most effective means of implementing the various principles of nonviolence. No generic formula or universal set of actions—including issues, strategies, and techniques—can be devised to fit all conflicts; for example, the specific strategies and actions that worked in India were unique and different from those applied in South Africa and Poland.

Assumptions on Nonviolent Resistance in Palestine

Although state violence and ethnic conflict have increased after the Cold War, nonviolent campaigns as a means to pursue equal human rights, remove violence, and achieve peace have also increased. In Kosovo, East Timor, South Africa, Macedonia, the United States, and European countries, organized campaigns of nonviolent protest have been launched to oppose wars and contribute to the liberation of oppressed communities. Palestine and Israel are not exceptions. In the past two decades, several nonviolent movements or organizations have emerged to take part in the overall struggle to end the Israeli occupation in the West Bank and Gaza.

This chapter focuses on the activities and accomplishments of such organizations, and the obstacles facing them in their struggle to end the occupation. Before discussing these themes, it is essential to clarify a few assumptions about nonviolence in Palestine. First, Palestinian nonviolent resistance of the Israeli occupation has been going on since the 1967 occupation of the West Bank and Gaza. Palestinian nonviolent resistance has been instrumental in sustaining a high level of popular resistance to the occupation throughout the years, as well as the public's consistent rejection of annexation or co-optation policies. Such refusal is expressed daily in symbolic or actual resistance, both individually and collectively. When these activities are recognized and framed as intentional acts of resistance, a more direct campaign can be launched and organized more successfully. Abdul Jawad Saleh stresses that despite the military occupation, Palestinians have resisted nonviolently in many ways, including simply trying to build a sustainable Palestinian society and economy. "The popular idea that such a movement has never existed is another attempt to erase its very real existence."[5] To minimize nonviolent resistance among Palestinians, Israeli occupation has systematically dismantled and discredited moderate political forces in the occupied territories.

Indeed, during this current intifada, Palestinians have employed many nonviolent activities in resisting the occupation, including nonviolent demonstrations, sit-ins in the streets, joint prayers in streets, periods of silence in public, stopping all movement in the streets, boycotting all Israeli products, joint nonviolent protest with Israeli peace forces on both sides of the checkpoints, signing and sending protest papers to embassies and international organizations demanding movement against the occupation, and holding national and international conferences.

The above activities comprise a wider conceptualization of nonviolent resistance, one that corresponds with Scott's definition by escaping the narrowness of associating nonviolence resistance only with direct action campaigns and focusing on the participants' intention. Scott's nonviolent resistance includes "any act (s) by member (s) of subordinate community that is or are intended or either to mitigate or deny opportunities to maintain control (land, economic, political, or any other forms of control) by super ordinate force (system or structure) or to advance its own claims (for independence, freedom, respect, etc.) vis-à-vis those super ordinate forces."[6]

The main challenge facing the Palestinian national movement has been its inability to frame Palestinian resistance—internally and externally—in terms of its nonviolent nature. Instead, the Palestinian leadership and a small number of armed groups indirectly played into the hands of Israel's government and other international forces (such as the media) by either highlighting their ineffective use of arms or by accepting the characterization of Palestinian resistance as mainly violent.

Thus, the first objective of any nonviolent campaign in the occupied territories should be to highlight and recognize the long history of nonviolent resistance used by Palestinians daily. It should be emphasized that the effective daily actions include maintaining internal solidarity, finding alternative routes around checkpoints, continuing to harvest olives, holding strikes, boycotting, refusing to cooperate with Israeli civil and military administrations, protesting, blocking roads, hanging Palestinian and black mourning flags on electric-power poles, educating foreign audiences about the impact and nature of occupation, and continuing to visit relatives despite Israeli blockades and curfews.

A second assumption about Palestinian nonviolent resistance is that local leaders and activists have enormous experience in organizing nonviolent actions. Some falsely argue that outside forces are needed to create nonviolent Palestinian strategies because Palestinians lack the knowledge or techniques to organize or carry out a nonviolent campaign. Ghassan Andouni counters by stating: "You do not come to people [the Palestinians] with a 400 year–old struggle and start preaching to them. You need to find space to engage, and you need to engage in your way, and people will watch you. And then, after a while, people either will deny you space or appreciate your work."[7] Since 1967, Palestinians have engaged in collective mobilization and nonviolent organization at the community and national level through, for instance, labor unions, social committees, political parties, and women's and youth organizations. All of these local organizations were the base for launching and maintaining the nonviolent campaign of the 1987–1992 intifada.

A third assumption is that an effective nonviolent grassroots campaign has to be accompanied by committed political leadership to engage in formal negotiation. Nonviolent campaigns alone cannot end the occupation. Like other cases around the world, for nonviolence campaigns to be effective, other political reasons are necessary (for example, international actors, local and national political leadership).

Fourth, it is important to acknowledge that both international law and the Universal Declaration of Human Rights give the right to armed struggle in resisting an occupying force. However, many analysts and peace activists deny Palestinians their right to use arms against the Israeli occupation, and legitimize only the use of nonviolence. When Palestinians use nonviolent strategies they are not necessarily denouncing or surrendering their right to resist occupation, but they are voluntarily choosing different means.[8] For example, International Solidarity Movement (ISM) coordinators have stated on various occasions that while they emphasize nonviolent resistance, the Palestinians have the right to use arms in resisting the occupation.[9] As one ISM leader states,

> I am not against legitimate armed resistance—I think everyone has the right to defend themselves—and certainly you hear people advocating for only armed resistance, that is the only way to liberation, and that has worked in many other countries. But I believe there needs to be an active Palestinian nonviolent resistance movement—I believe it is more powerful. I do not believe we can stand up to the Israeli military with weapons.[10]

The above assumptions suggest that the discussion of nonviolence in the Palestinian context should be focused on how to improve, upgrade, or further systematize the nonviolent activities already carried out by Palestinians in their daily lives and by many grassroots organizations or communities. Further, the discussion should include ways to evaluate the impact and effectiveness of nonviolent strategies that have already been used.

Nonviolent Resistance in Palestine

Scholars and activists of nonviolence consider the 1987 intifada as the most successful example of the organized nonviolent campaigns by Palestinians in their long history of resistance. This intifada, contrary to the myth of its being a sudden event, has historical roots and a long record of preparation. The roots of the intifada date back to the 1970s, when a strong popular movement emerged after the defeat in the Six-Day War of 1967 and many new professional and political institutions (e.g., women, health, agriculture) took a leading role in the rebuilding of the Palestinian society under occupation. Obviously other regional and international factors led to the eruption of the uprising, including the indifference of other Arab powers to the Palestinian situation, especially the sense of abandonment during the Lebanon War in 1982. Further, there were the undermining of the PLO role by the US government in supporting the Jordanian-Israeli formula; after the 1985 agreement between Arafat and King Hussein; Jordan's attempt to weaken the PLO role through controlling the allocation of resources in the occupied territories; the rise of the Islamist movement; and the neglect or avoidance of the Palestinian issue by the Reagan-Gorbachev Summit.[11]

In response to the Israeli policy of partial annexation and Jordanian linkage, Palestinians developed an organizational infrastructure to rely on themselves (socially, politically, and even economically). Examples of this infrastructure include the Patriotic Front in 1973–1975, the National Volunteering Committee in 1974, the Palestinian National Front, and the National Guidance Committee in 1981 (which was dissolved by Israel in 1982). By the end of the 1970s, all the Palestinian political factions created their own women's organizations and were actively mobilizing women for political and national activities.[12] In two decades, these organizations and many other professional institutions cultivated the values of solidarity, resistance, service, and steadfastness. In addition to this organizational structure, some educational and nonviolent consciousness-raising activities were initiated by the Center for the Study of Nonviolence in Jerusalem and the Committee Against the Iron Fist Policy. These groups translated into Arabic the strategies and techniques, as well as the philosophy, of nonviolence as adopted by Martin Luther King, Mahatma Gandhi, and Gene Sharp.[13]

In December 1987, there was a mass protest in response to two events: the truck accident in Gaza that killed several Palestinians and the subsequent shootings of demonstrators in Balata refugee camp. Despite the massive and sweeping repressive measures of the Israeli army led by Yitzhak Rabin, within a month the Palestinian grassroots movement managed to cultivate an underground, unified leadership and began issuing fliers and leaflets to guide the first direct, explicitly nonviolent Palestinian national resistance campaign. Although the uprising was eventually sustained by many strategies and activities, initially the core infrastructure consisted of popular committees that operated on the local level to respond to the social, economic, and political needs of the communities.

The major impact of the Palestinian uprising was political, not economic. It caused many Israelis to question the excessive force used to repress Palestinians, thereby sensitizing public opinion to the Palestinian quest for national self-determination. It assisted in mobilizing the Israeli political left (especially small protest groups), which demonstrated and conducted other solidarity activities, and it introduced the two-state solution into mainstream Israeli public opinion. Worldwide, the uprising brought the Palestinian issue to front-page news and internationalized the Palestinian fight for independence. Internally, the uprising brought enormous pride, empowerment, and unity to Palestinian communities and established a strong voice for the Palestinians in the occupied territories in determining the Palestinian national agenda (through coordination with exiled PLO leadership).

Several factors contributed to the success of the nonviolent resistance campaign in the first two years of the intifada. The diverse composition of the unified underground leadership allowed it to continue even when many top leaders were arrested. Strong links to the grassroot communities enabled leaders to sense the national mood; a well-trained political cadre operated throughout the PLO factions in the occupied territories; and the close contact and coordination (at least in the first two years) between the PLO leadership and the local leadership (including Islamic resistance groups) brought greater effect internationally and locally.

Nonviolent resistance during the intifada was comprehensive, manifesting itself in the economic, social, and political arenas. The national daily strike challenged Israeli control by closing businesses at noon and conducting daily marches. In general, Palestinians deployed eighty-seven types of nonviolent activities (out of 168 identified as applicable to the Palestinian context by Gene Sharp).[14] The leaflets put out by the unified leadership called for many activities, including creating alternative institutions to reduce dependence on the Israeli occupation, defying Israeli school closings, boycotting Israeli products, displaying the Palestinian flag, holding symbolic funerals, blocking roads into settlements, and withholding taxes. As mentioned earlier, none of these activities were totally new to the Palestinian context, their having been employed before the intifada. Although the Palestinian merchants' strike was the most prevalent form of economic noncooperation, tax resistance was particularly successful in Bethlehem, Beit Sahour, and Ramallah. The intifada cost the Israeli economy 120 million dollars per month, of which 88 million was indirect economic cost. Obviously, the economic strategies of noncooperation subjected the Palestinian community itself to enormous hardship, and an alternative labor market, along with small home-based health clinics and schools, were created to ease the burden.[15]

Other manifestations were reflected in social boycotting and suspension of all sports and other activities, which conveyed a "stay-home" resistance message. Marches and protests were a major tool, with messages framed by the Palestinian leadership. Political activities were in the form of rejecting any contact with Israeli military authorities and defying school closings, curfews, taxes, and other occupation laws.

The symbolic expression of nonviolent resistance, through graffiti or displaying the Palestinian flag, was extremely effective in sending a message of steadfastness and rejection of the occupation. Alternative institutions, both economic and social, were created through the work of popular committees and included agricultural organizations and cooperatives, health clinics and medical services, educational committees, and judicial institutions. (The work of these committees and institutions was not fully or perfectly monitored nor was it ethically grounded, especially in the punishment of collaborators or settling social and family disputes.)

This brief summary illustrates that the first intifada offers many lessons and insights in nonviolent resistance. Although such experience is still relatively underdocumented, it is available to activists and leaders engaged in the liberation movement.

Current Palestinian and Israeli Nonviolent Resistance: Actions and Obstacles

By September 2000 Palestinians were frustrated and angry, and saw no hope in good-faith negotiations. The Camp David talks had not produced any hope; on the contrary, Arafat and the Palestinians were yet again portrayed as missing a historic opportunity. On the ground, the reality of the Oslo Accords was worse than before them. Economically, Palestinian areas were suffering from worsening economic conditions (e.g., the lowest ever employment rates since 1990),[16] and were strangled by their lack of mobility under the Israeli military and security arrangements. Politically, neither the United States nor the Arab countries could offer any glimpse of hope for serious implementation of the peace accords, and the Palestinian Authority (also being perceived as corrupt) appeared ineffective in negotiating any relief from the occupation. Between 1993 and 2000, while territories were offered, the Israeli matrix of control remained intact. In fact, the Israeli settlements expanded considerably (i.e., 90,000 housing units, including 30 new settlements and 250 miles of bypass roads), 1,200 houses were demolished, 200 square kilometers of farmland and pasture were expropriated from Palestinian owners, more than 100,000 olive and fruit trees were uprooted, and Israel began constructing a barrier for a unilateral separation plan.[17] In this context, Ariel Sharon's provocative visit to the Al Aqsa Mosque with thousands of security guards and police triggered a massive Palestinian protest that marked the beginning of the second intifada.

Palestinians took to the streets and launched daily protests and other nonviolent activities. However, a few small Palestinian factions engaged in armed resistance that involved shooting at both Israeli civilians and soldiers. The Israeli response gradually escalated, and by March 2002 it launched its massive attack, Operation Defensive Shield, in which 500 Palestinians were killed and fifteen injured, and the Palestinian Authority security and administrative offices were completely destroyed. Arafat's compound was under siege and eventually destroyed, confining him and his aide to two rooms. At the same time Israeli forces began constructing a physical wall separating the West Bank from Israel. The consequences of this "apartheid wall" have been devastating to Palestinian communities, which as a result have been contained in 40 percent of the territories and divided into smaller ghettos. The wall has been described by many Palestinians as the most tragic event since the 1948 Naqba.[18]

The Al Aqsa intifada has affected the Israeli economy, tourism, and Jewish immigration to Israel. Collective and individual fear and insecurity have resulted from Palestinian suicide bombers in Israeli towns and cities. Since the outbreak of the intifada, at least twenty-three suicide bombs have killed hundreds of Israelis. Claiming that the Palestinian Authority leadership is unwilling to stop the suicide bombings by disarming Hamas and the Islamic Jihad, Sharon's government gained support to crack down on the Palestinians and to erect the apartheid wall. In unintended cooperation Hamas and Ariel Sharon have succeeded in hijacking the peace process, or what was left of it after Netanyahu came to power in 1996.

The voices of Arabs and Jews who believe in the possibility of living together in two independent and separate states have been kidnapped and trapped by the rhetoric of war and violence of the 1970s and 1980s. As in the years before the 1993 Oslo Accords, when the ruling Likud Party under Yitzhak Shamir refused to negotiate with PLO leaders, feelings of helplessness and hopelessness have affected people on both sides. Many are left asking what can be done to return to negotiations or even to reach a cease-fire.

Despite the association of this second intifada with suicide bombing and armed resistance, there has been strong continuation of Palestinian nonviolence in their daily defiance of and resistance to the occupation. Nonviolent actions include many active Palestinian NGOs that work on peacebuilding, human rights, and conflict resolution. Despite this wide range of activities, in comparison to the 1987 intifada, this uprising lacks the general image and voice of massive nonviolence. The following section explores some of the factors that contribute to such a reality.

Palestinian Authority Trap and Absence of Leadership

A major factor of the success of the first intifada was the presence and cultivation of a local unified leadership, which orchestrated and framed the initial massive, spontaneous resistance activities at the grassroots. The local, underground leadership provided direction and clarity for the goals of the intifada and coordinated with the exiled PLO leadership. Since Oslo, this leadership has been marginalized or co-opted by the returning exiled leadership that came to dominate. Thus, from its early stages, the current intifada has lacked top Palestinian leadership framing the community resistance in nonviolent terms. The failure of the Palestinian leadership (both of the authority and opposition groups) to unify at an early stage of the second intifada resulted in fragmentation and prevented it from launching a systematic campaign against the Israeli incursions into Palestinian-controlled areas. There were several meetings of the Islamic and National Coordination Committee (comprising top faction leaders in Gaza and the West Bank, including Marwan Bargouthi, who was jailed by Israel in 2001) in which the leaders discussed coordination, networks, and strategies for managing the 2000 uprising. Despite their late endorsement of the nonviolent strategies and action carried out by the ISM and other groups (especially after activists took over the Surda checkpoint for a few hours), such meetings were not effective in producing a national leadership committed to nonviolent resistance.[19] In addition, in comparison to the underground Unified National Leadership of the first intifada, the structure and nature of the Al Aqsa Intifada coordination committee conveyed the negative image of a forum of factions competing for control and thus failed to gain trust and credibility in the Palestinian streets. Such factors have to be viewed within the context of Israel's role in destroying the authority's capacity to rule. The Israeli military launched a massive continual assault on civilians and any form of mobilization; this included the destruction of the Palestinian security and police forces, administrative officers, and military and security installations.

The Oslo II track of negotiation and its aftermath established the Palestinian political leadership as the only form of resistance and sole legitimate authority in dealing with the Israeli government and occupation. However, this authority could not deliver any significant concessions or improvements in either security or economic development. In addition, the internal corruption scandals left the Palestinian community trapped between an occupation force and a symbolic system of authority ineffective in its negotiation policy and blocking other resistance forces from emerging. During the 1987 intifada, many Palestinians knew of the corruption in the PLO, yet they believed that such structure would be reformed and take a different role in the state-building process. This hope faded in the post-Oslo period, and the authority lost a great deal of credibility and legitimacy among the people. By claiming the sole legitimacy for negotiation and leadership with Israel, the authority leadership blocked the emergence of a local leadership—grassroots or elite—to lead a more massive direct-action campaign against the occupation. Several Palestinian leaders have called for dismantling the Palestinian Authority as a way out of the trap of having a political leadership with no power or legitimacy, locally or internationally.[20] Yet the authority's existence provides Israel and its allies with an opportunity to manipulate it as a counterpart for both negotiation and war.

Militancy and Arms in the Early Stage of the Al Aqsa Intifada

With the creation of the Palestinian Authority and its security branches, more small arms were introduced into the Palestinian society. Thousands of Palestinian security forces members carried small arms to ensure internal security and used them as early as 1996 in a confrontation with Israeli forces over the "tunnel opening." The uncoordinated and sporadic armed resistance that erupted in the early stages of the intifada in September 2000 poses another obstacle to framing the current resistance in a nonviolent perspective. The existence of small armed groups under different security forces and the creation of the militant force of Fatah (Al Aqsa Brigade) suppressed grassroots initiatives and a popular resistance campaign. This has confined organized resistance to a select underground group of armed men, who also rule the Palestinian streets and dictate social and political life.[21]

The sporadic and unorganized shooting at Jewish settlements in the suburbs of Jerusalem gave Israeli forces the pretext to invade Palestinian towns and cities and to escalate its assault against civilians in these areas. Although ineffective in facing the Israeli army, Palestinian gunfire created fear among civilians, unleashed Israeli forces, and allowed the Israeli government and military propaganda to portray the intifada as a war (thereby granting Israel international legitimacy for using heavier weapons). The

Israeli response did not distinguish between shooters and protesters (especially evident in the killing of thirteen in Israel). This lack of distinction between armed and unarmed resistance and the lack of international accountability, holding Israeli forces responsible, prompted many Palestinians to argue that nonviolence is ineffectual. On these grounds, the ISM and Grassroots International Protection for the Palestinian People began working on introducing an international civilian solidarity presence among Palestinian protesters to force the Israeli military to distinguish between civilians and armed resistance.[22]

Internally, the shootings confined resistance to a minority of underground militia groups that isolated and marginalized the role of the masses in resisting the occupation. Thus, participation in funerals became the Palestinians' primary formal mobilization framework instead of a more organized nonviolent mass movement. The availability of arms and the sporadic shooting and militancy also have had a far-reaching impact on the disempowerment of Palestinian youth, who constituted the base for the 1987 intifada mobilization. Many Palestinian youths have turned into observers for the militants, and some who enrolled in such factions were handed small arms. Militarizing young Palestinians will have more devastating future consequences even in an independent Palestine.

Suicide Bombings

Like the sporadic shooting, suicide bombings have had many negative consequences for the resistance movement. From a nonviolent perspective, suicide bombings are morally and tactically wrong. Killing Israeli civilians indiscriminately creates fear and insecurity and further increases Israeli public hatred and mistrust of Palestinians. Suicide bombings also isolate the Israeli peace camp and reduce its effect on policy or public opinion because it provides an opportunity to dehumanize Palestinians and inflame hatred for their cause, too.

The bombings and their planners blocked and delegitimized nonviolent popular campaigns by exposing Palestinians to a new level of violence and contributing to the degree and extent of Israeli military retaliation. In addition, establishing and supporting a culture of resistance that celebrates suicide attacks as "heroic" acts might have given some short-term acceptance for the need to retaliate against the Israeli military forces, yet in the long term such bombings damage the Palestinian community's social, religious, and cultural norms. Outside the region, bombings provide the Israeli government with political justification for continuing its use of excessive military force, selective assassinations, and collective punishment while at the same time achieving a measure of sympathy from abroad. Although portrayed otherwise, suicide bombings are a relatively recent phenomenon in the Israeli–Palestinian conflict. Images of Israeli children and civilians in the aftermath of the bombings have captured the front pages of news outlets worldwide. Israeli military operations are always reported in light of these attacks and are thereby legitimized. Nonviolent forms of resistance do not provide a similar justification for retaliation, and thus rarely make it to the front pages of mainstream news.

The suicide bombers have provoked an enormous environment of fear of and hatred for Palestinians and their leaders among Israelis, and have made it much more difficult for those who sympathize with the Palestinian national aspirations to fully express solidarity with Palestinians as victims. The scenes of body parts being collected in Israeli streets are more apparent in the Western media than those of Palestinian children, women, or soldiers executed by the Israeli army. The suicide bombings disengage the Palestinian public and make it a passive victim to Israel's assaults. It is true that many Palestinians support the bombings; however, such support is also passive. It feeds on vengeful feelings that are often destructive, and provides temporary relief from their sense of disempowerment. Even though many Israelis and Palestinians believe that Israeli forces were waiting for any provocation to enter the Palestinian territories in order to execute the Sharon plan, the suicide bombings undermine diplomatic efforts to seek a high moral ground when the entire Palestinian population is under severe attack. In addition to the immorality involved in suicide bombing, the act has overshadowed any peaceful or nonviolent actions taken by Palestinians.

Nonviolent Direct Actions in Israel

As with the first intifada, the nonviolent direct-action activities in Israel continue to be associated with fewer and smaller organizations, in contrast to other Israeli peace groups that have been widely publicized in research, books, and alternative media. Since the early 1980s, Israeli society has produced hundreds of NGOs focusing on Arab-Jewish relations inside Israel and issues of peace, coexistence, and dialogue. Millions of dollars and human resources are invested in the operation of these organizations and their field (e.g., Abraham Fund Initiatives). In the post-Oslo period, some of these organizations began launching peace programs with Palestinians in the occupied territories. The work of these groups remained within the realm of peace education, dialogue, and Track II diplomacy and avoided direct confrontation with the occupation forces.

Various factors can explain the lack of a sustainable and effective Israeli nonviolent direct-action movement. First is the manifesto of Israel's largest and most dominant peace group, Peace Now, which has determined from its inception to remain within the mainstream Zionist ideology of security. The group avoids any direct confrontation with Israeli military forces on the ground, yet it opposes many government policies such as settlement expansion, human rights violations, and collective punishment. Despite their active protest through the years, Peace Now leaders are extremely careful to remain within the national consensus on such crucial issues as support of the military (with so many of the leaders serving in the army or reserves, for example).[23] When Israeli peace groups refrain from confronting the military or other core foundations of the occupation, the groups, in fact (as some Israelis have pointed out), demonstrate their own adaptation to the occupation and the Israeli government's manipulation of their actions. This sentiment is captured by Tom Segev, the well-known Israeli journalist and author, who says that "these voices condemning the occupation are exploited to serve the Israeli myth and, paradoxically, facilitate the perpetuation of the occupation and expansion of settlement."[24] As Adi Ophir said in 2002, the left in Israel quickly slid to the right:

> It was a left that had never internalized the fact that the occupation is the point of departure; that ending the occupation is a condition of reconciliation—not vice versa. Had the peace camp torn itself away from the segment of Israeli society that maintains the occupation in its acts, its way of life, its person and property, an agreement might have been reached years ago, lives might have been saved, some of the destruction and ruination might have been prevented.[25]

Another Israeli scholar and activist offers the following critique of Peace Now and the response of its peace coalition to the second intifada:

> This coalition [is] made of two blocs. The major one, led by Peace Now, has very little chance of providing a significant alternative. It [is] genuinely convinced that [Ehud] Barak made the most generous offer possible to the Palestinian side and that Arafat disappointed them. . . . They never clarified to themselves or to the Jewish public what "peace" entails. As far as one can tell, it does not involve a solution to the refugee problem, a change in the status of the one-million-strong Palestinian minority in Israel (on whose vast support Peace Now relies for its demonstrations) or full sovereignty for the future Palestinian state.[26]

Ilan Pappe criticizes this peace camp for grounding its opposition to the occupation in terms of the corruption it brings to Jewish society, rather than as a crime against Palestinians, and certainly "not as a continuous evil that began with the ethnic cleansing of 1948." This perspective—which comprises the majority of the peace camp—marginalizes and delegitimizes the non-Zionist Jewish organizations and most Israeli Palestinian parties, which offer an alternative by arguing that the apartheid characteristics of Israeli policies toward the Israeli Palestinian minority and the historical context of

Israeli actions against Palestinians (including in 1948 and 1982) have to be recognized and acknowledged as a condition for genuine reconciliation with Palestinians.

A second factor explaining the lack of a sustained Israeli nonviolent movement is that nonviolent direct action requires a higher level of risk for peace activists, who are under a constant threat of arrest. The Israeli peace movement in general has relied on followers and organizers from the middle and upper classes, who are often professionals living in well-to-do communities, which increases the cost of their open dissent from the national consensus.

Third, Israel's militarized society and economy has created a strong dependence on security clearances. Most employment and career opportunities require military and security approval and compliance. Nonviolent direct-action activities often involve challenging laws and policies and confronting these security arrangements.[27] Thus, it is not surprising to see that Israeli peace groups have built their work around the Israeli–Palestinian conflict with the notion of security and peace, while Palestinian groups have focused on human rights and freedom. These are two different approaches to peace work, since "the dynamic of achieving freedom is different from the dynamic used to achieve peace."[28] However, most of the groups who work on nonviolent direct action with Palestinians have made the shift from focusing on peace and dialogue to focusing on freedom and liberation (see, for instance, Committee for House Demolition, Rabbis for Human Rights, Ta'ayush). Rabbi Ark Asherman from Rabbis for Human Rights captured this shift when he declared after being prosecuted by the Israeli court for his nonviolent actions that "now I feel as a member of a freedom movement."[29]

A fourth explanation for the lack of a sustained movement is the interdependence between Israeli and Palestinian peace and resistance movements. The withdrawal or weakness of one often affects the other because either can be used by those advocating violence to claim that "there is no partner on the other side." Thus, the lack of a massive Palestinian civil-based nonviolent mobilization is another factor weakening Israeli nonviolent direct-action groups. This is especially a factor during the second intifada with many Palestinian peace and nonviolence groups hesitating to work or even coordinate with Israeli peace groups. For more than fourteen months the Palestinians NGOs (as instructed by the Palestinian Authority) formally boycotted any form of joint activities with Israeli peace groups. Such interdependence was felt previously, when Israeli peace groups and activists withdrew in 1991 during the first Gulf War and accused Palestinians of supporting Saddam Hussein. In addition, the lack of protest in the Israeli peace camp in the post-Oslo period was attacked by Palestinian peace activists.[30]

Nonviolent Direct Actions in the Al Aqsa Intifada: Beyond Adaptability Toward an Active-Resistance Campaign

Despite the above contradictions and limitations to developing nonviolent mass mobilization in both the Israeli and Palestinian communities, there are a few active groups who have devoted significant efforts to challenging the occupation forces on a daily basis and building nonviolent capacities on the ground. The main characterization of nonviolent direct action by both Israelis and Palestinians is to create and operate resistance to and rejection of the occupation and to put pressure on the system and forces of occupation instead of adapting to its oppression. So when Israelis, Palestinians, and international activists manage to dismantle a small checkpoint, they are sending a powerful message of active resistance, as opposed to finding alternative ways to bypass the checkpoint. Palestinians have a long and solid repertoire of activities to draw from in dealing with the occupation, which range from passively living with the conditions and finding ways to adapt to it to finding ways to handle the restrictions without directly confronting the occupation. Palestinian nonviolent direct-action groups are aiming to achieve a wide civil-based resistance by drawing on both symbolic and actual acts of resistance. Providing the average Palestinian person with hope that this type of resistance is effective and successful has been the main challenge facing these initiatives.

Direct Nonviolent Action by Palestinians and Foreign Volunteers

There are many Palestinian organizations involved in or supporting advocacy, human rights, peace, dialogue, and joint projects with Israeli peace groups. The work of these organizations contributes to the development and sustainability of nonviolent culture in the Palestinian resistance, yet few of these organizations have consciously and explicitly framed their activities within the context of nonviolent resistance.

The Palestinian Center for Rapprochement Between Peoples (PCR)

The Palestinian Center for Rapprochement Between Peoples (PCR) is one such organization. It was founded in early 1988 by a group of Beit Sahour activists to lead their community in nonviolent actions. Among their well-known acts of defiance were the burning of Israeli identification cards, strikes, protests, tax revolt, prayer for peace, launching several dialogue groups, and leading a four-year campaign against the establishment of the illegal Israeli colony of Har Homa at Abu Ghoneim mountain near Bethlehem. During this intifada, the PCR intensified its nonviolent activities especially after Israeli soldiers killed three residents and damaged 200 houses. In response, the PCR organized a march to the Israeli military station, joined by the Israeli peace group Gush Shalom and many other international delegates, on December 28, 2000. The protest ended with the planting of a Palestinian flag on the military watchtower. The nonviolent campaign of PCR took a significant turn with its leaders' emphasis on inviting foreign observers and activists to Palestine and providing nonviolent training for Palestinian activists. The International Solidarity Movement and Grassroots International Protection for the Palestinian People are two international initiatives that PCR has contributed to their formation.

The International Solidarity Movement (ISM)

ISM's campaign has been the largest (having brought over 1,000 foreign activists) and most visible among the international nonviolent action groups. Led by local and international volunteers, ISM began its activity in March 2001 with an international presence in the village of Hares to protect local Palestinians from settlers and the Israeli army. This action was followed by a group of foreign volunteers camped outside the Arafat compound when it was first targeted by the Israeli army. In July they sat in some homes in Beit Sahour that were under attack by Israel. However, the official campaign call was issued in August 2001 for fifty foreigners to protest the closing of and attack on the Palestinian Orient House in East Jerusalem. The arrest of the international participants along with many Palestinians was widely covered by Arab and Israeli media. ISM activities have ranged from direct confrontation with Israeli soldiers while they demolished houses, removing roadblocks, planting olive trees, and accompanying Palestinian farmers to their olive fields in the harvest season. After the Israeli invasion of Palestinian towns in the spring of 2002, ISM shifted most of its activities to humanitarian aid (especially when the UN and Red Cross were not responding to the humanitarian crisis in the territories).

One of the successful cases of ISM's work was its coordination with Beir Zeit University students and some Israeli activists to plan and actually take control of the Surda checkpoint near Beir Zeit University. During the few hours of their control of the checkpoint, thousands of Palestinians managed to go through it. "The experience of Surda showed many people that the Israeli military is not all mighty and it broke many of the psychological barriers against the nonviolent direct action."[31] In fact, the Islamic and National Coordination Committee of the intifada took notice of the event and endorsed the nonviolent action campaign after the event.

In addition to the intended physical protection of ISM presence on the ground, Huwaida Araf described additional effects: "At the minimal level, it has greatly raised the morale of Palestinians. We have a big feeling of isolation. . . . So when we see civilians from other countries come and be willing to put their time, their energy, their resources and their bodies on the line, it lessens that isolation."[32]

ISM leaders are careful in defining their contribution as outsiders and maintaining that they "help support the nonviolent Palestinian resistance by tapping into the resource that internationals can provide—global attention."[33] However, probably the most significant factor in the visibility of the ISM has been the targeting of its active members by the Israeli security forces, especially after the killing of Rachel Corrie, one of its foreign volunteers in Gaza. Many of ISM's members and volunteers have been banned from entering Israel or the occupied territories. In addition, in the fall of 2003, Israeli forces began requiring all foreign visitors to Israel to sign a document prohibiting them from entering the occupied territories. Such a policy reflects the wide impact that ISM and its members have had on the occupation policy.

Grassroots International Protection for the Palestinian People (GIPP)

Similar to ISM, this initiative was inspired by local Palestinian NGOs and leaders who invited several foreign delegations to Palestine in March 2001 to visit refugee camps, hospitals, and demolished homes, as well as to Israeli settlements and bypass roads. Many Palestinian organizations supported the initiative, among them the Palestinian NGOs, YMCA/YWCA, Palestinian Council for Justice and Peace, Members of the Palestinian Legislative Council, Sabeel Ecumenical Liberation Theology Center, Palestinian General Union for Charitable Society, General Union of Palestinian Women, and ISM.

The initiative was launched after the United States vetoed the United Nations (UN) resolution to send international peacekeepers to the occupied territories. The call for protection was brought to the UN by Palestinian and Arab leaders at a time when Palestinians feared that Israeli forces were planning to conduct a massive invasion along with the start of the US attacks against Iraq. Mustafa Bargouti spearheaded the campaign and initially focused the work on bringing European diplomats and government officials to witness and monitor violations of Palestinian human rights by the Israeli military. However, the initiative expanded and, with international partnerships, it brought hundreds of officials and over 2,000 foreigners into Palestine. The stated goals of GIPP were as follows:

1. Manning areas leading to and/or around the Israeli roadblocks, in order to help the Palestinians to cross, and to witness Israel's violation of human rights.
2. Living in the threatened population centers that are in the greatest danger of Israeli collective terrorism (e.g., home demolition, land confiscation, mass murder, arrests, mass expulsion) under the distraction of a regional war. Areas close to the "wall of hate" constructed by Israel, containing over thirty Palestinian villages and more than

75,000 people, were of primary focus because they were under threat of ethnic cleansing/expulsion/transfer (internally or across the borders), and organizers felt that the presence of international delegates, as witnesses, could prevent such violations of international law.

3. Assisting with emergency teams and convoys helping the needy by distributing medicine, food, water, cooking fuels, and clothing to those under Israeli curfews.

During the first months of the Israeli invasion of Palestinian territories, the GIPP project welcomed over 800 international volunteers, who accompanied ambulances and provided humanitarian aid to Palestinians living under curfew.[34] Eventually the work of GIPP and ISM began converging, especially on the ground when international volunteers responded to calls to protest Israeli actions.

In the above initiatives,[35] outside activists played a crucial role in implementing nonviolent direct action. Coordinated by local leadership, thousands of foreigners poured into the Palestinian territories. Their activities included accompanying ambulances targeted by the Israeli army, staying in Palestinian homes to protect them from Israeli intrusion, and carrying food and medicine to 150 Palestinians under siege for forty-three days in Bethlehem's historic Church of the Nativity. In early 2004, many of the international activists, especially ISM volunteers, began assisting in organizing villagers in Beit Suriek, Budou, and Bodrus in facing the dividing wall on the West Bank. For three months they managed to march with hundreds from these villages and many Israeli activists (especially form Gush Shalom) and to confront the Israeli soldiers. On several occasions the soldiers and bulldozers were challenged by the nonviolent direct actions (see Gush Shalom and ISM reports).[36]

The effect of the international solidarity groups on the process of political change and resistance has been best captured by Mark Schneider (an international activist), who claims that it has "humaniz[ed] the Palestinian people's plight through personal stories shared by internationals with their home communities, expanded the breadth of coverage of Palestinians' experience of occupation in both alternative and mainstream media, and demonstrated a commitment to international solidarity that both the common Palestinian people and their leadership appreciate and want to see expanding."[37]

Despite the increasing Palestinian participation in GIPP and ISM, according to local Palestinian nonviolent coordinator Ghassan Andoni: "Most of these groups have national organization but are more effective at the local level. We haven't yet arrived at the level of national planning for civil-based (nonviolence) resistance. We still lack the national Palestinian infrastructure needed to reach that point."[38] The work of the nonviolent direct organizations, especially ISM, has been in the rural and most underdeveloped and poorest areas of Palestine. There is still a lack of strong engagement from the Palestinian middle class and NGOs and civil-society groups with well-educated constituencies. Andoni explains that the major base for ISM is from the refugee camps and poorest areas, which has affected ISM's social outreach. "Civil society as reflected in the NGOs in major cities involves middle-class, educated Palestinians, and has not contributed enough to the Intifada; they have been more detached than engaged. Their lack of participation certainly deprives the civil-based resistance of certain sources of strength."[39]

There are other current Palestinian initiatives that focus on capacity building through training workshops. For example, Holy Land Trust began offering nonviolence workshops (led by local and international experts) in Bethlehem, Beit Sahour, and Ramallah.[40] Finally, for over a decade Johnathan Kuttab and the Center for Nonviolence in Jerusalem have been operating the Library on Wheels for Nonviolence and Peace, which has offered many Palestinian children the opportunity to read material on nonviolence. In addition, MEND (Middle East Nonviolence and Democracy) has been actively promoting, educating, and building capacity for nonviolence in Palestine.

Middle East Nonviolence and Democracy (MEND)

MEND was set up in 1998 in East Jerusalem to promote nonviolence and democracy. It is a dynamic Palestinian institution working with education and with innovative techniques to promote empowerment and participation, and thereby promote peace in the region by helping and encouraging people to stand up to violence with nonviolence; that is with assertiveness, self-esteem, and dignity. In partnership with various international organizations MEND developed various projects. Some of MEND's activities have been schools/community education on nonviolence in the greater Jerusalem area, Ramallah, and Bethlehem, which includes using psychodrama counselors with students, teachers, and families. In active nonviolence training, MEND has already given a month-long intensive training to a group of mid-level activists in the Jerusalem area, Ramallah, Tul Karem, and Jenin. MEND has just published one of the first training manuals on active nonviolence in Arabic, and it is already in demand. One of MEND's pioneer projects is the production of a radio soap opera to promote nonviolence among Palestinian youths, which was launched in June 2003, and is currently recording its second series. MEND is training a wide cross-section of women in the Bethlehem area in active nonviolence and participatory video production. The project has put out two short films on women role models which were broadcast on local television; in partnership with Search for

Common Ground (United States) and the Truman Institute (Hebrew University, Jerusalem), completed a joint project with empowerment of women activists. Volunteers for nonviolence developed a group of young volunteers, MENDERS, who now work in their communities in a variety of ways, especially as advocates for nonviolence through theater and art. They write and produce their own quarterly newsletter, *IMPACT,* which is distributed in the West Bank. In the area of emergency help MEND responded to the continuing situation by working extensively on crisis management and counseling with front-line schools in the Bethlehem and Ramallah areas; by distributing clear and simple public-service announcements on such vital concerns as basic first aid and the dangers of landmines; distributing donations for children; building playgrounds; helping rebuild roads; and replanting uprooted trees. As the separation wall starts to dominate the landscape and political and personal futures, MEND has started work to help those most adversely affected by the wall to get together and regain their sense of community and explore ways to cope. MEND promotes better understanding between Palestinians and Israelis through a series of educational materials to accompany the Shara'Simsim/Rehov Sumsum, groundbreaking Sesame Workshop production. In this vein too, MEND has produced a series of bumper stickers in Arabic and English and Hebrew and English to encourage reflection among both Israelis and Palestinians about their common needs and shared values. The two most recent stickers in this series say, "We are all human beings" and "Life is worth living."

Israeli Nonviolent Resistance
Like the Palestinians, Israeli mainstream peace and nonviolence groups (e.g., Peace Now) have mainly focused their work on vocal peaceful protest. Thousands of people have participated in their marches and demonstrations, rejecting the occupation and calling for a Palestinian state. Yet members of the majority of such groups have also adapted to the conditions and restrictions generated by the occupation forces in Israel. For example, most of these supporters do not stop using bypass roads, buying products from the occupied territories, serving in the regular or reserve army, or obeying military and civilian court decisions regarding occupation policies like home demolitions (despite the fact that there are such campaigns). Fewer have engaged in nonviolent direct-action campaigns aiming at, for instance, total or partial refusal to perform military service in the occupied territories.

Among the most controversial nonviolent direct actions used by Israeli peace activists in their struggle against the occupation is the refusal to serve in the Israeli army. Professor Yeshayahu Leibowitz was among the first Israeli peace activists to call for such a stand in the late 1970s.[41]

The phenomenon of refusal is gaining ground in the Israeli army, and thus far refusers include a group of at least twenty-seven reserve pilots, four former chiefs of Israel's powerful domestic security service, the military's current chief of staff, and a separate list of 574 army reservists. In addition, by spring 2002 there were a thousand former officers, among them generals, who called on Israel to withdraw unilaterally from the territories.[42] The statements by reservists are being organized by Courage to Refuse. Due to the militarization and the sacred status of security forces in Israeli society, the call and practice of refusal to serve often shocks the public.[43] Although the number of soldiers who refuse to serve has been relatively very low, it still receives wide media coverage in Israel and abroad, especially when the refusers are associated with elite military units,[44] such as the recent group of pilots who refused to bomb any targets that endanger Palestinian civilians. In a more surprising action, three officers and ten soldiers of the army's most secretive unit, the Sayeret Matkal, general staff commandos, a unit specializing in counterterrorism, assassinations, and rescue missions, stated in their letter to Ariel Sharon: "We have long ago crossed the line between fighting for a just cause and oppressing another people." The group's stated motive for refusal was a "deep fear for the future of Israel as a democratic, Zionist, and Jewish country and out of concern for its moral and ethical image." These soldiers accused the Israeli government of "depriving millions of Palestinians of their rights" and using soldiers as "human shields for the settlements. . . . We will no longer butcher our humanity by taking part in an occupying army's missions."[45]

Yigal Shochat, an Israeli pilot who supports selective refusal said this:

> People who serve in the territories in their compulsory service return as reservists, and their children are also stationed in the same places. The new generation does not even know the Palestinians because of the lengthy closure, and to them, the territories are like Lebanon. Apartheid against the Palestinians is practiced by one generation to the next. And not only by settlers—by all of us. If there are no terrorist attacks, we do not even remember that the Palestinians exist.[46]

The debate over refusal has centered on several arguments, including the typical argument that no one can be a pacifist because the world still needs defense forces and armies to establish order and protect us all from external threats or irrational dictators.

A second argument holds that refusing to perform military service undermines the democratic order of the state and threatens it with total collapse. For example, settlers or even other army officers would have the same right not to obey the army's orders and carry out the evacuation of the settlements. Third, the Israeli army would be left in the hands of corrupt and immoral soldiers if all those who disagree with the occupation refuse to serve. In this case, the misconduct of the soldiers and their brutality in dealing with Palestinians would become the norm.

Yesh Gvul activists and other supporters have responded to such claims by arguing that many soldiers have convinced them that it is almost impossible to withstand the pressure inside the army. The brainwashing in the army machine is intense and unrelenting; those in the higher ranks are more and more like robots with blunted senses, the products of the occupation. Second, Yesh Gvul states that the occupation itself has become a monster that nobody can serve without losing his humanity. When the members of the "cream of the Israeli army," Sayeret Matkal, say so and refuse to continue, their testimony is persuasive. When combat pilots revolt against their commander, who has said that he "feels nothing but a slight bump" when he releases a bomb that kills women and children, respect is due them. Does this refusal prepare the ground for the refusal of right-wing soldiers to help in evicting the settlers? In response to this challenging question, some peace activists emphasize that the right of a soldier to refuse to take part for reasons of conscience must be ensured. Is the denial of this right a blow against democracy? This is a blow for the good. Israeli democracy is being whittled away with every day of occupation. We are witnessing a continual decline: the government had become Sharon's kindergarten, the Knesset attracted general contempt, the Supreme Court had largely become an instrument of the occupation forces, the media were marching in step. It is the refusers who introduced a moral dimension into the public discourse.[47]

Ishai Menuchin, chairman of Yesh Gvul, has stated, "my commitment to democratic values caused me to act against the occupation—to sign petitions, write ads, and take part in demonstrations and vigils. But those acts of opposition were not enough to absolve me of having to make a moral choice about participating in the occupation as an officer and ordering others to do so."[48] Michael Ben-Yair, the Israeli attorney general under Rabin, Peres, and Netanyahu (1993–1996), supported such claims. "In [refusers'] eyes, the occupation regime is evil and military service in the occupied territories, which places soldiers in situations forcing them to commit immoral acts, is evil. Thus their refusal to serve is an act of conscience that is justified and recognized in every democratic regime."[49]

The major assumption made by supporters of these strategies is that the impact of this nonviolent direct action is cumulative, and with one act inspiring the next and one military unit influencing another, it is bound to have a lasting effect on the general public. There are no clear indicators that for refusing to perform military service there will be an impact on government policy, yet peace activists and analysts emphasized that Sharon's threat to isolate the Palestinian Authority is affected by "the criticism from within the Israeli military and security forces."[50]

Yesh Gvul (There Is a Limit)

An Israeli peace group that has shouldered the task of supporting soldiers who refuse assignments of a repressive or aggressive nature. The brutal role of the Israel Defense Force (IDF) in subjugating the Palestinian population places numerous servicemen in a grave moral and political dilemma because they are required to enforce policies they deem illegal and immoral. The army hierarchy demands compliance, but many soldiers, whether conscripts or reservists, find that they cannot in good conscience obey the orders of their superiors.

The group is among the first peace groups to introduce conscientious objection during the war in Lebanon in early 1982 when 168 soldiers were jailed and many others were discharged. With the outbreak of the first Palestinian intifada in 1987, the group expanded its call to the West Bank and Gaza, and close to 200 of its followers were jailed, too. In the current uprising hundreds of reservists have refused assignments, and over 100 have been imprisoned. Also, for the first time, significant numbers of young conscripts have also declined to take part in the campaign of repression. Those who elect to refuse get our full moral and material backing, ranging from financial support for families of jailed *refuseniks* to vigils at the military prisons where they were held. Whenever a refusenik is jailed, we bring his protest to the public notice as a model for the broader peace movement and for other soldiers in a similar dilemma.

Ta'ayush ("Living Together")

Ta'ayush is an Arab-Jewish joint grassroots movement created in Israel in November 2000, during the early stages of the second intifada. The activists sought to develop forms of Arab-Jewish nonviolent action from below in order to subvert ethnic segregation and discrimination in Israel. They emphasize going beyond the usual forms of political protest (e.g., the use of texts and symbols) and working within local communities on concrete projects.

Ta'ayush is by definition a nonviolent direct-action movement. While many Ta'ayush activists oppose violence, any violence by principle, many others just consider the nonviolent methods as the only strategic choice possible for developing a joint Arab-Jewish alternative. These two currents of opinion, however, understand that Palestinian violence arises from the violence of the occupation. Given the existing power relations, there is not an equivalence or symmetry of violence from the two sides. However, there are symmetric tragic results from the point of view of the innocent victims and the negative consequences of the violence to the possibility of achieving just peace in living together, in a ta'ayush kind of relation.

Another Israeli group that has protested and introduced a new level of nonviolent action is labeled "The Anarchist." The nonviolent though militant group focuses on protest at the Separation Fence/Wall. The 22-year-old Gil Na'amati was the first Israeli peace activist to be shot in the leg by the Israeli army. His injury was widely covered by the Israeli media and ignited public debate surrounding the limits of protest and nonviolent direct actions in Israel. However due to the nature of the anarchist group, Israeli public and mainstream peace groups were quick to blame the protester for provocative and irresponsible behavior.[51]

The Campaign for Civil, Nonviolent Actions: Lessons Learned

Both Israeli and Palestinian peace groups have identified the need for a Palestinian and Israeli civil, nonviolent, direct action campaign that can pose a serious challenge to the occupation forces. The existing initiatives and extensive experience of Israeli and Palestinian peace groups offer a solid foundation for this kind of activism. However, several obstacles stand in the way of such a campaign: first, there is clear recognition among Palestinian and international peace activists that the mere presence of the PNA in its current configuration impedes the sustainability and expansion of a civil, nonviolent action campaign. Ali Abunemeh offers the following support for this realization: "What is needed is a strong, popular campaign of resistance based on nonviolence and civil disobedience, and involving the entire Palestinian population. Such a strategy would be unable to eliminate all violence, but would offer hope to the would-be suicide bombers and a powerful moral challenge to the occupier. It might also help transform passive global support for the Palestinian cause into concrete action. Such a strategy cannot emerge, however, as long as Arafat and his failed Oslo leadership hang on, neither offering leadership nor moving out of the way so that fresh leadership—one not anointed by Israel or United States—can rise."[52]

Thus, the major challenge facing the local leadership is how to engage those forces in the PNA that can support such a campaign without risking the movement's credibility and legitimacy in refugee camps and other Palestinian communities where there is a great deal of mistrust of the PNA's intention and effectiveness. Mubarak Awad and Johnathan Kuttab suggest that PNA involvement should be within the context of a broader social re-engagement with political issues on the grassroots level. They suggest that "for this [nonviolent direct action] strategy to succeed, it must be adopted on a massive scale by large segments of the Palestinian population and by the Palestinian National Authority itself. It must involve a strategic, long-term commitment and not simply be symbolic or episodic in character. To achieve this commitment, we need broad public discussions involving unions, students, civil society institutions, and the local Palestinian media. Political discussion within the community must be revived so that participation is universal and everyone has a voice instead of a gun."[53]

Local Palestinian leaders of NGOs, or of political factions like Fatah, PFLP, and the People's Party, have cooperated with MEND, ISM, and GIPP campaigns. Such linkages are crucial and must be expanded in the process of widening the base of the civilian resistance. There has also been symbolic support and recognition by Arafat's circles (especially during the siege) of the important role that such a campaign plays in the Palestinian resistance. This support—actual or symbolic—is important, because without the leadership's backing, it is difficult to mobilize significant numbers in the Palestinian communities to join the nonviolent resistance. The potential power of such support was evident in the spring of 2002 when the Israeli army surrounded Arafat's compound and Sharon gave an ultimatum for Arafat to leave or be bombarded. Within hours of this ultimatum, thousands of Palestinians were roaming the streets of Ramallah on their way to the compound. Thousands of others were protesting in the remaining Palestinian cities and towns. Repeating the tactics of Latin American nonviolent movements, these protesters banged on kitchen pots and household utensils to register their rejection of the ultimatum and offer support to their besieged leadership. Hundreds of these demonstrators camped for a few days outside Arafat's compound. Israeli military forces refrained from an attack, and Sharon's ultimatum was reversed. In combination with international political pressure, the protest on the ground sent a powerful message to both Israel and the international community. The event illustrated the potential of the Palestinian leadership's ability to bring people to the streets on specific issues with successful results. A similar strategy was considered for opposing the Israeli ban on Arafat's visit to Bethlehem during Christmas 2001. However, the PNA leadership did not adopt this course of action, which might have mobilized thousands to march with Arafat to Bethlehem.[54]

"Nonviolence Cannot Work with Israeli Occupation"

Within the Palestinian national liberation movement there have been three camps in the debate over using violence as a means to advance the cause of Palestine. The first group (led by Hamas) refuses to place any limits or conditions on the forms of resistance used and has supported all forms of struggle—including suicide bombings—regardless of geography or the nature of the target. A second group includes those who have supported specific forms of armed struggle, depending on geography or the nature of the target. Groups like People Party and even factions of Fatah have agreed to limit their attacks to the Israeli military or settlers in the occupied territories only. The third group includes those who have consistently called for nonviolent actions and strategies regardless of the physical nature of the target (for example, underground leadership of the first intifada, active NGOs endorsing nonviolence). Obstacles to nonviolent methods are often raised by the first two camps, which places the third camp in the defensive position of demonstrating that nonviolence is practical and effective in the Palestinian-Israeli case.

The cruelty and inhuman nature of the Israeli occupation is often cited as a central factor in justifying armed struggle and suicide bombing, and in delegitimizing nonviolence in the case of Palestine. The fierce attack launched by the occupation against Palestinians is reflected in the fact that during the first three weeks of Al Aqsa Intifada, before the wave of terrorist attacks against Israelis even began, the Israeli Defense Forces, according to army records, fired one million bullets.[55] Proponents of this argument emphasize that the Palestinian situation is unique and does not resemble other conflicts or occupation systems in which nonviolence has been used. They argue that although "every conflict and every liberation movement is unique, the Palestinian case is an exception among the exceptions and unique among special cases too."[56]

Munier Shafiq, an Islamic analyst debating nonviolence, argues that "nonviolent resistance does not work in the Palestinian context. Since 1917 through 1948, 1950, 1967, 1968 up to today, Palestine has experienced the highest forms of peaceful struggle or 'direct nonviolence.' Palestine is famous for its protest, conferences, negotiation, petitions. Palestinians used nonviolence in their six months (in 1936) 'longest peaceful strike known to any people.' All of these actions have failed and led to no signs of success if these efforts were to continue. The main reason is the nature of the Zionist project, the commitment of the British and other superpowers to it; namely the establishment of the Hebrew state and evacuation of the land from its owners/ inhabitants." According to these claims, not only did the nonviolent campaign of 1936 fail to realize any major political gains, but Palestinian leaders of the intifada of 1987–1992 and the "Return Ship" in 1988 failed too.[57]

Supporters of this claim assume that the Zionist occupation is inherently not subject to (or not affected by) the values that underlie the human and spiritual or pragmatic nonviolence action. Thus according to the above claim,

- Israelis who support occupation are people who will not be affected by moral appeals. "The only language they understand is violence."
- Sanctity of human life is not part of the Israeli occupation or society value system: "Arab lives for all Israelis are cheap and have no value at all."
- Israelis lack moral responsibility and are incapable of distinguishing between the different forms of violence generated by the occupation.
- Israelis lack an internal conscience to guide judgments of their behavior and attitudes toward Palestinians.
- Israelis lack any sense of justice that can lead them to realize the injustice imposed on Palestinians.

When Palestinians use the above assumptions as a basis for negating the feasibility of nonviolent direct action, they contribute to the dehumanization dynamics between Israelis and Palestinians. Such rationalization often leads to supporting not only armed struggle, but all forms of suicide bombing.

"Hezbollah's Form of Resistance Is the Only Effective Way"

Since the Israeli withdrawal from Lebanon in 1999, the credibility and legitimacy of Hezbollah-style armed struggle has considerably increased among Palestinian factions and has penetrated public opinion, especially through Hezbollah's satellite television channel *Al Manar.* Several points can be debated on this issue: first, Israel never settled Southern Lebanon, nor did it ever consider it part of Greater Israel. Consequently, Zionist ideology and Jewish religious factors did not play a role in Israel's presence. Second, the Israeli-Palestinian conflict has been framed as an existential and communal one; thus the debate on territorial concession is often associated with existential fears and identity formation. Hence, Palestinian suicide bombings and armed struggle have been successfully portrayed as an attack on the state of Israel's right to exist rather than as a border dispute. Nonviolent action cannot be misunderstood or misrepresented as an attack on Israeli existence and thus will either push Israel's silent majority toward peace, or at least deprive the Israeli government of its silent support. Another distinguishing factor between Hezbollah and Palestinian militias is the former's direct support from regional powers such as Iran and Syria, who provide the resources for such operations. Palestinian factions lack this direct support.

"Will This Work or Haven't We Tried It?"

One of the popular arguments among Palestinians opposing the civilian-based nonviolence movement, especially among those who were active in grassroots committees, is the belief that the method was tried in the 1987 intifada and failed. This argument is either based on the notion that the intifada was effective on the grassroots level, but was "sold out" by Palestinian politicians who negotiated a "bad deal," or the activities did not lead to the removal of the occupation regardless of the Palestinian leadership's behavior. Such feelings of disempowerment regarding the experience of the 1987 intifada have been encountered by ISM activists in their efforts to mobilize communities in villages prior to spring 2003.[58] Nonviolent activists developed two major responses to these arguments. First, a nonviolent campaign cannot be judged by two or three years of action, because it is part of a longer-term path of resistance. The 1987 intifada produced considerable gains on both the Israeli and international fronts, including raising awareness among Israelis of the consequences of the occupation, legitimizing the two-state solution as opposed to autonomy or the Jordanian option, and internationalizing the Palestinian plight. Second, the nonviolent campaign in the 1987 intifada would have resulted in more political gains if Palestinian and Israeli nonviolent peace groups continued to pressure and monitor their own leaderships during the negotiation process instead of leaving the outcome to politicians only. The role of the peace and nonviolence movements does not end with the start of negotiation or signing of an agreement.[59]

Despite these arguments, many skeptics continue to ask for illustrations of success and the impact of nonviolent movements. After providing many successful examples of civilian-based nonviolent direct action campaigns in Poland, India, Kosovo, Norway, Denmark, and South Africa, there are three other arguments used by activists to convey the need for the resurgence of such a campaign in Palestine and Israel. First, there are no guarantees of success that can be given by nonviolent direct action groups. Second, the cost of violent approaches on both sides can be easily demonstrated as a lose-lose approach, especially for the Palestinian community, while nonviolent direct action can save both lives and resources. Finally, Israeli military strength is unmatchable by Palestinians; violent tactics restrict the battle to the military arena, thereby avoiding international law or morality, both of which favor the Palestinian cause.[60]

Debating the Strategy

While sharing the overall objective of a civilian-based nonviolence campaign, activists and organizations have been divided on the strategies and methods to apply. The primary goal of Palestine's nonviolent campaign is the liberation and creation of a state. Thus, despite the acceptance of the fact that Palestinians have repeatedly used nonviolent direct-action campaigns, some continue to argue that nonviolent direct actions—even while they may eventually succeed—take a long time, which Palestinians do not have. The occupation is so brutal in its impact on all areas of Palestinian life (land will be lost, increase in refugees, more settlements, population transference) it is a matter of physical survival. Activists list many indicators of success to illustrate the effective role that nonviolent strategies have produced in the Palestinian fight against the occupation. However, when using the liberation of Palestine and the creation of a viable independent state as the sole criteria, analysts and critics of the nonviolent movement are quick to conclude that these strategies have not only failed, but have possibly derailed the liberation movement.

A typical response to this obstacle is the belief that a nonviolent resistance approach cannot be created in one day or month, but has to emerge as a result of two stages: first, an investment in further training and education of Palestinian grassroots and nongovernmental organizations in the value and methods of nonviolence; second, the selection of a feasible objective or issue to address, one that the Palestinian public can relate to and connect with. This objective should allow for the mobilization of youth, women, and elders and should not define success solely in terms of Palestinian independence. Palestinians have to find their own concrete objective issues to rally for, ones that would be equivalent to Gandhi's salt tax campaign, elections for the

Polish Solidarity movement, and the Chilean campaign of nonviolence. The issues cannot be the removal of the Israeli occupation or dismantling the settlements, for they are long-term objectives. Rather, the nonviolent campaign ought to have a shorter-term focus in order to keep people on board and keep them feeling that they have achieved some tangible goals on the path toward long-term social change. Identifying a series of these issues to illustrate the defiant resistance of the Palestinian population to the world and the Israeli public is a crucial step that can only be devised by Palestinians themselves. In this process of preparation, the civilian and political leadership has to design a contingency plan for each of these issues depending on the Israeli reactions to the nonviolence campaign.[61]

"Nonviolence Contradicts Islam"[62]

The argument that Palestinian Islamic religious and cultural values and norms oppose and contradict nonviolent methods has been raised inside the occupied territories, in Israel, and abroad as well. Muslim scholars have debated the nature of Islamic resistance, especially after the use of suicide bombs in September 11, Iraq, Palestine, Russia, and Indonesia. The two primary questions that peace activists are asked in the Muslim world when introducing Islamic nonviolence resistance are: Do nonviolent methods work in an Islamic context? And is Islam theologically compatible with the practice and philosophy of nonviolence?

To understand the compatibility of Islamic values and beliefs with nonviolence, we have to first dispel the myth that nonviolence is a form of surrender in which the oppressed or victim waits to be slaughtered and accept such a fate. This misperception of nonviolence has been mistakenly associated with peace work or groups. Khalid Kishtainy, Khalis Jalabi, Jawdat Said, and Imam Mohammad al Shirazi (pioneers of nonviolence in the Arab world) have used "civic jihad" as a term to avoid *La Unf* (non-violence) in Arabic which has a negative connotation of surrender and passivity.[63] Nonviolence is about active rejection of violence and full engagement in resisting oppression through means that challenge domination and any other form of injustice, without inflicting injuries on the opponent. For example, when Palestinians in the early phase of the intifada (1987–1989) adopted nonviolent resistance, they were rejecting the Israeli occupation, actively fighting its oppression, and not surrendering.

There is a complete compatibility between such methods of nonviolence and Islamic values and beliefs that instruct the faithful to resist injustice and oppression, and pursue justice and *sabr* (patience), protect the sacredness of human dignity, and be willing to sacrifice their lives for this cause. To fulfill and follow these values, the Islamic approach to nonviolence can only be based on active rejection and resistance of *zulm* (aggression) and injustice. If we accept the assumption and belief that Islam emphasizes resistance and pursuit of justice, then the real question becomes: Can non-violence be an effective tool for resistance?

There are many examples by which we can illustrate the use of non-violent methods in Islamic history and context. Probably the best known example is the thirteen years of nonviolent struggle and resistance of the Prophet (PBUH) in the Meccan context. No single violent act or expression was used or even legitimized by the Prophet or his early followers. Muslims were not passive and they did not surrender to their fate; on the contrary, they preached their message and faith and confronted nonbelievers on a daily basis.

The opposing argument is that Muslims later fought many battles and chose to defend themselves using swords and other weapons. But their intention and guiding Islamic teachings were not a struggle or jihad to kill or physically eliminate the others. On the contrary, the objective was to defend the faith and pursue justice, protect human lives, and accept death as *Shahada fi Sabil Allah* ("martyrdom in the cause of Allah"). Within that context Caliphs Abu Bakr and Ali preached their famous instructions to their military not to kill older men, women, children, animals, or trees.

Considering modern weapon systems and the massive destruction that even the smallest war will cause, it is clear that any violent act using such weapons will be violating the above Islamic teachings. In the case of Palestine, nonviolent resistance provides us with an opportunity and framework to resist and to pursue justice without inflicting physical harm or suffering on the "other." The power of Islamic nonviolent resistance is its appeal to the morality and humanity in every person, even the occupying soldiers. It is human *fitra* (nature) to know and discover the right and sacred in God's creation. Islamic nonviolent methods through unity and steadfastness can "force and persuade" the aggressors of the just cause.

Such methods, if organized and designed correctly and implemented systematically, can mobilize far broader segments of the Palestinian people in resisting oppression and provide the resister, or *mujahid,* with a sense of power and dignity far more than the effect that a suicide bomb leaves in the mind and heart of the same mujahid or his supporters. Such nonviolent methods can also prevent further dehumanization of Palestinians and Muslims around the world and convey a more powerful and sacred Islamic message of resistance.

Abdul Ghaffar Khan, the Muslim Pashtun tribal leader who was imprisoned by the British for over fifteen years, managed to mobilize 100,000 Muslim soldiers who each signed a ten-point pledge in which they swore to serve God, sacrifice their life and wealth for their people, oppose hatred, live by nonviolent principles, and not expect or desire reward for the service. As a devout Muslim leader, he unleashed the nonviolent force of Islam: "I am going to give you such a weapon that the police and the army will not be able to stand against. It is the weapon of the Prophet, but you are not aware of it. That weapon is patience and righteousness. No power on earth can stand against it." Palestinians can follow the same path in mobilizing hundreds of thousands of nonviolent soldiers instead of relying on small armed groups or individual bombers.

When examining Muslim societies and governments around the globe, their efforts or race to arm themselves in the name of liberating Palestine have been disastrous to their people and have brought internal destruction and victimhood. Similarly, when resisters use violent strategies, it becomes impossible to draw a clear line of when violence is legitimate and when it is not. Palestinians have used violent means internally to settle their differences in Lebanon. An Islamic nonviolent resistance approach and framework can eliminate the possibility of internal Muslim wars and violence too.

There is no lack of Islamic values of nonviolent resistance or historical examples of such practices in Islamic history and tradition. There is a need to widen a campaign of systematic efforts to theologically continue conceptualizing and articulating the Islamic nonviolent resistance philosophy, and to support the emerging efforts of establishing global and local Muslim nonviolent resistance movements to confront the current "Islamophopia" sweeping the world and to engage the masses in supporting the liberation of Palestine.

Palestinian Nonviolent Direct Action and Joint Participation

It is imperative that Israeli and Palestinian supporters of solidarity and nonviolent direct action coordinate and conduct joint actions. This principle and its practice are essential for the success of movements on both sides. However, such cooperation has its challenges, including language, meeting places (groups often meet on the Israeli side), negotiating internal organizational power relations, decisionmaking practices, and restrictions imposed by the reality of the occupation (what an Israeli can do versus what a Palestinian cannot do). In joint binational activities the decisionmaking processes used for selecting group action is constantly tested and challenged by the limits of binational partnership. Coordinated action, the impact of activities and their meaning, are continuously considered according to the evaluative standards of the three communities (Israeli-Jews, Palestinians living in Israel, and the Palestinians under occupation).

The experience of Ta'ayush, an Arab-Jewish joint group, offers some insight into these challenges:

> We also understood that just creating a joint Arab-Jewish group is not enough, by itself, to enable us to make a real contribution to establishing peace and equality. During the first discussions it became clear to us that we have to break with the old concept of "co-existence." Co-existence, and many of the joint dialogue groups based on this concept, served, intentionally or even unconsciously, to perpetuate unequal relations of power between

the two communities. They civilized them through dialogue without questioning them. Moreover, for some of us, co-existence meant a search for civilized patterns of interaction between antagonist communities, while tacitly accepting the essential division into two different—and often opposing—national-ethnic groups, one of them occupying the position of the dominant majority and the other that of a subaltern minority. Co-existence initiatives mitigated some of the segregation practices and offered a much fairer treatment to the minority; this is important. But they are based on the acceptance of the supposedly ascriptive identities as something immutable, as well as the Jewish identity of the State of Israel.[64]

Joint activities are the main window through which an image of the reality of the occupation can be transmitted and framed in a constructive way for political change in Israel. As in the struggle against South African apartheid (when white South Africans needed to be confronted with the reality and consequences of apartheid), the nonviolent resistance can be moved to the Israeli majority's streets and homes, in ways that cannot be manipulated to justify aggression. Nonviolent resistance leaves the Israeli government and policies with no justification of or escape from their acts of injustice against the Palestinians. For many Palestinians, joint activities allow humane forms of interaction with other types of Israelis and prevent further dehumanization.

Notes

Special thanks to Mubarak Awad, Eitan Alimi, Edy Kaufman, Walid Salem, Lucy Nusseibeh, and Maiai Carter, who have read the various versions of this chapter and made constructive comments. I am also grateful to Juliette Verhoeven and Lambrecht Wessels for their support and input.

1. H. Tom Hastings, *Meek Ain't Weak: Nonviolent Power and People of Color* (New York: University Press of America, 2002).

2. Mohammed Abu-Nimer, *Nonviolence and Peace Building in Islam* (Gainesville: University Press of Florida, 2003).

3. Martin Luther King Jr., "Nonviolence and Racial Justice," *Christian Century* (February 6, 1957): 165–167.

4. Mulford Sibley, *The Political Theories of Modern Pacifism: An Analysis and Criticism* (Philadelphia: American Friends Service Committee, 1944), p. 21.

5. Abdul Jawad Saleh, "The Palestinian Nonviolent Resistance Movement," *Live from Palestine,* Nancy Stohlman and Laurieann Aladin, eds. (Cambridge: South End Press, 2003), p. 49.

6. James Scott, *Weapons of the Eak: Everyday Forms of Peasant Resistance* (New Haven, CT: Yale University Press, 1985).

7. Stohlman and Aladin, p. 184.

8. Certain Israeli peace activists, too, have recognized the Palestinian right to resist the occupation: "The occupied party's resistance to the occupier is its moral right. Its violent resistance to the occupation is a direct result of the violence of the occupation itself." Adi Ophir, "A Time of Occupation," in *The Other Israel Voices of Refusal and Dissent,* Roan Carey and Jonathan Shainin, eds. (New York, The New Press, 2002), p. 61.

9. Howaida Araf and Adam Shapiro have stated that such position allowed them to get more credibility among Palestinian public in support of nonviolence (American University, March 2003).

10. Stohlman and Aladin, p. 67.

11. David McDowall, *The Palestinians: The Road to Nationhood* (London: Minority Rights Publications, 1994), pp. 96–98.

12. Souad Dajani, *Eyes Without a Country: Searching for a Palestinian Strategy of Liberation* (Philadelphia: Temple University Press, 1995), p. 67.

13. Mubarak Awad, "Nonviolent Resistance: A Strategy for the Occupied Territories," *Journal of Palestine Studies* 13, 4 (Summer, 1984): 22–36.

14. Gene Sharp, *The Politics of Non-Violent Action,* vol. 2 (Boston: P. Sargent, 1973).

15. Yossi Melman and Dan Raviv, *Behind the Uprising: Israelis, Jordanians, and Palestinians* (Westport, CT: Greenwood, 1989), p. 200.

16. Sara Roy, *The Gaza Strip: The Political Economy of De-Development* (Jerusalem: Institute for Palestine Studies, 1995).

17. Jeff Halper, "The Key to Peace: Dismantling the Matrix of Control," in *The Other Israel Voices of Refusal and Dissent,* Roan Carey and Jonathan Shainin, eds. (New York, The New Press, 2002), 37.

18. *Washington Post,* February 11, 2004.

19. The Coordination Committee invited one of the Palestinian local leaders of the international solidarity nonviolence campaign to debrief and be a liaison for such a campaign. For details of these meetings see January 2001 coverage in *Al Ayam, Ha'aretz,* and *Jerusalem Post.*

20. Several members of the Palestinians legislative council called for dismantling the PNA structure in December 2003 (see *Ha'aretz,* December 2003).

21. See Palestinian Human Rights Monitoring Group report by Bassam Eid and Gaza Center for Mental Health Directors report by Eyad Sarraj.

22. Adam Shapiro argues that such actions were effective in reducing Israeli military shooting at Palestinian protesters when foreigners were spotted in the middle. A tragic exception occurred when in April 2003 Tom Hurndal, a British ISM volunteer, was shot in the head and later died in January 2004.

23. David Hall-Cathalah, *The Peace Movement in Israel 1967–1987* (New York: St Martin's Press, 1990); Mordechai Bar-On, *In Pursuit of Peace: A History of the Israeli Peace Movement* (Washington, D.C.: United State Institute of Peace Press, 1996).

24. Tom Segev, "Foreword," in *The Other Israel Voices of Refusal and Dissent,* Roan Carey and Jonathan Shainin, eds. (New York: The New Press, 2002), p. xi.

25. Ophir, p. 58.

26. Ilan Pappe, "Break the Mirror Now," in *The Other Israel Voices of Refusal and Dissent,* Roan Carey and Jonathan Shainin, eds. (New York: The New Press, 2002), pp. 113–114.

27. Orna Sasson-Levy, "Feminism and Military Gender Practices: Israeli Women Soldiers in 'Masculine' Roles," *Sociological Inquiry* 73, no. 3 (2003).

28. Stohlman and Aladin, p. 70.

29. Ascherman, joined by two others, went on trial for interfering with police during demolitions of two Palestinian homes. In one case, he blocked a bulldozer and in another, he refused to leave the roof of a house designated for destruction. The houses were destroyed on the grounds they were built without permits. See Ben Lynfield. "Activist Rabbi Faces Trial in Israel," *The Christian Science Monitor,* January 20, 2004.

30. Mohammed Abu-Nimer, *Nonviolence and Peace Building in Islam* (Gainesville: University Press of Florida, 2003).

31. Cynthia Johnston, "Palestinian Town Claims Victory for Non-Violence," Reuters. *Washington Post,* March 19, 2004.

32. Stohlman and Aladin, p. 69.

33. Huwaida Arraf, quoted in ibid.

34. Ibid., p. 59.

35. A third initiative has been launched by Nonviolent Peaceforce, which uses interpositioning, accompaniment, presence, and witnessing as the main tactics in working for peace (David Grant and Juliette Verhoeven, Nonviolent Peaceforce, Washington D.C., Fall 2003).

36. See ISM and Gush Shalom reports. Sami Awad, Huwaida Arraf, and other Palestinians and US trainers have been responding to calls for nonviolence training in various Palestinian communities. Awad conducted training for students in Jenin area and declared that "the majority of Palestinians are not involved in acts of violence and armed resistance against Israeli occupation . . . a growing majority is calling for nonviolent resistance," Jonathan Curiel, "Palestinian Activist Touts Nonviolent Resistance to Occupation," *San Francisco Chronicle,* June 12, 2003.

37. Mark Schneider, "International Direct Action: The Spanish Revolution to the Palestinian Intifada," in Stohlman and Aladin, p. 85.

38. Stohlman and Aladin, p. 182.

39. Ibid., p. 182.

40. Based on correspondence with Lucy Nuseeibeh, March 2004.

41. He refused to receive the prestigious award of Israel Prize when the committee debated awarding him the prize following his call to refuse service in the occupied territories and compared the Special Units of the Israeli army to the Nazi SS.

42. Anthony Lewis, "Introduction," in *The Other Israel: Voices of Refusal and Dissent,* Roan Carey and Jonathan Shainin, eds. (New York: The New Press, 2002).

43. It was a letter from hundreds of army officers that placed enormous pressure on Begin to negotiate with Egyptian president Anwar Sadat in early 1977, and the letter is recognized as a trigger for the mobilization of Peace Now as a political movement for peace since 1970s.

44. In January 2004, a group of Israeli pilots declared that they would no longer follow commands to bomb Palestinian civilian targets.

45. *Jerusalem Post,* December 20, 2003.

46. Yigal Shochat, "Red Line, Green Line, Black Flag," in *The Other Israel Voices of Refusal and Dissent,* Roan Carey and Jonathan Shainin, eds. (New York: The New Press, 2002), p. 130.

47. See the *Jerusalem Post* and *Ha'aretz,* December 27, 2003.

48. Ishai Menuchin, "Saying No to Israel's Occupation," in *The Other Israel Voices of Refusal and Dissent,* Roan Carey and Jonathan Shainin, eds. (New York: The New Press, 2002), 124.

49. Michael Ben-Yair, "The Six-Day's War's Seventh Day," in *The Other Israel Voices of Refusal and Dissent,* Roan Carey and Jonathan Shainin, eds. (New York: The New Press, 2002), p. 15.

50. Ibid.

51. Adam Shapiro Interview, American University, December 12, 2004.

52. Ali Abunimeh, "On Violence and the Intifada," in *Live from Palestine: International and Palestinian Direct Action Against the Israeli Occupation,* Nancy Stohlman and Laurieann Aladin, eds. (Cambridge, MA: South End Press, 2003), p. 59.

53. Jonathan Kuttab, "Why Nonviolence Campaigns Are Effective—Nonviolent Resistance in Palestine: Pursuing Alternative Strategies," *CPAP,* March/April 2003.

54. Mubarak Awad and the author discussed the march to Bethlehem with members of the Palestinian leadership (*Nonviolence International,* December 2002). In addition, hundreds of international solidarity groups and Palestinian activists associated with nonviolence urged the Palestinian Authority leadership to launch the march to Bethlehem, February 10, 2004.

55. Yetzhak Laor, "A Report Published on September 6, 2002," *Ma'arive* (a right-wing newspaper) September 6, 2002.

56. Responses from direct nonviolent action discussion group in Jerusalem, March 2003.

57. Shafiqu Muneer, http://Islamonline.net/Arabic/contemporary/2003/12/article01e.shtml, 2003. Some Palestinian factions and activists attempted to organize a massive return of refugees to Palestine using ships from Lebanon and Cyprus. However, the efforts to organize such symbolic acts were not completed, http://Islamonline.net/Arabic/contemporary/2003/12/article01e.shtml.

58. Adam Shapiro Interview, American University, December 12, 2004.

59. Mordechai Bar-On (*In Pursuit of Peace: A History of the Israeli Peace Movement,* Washington, D.C., United States Institute of Peace Press, 1996) and other Israeli authors have documented the fact that Israeli peace groups stopped their efforts and protest after the Oslo declaration of principles.

60. Jonathan Kuttab and Mubarak Awad, March, 2003.

61. Mubarak Awad and Abu-Nimer, Search For Common Ground Newsletter, March 2003.

62. Portions of the following discussion have appeared as an earlier draft in Mohammed Abu-Nimer, "Islam Does Not Correspond with Nonviolence: Nonviolence in the Islamic Context," part of series of views on "Nonviolence," *Al Hayat Newspaper,* August 17, 2003, published in partnership with the Common Ground News Service (CGNews).

63. Khalid Kishtainy, *Dalil Al Muatuin Al Madani* ("Citizen Manual for Civil Jihad") (London: Al-Radid, 1998); Khalis M. Jalabi, *Sikulujiyyat al-Unf wa Istratijiyyat al-Amal al-Silmi* ("The Psychology of Violence and the Strategy of Peaceful Action") (Damascus: Dar al-Fikr, 1998); Jawdat Said, "Peace—Or Nonviolence—in History and with the Prophet," paper presented at the Forum on Islam and Peace in the Twenty-First Century, American University, 1997.

64. Gerardo Leibner, unpublished conference paper, May 2003.

7

Two Peoples, One Civil Society

Shalom (Shuli) Dichter and Khaled Abu-Asba

This chapter deals with whether cooperation between civil society organizations comprising both Palestinian[1] and Jewish citizens of Israel have a chance to promote reconciliation in the region and, if so, to what extent?

Between the Mediterranean Sea and the Jordan River there exists, in effect, a conflict within a conflict. There is the broad conflict between the state of Israel and the Palestinian people that harbors an internal conflict within the state of Israel, between the Palestinian Arab citizens and the Jewish majority. Citizenship in Israel serves as an arena for this conflict. These two conflicts are interconnected, yet, so far, the broader conflict has significantly influenced the internal conflict in Israel, while the influence of local relationships on the broader situation has remained limited. Could reconciliation of the internal conflict in Israel positively affect the reconciliation of the overall conflict? Should civil society be expected to act as a catalyst in this process, and in what way?

In order to shed light on the reasons that currently hold back the Israeli civil society from fulfilling a more meaningful role in the Israeli-Palestinian conflict, we will examine the implications of the lack of state neutrality toward various groups within its borders. Today, the population of the state of Israel is made up of 81 percent Jews and 19 percent Palestinians, and these numbers are not expected to change over the next twenty years. Inside its borders, the state of Israel discriminates between its Jewish and Arab citizens, the discrimination itself also serves as a factor of conflict between them. But could the citizens, on their part, avoid entering the pattern of conflict imposed on them by the state?

Since civil society fashions its worldview and defines its needs independently of the government, we believe that a meaningful and constructive role is meant for civil-society actors in Israel. Civil society in Israel has the potential of constructing a viable alternative to the existing policy, both between Jews and Palestinians inside Israel, and between Israel and the Palestinian people as a whole. Nevertheless, past experiences point to a difficulty in realizing this role.

Civil society constitutes a broad arena for Jewish and Palestinian activities that promote relations between the two groups that may lead to true equality. Yet, in reality it does not fulfill this role. Most of the joint Jewish and Palestinian activities are still played out in marginal areas such as youth and children's activities, culture, and society, but are not intended to change government policy.[2] In this chapter we discuss this issue, examine the factors leading to the restricted role of civil society in Israel, and finally propose a possible way of changing this situation.

Relationships Between Jews and Palestinians in Israel as an Impetus for Organizations' Participation in the Peace Process

The reality in Israel is in fact binational because the two basic elements of the population are Jews and the Palestinians. The formality that both are citizens of the state did not succeed in softening the sting of the built-in, historical conflict between the two groups. On the contrary: citizenship in Israel has become one of the arenas of the Jewish–Palestinian conflict in the region. There is a deep-seated disagreement in this arena, between the Israeli state and the Palestinian citizens regarding their lack of access to state resources.[3] Furthermore, Palestinians in Israel do not see eye to eye with Jewish citizens about the former's inferior social status.

Jews and Palestinians are the two main groups in the country, akin to two tectonic plates resting beneath the surface of Israel's historical and political reality. More than any other conflict or "split," the conflict between them will be the one to determine the future of the state. In this situation any above-ground structure in the state of Israel—social, economic, organizational, political, or cultural—will be affected by the nature of the relations between these two forces, and mainly by their movements caused by the friction between them.

It is commonly assumed that there exists a fundamental disagreement between Palestinians and Jews in Israel regarding the definition of the state as Jewish. This disagreement is based on the assumption that the roots of the institutionalized division between Jews and Arabs, as well as the reality of a "lesser citizenship" of Palestinians in Israel, lie in the very definition of the state as "Jewish," serving as the main tool to fulfilling the aspirations of the Zionist movement. According to this approach, possibility of equal citizenship between Israelis and Palestinians in Israel does not exist as long as the state is defined as Jewish and its symbols are Jewish. The symbols, and more important, the definition express the exclusiveness of the Jews in the context of Israeli citizenship.

On the other hand, it has been claimed that the test of Israel's equal treatment of its Palestinian citizens is essentially practical and does not stem from the official definitions of the state. According to this approach it is this practical test that steers Palestinian public opinion in Israel. This approach claims that acting consistently to close the gaps between Jews and Palestinians in Israel may bring about a significant turnabout in the Palestinian public's attitude. Figure 7.1 illustrates a monitoring of Palestinian public opinion regarding its willingness to accept the Jewish and Zionist definitions of the state. The figure clearly shows that in 1995 such a turning point took place: an increase of about 100 percent in those who accept the Jewish-Zionist definition of the state. The reasons for this turnaround at the time are varied: (1) Progress in the Israeli-Palestinian peace proves projected positively; (2) Prime Minister Rabin used a "safety net" provided by Arab members of the Knesset to pass the Oslo Accords in the Knesset and ensure support for the agreement; and (3) The Rabin administration recognized the discrimination against Palestinian citizens up to that time and began implementing practical measures to close the gaps, particularly in the area of physical infrastructure.[4] These three factors, one of which is external and the other two internal, probably caused the Palestinians in Israel to assume that state's conflict with their people was being settled, while they were also beginning to assert their status as citizens in the state.

Figure 7.1 indicates a halt in the government's policy of development from the mid-1990s on. Despite the changes that occurred in the status of Palestinians in Israel in their quality of living and in education, as well as in areas of society and culture, their sad state did not change. This misery comes mainly from a consensus among the Jewish majority in Israel that views citizenship as exclusive to Jews. From this stems, in practice, the marginal status of Palestinian citizens.

Since Israel's creation, its Palestinian citizens have been perceived as a security or demographic threat who will some day outnumber the Jews. The military rule over the Palestinian citizens for the first two decades was replaced by a tight security supervision by Shin Bet, mainly through the education system. For many years, the classical sociological approach to research of Arab Palestinian society in Israel has been dominant. This approach argues that intensive contact with the modern Israeli society is the main factor in advancing the development of an underdeveloped Palestinian Arab society. That is, the traditional culture and social structure of the underdeveloped society is the main factor that delays this development: the internal characteristics of Arab society in Israel, particularly its traditional nature, are the central variables that explain its marginal place in Israeli society. This view has been criticized by such prominent researchers as the sociologist Rozenhak,[5] mainly for its view of Arab Israelis' place in Israel in terms of friction between traditionalism and modernism, and for neglecting

**Figure 7.1 Does Israel Have the Right to Exist as a Jewish-Zionist State?
A Multiyear Poll of Arab Citizens**

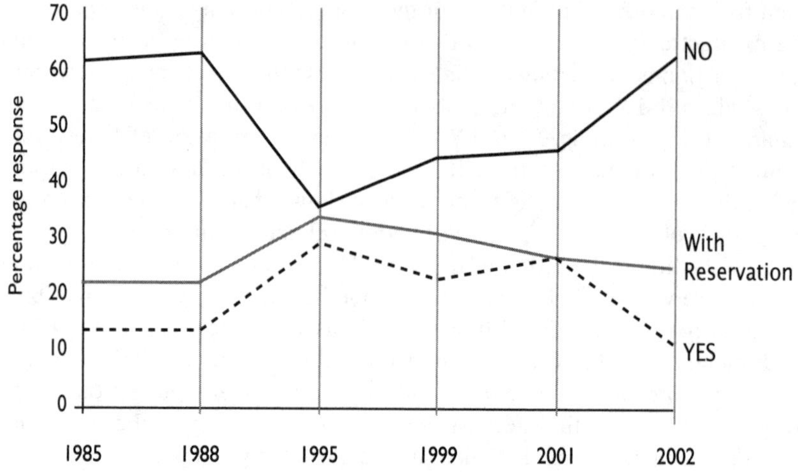

Source: Survey conducted by Sammy Smooha, Haifa University.

to examine the condition of structural subordination of Arabs in Israel more fully and deeply. In other words, numerous mechanisms, from security forces to teachers in state schools, have contributed to preserving the existing balance of powers in which the Jews are the main benefactors of the state and their perception of their treatment of Palestinians is tolerance and benevolence. This, then, is an acceptance that arises not from acknowledging the principle of pluralism, but as a tactic to perpetuate the existing situation.[6]

Under the historical conditions that exist here, and especially under the shadow of the "tectonic relations" between Jews and Palestinians in Israel, it seems that this delicate fabric may be torn by the slightest movement beneath the ground of Israeli reality.[7] And yet so immense is the Jews' difficulty to deal with the issue that they would prefer to leave the inequities intact—as well as the resulting friction to which they are subject—if only so as not to engage in a fundamental change in the relationship. It seems that there is a great apprehension among Jews of altering the form of the relations because, in their view, it may cost them their favored position in Israel. Moreover, the Jews fear very much a loss in principle as a result of a just sharing of national resources with the Palestinian citizens. This loss is not simply material, but a surrender of the very advantage perceived as the essence of the Jewish existence in Israel as the sole Jewish state in the world.

This has to do not only with Jews as a whole, but also with most of those who labor to bring Jews and Arabs closer. Of all organizations that deal with Jewish-Arab relations, only 4 percent work to truly change the reality by challenging the discriminatory system.[8] The rest work within the perception of existing power relations. The dominance of Jews in these organizations is no secret, which helps explain why only 4 percent strive for a true change. Below are some of the findings of the Israeli Institute for Democracy from 2003 that show how difficult it would be to change Israeli Jewish public opinion:

- 53 percent of the Jews in Israel oppose equal rights between Jewish and Arab citizens
- 57 percent of the Jews in Israel support government encouragement of Arab emigration from Israel
- 69 percent of the Jews in Israel oppose Arab participation in governing coalitions
- 77 percent of the Jews in Israel think that there must be a "Jewish majority" for crucial national decisions

Palestinians in Israel do not share in feeling an ownership over the state, and also are not an actual part of the Palestinian struggle. Since they lack status and genuine power in the Israeli public sphere, they have no influence on the agenda in this context. They are perceived by large segments of the Jewish public as a "fifth column." Furthermore, if they did take part in the Oslo process, it was only as a parliamentary safety net, that is, in a passive role at best. In addition, Jews do not consider them a real part of the Palestinian struggle, which is characterized as multidimensional—political and military—none of which the Palestinian citizens of Israel are part of. Their partnership in the struggle is reflected only in the civil aspect: aid shipments of money, food, and medicine, and the holding of demonstrations in support of their brothers across the Green Line.

The Oslo process constituted a watershed for Palestinians in Israel. They were not included in the process by either side, Israeli or Palestinian, accentuating their marginality and mostly their sense of isolation. These sentiments brought about a renewed process of examining their collective identity. In the winter of 1993–1994, the Arab Supreme Monitoring Committee in Israel held a series of public seminars aimed at redefining their identity and the needs of Palestinians in Israel. By doing so, the Palestinian leadership in Israel began a decade of Palestinian institutional recuperation.

And yet this recuperation is not necessarily steered by the committee. The new wave in which national identity was consolidated, the "stand-tall generation," strengthened the abilities of the Palestinians in Israel to organize.[9] They fill the ranks of associations for self-help, advocacy, and the struggle for equality inside Israel. At the center of this process is the establishment of dozens of new associations and the sharpening of internal historical discussion in the society. With the assistance of those from their parents' generation who have not been worn down trying to assimilate themselves into the state, the activists in these associations steer the internal discourse toward empowerment and a shift in discourse with Jews. In other words, it is a powerful positioning of the self that does not accept the reality of inequality but strives for equality in all senses: the citizens versus the state and the personal and collective in the discourse with Jews.[10]

In contrast to this approach, some researchers attribute only little stability to this development. Eli Rekhess holds that since 1993 parallel processes have begun, both in ripening social and economic changes among the Palestinian population in Israel and in the beginning of a reconciliation process between Israel and the Arab world.[11] Rekhess calls the relations "shifting sands," meaning a fluid, dynamic condition resulting from the influence of internal and external factors.[12] According to this approach, movements in Palestinian society are reactions to the Israeli government's actions and do not necessarily develop from internal processes.

The October 2000 events in which the police shot dead thirteen demonstrators in demonstrations held by Arab citizens of Israel, marked another milestone in the relations between the two populations, and had a great impact on the awareness of Palestinian citizens of majority-minority relations and Israel's treatment of the Palestinian minority.[13] According to Ghanem,

> The discomfort of the Palestinian citizens as citizens in the state was expressed in the massive confrontations of thousands of them with security forces after the killing of the Palestinians in Umm El-Fahem. When the issue is the rights of the Arabs in Israel, the Jewish political leadership stands as one in order to explain and justify the government policy, and refrains from protecting the Arab minority in Israel.[14]

In opposition to this view, Neuberger claims that characterizing the Israeli-Jewish society as one standing against the Arab minority is erroneous. He believes the Israeli-Jewish society is a society polarized between the religious-hawkish "national camp" and the secular-dovish "peace camp". Each of these camps has a different approach toward the Arab minority. Thus, when the relations between the Arab minority and the Israeli Jews are analyzed, one has to take into account the diversity of each Israeli-Jewish camp.[15]

We assume that the growing trend of open and authentic dialogue that takes place both in academia and in civil society acknowledges the conflict and relies on each side's ties to its own identity and interests could build more fruitful relations between the Jewish and Palestinian organizations as well as cooperating organizations. The fruitfulness of these relations will be tested by the ability of these organizations to influence their environment in civil society and to influence the policies of the government.

Different Organizations in Israeli Civil Society

Within the conglomerate of civil-society organizations in Israel, only a few are involved in the peace process between Israel and the Palestinian Authority. There is a clear distinction in Israel between organizations that look inward to the structure and quality of citizenship in Israel and those that view overall Israeli-Palestinian relations as the focus of reference. Before briefly surveying the types of organizations, we will outline the structural relations between Jews and Palestinians in Israel that influence possible partnerships.

Genuine joint action in the civil society in Israel is supposed to reflect the interests and agendas of both sides, assuming the over one-hundred-year-old conflict built into them. One can expect the organizations' agenda to be consolidated and to reflect both sides' perception of reality while authentically representing the "magnetic field" they come from, even in the territory of joint action. Because of the relatively democratic and tolerant atmosphere in Israel, one would expect the growth of many such partnerships that could indicate a possible partnership between Jews and Arabs, not beyond the realm of options in the Middle East. Yet this is not the case in reality, and we must examine why.

To the Palestinian citizens, civil-society work in Israel is a framework alternative to the missing state services (see the following "Palestinian Civil Society in Israel"), as well as a framework for the struggle against the state for attaining equality. To Jews, on the other hand, the state has already taken upon itself the national task, leaving them supposedly "free" to engage in partnerships with Palestinians. Yet this is not the case, since there are so many barriers, chief among them the commitment of Jews to the state and the Zionist project in its traditional sense, that is, the establishment of Jewish hegemony in the country through a Jewish state. Most civilian co-operation with Palestinians are subordinate to this mission.

There are many Jewish organizations that employ Arabs, and a number of Palestinian organizations that employ Jews, yet few are the organizations truly joint to Jews and Palestinians in Israel and even fewer are organizations that share ownership, meaning a joint Jewish-Palestinian executive board. As a result of equal distribution of power in an organization, such organizations must form an agenda shared between Jews and Palestinians. This is no easy feat, since each side brings its own solid, particular identity, and does not compromise in this simply for the sake of partnership, in genuine joint organizations points of disagreement arise constantly.

The raison d'être for these organizations is the very fact of partnership between two sides engaged in a conflict and is based on politics of identity. The main objective of these organizations is to use their partnership as leverage to affect government policy and the face of society. Joint organizations, such as the Jewish-Arab Center for Economic Development, the Sikkuy Foundation, Neve Shalom, Osim Shalom, and others, may engage in projects with Palestinians in the occupied territories, yet their main focus of attention is moving the internal Israeli reality toward equality among all citizens. These are civil-rights organizations that base their actions and demands on change for citizenship in Israel.

In contrast, the organizations that actively involve themselves primarily in human rights issues are not under joint sponsorship. These include the Association for Civil Rights in Israel, Adalah, B'Tselem, Physicians for Human Rights, the Arab Human Rights Organization (based in Nazareth), and others. Such organizations have taken up an agenda based on universal principles, and so the identity of the activists is supposedly irrelevant, since by the universal nature of their actions the activists see themselves outside the confines of identity politics.

Ta'ayush, however, is an exception. Being a genuine joint organization, it recognizes identity as a fundamental element of political action, yet its agenda is broader and deals with both citizenship in Israel and peace between Israel and the Palestinians. Therefore Ta'ayush is not constrained as a civil- or human-rights organization. It is not a parliamentary political movement with an agenda even broader than those of Gush Shalom and Peace Now, which focus on promoting peace between Israel and the Palestinians as a whole.

Other organizations involved with the relations between Israel and the Palestinians (e.g., IPCRI, ECF, the Peres Center for Peace) do not consider civil society in Israel their main objective, but work mostly with Track II diplomacy and accelerating the processes between Israel and the Palestinian Authority. This is why it is difficult to associate them with the actions of civil society in Israel. Two exceptions in this context are the Geneva and Ayalon-Nusseibeh initiatives, which recognize the public as an important target for change, yet since these are partnerships between Jews from Israel and Palestinians who are not citizens, they will not be included in this discussion.

The scarcity of joint organizations reflects the Israeli reality, in which Jews and Arabs rarely share the public space. Therefore, it must be asked why, among the Jews, there is not a growing recognition of the necessity of including the Palestinian citizens in the state and establishing healthy relations with them. The question is especially acute in light of structural changes in the Israeli-Jewish society dealing with greater pluralism.[16] It seems that each example of substantial debates that created historical reversals in Israel was somehow tied to a solid foundation in the Jewish-Zionist (or Israeli) consciousness and ethos, whether it be the settling of the land of Israel or the sanctity of lives of the boys being sent to battle.

Yet it remains difficult to point out deep foundations in the Jewish-Zionist ethos that can serve as a cornerstone for civil discourse. Some exceptions include remarks and writings of Theodor Herzl, remarks by the first president of Israel, Chaim Weizman, and the obscure mention of civil equality in the new nation's declaration of independence. Support for civil equality can also be found in the Jewish sources, yet in recent decades these serve aggressive Zionism more than any humanistic ethos.

In Israel's formative years, no civic discourse was created, nor was any organized philosophy to which one could turn today in attempting to consolidate the state's civil character. One philosophy set down by a significant ideology was that of the Shomer Hatzair, a settlement movement that expressed in the 1920s, 1930s, and 1940s a brotherhood of peoples based on socialism. Yet in practice the movement proved to be quite the opposite, aligning itself with Zionist mainstream thinking that ignored the possibility of a shared, equal life with the Palestinians based on joint citizenship.

Despite the claim that a civil society is developing in Israel, the crucial test will be its ability to include all of its citizens with no regard to nationality, even if the state fails to do so. Passing this test is still far away because civil discourse over a joint life with the Palestinians has not yet become concrete yet, nor, of course, has any action toward such an existence.

Yael Yishai has argued that the main attitude of the state toward Jewish civil society has been characterised since the 1980s by "passive exclusion," an attitude of live and let live. According to Shany Payes, such benign attitudes do not apply to Palestinian NGOs in Israel, which operate under continual pressure from the state authorities, wielding everything from threats of job losses to investigation by the police.[17]

Palestinian Civil Society in Israel

In Israel the Oslo Accords gave birth to a process already undergone by the Palestinian minority in Israel, that is, consolidating a sense of a unique collective and a repositioning of the relations with the state (i.e., challenging the relations of control vis-à-vis the Jews).

Data show that Arab civil society organizations make up about 4.5 percent of all NGOs in Israel. This percentage is significantly smaller than their population ratio in Israel (19 percent). Moreover, the number of Arab organizations supported by government offices is minuscule. Only a small fraction, numbering forty-three Arab organizations, qualifies as a public institution in order to receive donations. In comparison, 3,800 Jewish organizations qualify. In recent years there has been an accelerated increase in third-sector organizations among the Palestinian population in Israel.

The autonomous growth of the third sector in Arab society is linked to an attitude toward the Arab population, though citizens of Israel, as an unwanted, hostile element. This attitude is reflected in the government's priorities and creates hardships that remain absent from the overall Israeli public's agenda. The accelerated growth of the third sector can be explained by specific reasons:

- The third sector's lack of commitment to services in Arab society, and/or the incongruity of services by Jewish organizations to the unique culture of the Arab-Palestinian population
- The Palestinian population's lack of accessibility to government offices
- An under-representation of Arab social capital, specifically among the intellectuals, in institutionalized areas of the state

Palestinian members of the Knesset may be able to deliver a piece of the pie of the state's resources that their voters deserve, thus gaining access to resources and budgets through the different Knesset committees. The Knesset serves as an "open market" for deals between parties and members, who work for their voters. Each party looks after its voters by cutting deals with other parties, even when it is outside the coalition government. It is able to do so because all sides are aware that during the next administration it may be part of a coalition government and thus will be able to return favors to other parties that are part of the new government but may not be afterward. Herein lies the problem: Palestinian members of the Knesset are unable to return any favors during future administrations because they are never part of a coalition government. Aside from minute parliamentary manipulations, they lack any real power in the Knesset, and if they wield any power it is limited to giving speeches in the general assembly. This is why parliamentary action has ceased to be held in high regard, while the Palestinian population in Israel no longer expects it to instigate a genuine change.

In contrast to ineffective parliamentary action, the importance of civil-society organizations has only increased. While Jewish civil-society organizations complement government action and work closely with it, identifying with the Zionist "general goal," Palestinian civil-society organizations stand against the government. Even when achieving what the government has failed to accomplish (the Palestinian Galilee Society for Health Research and Services, for example, has built clinics for mothers and children), they do it not through coordination and cooperation, but for lack of choice and as a protest to encourage the government to do its job.

This provides a true window for setting projects in motion and matching services to the needs and the culture of Palestinian society in Israel. Such Palestinian organizations as the Galilee Society, Association for Student Guidance, Women against Violence, and especially the Islamic Movement, which has created a wide network of social services particularly for children, are all a hybrid array of welfare, education, and health services. The exclusion of the Arab population has led to the development of autonomous welfare services that not only aid the state in providing services, but also provide employment to a wide stratum of academics. These organizations often complement or substitute for the state not because of liberal ideology, but solely as a constraint.

Compared with organizations that provide services, there are a small number of advocacy organizations in Palestinian society (although the proportion of advocacy organizations among Arab NGOs in Israel is double the rate among their Jewish counterparts). These organizations are universal in that they provide for the entire Arab population throughout the country. This is evident in the frequent use of "Arab" in the organizations' titles. Women's organizations that advocate feminist ideas are an exception.

Most Jewish organizations disregard the Arab population, while only a small number of advocacy organizations, such as the Association for Civil Rights, are equally committed to both populations.

Jewish-Palestinian Relations in Israel and Their Effect on the Development of Civil Society

A society in conflict is in fact a society of sectors that clearly defines who is in and who is out, who belongs to one camp and who does not. Some claim that the relations between the two populations in Israel are headed for an inevitable collision,[18] while others argue that both groups use a strategy of mutual accommodation.[19] Either way, to take a step toward a civil society common to both Jewish and Palestinian citizens, there is no doubt a need for an honest and prolonged dialogue between the two publics. Examination of the existing limitations that delay the integration of Palestinian citizens into Israeli society must be examined.

The conflict between the two communities inside the Green Line is mostly nonviolent but is continual. The struggle between the national Palestinian movement and the national Zionist movement influences greatly the status of the Palestinian minority in Israel. Even though the Arab minority's claims and status were never of a high priority in Israeli public policy, at local and regional levels there have been many changes in the relations between Jews and Arabs.

One central change is the elimination of military rule in 1966, yet its ramification came into full effect ten years later—particularly on the first "Land Day" in March 1976, when six protesting civilians were killed by Israeli security forces and the consequences of that episode.[20] The 1970s were a time when economic changes in Israeli society began taking root, namely democratization, the strengthening of Israeli news media, various globalization processes, privatization and economic growth, the strengthening of human rights, and a growing awareness among the Arab population of its ability to use both political and legal mechanisms.

In Israeli academic circles there is a widespread theoretical attitude toward the friction between nationalism and nationality in the state of Israel, and in that context, toward the Jewish–Palestinian conflict in the state. This view claims that the essence and definition of the state as Jewish creates the structure that prevents equal citizenship: without tackling them, talk of taming the conflict is useless. Others argue that the struggles that touch people's lives enough to answer their expectations and aspirations are good to sustain relations that can be lived with for many generations.

Yet between the option of revolution and slow change, there lies the widespread option in Israeli civil society, which is to preserve Jewish control in Israel in "pleasant ways" (i.e., through "the coexistence culture").

Dialogue Between the Ruler and the Ruled

Since the creation of the state, dialogue between Jews and Palestinians in Israel has taken place informally in different frameworks—at workplaces and universities, in trade and business, in the media, and so on. One of its central characteristics is the unequal relations between ruler and ruled. These relations were underlined first by military rule and then by that of the security forces, the education system, and other elements of the state, which were perceived by the Palestinians more as mechanisms of control than service-providing systems. Thus, the relations between those meeting on the street, in the hospital, or in the business place have been shaped according to the relations fixed by the state from its inception. Throughout the years a pattern of controlled behavior was created among Palestinians, which was construed by Jews as a "common" behavior. This situation was cultivated by the state and supported by the Jewish public.

The Dialogue and Its Results

During the 1980s different plans for a structured, literal dialogue were developed. These rose to the surface along with Palestinians' discontent with the situations having been imposed on them. These initiatives remained marginal to the general public, both Jewish and Arab, and were attended by a few dozen youths who would occasionally aid in facilitating larger circles composed mostly of high school students. Though it is not unlikely that tens of thousands of students participated in different dialogue workshops over the years, this dialogue remained marginal in the Arab public's experience. The different dialogue initiatives may have eased the hostility and resentment that accumulated in the wake of the imposed "coexistence," but they failed to bring about a genuine change. Therefore, one should add, they also created a sense of disappointment that may have aggravated hostility.[21]

For the Jewish participants this meant an effort to have the Palestinians accept the former's presence in the country. The structures were Jewish, as naturally were the initiatives and the planning. During most meetings the power relations echoed those outside this framework of dialogue: from researchers' analyses we learn of the majority's dominance instead of the minority's passivity.[22] These were not areas where the situation of control was confronted but rather where it was perpetuated. Research recommendations from the 1980s have never been implemented in a way that allows an essential transformation. Research from a decade later points only to a very small change in educational patterns of action, which remains more rhetorical than practical. Those Palestinians who took upon themselves dialogue with the Jews and who were expected to deliver results usually came back to their public with words only. In the eyes of the "proud generation," this generation that tried to communicate with the Jews and assimilate is regarded as the "eroded generation."[23]

During the 1990s, the majority of communication frameworks served only to preserve the existing reality through ongoing talks, while only a small, brave part of the Palestinian population worked to create a partnership through genuine dialogue. Generally speaking, while Jews acquired friends on the personal level, and gained sympathy for their Palestinian friends on the political level, only a few engaged in a dialogue intended to bring about an open, civil struggle for the equal distribution of national resources.[24] Jews continued to benefit from the relatively large portion of the pie without opposition. The Palestinian share, as already mentioned, remained the ongoing and accumulating disappointment. Furthermore, most efforts during the 1980s and 1990s were made by the young rather than adults.

The historical creation of a "delicate fabric" of relations had been minimal and impoverished.

The aforementioned has played a large part in the range of activities in Israel's civil society, which is particularly evident in the most recent Jewish-Arab activity in 2003. Indeed, the array of activities aimed at preserving the current situation is very developed, and in this context we will try to examine what confronts those who continue to strive to change the situation in civil society.

Civil Society as a Framework for the Struggle for Equality

Civil-society organizations are engaged mainly in a struggle based on shaping an ideological view of the character of the state. As opposed to representatives in parliament and political parties, civil-society organizations are not bound to definitive political solutions. Therefore, their commitments and real abilities to obtain those solutions are very limited and derive from their degree of pressure and indirect influence on those in office in parliament and administration.

In Israel, the ideological challenge against the state is channeled by political parties through the institutional political system. In this area almost any stance regarding the future of the political framework is legitimate, yet already in 2001 the central election committee disqualified the candidacies of Ahmad Tibi and Azmi Bishara to the Knesset, as well as the Balad Party, because the committee did not accept their positions on future political settlements. Israel's Supreme Court overturned the committee's decision a few weeks later. Civil-society organizations, however, usually refrain from voicing a clear political stance and, therefore, involve themselves mainly in social-justice issues.[25] Yet it is exactly those questions dealing with equality between the Jewish majority and the Arab minority that are on the fine line between purely social issues that do not challenge the political structure and totally shake up the state's structure.

In Israel's declaration of independence there is an unequivocal declaration covering full equality among citizens, but the definition of the state itself is "Jewish."[26] One could assume that a contradiction between these two declarations is innate, and indeed the first fifty-six years of the state's existence do show that there is still no full equality between the Jewish and the Palestinian citizens. However, almost half a million citizens who are not Jews according to Jewish law who have emigrated from the former Soviet Union have been granted citizenship by Israel's Law of Return. Israel's Jewish identity does not get in the way of receiving such a large number of non-Jews, since it grants civil rights and even immigrant assistance to many such non-Jews. Ian Lustig claims that for this reason Israel is not a "Jewish state" but rather a "non-Arab state," although in reality these non-Jews have joined in the Jewish collective in Israel.[27]

The social structure in Israel is in reality binational (dual-ethnic), Jewish and Palestinian, and the atmosphere in which this shared citizenship exists is that of fundamental disagreement over the state's own identity. Over the past fifty-eight years the Palestinian minority in Israel has suffered sweeping institutionalized discrimination in all areas of life, because the state's main project since its inception has been the creation of a political framework for the Zionist movement and for the Jewish people.

As noted in the context of Jewish public discourse, central to civil-society elements to generate change is its ability to influence Jewish public opinion. We are now searching for a way to energize Jewish activists for the mobilization of the entire Jewish public in Israel.

According to Israeli law there should be full equality between Jewish and Palestinian citizens, yet the policies of all Israeli governments have been sweepingly discriminatory. Only in September 2003, with the publications of the Or Committee's report, was this discrimination officially recognized and its amendment placed at the top of the government's agenda by that very committee.[28] And still, despite its moral, constitutional, and political legitimacy, the promotion of full equality between Jews and Palestinians in Israel is often perceived as a challenge to the state's definition—perhaps for lack of consensus among members of the Jewish public. As of 2003 there was yet a majority of Jews (53 percent) in Israel that objected to equal rights for Palestinian citizens.[29]

A central reason for Jewish citizens' hesitation to engage in a genuine struggle for equality with Israeli Palestinian citizens lies in a basic feeling of cultural identification. Jews active in the realm of civil and human rights do so out of a broad human and political perspective, and though they belong to the collective Jewish society they nevertheless see themselves as part of other "magnetic fields" of identity, such as humanistic and universal values. Some of the Jewish activists even express discomfort at belonging to the collective society in Israel.

During the continual contact with Palestinians some Jewish citizens find the allegations against the collective Jewish society so hard to bear that they detach themselves and become non-Zionists. In this sense they feel not as part of the problem but as part of the solution. On the other hand, those among the activists who acknowledge their belonging to the collective society accept living in constant disharmony.

One of the basic qualities of a civil society is its ability to separate itself from the state and identify and promote civil interests divorced from or even contrary to government interests. It seems that on the Jewish side there is still no adequate distinction between the state and the civil organizations. Recent public opinion polls show that one of the greatest fears among Jews is that if full equality with Palestinians is implemented, the former will lose their exclusiveness in the state.[30] Thus, although in Israel "legitimate" challenges to the state's structure are those that are channeled through the parliamentary system, the struggle for equality within civil society is often considered a challenge to the state structure itself, perhaps even to the state's very existence.

The question we pose to conclude this chapter is how can the Jews who are strongly connected to their collective society be recruited to a civil struggle in favor of equality for Palestinian citizens of Israel? It seems that the recruitment of merely those Jews who see this as an authentic Jewish interest may turn the tables in their own public in Israel, and outside, for the sake of ordinary citizenship in Israel.

Influence of Jewish-Palestinian Partnership in Israel and on the Peace Process

Until now it seemed that partnerships between Jews and Palestinians in Israel did not exert a critical influence on the resolution of the overall conflict. However, we can use the 1990s as a time to examine the possible influence that resolution of the overall conflict between Israeli Jews and Palestinians had on their common society. It should be asked whether the beginning of the process toward a solution in the mid-1990s, or at least the feeling it brought, aided in building relations between Jews and Palestinians in Israel.

It seems that this period of crystallization of the particular Palestinian identity in Israel, and perhaps the Oslo process as well, acted as a catalyst to the unique self-determination of the Palestinian citizens in Israel. At a Nazareth convention in January 1994, Professor Majid al-Haj protested against the disregard of Israel's Palestinian citizens in the Oslo Accords and claimed that "if we are not part of the solution, we will remain a part of the problem." As mentioned before, in 1993–1994 the Supreme Monitoring Committee began an internal examination process that led to the establishment of various other committees. Dozens of advocacy and self-help organizations emerged, and by 2001 the Palestinian civil society had managed to win effective international exposure for its agenda at the Durban Convention in South Africa. One of the most invested moves in building the self image of the Palestinian collective in Israel was its placement within the Arab world. Activists for such organizations as Ittijah attended international forums in Arab countries not only as representatives of the Palestinian society in Israel but of those in Lebanon and Jordan as well. In April 2004 the Arab League discussed the issue of "the Arabs of 1948." Some representatives of civil organizations (primarily Ittijah) participated, yet the head of the Supreme Monitoring Committee declined the invitation, claiming this was not the place in which to promote the interests of Palestinians in Israel; the domestic arena was the proper forum. Nevertheless, elements of civil-society organizations in Israel continue to operate on the international scene. From a group forgotten by the Arab world after 1948 (and only to be subsequently condemned by it), the Palestinian citizens of Israel may yet become a forceful element in the inter-Arab civil arena, providing that this action remains consistent.

Until recently the open forum of civil society in Israel generally allowed freedom of movement, creation, and assembly, which are more restricted in Arab countries. And yet, as a whole, Palestinians in Israel are always suspect, the government always watching them. This is in fact a direct continuation of the military rule under which the Palestinian citizens lived for the first nineteen years of Israel's existence.

People as a Bridge to Peace

It used to be expected, and still occasionally is, that the Palestinian citizens of Israel would serve as a bridge for peace. This expectation assumes that their knowledge of both Hebrew and Arabic can serve as a mediating tool between the Zionist movement and the national Palestinian movement. This simplistic perception fails to take into account numerous historical-political forces that exist. Nevertheless, by its nature civil society is not obligated to align itself in accordance with the historical rules and identifications, and is freer than the state in determining the future. In this light, we will attempt to draw out what is necessary to happen in order for civil society in Israel to be an effective element in the advancement of the peace process.

The civic meeting point in Israel is more an existential must of the two collectives, rather than a "celebration of differences" between immigrants-of-choice as in the West. The common civil structure in Israel was created as a result of a collision between the two national movements, and continues to reflect that conflict. Therefore the creation of one national identity such as "Israeli" is simply impossible. Access to such common space is hesitant and under suspicion from both sides. Thus, the nature of Israeli shared citizenship that includes both Jews and Palestinians must be of rather technical nature, and should include as least as many elements of group identity as possible.

However, could a partnership in the framework of citizenship in Israel positively reflect and assist in promoting relations between both peoples as a whole? For such a partnership to be effective, the unique identity of each partner must find full expression in any common civil-society framework, for trust must be gained so that a common framework can actually include both identities. Those who approach the creation of these partnerships carry responsibility and a commitment toward their collective groups, and are therefore expected to sharpen their particular identities within the common framework.

A few hundred Israeli activists have been trying to build partnerships of different types in different fields. Is there a connection, a mutual influence, or a one-directional effect of organized civil relations between Jews and Palestinians in Israel on resolving relations between the state and the Palestinians as a whole? This question has two aspects:

- For a positive experience of Palestinian citizenship in Israel to have a ripple effect on relations between Israel and the Palestinian people as a whole, Palestinian citizens must feel at ease with their Israeli citizenship in all respects—apart from the state's conflict with their Palestinian fellows. For this to happen the state must completely alter its discrimination policy in a 180-degree turnaround and gain the Palestinian citizens' trust. Such a step would require a decade of strenuous effort.
- To serve as effective advocates to their people outside the state, like US Jews are to Israel, the Palestinian citizens in Israel should be included in all state systems; otherwise their voice will lack any real value.

Following is an illustration of two models of the relations between the state and the Palestinian citizens. To each of the models there is a consequence in the context of relations between the two peoples as a whole.

According to the first model, the state is a patron of the Palestinian citizens of Israel, who hold a "lesser citizenship" and do not enjoy equal rights (the present situation).

The possible outcome is the seclusion and dissimilation of the Palestinian citizens of Israel from the rest of the Palestinian nation and segregation within the more comfortable state, which provides a safety net of minimal social security and access to a more convenient way of life. In this situation some could become involved in aiding the Palestinian people on the civilian level, with professional consulting, or by community shipments of food donations and the like. Yet there is no chance of them having a positive influence on a process of peace between Israel and the Palestinian people.

The second model, the equal civic model within the state of Israel, is manifested in the realization of at least four central elements:

- Full civic equality between Jews and Palestinian, including collective rights
- Sound personal and group-related social relations
- Proper representation in all the state systems and the private-market sector
- Legitimacy and the inclusion of Palestinian citizens in the state of Israel and its definition

The possible outcome is a ripple effect, a projection outward of trust and security in the Jews' ability to live alongside Palestinians, respecting them as a party that lost in the 1948 war but was not completely crushed as a result; the establishment of the sense of personal and collective confidence in the state; the use of the sense of security in the state as leverage to bridge over the Palestinians' two political poles; and the state of Israel as the strong anchor of civilian belonging on one hand and the strong historical and cultural belonging to the Palestinian people on the other.

It should be asked whether a common, equal, and healthy citizenship within a democratic regime sets a proper example for the framework of relations between the peoples as a whole. Or, in other words, would a successful example of a common life inside the state of Israel pave the way to a framework of a common, Jewish-Palestinian life in two states between the sea and the river? The answer to this question is complex: in the short term—no. Yet in the long term it seems to be so. For the civil society to realize its potential as a structure for identification that permits ongoing conflict, yet which does not bleed, certain minimal conditions that were described in the second alternative, the civil equality alternative, must exist. Civil society has the ability to become the catalyst for these changes.

In the context of the complicated situation, the stagnation, and the deterioration, Jewish and Palestinian civil society is closer than ever to presenting a qualitative alternative to this situation. The model of a civil state is not too far away, and could include both sides of the conflict. In order to set this change in motion, the Jewish, Palestinian, and especially the joint organization, must consider their next steps wisely.

Conclusion: A Local Civil Society or an International One?

Up until now common citizenship in Israel does not provide an encouraging message and valid examples of Jews and Palestinians living together Middle East. Yet, if this is specifically defined as a goal, a broad effort could assist in establishing the desired model of a shared and inclusive civil society that constitutes a workable alternative. To achieve this, there must be patience for a decade of coordinated, strenuous work; coordination between the professional, organizational, and academic forces; and consistent, extensive funding.

Civil society, then, is not obligated to align itself with dominant streams in different countries. Its relative freedom allows it to make ties and base local changes on a joint effort that is international. Therefore we must wait no longer, and must turn to the international civil society for urgent help. Today, this civil society helps in various initiatives in Israel, but the assistance could be coordinated among all the elements as much as possible, without damaging any possibilities.

Aside from the funds needed for the advancement of this process, civil-society elements could share the knowledge gained from successes and failures in other countries.

The global civil society, as well as governments that give foreign aid, regard the change needed in Israel as very important, yet they all consider Israel as a developed country that does not need aid from outside. This is financially and economically true, but in terms of an index of conflict zones, the state of Israel itself is a conflict zone beset by one of the most intractable conflicts because it is built into the state's very structure, and so Israel is underdeveloped.

Notes

1. In this chapter the terms "Palestinian citizens" and "Arab citizens" will both be used in reference to the Arab-Palestinian minority, indigenous people in Israel, who make up about 19 percent of the population.

2. Yael Yishai, "Civil Society in Transition: Interest Politics in Israel, *Annals* 555 (January 1998): 147–162.

3. S. Dichter, ed., *The Sikkuy Report,* 1992–1996.

4. Ibid.

5. Z. Rozehak, "New Developments in Sociology of Palestinian Israeli Citizens: An Analytical Overview," *Megamot* (1995): 167–190.

6. Y. Peled, "Strangers in Utopia: The Social Status of the Palestinians in Israel," *Theory and Critique* (1995): 3, 21–35.

7. S. Dichter, ed., *The Sikkuy Report,* 1992–1996.

8. Y. Korin and A. Abu-Zaidan, *The Book of Organizations Working on Jewish-Arab Coexistence in Israel,* Forum for Civic Agreement and the Abraham Fund Initiatives (2003).

9. Dani Rabinovitz and Haula Abu Bakar, *Hador Hazakuf* (Keter Publishing, Jerusalem 2002).

10. Shany Payes, *Palestinian NGOs in Israel: The Politics of Civil Society* (London: IB Tauris, forthcoming).

11. Eli Rekhess, director of the Moshe Dayan Centre for Middle East Studies.

12. Ibid.

13. Nadim Soltoni, "Citizens without Citizenships," First Mada Annual Political Supervising Report: Israel and the Palestinian Minority 2000–2002 (2002).

14. Asad Ghanem, Paper for the Investigation Committee of the Clashes between Security Forces and Israeli Civilians (2000).

15. B. Neuberger, "The Arab Voice: Between Integration and De-legitimacy," in A. Reches, ed., *Arabs in Israeli Politics: Dilemmas of Identity*, pp. 31–39.

16. Benjamin Gidron, "Not-for-Profit Organisations in Israel, 1991," *Theoretical and Historical Review* (Jerusalem: Bureau of Statistics, publication 1016, in Hebrew, January 1996), p. 23.

17. Payes (forthcoming).

18. Elias Zeidan and As'ad Ghanem, *Donation and Voluntarism in the Arab-Palestinian Society in Israel* (Beersheba: Israeli Centre for Third Sector Research, Ben Gurion University in the Negev, February 2000), p. 15.

19. Asad Janem, "The Palestinians in Israel as Part of the Problem and Not of the Solution: Their Status in Times of Peace," *State, Government, and International Relations*, 1997: 123–154.

20. S. Smooha, "Ethnic Democracy: Israel as a Prototype," in P. Genosar and A. Barnea, eds., *Zionism: A Contemporary Debate* (Beer Sheva: The Center for the Heritage of Ben Gurion), pp. 277–311.

21. Earth Day came about following the massive expropriation of private lands belonging to Arab citizens in the Galilee, in order to build Jewish settlements on them.

22. Haviva Bar and David Bergel. "Living with the Conflict," pp. 238–241.

23. Ibid., pp. 242–247.

24. Dani Rabinovitz and Haula Abu Bakar, *Hador Hazakuf*, pp. 39–46.

25. Bar and Bergel, p. 214.

26. Yael Yishai, *Between Recruiting and Reconciling Civil Society in Israel* (Jerusalem: Carmel, 2003), pp. 105–107.

27. Shulamit Aloni, "A Citizen and His State," *Maarachot*, 1985, p. 58.

28. Ian S. Lustick, "Israel as a Non-Arab State: The Political Implications of Mass Immigration of Non-Jews," *Middle East Journal*, p. 53.

29. Or Committee Report.

30. Asher Arian, "Survey by the Israeli Institute for Democracy" (Jerusalem, 2003).

8

Looking Back, Looking Forward: Toward Transforming the Conflict

Edy Kaufman, Walid Salem, and Juliette Verhoeven

This closing section reviews and processes the vast amount of information about the impact of Israeli and Palestinian civil society on the Middle East conflict over the last decades. Adopting a multiple source approach, it collects conclusions drawn in the preceding chapters of the book; reviews the recommendations and conclusions of other relevant books and articles; considers the successful experiences of peacebuilding in other parts of the world; and draws on the fruits of a brainstorming session that included both contributors and reviewers of this publication.

Many of the "lessons learned" presented in this chapter reflect the current pessimism arising from the lack of progress in official Palestinian/ Israeli negotiations. But we need also to remember that peacebuilders in both civil societies have made important positive contributions toward the advancement of mutual recognition and the limitation of human rights violations. Nor should we forget that they have provided many creative ideas for helping resolve permanent status issues. It has been said that even the mere fact that ties across the divided continue to exist proves that peace is possible.

Even in these difficult times, we recognize that there is no life to a peace movement without the belief that peace is possible. We know that there are formulae that can be acceptable to moderates and pragmatists on both sides. Even if much of what is happening now is an antiwar protest, it is just a phase, as long as there is faith in peace.

The Context of Peacebuilding Work
Focusing on the last decades reveals that while we have often looked at the impact of peace forces on the overall relations between Palestinians and Israelis, the question could also at times be usefully inverted to explore the impact of the situation on peacebuilding behavior.

A shift in priorities from "how to make peace" to "how to stop war" has occurred within the context of this conflict for both civil societies and newly emerging NGOs, who are now concerned with formulating, conveying, publicizing, and disseminating key ideas for mutual recognition. Early in the 1990s a solution based on the acceptance of self-determination for two states initiated a process of reconciliation at the people-to-people level. One of many Track II initiatives occurred in Oslo, and, in September 1993, triggered the historic agreement formalized on the White House lawn between Prime Minister Rabin and President Arafat. When, in summer of 2000, the Camp David negotiations and their aftermath collapsed, many of us working for peace felt as though we had been plunged into an abyss. The subsequent eruption of the Palestinian uprising after Sharon's provocative visit to Al-Haram Al-Sharif, and the impact of state terror and group terror against Palestinian and Israeli civilians, not only had a huge impact on the participation of the general public in the peace process but also weakened and diminished the peace camp itself. Suicide bombing and massive Israeli military operations that led to large numbers of innocent casualties constitute crimes against humanity and have a chilling impact on the already tenuous cooperation between the two camps.

In fact, disillusionment on both sides has been overwhelming and has been reinforced by mutual recriminations for the failure of the Barak/Arafat leadership to come to an agreement. The Oslo Peace Process raised expectations for security and economic "peace dividends," although the disappointment of those failed expectations is felt most keenly by the Palestinians, who endure almost daily incursions by the Israeli army into their areas. Within this context, the centrality of the sense of personal, rather than purely national, security within civil society and the public at large needs to be addressed as a primary issue.

At the initial stages, the Israeli unilateral pullout from Gaza and the electoral defeat of the hardliners in the remains of the Likud Party in the March 2006 elections could incrementally provide some minimal change. But the coming into power of Hamas in the January 2006 elections makes more difficult than ever dialogue at the official level. The non-partner policy of the new Kadima Party with the Palestinian president Abu Mazen creates an additional obstacle to moving forward.

On the one hand, despite the gradual development of a space for dialogue and joint cooperation between Israeli forces and Palestinian forces that began in 1974, the second intifada caused a backlash. The Palestinian position was a reaction to the Israeli's repressive policies against the Palestinians and the inability of the Israeli peace movement to change these policies. Furthermore, Prime Minister Sharon's refusal, as a matter of policy, to negotiate with the Palestinian National Authority (PNA) at any level affected the will to legitimize contacts at the civil society level. These painful setbacks to normalization occurred mainly in the first year of the intifada. During this period Palestinian officialdom halted relations with the Israeli mainstream and maintained contacts only with those groups that were willing to provide unconditional solidarity with the Palestinian's increasing suffering.[1] Paradoxically, the rising death toll indirectly revived the hope of peace by providing a stark manifestation of the cost of conflict.

On the other side of the political spectrum, the extremist powers and factions in both communities have united indirectly on the basis of their unwritten agreement to continue violence, state- and group-terrorism, the continuation of the occupation, hatred, and the demonizing of the "other." More often than not, their dominant strategies—often in defiance of national and international law—and their fanatic dedication to "the cause" have proved better able to dictate the course of events than the peace forces. Although representing a minority in both societies, their militancy forced the moderates on both sides to participate only reactively by exposing human rights violations, demanding respect for life and property, declaring the illegality of the settlements, appealing against intimidation, and calling for freedom of expression and the resumption of negotiations. These were for the most part expressions redressing negative acts of the extremist forces that by commission or omission have been endorsed by the governments of both sides over the years.

Paradoxically, although the extremists on both sides do not coordinate their acts, they effectively escalate the situation in tandem. Their strength lies in using, with impunity, illegal means and a fanatic commitment to invest their lives—literally—in the attainment of their objectives: the denial of the existence of the other. But the level of intensity is one factor among many, including their better access to the sensationalist media. On the other side, as we have noted, the peace forces that have coordinated their national and bilateral work have been mostly reactive. Although larger in number—with notable individual exceptions—the overall personal level of commitment of those interested in peaceful resolution is low.

Torn between the forces of war, violence, and unilateralism on the one side and an appeal for humanity, historic compromise, and reconciliation on the other, the majorities in both societies have been looking for peace, but more passively.

The current paralysis of the process leading toward a two-states solution only reaffirms the need to look back critically into the roles of civil societies, to learn from failed attempts and missed opportunities, and to take encouragement from the positive experiences. The sense of urgency behind this need for critical introspection is triggered by the suffering of the Palestinian people as a whole—who are now exposed to the worse consequences of the occupation—and the fears and sorrow arising from the deaths of both Israelis and Palestinians.

Methodology

The editors have tried to organize and frame the acquired knowledge on Palestinian/Israeli peacebuilding by using the term *linkages* to identify the input of their work to other parts of their respective societies. This framework aims to provide a comprehensive and "exclusive" categorization so that we can draw lessons learned by focusing on work *done* as well as *not done,* that is, looking at best practices not only on past and present records but also projecting new ideas toward the future. Such a logical framework presents the actual and potential linkages—conscious or not—between Israeli and Palestinian peacebuilders themselves, in their contacts with decisionmaking elites and public opinion/mass audiences within their own societies and across the divide. It also looks into the interaction of both sides separately and together with the international community at large. We also want to make sure that the lessons learned come with some sense of the shift from a "pro-peace" to an "antiwar" reality and conclusions about what should be done now. We will first display the framework graphically and then deal with the linkages individually.

The dotted lines in Figure 8.1 indicate links that are weaker than the solid lines. As we can see the originators of the peacebuilding linkages are both the Palestinian and Israeli civil societies, and their strength has been mutual cooperation (linkage 1). Normally we tend to concentrate on the direct vertical ties toward their own decisionmakers (linkages 2, 3) and public opinion (linkages 4, 5), including people who participate or support these initiatives and those who disseminate these ideas. We tend to focus less on the attempts to influence each other's decisionmakers (linkages 6, 7) and public opinion (linkages 8, 9) with the hidden cooperation of their counterpart peacebuilders. The presentation of a categorization of societies in three levels does not show the intermediate actors. Quite a few elected politicians and candidates, often in opposition to the main leadership, have been closely involved with the peacebuilders. Also it is difficult to distinguish between full- and part-time peacebuilders, those Palestinians and Israelis who have sporadically participated in some joint or unilateral activities from the activists.

International actors are not considered in this book, and the few lessons mentioned in this chapter should serve only as a reminder of what still needs to be done. Consequently, the references to the international actors (intergovernmental, governmental) have been clustered in one link (10) together with national NGOs, and local and worldwide public opinion. Given the constraints of this book, we have to accept some simplification of the large volume of interactions of peacebuilders with the global community. A more systematic framework of constructive inputs from abroad needs to be prepared with the participation of the most active governmental and non-governmental organizations worldwide. Lessons also need to be learned about the relation to the international civil society as a potential

Figure 8.1 Peacebuilding Linkages

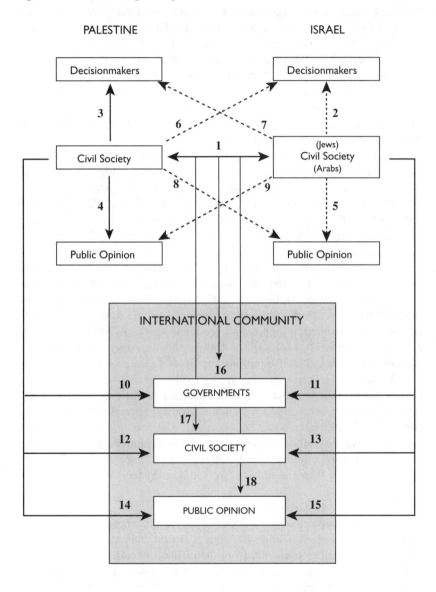

player in Israel-Palestine at a time when the need for third-party participation seems to be more important than ever. While the Palestinian civil society can be taken as a whole, a deeper look into Israeli counterparts includes a Jewish, Arab, and sometimes a common action component, creating additional difficulties in categorization. Lessons about the impact these activities have upon the Israeli/Palestinian peace process are also summarized in one link (linkage number 11).

In this final chapter we will not repeat the conclusions arrived at in earlier chapters but will nevertheless stress some of the more important points arising from those more specific accounts.

If we choose to regard the cup as half-full rather than half-empty, we can note that during the current intifada, the groups working vertically with each other within the Israeli and the Palestinian societies are meeting horizontally with their counterparts across the divide, whether directly or indirectly. Although the relative weakness of the peace forces, with the added desertion of former activists and the scarcity of new "recruits" to the cause, also needs to be recognized.

In the background of civil society interactions, we include sectorial actors covering women, journalists, youth, professional groups (medical, social workers, teachers), business, and artists, as well as activities in the fields of training, interfaith relations, community relations, public health, education, environment, media, and academic research. Although no specific mention of lessons learned for such sectors appears in the framework, we have incorporated their input into the field of peacebuilding.

We also try to uncover the types of relations between civil society organizations and decisionmakers on both sides. Although some of the interactions have been conducted simultaneously, normally the encounters with the leadership have occurred separately. The nonviolence issue will be tackled during the analysis of the solidarity work, joint work, and the work of civil society in both societies. Finally, when we discover that a lesson is relevant for more than one linkage, we add a reference when appropriate.

1. Civil Society to Civil Society

While we often cluster both civil societies together, we need to recognize the asymmetries that provide more freedom of action and means to implement ideas on the Israeli side in contrast to the difficult overall conditions of the Palestinians under occupation. The physical and psychological constraints placed on the peacebuilders there leads to complications and doubles and triples the amount of work necessary for peacebuilding in that context. These differences place a higher burden on the side of the occupier's civil society. Given such imbalances, the larger social responsibility of the Israeli counterpart needs to be acknowledged and taken up by Israeli civil society. Yet, the need for reciprocity is an important trigger for action on both sides, through finding ways to express humanity toward the other.

While recognizing the physical, social, and political constraints on the Palestinian counterparts, these constraints must not be accepted as a given. Rather they should be dealt with by struggling for the freedom to work for peace, within their own society, and through the support of Israeli activists' and the provision of international protection both in terms of solidarity and demands on the authorities. All of these individual and group demands need to be seen within the framework of the struggle to bring an end to the occupation.

There have been some joint initiatives in both communities, such as the Nusseibeh Ayalon and Geneva Accords, as well as field actions against occupation. However, on the Palestinian side these have been mostly hidden from the public eye, thereby diminishing the initiatives' participatory nature from general public perception. Consequently, the importance of building bridges was not fully understood or appreciated. One of the Israelis' failures, in deference to the Palestinian partners, was to go along with this course instead of finding a creative solution to the problem. The "people-to-people" programs were never normalized, public exposure was limited, names were hidden, meetings were held abroad, and so on. The general ignorance about the scope of activities wasn't only due to the lack of media coverage, but the participants also failed to promote the message. The lesson here is thus to concentrate on more grassroots and open cooperation, and on NGO projects that are more publicly oriented than only inward looking.

There is a need to understand the dilemma of peace-oriented organizations and individuals from both sides if more energy is to be spent meeting *across* the national divide at the expense of working *within* their societies. We need to respect alternative sets of priorities, and take into consideration the problems of marginalization faced by groups within their own constituencies. It is also important to stress that civil society organizations need to approach their intra- and inter-community tasks with the same level of seriousness, setting and shifting their priorities according to strategic planning.

During the second year of the Al Aqsa intifada, the peace movements, in general, began to return to their earlier relationships, and to a feeling that there was no alternative but to develop partnerships between the two communities. Anything else would simply provide additional support for the propagandist claims that there "is no partner on the other side," and that it is more effective to do things unilaterally. Therefore, a positive trend began with the recent development of joint peace appeals and plans: the People Peace Campaign and the Israeli-Palestinian Peace Coalition preceded the Nussiebeh-Ayalon agreement, the Geneva Accords, One Voice, and the Palestinian-Israeli Action Group for Peace. But the emergence of these joint efforts paled in significance alongside the increasingly aggressive strategies of the extremists on both sides. This reality demonstrates a problem in the public perception in both societies, but it also represents one of the most important deficits in the work of peace organizations.

We need to understand four trends that continue to exist within both camps regarding joint cooperation. Delineating the separate trends can help us design different approaches and reduce internal confrontations.

There are those who are eager to continue cooperation in spite of all the adverse circumstances. The number of these dedicated activists may now have been reduced.

There are those who favor a two-state solution immediately without any gradualism, in order to separate from each other. This group is not interested in cooperation in the near future, which could leave the door open for future reconsideration or backsliding.

The third position—the majority within the Palestinian peace-oriented organizations—consists of those who still think that it is possible to have selective activities, and/or to conceal them so as not to provoke the majority who are against joint activities.[2] It may be acceptable if Israelis come to participate in solidarity activities with the Palestinians, for example, via videoconferences between the two parties. It is possible to have joint nonviolent actions against occupation, but other activities will be considered normalization activities.[3]

Finally there is the group that believes normal joint activities can take place only after peace is reached and two states have been established for the two peoples, despite the obvious truth that there is good reason for both sides to struggle nonviolently and separately for an end to the occupation after which reconciliation would be possible.[4]

These different approaches to cooperation have often been advocated in an adversarial manner, with the result that much energy is wasted on internal conflict within the peace camp. The tactical or strategic preference of a particular course of action should be respected as long as it moves along the same direction of struggling for a *just peace for both nations*.

On the Israeli side, the place of peace groups within civil society is heavily influenced by the middle- and upper-class nature of its membership. This has tended to deter other social organizations from supporting this work. One problem lies in the failure to connect the cost of militarism and occupation to the increasing limitations of the welfare state within Israel and the impoverishment of large segments of society. The highest priority should be given to finding effective incentives and programs for training and socializing young and potential leaders of development towns and underprivileged neighborhoods in the advantages of peace for their own futures and that of their communities. Efforts should also be made to develop tolerance within Israeli society, toward both other Israelis and toward the Palestinians.

On the Palestinian side, the main characteristic of civil society—including the peace organizations—is that it was created in the absence of the state, yet still carries the burden of the state. Consequently, Palestinian civil society can be divided between those organizations that are annexes of the

PLO and its factions—including some unions, federations, and grassroots organizations—and those that are independent organizations formed mainly after the creation of the PNA. Top priority should be given to the development of social programs to the Palestinian peace organizations that involve people in peace activities connecting to the recognition of their own needs.

A related criticism stresses that the Israeli peace movement, by virtue of its predominantly Ashkenazi membership, remains vague about the need to incorporate a Middle Eastern identity as a significant aspect of its composition. Even if one agrees that, as a reflection of their society, Israelis should not have to choose between Europe and their surrounding culture, the general lack of enthusiasm for Arab culture and language has been an obstacle to the perception of Israel as an integral part of the region. A stronger alliance could be built by promoting the learning of the Arabic language, and developing an appreciation of the broader region in which it wants to be accepted. At the same time, we need to be wary of the claim that unless Israeli society becomes a part of the Middle East, there can be no peace. While peace can be reinforced by such trends, it is not contingent upon achieving it.

It has become clearer that professional relations (medical, education, environmental) have a good chance of prevailing even under adverse conditions because, in addition to the peace orientation of the participants, there is an additional shared identity across the divide based on their own career patterns. From different areas of concrete cooperation, the medical/humanitarian area has continued to be perceived by large segments of the population on both sides not only as legitimate but effective.

Similarly, shared gender and age identities can be a strong bond for continuous cooperation. With some ups and downs, women's organizations have continued to cooperate. While there has been a general decrease in the level of joint activities during the second intifada, it is important to stress that a smaller decrease occurred in the cooperation between women's organizations from both sides that were able to join forces. One of the successful stories in this regard is the Jerusalem Link's (Bat Shalom and Jerusalem Center for Women) joint initiative. The potential of women's appeals needs to be further explored.

Joint Israeli/Palestinian organizations should be encouraged. This is not only a priority in terms of showing in a microcosm that Arab/Jewish coexistence is not only a slogan but also a reality, but, since binational cooperation is a prerequisite for their continued existence as NGOs, such organizations have a greater chance of surviving difficult times. In Chapter 4, Mohammed Dajani and Gershon Baskin recommend other lessons regarding the issues of civil-society joint ventures and the development and sustainability of such organizations.

Joint Palestinian-Israeli cooperative ventures have not found broad participation. Although many joint activities are held, only 0.5 percent of

The Jerusalem Link

The Jerusalem Link is the coordinating body of two independent women's centers: Bat Shalom—The Jerusalem Women's Action Center, located in West-Jerusalem, and Marcaz al-Quds la l-Nissah—The Jerusalem Center for Women, located in East Jerusalem. In 1989, a meeting was convened in Brussels between prominent Israeli and Palestinian women peace activists. The meeting initiated an ongoing dialogue that in 1994 resulted in the establishment of the Jerusalem Link. Bat Shalom and the Jerusalem Center for Women share a set of political principles that serve as the foundation for a cooperative model of co-existence between their respective peoples. Each organization is autonomous and takes its own national constituency as its primary responsibility—but together they promote a joint vision of a just peace, democracy, human rights, and women's leadership. Mandated to advocate for peace and justice between Israel and Palestine, they believe a viable solution to the conflict between the two peoples must be based on recognition of the right of the Palestinian people to self-determination and an independent state alongside Israel, Jerusalem as the capital of both states, and a final settlement of all relevant issues based on international law.

Jerusalem Link Declaration

We, Palestinian and Israeli women, united in a joint effort to bring about a just, comprehensive and lasting peace between our two peoples, affirm our commitment to working together within the framework of The Jerusalem Link for the rapid realization of our common vision of peace. This effort is based on the following principles:

1. Recognition of the *right to self-determination* of both peoples in the land, through the establishment of a Palestinian state alongside Israel on the June 4th, 1967 boundaries.

2. The whole city of Jerusalem constitutes *two capitals for two states.*

3. The *Oslo Declaration of Principles*, signed on September 13, 1993, and all subsequent agreements *must be implemented immediately* and in their entirety.

4. Permanent *settlement negotiations* must resume without any delays on the basis of the agreed agenda of the Declaration of Principles, the terms of reference being all relevant UN resolutions, including 242 and 338.

5. It is our conviction that *all Israeli settlements* in the Palestinian territories occupied in 1967 *are illegal*, as stipulated in international law, and violate the requirements of peace.

6. A *just solution* to the Palestinian refugee question is an essential requirement for a stable and durable peace. This solution must honor the right of return of the Palestinian refugees in accordance with UN resolution 194.

7. *Respect for international conventions*, charters and laws, and the active involvement of the international community in the peace process are crucial to its success.

8. The realization of political peace will pave the way for mutual understanding and trust, genuine security, and constructive [cooperation] on the basis of *equality and respect for the national and human rights of both peoples.*

The Jerusalem Link (con't.)

9. *Women must be central partners in the peace process.* Their active and equal participation in decisionmaking and negotiations is crucial to the fulfillment of a just and viable peace.

10. We women are committed to a peaceful solution of our conflict, also as a means for the promotion of *democratic and non-violent norms and for the enhancement of civil society.*

11. A peaceful solution of the Palestinian-Israeli conflict and Israeli withdrawal from all occupied Arab territory, including Lebanon and Syria, are *prerequisites for a just and comprehensive peace.* This will pave the way for a region characterized by good neighborly relations and regional [cooperation].

A Summary of the Jerusalem Link Joint Activities

2003: Palestinian and Israeli Women's Silent Vigil against Occupation.

April 15, 2003: Issued, together with Bat Shalom, a joint declaration entitled "Palestinian and Israeli Women demand immediate end of Occupation." 2003: Women's International Peace Activist Network (WIPAN): JCW is working jointly with Bat Shalom on building this network as an extension of their work toward a just and lasting peace.

2003: Internal Political Dialogue.

2003: Training Programs on Conflict Resolution.

March 8, 2003: Delegations to embassies consulates.

2000: Presentation and discussion of the film "Truth and Reconciliation"

March 8, 2000: Joint demonstration

1999–2000: Creating Dialogue Through Video

1999: Seminar, "Women Engendering Democracy And Peace"

1999: Updating of JL principles (Jerusalem).

1999: Women Making Peace project, a joint project between JCW and Bat Shalom.

1999: Women's Day Panel on the implication of Israeli Elections, held at Dar al-Tifl Al-Arabi, March 8. Prominent Palestinian and Israeli figures attended.

Israelis and Palestinians participated in NGO joint ventures.[5] If we add the success of Nussiebeh-Ayalon in collecting 300,000 signatures from both sides, the Geneva Accord's 40 percent support in Israeli public opinion, and 25 percent out of the 73 percent of the Palestinians who have read the text of the accord,[6] the percentage of participants increases. However, a signature or a vote does not necessarily imply support for joint activities. Some conclude that the peacebuilding work requires a larger investment from the international community; unfortunately funds are not made available by Israeli and Palestinian authorities. Even if program improvements are made, the lack of any "economy of scale" necessitates broadly increased funding.

The issue of the multiplicity of the peacebuilding NGOs can be seen as a blessing or a problem. On the negative side, fragmentation of effort is demonstrated in the lack of coordination, lack of cooperation within and across the national divide, competition for scarce financial resources leading to mutual delegitimatization and understaffing, and a lack of voluntary participation. Such negative momentum must be counteracted in order to make real progress.

On the positive side, we should stress the benefits of diversity and make the best of the realities on the ground. Varying perspectives have resulted in ideological or strategic differences within the peace forces on both sides. These different preferences are often genuine: some groups demand an understanding of the root causes of conflict while others call for strategies that focus on consensual criteria for solving the existing conflict. Some focus on research while others expect immediate action.

Pluralism may thus be a positive fact of life, giving room for a variety of perspectives in the peace camp. Peace activists often develop consensus more effectively when working face-to-face in a small nucleus of people rather than in hierarchical structures. Hence, each NGO is limited in what it can do, and it often cannot expand beyond a limited scope. Therefore, the more groups the better, as long as they cooperate more than they compete with each other.

One way to overcome these obstacles to cooperation is by building coalitions. There is a need to work together within and across the divide on themes of mutual concern. Cooperation in lobbying for the specific goal of "expanding the pie before cutting it" when it comes to financial resources is vital. Information should be shared and work divided among the many organizations seeking support. Above all, it is essential to endorse, understand, and formulate a commitment to accept the pluralistic nature of the movements. It should be recognized that there are some who put more emphasis on means (nonviolence, human rights protection) and others on goals (peace planning, research on final status issues). There are also those who prefer to work on a national basis rather than jointly; those more interested in affecting policy (Track II); and those oriented toward working with the masses (people-to-people). So too there are more-radical groups who focus more on solidarity with the weaker side, and there are those who are moving in a slower path, incrementally exploring dialogue with a good chance that it may eventually translate into action. In effect there is a wide highway, in which different models of car are all running in parallel lanes at different speeds—but all toward the same destination.

There is a perceived need to generate a standard of cooperation, a set of principles that could provide a universal ethical foundation to the social responsibility that we all should uphold as concerned citizens and in our own professional lives. As physicians and health workers have codes of ethics to be applied in times of emergency, we may emulate and learn how to translate the idea of sectoral peace into the reality of other sectors of civil society. One possibility is for academics—who have had privileged access to higher education and who can affect important sectors of their communities—to develop a formula for combining their professional work with actions that express their commitment to overall human rights, democracy, and peace. A code of principles for working together across the divide can and should be developed and discussed with other peace-oriented colleagues.

Within this understanding of pluralism, dialogue can be seen initially as targeted at the less convinced while joint actions are designed for the converted. Hence, it is necessary to combine dialogue with activities or consensual themes in order to show solidarity, reciprocity, and that there is a partner on the other side. Dialogue activities taken in isolation could encourage unrealistic dreams that lead to frustration when they are thwarted by realities on the ground. But dialogue could be the first step toward a growing motivation to activism. In such a case, joint actions take on a new significance, hopes for change are raised, and belief in future coexistence is developed between the two sides.

There is also a need to combine the vertical approach, in which activists from both sides agree on details, and horizontal activities to interact with people from both sides, educating and learning from them. More important, it is vital to build programs according to real needs and interests. While the vertical approach might be cooperative, the horizontal is unilateral, although it can also be organized and agreed upon jointly in the vertical process.

Joint actions should take into consideration how to maximize the potential of nonviolent actions, as recommended by Mohammed Abu Nimer in Chapter 6, to involve a large segment of both societies. Partnership is possible and the notion that there is an alternative to violence must be successfully proven by nonviolent activities in order to counter the claims that violence is more effective. Historically the Palestinian people generally have supported nonviolence, given that the nonviolent activities were more intense and sustained than the sporadic violent activities conducted by self-appointed groups. But among those who support nonviolence, there are also NGOs that do not support cooperation. A better understanding of the potential of the nonviolent approach requires more study.

On the Israeli side a sustainable nonviolent campaign to influence decisionmakers and the public is a priority. The challenge is to convey that it is not enough to demonstrate the potential of such a strategy for an alternative vision of peace but to actively use it as a means for daily struggle.

Within civil society there has been a distinct lack of cooperation between the human rights and conflict resolution/peace NGOs across the national divide. Driven by differing paradigms, this lack of cooperation needs to be overcome by bridging the understanding of short- versus long-term views, individual suffering, and collective self-determination. The current construction of the wall/fence separating many Palestinians from their lands and all from Israel is leading to increased unity of action because it affects the territorial options for peace and involves individual human rights violations. Similarly the joint work against the checkpoints in the West Bank is highlighting both a humanitarian concern and a concern about the cost of security for the settlers who are in the occupied territories.

2. Israeli Civil Society and the Israeli Government

On the Israeli side, the peace movement relied too heavily on the government at the time that the Oslo process was involved in Track I. Israeli civil society made the mistake of refraining from criticizing the shortcomings of the Oslo agreement so as not to undermine its implementation. Furthermore, peace organizations were not sharp enough in criticizing the damage the process itself created in terms of human rights violations. Even if Oslo was not seen by all peacebuilders as a viable solution, the peace organizations should at least have insisted in meeting the deadline for the establishment of the Palestinian state in order to alleviate public frustration. At a more general level, there has not been a systematic strategy for addressing and empowering the peace-oriented decisionmakers and the leaders of government.

Some maintain that if women had been included in the negotiating process there may have been more awareness of human rights issues. Conversely, the high level of career and reserve military personnel involved in the negotiations failed to take into account the human dimension and only heightened the level of distrust.

Relevant to the next linkage (Palestinian Civil Society with the PLO/PNA), Track II endeavors have contributed greatly in previous decades to developing Track I and offering ideas, suggestions, and scenarios for the solution of the Israeli-Palestinian conflict. Track II was able to develop scenarios for all the permanent-status issues including refugees, Jerusalem, borders, water, environment, the nature of statehood for the two peoples, and for future joint cooperation, as well as future regional cooperation (see Chapter 5 by Menachim Klein and Riad Malki for more details). In the last years, the Ayalon/Nusseibeh and the Beilin/Abed Rabo Geneva Accords have generated a shared comprehensive plan for a permanent peace. They have also indirectly affected the Sharon government by expediting the formulation of their own political plan based on unilateral withdrawal from Gaza and three settlements in the West Bank.

The main challenge now seems to be in finding creative ways to influence the governments toward moving from the current impasse to the negotiation of the many alternative options. The issues of mutual recognition, the advantages of negotiations over unilateral dictates, and the possibility of ending violence could all benefit with Track II as a vehicle for the generation of new ideas. Government approval of shared conflict-resolution institutions would offer a more formal recognition of citizens' participation in peace negotiations.

It seems that while the focus of Track II during the peace process was to support the political decisionmakers with ideas and scenarios, it becomes important in times of engagement and disengagement to view the tasks of Track II differently. Four sets of scenarios that are urgently needed to be developed are: (1) scenarios for reconciliation between the two peoples and in relation with the entire region; (2) scenarios for promoting civil-society cooperation including those for new visions and approaches for joint ventures; (3) scenarios for the overall solution for disengagement in a way that preserves future cooperation; and (4) scenarios for the related issues of equality of citizenship in Israel and the region, the refugee issue, and the nationality/nationalities issue for every citizen in the two states.

The effectiveness of trying to influence peace-oriented policy from within or without the establishment depends on the intentions of who is in government, as well as on the personalities and approaches of the diverse individuals and groups within the peace movement. The key priority in this context is that advocates of alternative or combined modes of action do not insist that theirs is the only "right course of action" but, with a spirit of cooperation, advance in parallel down the same road, even at different speeds, but toward the same goals.

3. Palestinian Civil Society and the Palestinian Political System

The Palestinian political system is a combination of the PLO and PNA. The PLO represents all of the Palestinian people around the world, while the PNA represents the Palestinian people in the West Bank and Gaza Strip. Palestinian civil-society organizations working with Palestinians outside Palestine are interacting with the PLO, while the Palestinian civil-society organizations in the West Bank and Gaza Strip are interacting with the PNA. The PLO civil-society organizations, such as students and the Workers' Federation, have been participating in peace meetings with Israeli organizations since the 1980s. An important question in this context is, "To what extent were the Palestinian peace organizations, as part of the Palestinian civil society, able to influence the Palestinian Authority in relation to the peace agenda and peace work?"

Answering this question is difficult in part because the peace agenda in Palestine includes not only peace with Israel, but also democratization and peace within Palestinian society. The case for endorsing the assumption that democratic states do not conduct war against each other has been made in relation to this conflict.[7] Unfortunately, the link between struggling simultaneously for democratization and peace is not widely recognized within either civil society. Even if NGOs have differing priorities in each of these goals, making the connection in the planning and coordination of action is of great importance.

Palestinian peace-oriented NGOs were not able to effectively advocate for nonviolence when the militarization of the uprising dominated the landscape. Even now, the few NGOs involved in advocacy and training of nonviolence have been unable to gain even a verbal endorsement from either the PNA or individual members of the leadership. This failure has weakened the position of these NGOs. There is a pressing need to develop more influential nonviolence campaigns in order to be officially and formally endorsed by the leadership. This effort continues while the people are engaged in nonviolent action on a daily basis.

Given the absence of a professional bureaucracy, the PNA has co-opted a significant number of individuals from civil-society organizations to work in their areas of expertise, often working both in Track II and Track I, making the transmission of ideas smoother. On the other hand, officials of goodwill participated in the formulation of Track II agreements (Abu Allah in Oslo, Abed Rabbo in Geneva). This access to representatives of civil society makes for a favorable connection that needs to be systematically explored around the issues of contention in the negotiating agenda with the Israelis.

Peace education programs are now being kept secret, and yet, during the early stages in both the Israeli and Palestinian schools, peace education was very fashionable with creative material being produced by both NGOs and the schools themselves. There was, however, no systematic attempt to consolidate the effort. A serious attempt was made to generate a culture of peace, but this collapsed with the onset of the intifada. What happened in between? Why did this movement fail? How after years of ample funding did the whole process grind to a halt? A serious evaluation is needed to explore more effective ways of propagating the life skills that can socialize children into conflict transformation within their own communities and across the national divide.

It is important to separate out and understand the different actors within the PNA. During the initial stages of the Oslo process, Palestinian peace organizations worked in coordination with the PNA. There was always a group in the PNA that supported a particular NGO working on peace projects with the Israeli organizations, but the PNA had no united position toward peace initiatives. There are peace NGOs that are loyal to the PNA doing joint peace projects, while there is a lack of such support to the Palestinian independent NGOs, simply because they are independent or because they criticize the Palestinian Authority. It is necessary to find ways to encourage the PNA to develop a more consistent position toward peace activism.

These contradictory positions reflect different positions within Fatah (the main PNA organization) regarding peace projects with the Israeli side.

Much of Palestinian politics are run on an informal basis, and one can find that informally Palestinian officials are divided into five groups in this respect. One faction calls for the cessation of all projects (halting the normalization of relations in other words), while only continuing negotiations. For this group, the relationship with Israel is thus excluded from negotiations. The second group does not object to organizing Israeli solidarity activities with the Palestinians, sometimes with the participation of international activists in these activities. The third group consists of those who support the development of joint peace initiatives with the Israeli groups, but remain cautious about joint civil-society activities. The fourth group includes those from the PNA who support and participate in the joint ventures. The fifth and the final group consists of those who want the Israeli peace camp to help the Palestinians connect with the mainstream in Israel. There has not been a systematic effort to endorse the support of such groups as "allies from within the Palestinian establishment." Systematic efforts to this end should be undertaken by the NGOs.

The peace groups themselves can be criticized for their failure to advocate effectively with the PNA for their peace projects or to create public support for their work, although they were able to do a lot of media and mass public relations work on the issues of the militarization of the intifada, the chaos in the streets, and the violation human rights. These organizations also worked on the development of nonviolent strategies to opposing the strategies of violence, but, as Mohammed Abu Nimer notes in Chapter 6, they still need to develop a major nonviolent campaign that includes the PNA, grassroots organizations, NGOs, the media, influential leaders, international participation, and the Palestinians of the diaspora. He concludes that the nonviolent campaign needs to succeed in certain cases in order to develop the belief in nonviolence as an effective tool to counter violence.

The failure of the peace organizations in advocacy campaigns for peace and nonviolence contrasts with the greater success of democracy and human rights organizations in advocating democracy and monitoring human rights violations by the PNA. In a series of reports and cases presented to the monitoring bodies of the PNA and the international organizations, the work of these groups has been significant and influential, even during the period of the second intifada.

4. Palestinian Civil Society in Palestinian Society

A large group of Palestinian civil-society organizations (CSOs), in cooperation with Palestinian officialdom, was able to develop a peace discourse in the Palestinian National Council session of 1988. This peace discourse was built on the idea of having two states living beside each other in peace and cooperation. The challenge and the lessons for the present time are to develop more mainstream support in Palestinian society for such a program.

While some Palestinian peacebuilders, mostly at an individual level, have made efforts to reach out to public opinion through the media, the NGOs did not act as a coalition to publicize their understanding of the importance of working together across the divide for a just peace. The need to convey to the public that peace is a process and that no instant dividends could be expected was subordinated to private talks and was shared mostly with groups and individuals already closely associated with the peace process.

Another major concern is that the youth—a numerically large and actively engaged sector of society—has been overrepresented among the victims and perpetrators of violent conflict. Over the years, a significant minority of young Palestinians has participated in joint activities. A few of them have continued to work for peace with their Israeli and other Middle Eastern peers in spite of the difficult circumstances. However, many of them have been frustrated because of the closures and daily killing, and the absence of any hope for their futures. Hence, programs such as the Seeds of Peace organization have developed not only a personal enrichment program but a continuation of relations across the divide, and their work should be valued for its outreach and effectiveness. The challenge is to renew the trust-building process among those who were already exposed to the "other" and to find ways of working uninationally for the same goals, and to change the realities on the ground in order to offer hope to these young people. Creativity and sustained projects are necessary and are, in many ways, a long-term investment.

An important area that should not be neglected is working with university students and schoolchildren and their teachers. We need to recognize that books alone are not a remedy when there is a gap with the daily reality of an ugly confrontation with the "other." This reality may prove stronger than the text, while teachers themselves as the socializing element may feel the same sense of victimhood as their pupils. Hence, the focus on human rights education, civics, and conflict-transformation programs in the classroom, along with changes in the lives of Palestinians on the ground and an eventual acceptance of a new relationship between Palestinians and Israelis, may be an effective approach to bridging the gap.

After the formation of the PNA, the development and production of Palestinian educational textbooks began. Minor criticisms aside, it is important to note that the new curriculum generally included textbooks that concentrate on tolerance, civil rights, and other civic issues. The process of producing the new curricula continued even during the intifada. This process needs greater encouragement from peace organizations than is presently the case, and such groups should provide feedback to help develop its content.

Various polls taken in the last few years show that public opinion in both societies is fluid, on one hand supporting a two-states solution and nonviolence, and at the same time supporting the strategies of revenge for the killings done by extremists on both sides. The fluidity of public opinion demonstrates a significant deficit in the work of peace organizations. They have been unable to establish a positive view in public opinion calling for a two-state solution and to overcome, or at least diminish, the calls for revenge and violence.

The media as a whole fueled the level of conflict by providing a largely one-sided picture of the suffering, typically highlighting the victimization of its own side. Although peacebuilders have used op-ed pieces to publicize their views, the media should be utilized more widely.

We should draw inspiration from the joint work in the medical/humanitarian field and consider how to translate this into other "soft" areas of cooperation so that there remains a common ground for action even at times of violent conflict. Among others, environmental issues that know no borders and the shared "code of ethics" between different sectors, noted above, may be a platform for action in their respective fields (see Chapter 3 by Manuel Hassassian).

5. Israeli Civil Society and the Israeli Public

For a brief period, Israeli educational policy included work on the importance of peace in most schools. However, a change of government brought an end to this initiative. Israeli peace NGOs have not attempted to redress this setback, nor have they, with a few exceptions, been given sufficient access to the school system.

"Difficult" sectors of Israeli society have not been sufficiently addressed, particularly the new Russian immigrants, the religious community, and the settlers. Sporadic efforts with the latter need to be systematically sustained. Their needs have to be addressed as they are the ones who will be the most affected. In their discourse, the Israeli peace camp should avoid alienating the majority of the settlers who are not ideologically driven. The settlers will pay the price for the negotiations, so if they are not brought into the process then they will remain a significant obstacle.

The need to address the large segment of the "Oriental" (Mizrachi) Jews originating from Middle Eastern countries has been mentioned before. More in-depth brainstorming needs to take place, together with the encouragement of NGOs with close ties to this group. Work in economically marginal neighborhoods and development towns has been a total failure, with NGOs being unable to make the link between the economic underclass and peace work.

People-to-people initiatives must be analyzed carefully. One of the most important lessons learned is that the total surprise of the Israeli public at the collapse of the peace process (blaming Arafat) and the beginning of the militarized uprising was a sign of the failure of the peace movement in the Oslo period. While the general disenchantment of the Palestinians with the Oslo process was building up slowly, the dramatic change of events not only came as a greater shock to the Israeli side, but it also left many of the peacebuilders temporarily without the motivation, let alone the right message, to communicate to the masses. Until now, the pragmatic message has been stopping violence on both sides and bridging the divide through negotiations. In the quest to appeal to the political center in order to gain legitimacy, there is also a need to appeal to self-interest; the effect of violence and terrorism has damaged the legitimacy of alternative arguments about reconciliation and human dignity.

The Israeli peace movement has a history of mass mobilization at times of major crisis or raised expectations of change, as seen in the demonstration in Tel Aviv after the massacre at the Sabra and Shatilla camps in Beirut in 1982 (estimates range from 200,000 to 400,000 participants). Other landmarks have been the peace rally in which Prime Minister Rabin was assassinated and in May 2004 the "pull out from Gaza and start talking" demonstration in what is now Rabin Square, attended by an estimated 150,000. It is essential that NGOs, academics, and intellectuals help continue the momentum of broader public participation.

It should be recognized that Israeli public opinion is presently unfavorable to the peace organizations, which are often accused of being unpatriotic, as Tamar Hermann shows in Chapter 2. Hence, the combination of antiwar movements (from conscientious objectors to "mothers of soldiers" groups calling for an immediate pull-out from Gaza) and the appeal of "give peace a chance," may be a plausible mix for effective action in the short-term.

The statement that "There is a Partner—Peace is Possible" has been illustrated by the massive showing in the street via petitioning of the Ayalon/Nusseibeh national accord and the mailing to every single household (in Arabic and Hebrew) of the "Geneva Accords" in summary and full text. The Bereaved Families Forum's Hello Shalom/Salam campaign of connecting Israeli and Palestinians by phone reached the figure of 40,000 calls and more than one million minutes of conversation, providing a direct method of people-to-people interaction during very difficult times. Such initiatives have a slow but cumulative impact on both sides and should be pursued. The settlers and their supporters have conquered the streets with posters and car stickers. Perhaps the peacebuilders can do better, while also using tools that demonstrate a massive public participation.

Did Israeli civil-society organizations put as much effort into working in Israeli society as they did into working with their Palestinian counterparts? This and other questions addressing previous lessons cannot be fully answered without a proper evaluation, which has been the exception to the rule for most initiatives. We should encourage the civil-society organizations working uninationally across the divide to request external evaluation from friendly quarters and build on their constructive advice on better ways to perform in the future (see Chapter 2 by Tamar Hermann).

6. Palestinian Civil Society and the Israeli Government (including Track II)

One initiative in this context was the Palestinian NGOs' use of the Israeli High Courts to stop house demolition, ID confiscation, and similar human-rights violations in the West Bank, Gaza Strip, and East Jerusalem. The lessons learned here include the continuation of human-rights campaigns in Jerusalem, which brought in more Israeli participants and international participants, thereby increasing their influence. The submission of cases to the Israeli High Court by Palestinians became a controversial area as the court's rulings on such Palestinian issues had become more supportive to Israeli government policies since the beginning of the intifada.

The Palestinian East Jerusalem NGOs, in addition to taking issues to the Israeli courts, have also worked with the Israeli municipality in Jerusalem on complaints of East Jerusalem Palestinians and municipality taxes and house demolitions. They also worked with the Israeli National Insurance on insurance issues and with the Ministry of Interior office in East Jerusalem on the issues of ID confiscation and family reunification. This kind of work included advocacy campaigns, marches, demonstrations, sit-ins, and recourse to the courts when all the previous acts had failed. The Jerusalem-based organizations use these procedures because of the special situation of the Jerusalem residents whom the Israeli government considers "Jordanian citizens residing permanently in Israel."

An often neglected connection relates to "lobbying" of the various party leaders and members of the government coalition via Track II and periodic meetings. Even among the hardliners there are different shades and motivations, and dialogue can be useful. Talking to declared opponents of "normalization" may not seem legitimate, but conventional wisdom says that if the top officials of the PNA are willing to talk—with all the formal limitations of Track I—it is no less important for civil society to share the burden. What became known as Track I 1/2 can contribute to developing new ideas and opportunities. Occasional and discontinued attempts to engage in such exercises with Likud and Shas MKs have shown some level of receptivity, which should encourage the pursuit of further meetings.

7. Israeli Civil Society and the Palestinian Government

It is no secret that many individuals on the Israeli left had excellent personal relations with President Arafat and other members of Abu Ala's government and the Legislative Council. But in addition to their explanations to the Israeli public of the legitimacy of the Palestinian government's position, it is equally important for such "intermediaries" to use their knowledge of Israeli society to inform the Palestinian leadership as to how best to address their fears and concerns.

Israeli peacebuilders need to systematically approach the Palestinian political parties, including the fundamentalists (just as the Palestinians should address the Likud and Shas), and convey in clear terms the pernicious effect of violence against innocent civilians that amounts to terror, and the lingering fears and collective memory of attacks on the public in Israel. This has to be done in a manner that at the same time, and in parallel, condemns the Israeli Army's violent actions against Palestinian civilians.

8. Palestinian Civil Society and Israeli Public Opinion

Have Israeli organizations helped their Palestinian colleagues address Israeli public opinion? We first need to appreciate the physical limitations that have existed for several years in this regard. Apart from the Jerusalemites, the Palestinians cannot address Israeli public opinion directly because of the restrictions imposed on their freedom of movement. This exceptional situation and the fact that they need a special permit to come to their capital, Al Quds, is a deterrent for many potential participants. One lesson learned is to use electronic media and videoconferences to address Israeli society about the Palestinian suffering. But it is also important to use the Jerusalemite Palestinian activists to carry the stories of the Palestinians of West Bank and Gaza to the Israels. Storytelling, role-playing, films, and theatrical productions about both societies presented to the public on both sides is a hugely important tool. So far it has not been used enough to educate the two societies about the concerns and sufferings of each other in a way that confronts the official media's concealment of the issues (Israel), or exaggeration of them (Palestine). The fact that a significant number of prominent Palestinians are fluent in Hebrew facilitates direct contact, especially through television and radio interviews. Perhaps more difficult but no less important, is to increase the submission of op-ed articles to the printed media.

As much as the previous lesson is a priority to the Palestinians and Israelis, it is also an important element for both societies to hear voices of moderation and the sharing of their suffering expressed by academics, intellectuals, and activists from both sides. For pragmatic reasons too, such acknowledgment of shared victimhood facilitates the acceptance of the Palestinian demand for justice and the end of occupation and the Israeli demand for peace. The challenge is not only to explain the plight of one's side but also to present peace as a win/win situation for both sides. While confrontational rhetoric from the opponent travels fast, the empathy message may have to be repeated time and again to be perceived as authentic.

9. Israeli Civil Society and the Palestinian Public

Have Palestinian civil-society peace organizations helped their Israeli counterparts address Palestinian public opinion? Some such organizations are
working mostly within Israeli society to end the occupation and the oppression of the "other." Yet, with respect to helping Israeli peace activists connect with Palestinian public opinion, the problems of closures, permit
requirements, and the issue of safety of the Israelis coming to the West
Bank are obstacles to direct communication. Here, the lesson learned is to
overcome such problems by using the media for such initiatives, and by
using video-conferences as a tool for direct communication, with transla-
tion to each other's languages. E-mail communication is insufficient in this
area because most Palestinians still do not have access.

Although there are different evaluations of the work of these organizations by the Israeli peace groups, for the Palestinians the work of such
groups created a situation in which Palestinians can differentiate between
those Israeli enemies (the army) and those Israelis who are pro-peace. Such
activists in the West Bank are welcomed by the Palestinians as representatives of the face of Israel who want peace and cooperation.

More specifically, the "solidarity groups" who have protested nonviolently with Palestinians against the Israeli construction of the wall/fence in
Palestinian territory, even if marginal within their own society, have helped
counter the image that all Israelis are the Arab's enemy.

There have been few cases in which mainstream Israeli peacebuilders
have been able to share their concerns with the Palestinian public at large.
Experiences such as calling in to a Palestinian radio talk show or writing an
op-ed piece to a newspaper are rare and should be encouraged. While some
peacebuilders may be deterred from coming to what is perceived to be a
one-sided solidarity event, they should be persuaded that the Palestinian
peacebuilders are also able to reciprocate. The lesson learned from the work
of these organizations is that it is not enough for the Israeli peace movements to have dialogue with the Palestinians and to address the Palestinian
people directly or by media. Such activities will not be welcomed by the
Palestinians if they are not accompanied by actions against the atrocities of
the occupation; thus it seems that all the Israeli organizations involved in
peace activities with the Palestinians must also undertake at least some solidarity field actions, even if mainly symbolic.

10. The International Community at Large

Due to this project's constraints, we could not expand on all the linkages
that connect our two civil societies to the international, and we clustered
several of them into one overall link. Until now the international involvement with peacebuilders of both sides has been either from governments or

• *Machsom Watch*

Machsom Watch was founded in January 2001 in response to repeated reports in the press about human rights abuses of Palestinians crossing army and border police checkpoints. The excessive Israeli response to the El Aksa Intifada and the prolonged closure and siege of villages and towns on the West Bank provided the stimulus and the motivation for what at first seemed an impossible mission. The initiative of three women—Ronnee Jaeger, a long-time activist with experience of human rights work in Guatemala and Mexico; Adi Kuntsman, a feminist scholar who emigrated from the former Soviet Union in 1990; and veteran activist Yehudit Keshet, an orthodox Jewess—Machsom Watch now boasts 400 women members all over the country. The goals of the group are threefold:

1. To monitor the behavior of soldiers and police at checkpoints
2. To ensure that the human and civil rights of Palestinians attempting to enter Israel are protected
3. To record and report the results of observations to the widest possible audience, from the decisionmaking level to the general public

Membership in Machsom Watch is open only to women. Their quiet but assertive presence at checkpoints is a direct challenge to the dominant militaristic discourse that prevails in Israeli society. It demands accountability on the part of the security forces toward the civilian estate, something hitherto almost unheard of.

Machsom Watchers comprise a wide spectrum of ages and backgrounds, with a definite bias toward mature, professional women. All members are Israeli. The group is politically pluralistic within the context of opposition to the occupation and a commitment to human rights.

• *Ta'ayush, Arab-Jewish Partnership*

Arab and Jewish citizens of Israel live surrounded by walls and barbed wire: the walls of segregation, racism, and discrimination between Jews and Arabs within Israel; the walls of closure and siege encircling the Palestinians in the occupied West Bank and Gaza Strip; and the wall of war surrounding all inhabitants of Israel, as long as Israel remains an armed fortress in the heart of the Middle East. In the fall of 2000, citizens from both sides joined together to form Ta'ayush (Arabic for "life in common"), a grassroots movement of Arabs and Jews working to break down the walls of racism and segregation by constructing a true Arab-Jewish partnership. A future of equality, justice, and peace begins today, between us, through concrete, daily actions of solidarity to end the Israeli occupation of the Palestinian territories and to achieve full civil equality for all Israeli citizens.

Ongoing activities of Ta'ayush include the Campaign Against the Separation Fence—No To The Apartheid Walls; a donation campaign for Rafah families; a protest against some demolitions; solidarity activities with Yanun villagers; and solidarity activities with Palestinian residents in the Susya Region.

CSOs. In some cases this was limited to the role of donor, supporting Israeli/Palestinian joint projects; at times the third party acted as mediator, facilitator, or hosting partner to projects and Israeli/Palestinian meetings. The full potential of such links has not been maximized due to the disorganized nature of the global peace-seeking community. Even campaigns on issues such as the wall/fence or stopping the killing of innocent civilians have not been effectively coordinated at either the international governmental or nongovernmental level.

In the current phase of the crisis this third-party role is far too limited. International participation in Israeli/Palestinian projects should be increased, with involvement from the initial phases of design and continuing through the implementation and follow-up activities.

It is also important that in the definition of mutual concerns, the international participants can frame their perspectives in such a way as to promote ongoing responsibilities for the international participants. In this way international participation in the cooperation process will be transformed from an outsiders' artificial input, into an internal, and thus more influential one, and this is certainly what is needed during the present crisis.

Concerned visitors to the Holy Land often meet Palestinians and Israelis separately without thinking that by so doing they are separating rather than uniting. They should always encourage encounters with joint teams, not only those already working together, but with new potential partners that through this third-party initiative can get to know each other. The presence of a third party should not be used for the generation of an adversarial forum (as often happens in public meetings overseas), but both sides should be asked to look within and try to find common ground.

International participation can be developed in a way that avoids the usual kind of involvement, in which some organizations send groups and delegations to support one side against the other. This process simply helped blind each group to the other's rights. The lesson learned here is that international civil society and grassroots organizations are a powerful force, and they must come to Israel/Palestine not to work with one party against the other, but instead to work jointly with the peace movements of both sides.

From the perspective of the Israeli-Palestinian peace organizations, the process of competing for the partisan support of the international community has harmed dialogue and cooperation between the parties. Therefore the lesson here is that less competition and more joint activities with the international groups participating is most valuable.

Although it is difficult to calculate exactly, one can be certain that more money to settlements comes indirectly through US governmental support (by releasing the Israeli government from the need to cover the requirements of immigrants and citizens) than the estimated 60 million dollar earmarked for peace work between 1993 and 2000. To make sure that peacebuilding is a US policy priority, an uphill battle in Congress needs to be fought to ensure that any foreign aid bill that provides large funds for Israel include a substantial share earmarked for peacebuilding activities.

Overall, not enough money was provided for "people-to-people" activities. Some 98 percent of Israeli and Palestinian people have not been exposed to this activity. The Oslo negotiators on both sides did not give sufficient acknowledgment to the fact that this conflict is not only between two governments but also between two nations. It was only when looking for a role for third parties that the idea of people-to-people initiatives arose. Indeed, in this trilateral relationship, the Norwegians paid for all people-to-people programs with matching funding from Jewish benefactors. Both the Israeli and Palestinian authorities refused to pay for grassroots activities.

There is no question that the international community, both at the governmental and nongovernmental level, is extremely concerned with our Palestinian/Israeli conflict and that has not managed, so far, to maximize its positive influence in peacebuilding.

11. Palestinians in Israel, in Cooperation with the Jewish Israelis and Alone

One of the most important issues in this direction, as Chapter 7 by Khaled Abu-Asbeh and Shuli Dichter suggests, is dependent on the ability of Israel to build partnership relations based on integration and equality with the Palestinians living inside Israel. It is here the wisdom of the saying: "How far you can arrange relations outside your house depends on how far you can arrange them within" applies.

Another lesson comes from the fact that Israeli society was shocked and surprised by the uprising of the Israeli Palestinians in October 2001. The Israeli Palestinians in turn were shocked that the police killed thirteen participants while they are considered to be Israeli citizens, and thus to enjoy the same protection as any other citizen in the country. This mutual shock expresses the gap that needs to be bridged in the internal relations of Israeli society.

One of the lessons of the peacebuilding initiatives is that Israeli Palestinians are not only a bridge between Palestinians and Israelis, but are a unique group with their own needs and national narratives. They are not mediators, nor do they stand in the middle of the bridge, but they have the advantage of knowing the language, mentality, and concerns of both societies. Often this group is overlooked or subsumed into one side or the other. As a separate force that is dually connected, concerned, and intrinsically linked to the future of all sides, they can provide valuable insight. Therefore, they should be encouraged to air their grievances even if the emergency situation requires having a priority focus on improving the current impasse that makes life in the West Bank and Gaza so difficult. The issues of dual identity can be transformed from a minus to a plus if adequate dynamics and sensitivity are displayed.

One of the important lessons to be derived from the experience of the Israeli Palestinians relates to the role of the media. The Israeli media has failed to provide any coverage of their situation, and has done nothing to build any bridge between them and the Israeli Jews. A campaign to persuade the media to move in this direction is thus very important (see Chapter 7 by Khaled Asbeh and Shalom Dichter).

Final Remarks

Peacebuilders were able to influence both decisionmakers and public opinion toward peace in crucial stages of the Israeli-Palestinian conflict. Examples of this include the Israeli government's decision to withdraw from south Lebanon as a result of the continuous pressure of the peace movement in Israel as well as from the outside. The grassroots uprising of the first intifada put effective pressure on Yasser Arafat and the Nineteenth Palestinian National Council to eventually approve the two-state solution, while recognizing Israel was calling for the end of occupation in a fully independent Palestinian state. Another example is the Oslo agreement, and, last but not least, Prime Minister Sharon's plan to withdraw completely from Gaza was made under external pressure, but also as a right-wing response to the left's peace initiatives such as the Geneva Accords and the Aylon-Nussiebeh initiative.

In the area of public opinion, it is not an accident that 70 percent of both peoples support peace built on a two-state solution. Although this is fluid and combined with other contradictory trends in public opinion, this remains one of the achievements of the peace movement.

And yet, at this time, it seems that the effectiveness of the peace and conflict resolution organization in both societies is at a low point. While acknowledging their past contribution, it also demonstrates the work that was not done by the peace camps on both sides and formulates strategies for working for peace and ending the occupation, as a way not only to liberate the Palestinian people, but also to liberate the Israelis and safeguard the deteriorating democracy.

Another incomplete task has been the need to include the public at large in peace action. This requires not only personal courage, but also experience. Therefore it seems a desirable aim in the near future to bring the peace movements together in one peace front, where every movement will keep its own independent personality, but all will work together upon themes at the same time.

Another conclusion relates to Judaism, Christianity, and Islam. In a time of revival of religious ideologies, it is very important for the peace movements to use tolerant and nonviolent religious texts in the preaching of peace toward the faithful. If peacebuilding is a process of building and extending the constituencies for peace, it will be important for those religious peace activists already involved to bring devout believers in large numbers to peace work.

An interconnecting conclusion relates to nonviolence as a concept of conflict transformation. Nonviolence in this respect is needed by all, not only the Palestinians, in order to create a win/win situation. The Israeli population has to pressure decisionmakers for peace and to pressure the military not to use violent measures against Palestinian civilians. Nonviolence should be understood differently not only as a way to control violence and to show respect for universal human rights, but as a way of personal and collective struggle for legitimate objectives, from the school and the community up to the national liberation of both nations.

The final interconnecting lesson regards the future relations between the two peoples. The high level of hatred and mutual mistrust has projected an overwhelming feeling of pessimism for the prospects for peace in the near term. The challenge here is to build these relations on the cooperation called for by peacebuilders and not upon separation.

Thanks to the contributors to this book, we now know more about peacebuilding initiatives in Israel/Palestine. But more research is needed on the history of peace activism in Israel/Palestine, with every movement being researched from primary sources. Further research is needed on strategies for nonviolence in both societies, and for the development of a social and economic program for the peace movements that will connect the cost of war and occupation to the poverty of large sectors of both nations. Peacebuilders need to better reach public opinion on both sides, perhaps talking directly to the media of the other, if possible in their respective languages.

Reconciliation is traditionally seen as part of the postconflict era, after the signing of a peace accord. In this protracted dispute, there is a need to put the best minds to work together and discern how elements of reconciliation (healing, acknowledgment, apology, forgiveness, punitive justice) can be injected *now,* in the time of violent conflict. Otherwise, we may not reach a peace accord in our lifetimes.

Last but not least, the main challenge currently is to build these relations on the cooperation called for by peacebuilders and not upon separation, as now seems to be the prevailing norm. Lack of dialogue at the leadership level resulting from policies of unilateralism should not polarize the peacebuilders of both societies. Much to the contrary, after a rather self-critical diagnosis of the shortcoming in the past, it is now the time to brainstorm together how to translate the large common denominator of the two-state solution by the majorities in both societies into a gradual appeal for negotiations and implementation of such a goal.

We hope that this joint effort will be widely read by our peers and society at large and that translations into Arabic and Hebrew will follow in order to stimulate further thoughts on peacebuilding leading into action.

Notes

1. For such a critical position see Edward Said, "The Limits of Cooperation Between Palestinians and Israelis," *News from Within*, April 1994; Jonathan Kuttab, "An Exchange on Dialogue," *Journal of Palestine Studies,* 1986; and "Palestinian Israeli Civil Society Cooperation," *Nasif Mau'alem,* 1999.

2. For instance, one of the activists interviewed on October 2, 2003 (requesting anonymity) told one of the writers that it is possible to have joint activities on both sides of the checkpoints, but the statement was not announced publicly as being jointly prepared.

3. From the Palestinian side, the Palestinian Nongovernmental Organization Network (PNGO) released a statement on October 23, 2000, "to ask all Palestinian NGO's to withdraw from any basic joint projects with Israelis." A call was made also to the Arab NGOs "to halt all joint activities with Israeli organizations, until the end of the Israeli occupation and withdrawal from the lands occupied since 1967, including East Jerusalem, is realized."

4. The idea of postponing any relations with Israeli peace organizations until after the establishment of a Palestinian state extends the assumption that joint peace activities are marginal and cannot change the political map, and conversely, that they can be used by decisionmakers to claim stability even though occupation still exists. Professor Edward Said, who participated actively in joint Israeli-Palestinian endeavors, clarified this position as follows: "My position is predicated upon the goal of equality between the peoples, with the Palestinians enjoying the same rights that only the Israelis enjoy today. In order to attain this objective, there is only the path of direct struggle for an end to the Israeli occupation and denial of Palestinian rights. By contrast, the current [Israeli] approach of at one in the same time taking steps to prepare the ground for the continuation of the occupation while spreading promises of cooperation between some Israelis and Palestinians, seems to me false and deceptive. . . . Therefore we must strive first of all for the following two objectives: For an end to the occupation and for the development of independent institutions on a level equal to those of the Israelis. Only then will it be possible to seriously speak of cooperation. Until then, any cooperation constitutes capitulation to Israeli policy." Edward Said, "The Limits of Cooperation Between Palestinians and Israelis, *News From Within,* vol. x, no. 4, April 1994.

5. Israel-Palestine Center for Research and Information ((IPCRI), "Years of Experience in Strategies for Peace Making," *Yes PM,* December. 2002, p. 4.

6. Palestine Center for Policy and Survey Research, Poll Number 10, December 4–9, 2003.

7. Edy Kaufman, Shukri B. Abed, and Robert L. Rothstein, eds., *Democracy, Peace, and the Israel-Palestinian Conflict,* Boulder, CO: Lynne Rienner Publishers, 1993.

PART 2

Directory

Introduction to the Directory

The directory that follows presents profiles and contact information for about 80 organizations working in the field of conflict prevention and peacebuilding in Israel and Palestine. Because organizations working in the field of humanitarian aid, development cooperation, human rights, and democracy have increasingly incorporated the goals of conflict prevention and peacebuilding into their primary mandate, we have also opted to include organizations that, at first sight, might not be seen as conflict prevention and peacebuilding organizations.

Additional information on some organizations may be found in various of the preceding chapters. The shaded box that appears at the upper right of each profile presents the organization's main activities in conflict prevention and peacebuilding.

This directory focuses only on those organizations working for peace across the divide that the editors could identify throughout this project and were cooperative in providing information to us. It thus does not claim to contain information of all efforts for peace, initiatives, and organizations in Israel and Palestine.

Abraham Fund Initiatives

The Abraham Fund Initiatives is a nongovernmental organization based in New York and Jerusalem working to advance coexistence, equality, and cooperation among Israel's Jewish and Arab citizens. Founded in 1989, The Abraham Fund focuses its activities in three different arenas: (1) implementing advocacy and awareness campaigns to the public and policymakers to increase knowledge and encourage dialogue on the issue of coexistence; (2) funding and supporting grassroots coexistence projects in three key areas: advancing the professionalization of educators and leaders, coexistence education in the formal school system, and education for coexistence in the community; and (3) developing, managing, and sponsoring large-scale regional and national coexistence projects to encourage Jewish and Arab Israeli citizens to work together in achieving shared goals.

Yozmot Keren Avraham
15 Arlozorov Street
Jerusalem 92181
Israel

Tel: +972 (2) 566 5133
Fax: +972 (2) 566 5139
tafjer@netvision.net.il
http://www.coexistence.org/

Contact: Dan Pattir, Executive Vice President

Number of staff: 15

Publications: Advancing Coexistence and Equality among Jews and Arabs in Israel: a Platform for Action; The Effects of Participation in Co-existence Programs Supported by The Abraham Foundation on Jewish and Arab Youngsters, 2002; The Education System in the Arab Sector: Guidelines for an Advocacy Plan; and *An Evaluation of Jewish-Arab Coexistence.*

Adalah

Adalah ("Justice" in Arabic): The Legal Center for Arab Minority Rights in Israel, established in 1996, works to protect human rights in general and the rights of the Arab minority citizens of Israel in particular. Adalah addresses legal issues pertaining to land rights; civil and political rights; cultural, social, and economic rights; religious rights; women's rights; and prisoners' rights. Adalah's range of activities include bringing cases before Israeli courts and various state authorities; advocating for legislation; providing legal consultation to individuals, nongovernmental organizations, and Arab institutions; educating and publishing human rights reports on legal issues; and training stagiaires (legal apprentices), law students, and new Arab lawyers in the field of human rights.

P.O. Box 510
Shafa'amr, 20200
Israel
_____

Tel: +972 (4) 950 1610
Fax: +972 (4) 950 3140
adalah@adalah.org
http://www.adalah.org/

Contact: Hassan Jabareen, Advocate, Founder, and General Director

Number of staff: 20

Publications: Adalah's Newsletter. Adalah's Review. October 2000—Law and Politics before the Or Commission. Institutionalized Discrimination: Adalah's Report to the World Conference Against Racism, Aug/Sept 2001. Human Rights Guide for Palestinian Citizens of Israel (Arabic).

Adam Institute for Democracy and Peace

EDUCATION
ACTION

The Adam Institute for Democracy and Peace is a nonprofit organization working to break down stereotypes, enhance understanding of democratic principles, and promote peaceful coexistence. Established in 1986, the Adam Institute is currently working with the Israeli Ministry of Education to integrate peace education into the Israeli school curriculum. The Institute also trains young journalists from Israel, Palestine, and Jordan in accurate and honest reporting as a mechanism for preventing the perpetuation of stereotypes. Programs working directly with young people include democracy education for young Jewish and Arab Israeli, Palestinian and Jordanian leaders; the Promises Program to break down stereotypes between Jewish and Arab high school students; and democracy education for Jewish and Arab elementary students in northern Israel. The Adam Institute's International Center for Education for Democracy was founded in 1992 to promote networking and the exchange of research and workshop opportunities for Israeli and international educators.

P.O. Box 3356
Jerusalem 91033
Israel

Tel: +972 (2) 644 8290
Fax: +972 (2) 675 2932
adam@adaminstitute.org.il
http://www.adaminstitute.org.il

Contact: Laura Salem, Resource Officer
Number of staff: 80
Publications: Adam's Voice newsletter.
The Educational Process in Adam Institute Workshops, 1999. *The Right to Dignity and the Difficulty of Respecting Other,* 1998. *Incitement and Freedom of Speech,* 1997.

RESEARCH
EDUCATION
ACTION
ADVOCACY

Adva Center

Adva Center was started in 1991 and is a nonpartisan Israeli policy analysis center. Adva publishes position papers and *The Israel Equality Monitor,* covering policy topics such as education, health, housing, income distribution, and social welfare. Adva's Budget Analysis Project broadens public debate on national financial priorities, a more equitable distribution of government resources, and a more democratic and transparent budget-making process. Each year, Adva organizes an Alternative Debate on the Budget of Israel, held in the Knesset building with legislators and representatives of advocacy organizations. Adva also provides educational and outreach programs on budget and equity issues. The public health advocacy Hotline on Health Project helps resolve callers' health care related complaints.

P.O. Box 36529
Tel Aviv 61364
Israel
—————
Tel: +972 (3) 560 8871
Fax: +972 (3) 560 2205
advainfo@bezeqint.net
http://www.adva.org/

Contact: Barbara Swirski, Director

Number of staff: 7 and research contractors

Publications: The Israel Equality Monitor pamphlets. *The Role of the Knesset in the Budget-Making Process: A Critical Analysis and Proposal for Reform. Looking at the Budget.* Women's Economic Literacy/Gender Budget publications. Position papers on equity issues in the areas of education, health, housing, income distribution, and social welfare.

Arab Association for Human Rights

EDUCATION
ACTION
ADVOCACY

The Arab Association for Human Rights (HRA), founded in 1988 by lawyers and community activists, is an independent, grassroots, nongovernmental organization. HRA works to promote and protect the political, civil, economic, and cultural rights of the Palestinian Arab minority in Israel from an international human rights perspective. HRA has conducted local community and international campaigns to raise awareness, understanding, and respect for human rights and democratic principles; monitored violations of human rights and published and distributed reports documenting abuses; initiated and participated in local NGO coalitions concerned with the rights of prisoners and administrative detainees, land and housing rights, women's rights, and networking; facilitated community human rights education programs and events; provided legal assistance; advocated before United Nations bodies; and organized and participated in local and international training workshops and conferences. Additionally, HRA has conducted lectures and workshops for Palestinian secondary school students on human rights principles and standards and how they apply to the situation of the Palestinian Arabs in Israel.

Mary's Well Street
P.O. Box 215
Nazareth 16101
Israel

Tel: +972 (4) 656 1923
Fax: +972 (4) 656 4934
hra1@arabhra.org
http://www.arabhra.org/

Contact: Muhammad Zeidan, Director

Number of staff: 16

Publications: Fact Sheets on issues pertaining to human rights status of Palestinians in Israel. *Weekly Review of the Arab Press in Israel. The Right for Muslims to Take Part in Politics,* 2003. *The Unrecognized Villages in the Negev. Update: 2003. HRA Submission to the UN Human Rights Committee,* 2002. *Silencing Dissent: A Report on the Violation of Political Rights of the Arab Parties in Israel,* 2002. *Behind the Walls: Separation Walls Between Arabs and Jews in Mixed Cities in Israel,* 2005.

EDUCATION

Ariga

First opened to the public in 1995, Ariga is a web-based, free source of independent news from Israel, emphasizing the peace process, but also including poetry, painting, and other subjects of interest to its sole owner, publisher, and editor. The peace-focused subjects include "The Situation," a Monday through Friday report on Israel written daily by the site editor, as well as other analysis and commentary by Ariga contributors. A section lists resources such as human rights and peace groups operating in Israel and Palestine and a complete collection of significant treaties and historical documents relating to the peace process. Also included on the site are poetry, a Yiddish glossary, a Bible food cookbook, a small art gallery, and short stories and articles.

86 Shlomo Hamelekh Street
Tel Aviv 64512
Israel

Tel: +972 (3) 522 4687
Fax: +972 (3) 527 5131
rbr@ariga.com
http://www.ariga.com

Contact: Robert Rosenberg, Founder and Operator

Number of staff: 1

Publications: The Ariga Update newsletter.

RESEARCH
EDUCATION
ACTION
ADVOCACY

Association for Civil Rights in Israel

The Association for Civil Rights in Israel (ACRI) is a nonpolitical and independent body with the mission of protecting human and civil rights in Israel and in the territories under Israeli control. ACRI has been working since 1972. It is a membership organization focusing on (1) advocacy at public policy level; (2) pursuit of legal actions intended to set precedents favoring human and civil rights; (3) publication and dissemination of reports on human rights issues; (4) an educational program in both Jewish and Arab schools; (5) educational work aimed at social and community workers, security forces, and local and national decisionmakers; and (6) casework on complaints and requests for assistance from the public, including a public hotline.

P.O. Box 34510
Jerusalem 91000
Israel
Additional offices in Tel Aviv
    and Haifa
_____

Tel: + 972 (2) 652 1218
Fax: + 972 (2) 652 1219
mail@acri.org.il
http://www.acri.org.il

Contact: Rachel Benziman, Executive
Director

Number of staff: 45

*Publications: The State of Human Rights
in Israel,* 2003, 2004. *A Status Report:
Equality for Arab Citizens of Israel,* 2000.
*Fatal Force: Report on Police Brutality
During the October 2000 Riots that Killed
13 Israeli-Arab Citizens,* 2000. *Without
Justifiable Cause* [report criticizing police,
courts, and prison system in application of
the Arrests and Detention Law], 2000.

Association of Forty

The Association of Forty—the association for the recognition of the Arab Unrecognized Villages in Israel—was formally established in 1988 in the unrecognized village of Ein-Hod, by the local committee of the village, the inhabitants of unrecognized villages, and Arab and Jewish volunteers from all over the country. Among its goals are to obtain official recognition for the villages, to improve living conditions, and to claim full rights and equality for the Arab citizens of the state. Among the Association's activities are providing legal advice to the residents of the villages against Israeli policies of demolishing houses and confiscating lands; establishing a parliamentary lobby to raise the cases of these villages; and pursuing the governmental housing projects. They have also organized villages to provide their own needed infrastructure, such as paving roads; improving existing roads and connecting villages to the network of water, electricity, and telephones; operating kindergartens and clinics for mother and child care; and offering educational noncurricular activities for the schoolchildren of these villages. Public education campaigns include a monthly newspaper, photographic exhibitions, documentary films, study days, and local and international conferences.

Ein Hod
near Nir Etzion, 30808
Israel

Tel: +972 4 984 3335
Fax: +972 4 984 3336
a525@netvision.net.il
http://www.assoc40.org/

Publications: Sawt Al-Qura monthly newspaper. *Policy & Solutions* (online articles). *Mena Report,* 1996. *Markovith Report,* 1986.

ACTION
ADVOCACY

Bat Shalom

Bat Shalom is an Israeli national feminist grassroots organization of Jewish and Palestinian Israeli women working together since 1993 for peace grounded in a just resolution of the Israel-Palestine conflict, respect for human rights, and an equal voice for Jewish and Arab women within Israeli society. It is the Israeli side of the Jerusalem Link Women's Joint Venture for Peace. Its main activities are advocacy and grassroots campaigning for a just peace and against the occupation of the West Bank and Gaza Strip, including joint activities with Palestinian women's organizations. It also promotes action by international groups and individuals to these ends.

The Jerusalem Women's
  Action Center
P.O. Box 8083
Jerusalem 91080
Israel
Branch office in Afula

Tel: +972 (2) 563 1477
Fax: +972 (2) 561 7983
info@batshalom.org
http://www.batshalom.org

Contact: Molly Malekar, Director

Number of staff: 6

Publications: Joint Statements with the Jerusalem Center for Women and Annual and Additional Declarations

RESEARCH

Begin-Sadat

The Begin-Sadat (BESA) Center for Strategic Studies is a nonpartisan and independent institute, affiliated with the Political Studies Department at Bar-Ilan University, Israel. The Center was founded in 1991 and is named in memory of Menachem Begin and Anwar Sadat. The BESA Center provides policy-oriented research on matters of strategy, security, and peace in the Middle East. The BESA Center also sponsors conferences, workshops, lectures, symposia, and briefings for international and local audiences.

Bar-Ilan University
Ramat Gan 52900
Israel

Tel: +972 (3) 535 9198
Fax: +972 (3) 535 9195
office@besacenter.org
http://www.biu.ac.il/SOC/besa/

Contact: Efraim Inbar, Director

Number of staff: 24

Publications: BESA Bulletin (newsletter). Books related to security issues. *Armed Forces in the Middle East: Politics and Strategy,* 2002. *US Allies in a Changing World,* 2000. *Democratic Societies and Their Armed Forces: Israel in Comparative Context,* 2000. *The Politics and Economics of Defence Industries,* 1998.

ACTION

Beit Hagefen

Beit Hagefen—a municipal, national, and international center—was founded in 1963 to create a meeting place for social and cultural encounters between Jews and Arabs and to encourage and promote understanding and coexistence. The Center operates as a nonpartisan association and is supported and funded by the Haifa Municipality, the Ministry of Education Culture and Sport, the Ministry of Foreign Affairs, as well as private donors. Beit Hagefen sponsors a wide range of activities for both Arabs and Jews including: cross-cultural encounters for all age groups, courses, women's clubs, a library, an art gallery, an Arab theater, a training center for Education for Democracy and Coexistence, and a visitors center. Emphasis is placed on special events and activities such as: The Arab Book and Culture Month and the Hanukah-Christmas-Ramadan Festival.

2 Hagefen Street
P.O. Box 9421
Haifa 35662
Israel

Contact: M. Peri, Director General
Number of staff: 30
Publications: Catalogs

Tel: +972 (4) 852 5251/2
Fax: +972 (4) 852 9166
bhagefen@netvision.net.il
http://www.haifa.gov.il/beit-hagefen/

EDUCATION
ACTION

Beyond Words

Beyond Words is a nonprofit organization that operates a coexistence program developed in Israel over the past 10 years. The organization was set up between 1995 and 1996 and became official registered in 2003. The program enables Arab and Jewish early childhood educators, parents, and youth to overcome biases and release the feelings that otherwise hinder their ability to be close to those of different races, cultures, and religions. Activities include training programs in verbal and nonverbal communication, drama, dance/movement therapy, holistic massage, listening partnerships, and noncompetitive games. The Shchenim–Jiran initiative works to bring entire Jewish and Arab communities together in order to work with children at an early age to break down stereotypes.

P.O. Box 956
Kfar Vradim
Israel 25147

Contact: Nitzan Gordan, Founder
Number of staff: 13
Publications: Good News, Newsletter

Tel: +972 (4) 997 1151
info@beyondwords7.org
http://www.beyondwords7.org/

B'Tselem

B'Tselem (translated from Hebrew as "in the image of")—The Israeli Information Center for Human Rights in the Occupied Territories—is an independent Israeli nongovernmental organization founded in 1989 with the primary goal of documenting human rights violations in the Occupied Territories and of building a human rights culture in Israel. Findings are made available to the public through their website and issue-specific publications. B'Tselem conducts its own fieldwork and research and cross-checks analysis with relevant documents, official government sources, and information from other human rights sources. B'Tselem recommends and encourages changes in the Israeli government and military policies to ensure greater protection of human rights. Staff also brief the media, Knesset members, foreign diplomats, and researchers on their findings and analysis. Through these efforts, B'Tselem works to foster debate and discussion among the Israeli public and international community about the importance and application of human rights in the occupied territories.

8 Hata'asiya Street, 4th floor
Jerusalem 93420
Israel

Tel: +972 (2) 673 5599
Fax: +972 (2) 674 9111
mail@btselem.org
www.btselem.org

Contact: Rachel Greenspahn, Development Director

Number of staff: 29

Publications: Electronic newsletter and reports since 1989 on Administrative Detention, Attacks of Israeli Civilians, Deportation, Destruction of Houses and Fields, Economy, Family Separation, Freedom of Movement, House Demolitions, Human Shields, Jerusalem, Minors, Open-Fire Regulations, Palestinian Authority, Planning and Building, Separation Barrier, Settlements, Settlers' Violence, Torture, Violence by Security Forces, Water Crisis, and Workers from the Territories.

Bustan L'Shalom

ACTION

Bustan L' Shalom began in 1999 as a grassroots partnership addressing the plight of indigenous and marginalized people in Israel/Palestine. Members include Jewish and Arab activists, architects, eco-builders, and organic farmers promoting environmental justice and human rights. Bustan was created to address the environmental degradation and disappearance of the rural landscape in Israel/Palestine as a by-product of the continued territorial war and occupation. Their work raises awareness of systemic discrimination and the effects of globalization by creating sustainable civil and agricultural infrastructure. Activities include workshops, building camps, and eco-reality tours. They have built a medical clinic in Wadi el Na'am, provided needed medical supplies and basic needs to indigent Russian and Ethiopian families living at Givat HaMatowse Absorption Center in Jerusalem, helped to coordinate a weekly Interfaith Peace Vigil in the Old City of Jerusalem, and supported the Jahalin Bedouin community.

P.O. Box 6955
Jerusalem, 91060
Israel

Tel: +972 (53) 711800
info@bustanlshalom.org
http://www.bustan.org

Contact: Devorah Brous, Founder and Director

Number of staff: 11 volunteers

Center for Jewish-Arab Economic Development

RESEARCH
EDUCATION
ACTION
ADVOCACY

The Center for Jewish-Arab Economic Development (CJAED) is an Israeli nongovernmental organization that has aimed to close the gap between the Jewish and Arab sectors in Israel since 1988, striving to thus build the foundation for sustainable economic development and peace. Its programs include business development and cooperation projects, promotion of Palestinian women's entrepreneurship, small business promotion and financing, promotion of community involvement in municipal government and planning processes, and facilitating discussion of relevant public policy.

16 Galgalei Hapladah Street
P.O. Box 12017
Herzilya Pituah 46733

Israel
Tel: +972 (9) 971 9900
Fax: +972 (9) 954 0136
information@cjaed.org.il
http://www.cjaed.org.il

Contact: Helmi Kittani, Co-Director; Hanoch Marmari, Co-Director

Number of staff: 8

Publications: Center for Jewish-Arab Economic Development, quarterly newsletter

RESEARCH
ADVOCACY

The Council for Peace and Security

The Council for Peace and Security, established in 1998, is a nonprofit organization of experts on peace and security without political party affiliation. The Council brings together some one thousand volunteer members, each with a background in security and diplomacy. Members include former high-ranking officers in the Israel Defense Force, Mossad and Shin Bet security services, and Israel police; retired diplomats; directors general of government ministries; and academics from various fields. Members see supporting the Middle East peace process as a necessary component of national security. The aim is to educate the public on security-related issues in the peace process. The Council holds seminars and meetings on security issues and leads study tours to battle sites.

P.O. Box 1320
Ramat Hasharon 47112
Israel
_____

Tel: +972 (3) 548 1414
http://www.peace-security.org.il/

Contact: Maj. Gen. (Ret) Danny Rothschild
Number of staff: 8
Publications: Israeli-Palestinian Conflict:
The Way Ahead for Israel, 2003. Slippery
Slopes and Uphill Battles, 2003. Removing
Saddam Is Good Enough, 2003. Walking
the Beat in Gaza, 2003. Unilateral
Redeployment Did Not Lose in These
Elections, 2003. Various articles in
Hebrew and English by Council members.

Courage to Refuse

Courage to Refuse is a group of combat officers and soldiers in the Israeli armed forces who in 2002 signed the Combatants' Letter declaring that they will not serve in the occupied territories, stating that the occupation is immoral and a threat to Israel's own security. In the letter, the soldiers pledge their ongoing commitment to the security of Israel, but declare that they will take no part in missions intended to prolong the occupation. Signatories represent all units of the IDF and all sectors of the Israeli society. The members of the movement, often called "refuseniks," continue to do their reserve duty whenever they are summoned, but refuse to serve in the occupied territories. Over 280 members of Courage to Refuse have in fact been courtmartialed and jailed for periods of up to 35 days as a result of their refusal.

P.O. Box 16238
Tel Aviv
Israel
_____

Tel: +972 (3) 523 3103
info@seruv.org.il
http://www.seruv.org.il

Contact: David Zonshein, Co-Founder

Number of staff: 5

Publications: Monthly e-mail newsletter available through website. *Democracy, Obedience and Refusal,* 2004. *Bound by Their Conscience,* 2004. *The War's Seventh Day,* 2003. *Apartheid in the Holy Land,* 2002.

Defense for Children International— Israel Section

RESEARCH
EDUCATION
ACTION
ADVOCACY

Defense for Children International—Israel Section (DCI-Israel) was founded in 1987 by a group of Arab and Jewish educators, psychologists, lawyers, and social workers to promote and protect the rights of children in Israel and, under the effective control of the state of Israel, in the occupied territories. DCI-Israel advocates for free and adequate legal counseling and representation for minors in civil matters, runs pilot projects to train lawyers to represent children in civil cases, and promotes the establishment of legal counseling centers for minors. DCI-Israel also intervenes on behalf of children directly affected by the Israel-Palestinian conflict and monitors the situation of Palestinian and Israeli minors in Israeli jails, prisons, and closed institutions. Although it provides legal counsel to individual cases, DCI-Israel focuses on developing pilot projects for needed services. DCI-Israel is the coordinator of the Israeli Children's Rights Coalition, coordinates the Israeli NGO report to the UN Committee on the Rights of the Child, monitors implementation of international standards for children's rights, and participates in the Knesset Advancement of the Status of Children Committee.

2 Yzhak Elhanan Street
P.O. Box 8028
Jerusalem
Israel

Tel: +972 (2) 563 3003
Fax: +972 (2) 563 1241
info@dci.org.il
http://www.dci.org.il/home_en.asp

Contact: Philip Veerman, Director and Hadeel Younis, Acting Director

Number of staff: 8

Publications: Periodic Alternative Report to the UN Committee on the Rights of the Child. Juvenile Justice in Israeli Occupied West Bank: Lessons of the Joint Project of DCI-Palestine and DCI-Israel, 1995. Improving Health Care Access for Palestinian Children: Visions for the Future, 1994. A Situation Analysis of Palestinian Children in the West Bank and Gaza, 1992–1993. Uprooted Children: Final Report on the Situation of the Uprooted Jewish Children in Addis Ababa, 1990.

The Forum for
Coexistence in Negev—Dukium

The Negev Coexistence Forum—Dukium has sought, since 1997, to provide a framework for Jewish-Arab cooperative efforts through seeking equal human rights for Arabs living in the Negev. Dukium (Hebrew for "coexistence") acknowledges Israeli responsibilities in the denial of full civil rights to Arabs in the Negev. Projects include providing basic human services such as water irrigation to unrecognized villages; public action campaigns and cases through the Israeli high court of appeals; and general lobbying and letter-writing campaigns for Bedouins excluded from future expansion plans.

P.O. Box 334
Lehavin 85336
Israel
_____

Tel/Fax: +972 (8) 651 2850
info@dukium.org
http://dukium.org

Contact: Yeela Livnat, Coordinator and Sliman Abu-Zaed, Coordinator

Number of staff: 30

Publications: Internet newsletter, various PDF documents posted on the website pertaining to the needs of unrecognized Bedouin villages and unrecognized villages in the Negev.

Givat Haviva

Givat Haviva is an education, research, and documentation center, founded in 1949 by the Ha'Kibbutz Ha'arzi Federation. Its goals are to educate for peace, democracy, and coexistence; to resist racism and all forms of discrimination; and to foster greater understanding between different groups in society and among nations. Givat Haviva hosts conferences, seminars, and workshops with a faculty of Jewish and Arab educators. Its Moreshet Center, established in the early1960s, houses a collection of testimonies from concentration camp survivors and resistance fighters and is a leading research institute and resource center for the study of the Holocaust. The "Yad Ya'ari" Center focuses on the history and current issues of the kibbutz movement, the youth movement, and Israeli society. The campus facilities include classrooms, audi-toriums for conferences and events, guestrooms for hosting VIPs, a computer lab, a language lab, an extensive research library, 112 dormitory rooms, a swim-ming pool, and athletic fields.

Givat Haviva, Israel
M. P. Menashe 37850
Israel
Other international locations
    listed in the U.S., Canada, UK,
    Switzerland, Germany, Austria
    and The Netherlands.
_____
Tel: +972 (4) 630 9289/214
Fax: +972 (4) 630 9305
givathaviva@givathaviva.org.il
www.givathaviva.org.il

Contact: Alex G. Elsohn, Europe Director

Number of staff: 30

Publications: 2001 Survey—Attitudes of the Arabs to the State of Israel. The Al-Aqsa Intifada among the Palestinian Citizens in Israel: Causes and Results. Children Write for Peace, 2000. Planting in Rocky Ground: The History of "Ha'Shomer Ha'Tzair" Movement in Hungary from its Beginnings Until the Outbreak of World War II, 1927–1939. Hashomer Hatzair Political Posters, 1937–1967. "7 Roads": Theoretical Options for the Status of the Arabs in Israel.

Gush Shalom

Gush Shalom ("The Peace Bloc") was founded as an alternative to the Israeli mainstream peace movement in 1993 with the coming into power of the new Labor Party government headed by Yitzhak Rabin. The primary aim of Gush Shalom is to influence Israeli public opinion and lead it toward peace and conciliation with the Palestinian people, based on the following principles: putting an end to the occupation, establishing an independent and sovereign state of Palestine in all the territories occupied by Israel in 1967, establishing Jerusalem as the capital of the two states, recognizing in principle the right of return of the Palestinian refugees, safeguarding the security of both Israel and Palestine by mutual agreement and guarantees, and striving for overall peace between Israel and all Arab countries. Public information campaigns have addressed issues of Palestinian prisoners, refugee rights, Oslo agreement violations, house demolitions, boycotting of settlement products, and reestablishing the Green Line as the international border between Israel and the future Palestinian state. The Gush has held hundreds of demonstrations and carried out countless direct actions in response to day-to-day emergencies. Most of these were joint actions with Palestinians.

P.O. Box 3322
Tel-Aviv 61033
Israel
_____
Tel/Fax +972 (3) 556 5804
info@gush-shalom.org
http://www.gush-shalom.org/

Contact: Uri Avnery, Founder
Number of staff: 100
Publications: Weekly political advertisement in Haaretz.

HaMoked:
Center for the Defense of the
Individual

ACTION
ADVOCACY

HaMoked: Center for the Defense of the Individual, founded in 1988, is an Israeli human rights organization whose main objective is to assist Palestinians of the occupied territories whose rights are violated due to Israel's policies. HaMoked files legal claims, submits petitions to the High Court of Justice, endeavors to bring about changes in policy by the authorities, and supports legislative amendments that would improve the status of human rights in the territories and East Jerusalem. Policy areas include detainee rights, family unification and residency rights, freedom of movement, violence committed by security forces and settlers, home demolition, deportation, and respect for the dead. HaMoked also operates an Emergency Human Rights Hotline. HaMoked's website contains texts of Israeli laws and regulations, including those of the military government; international conventions; petitions to the Israeli High Court of Justice; claims for compensation for damages; decisions by Israeli and other courts; and other official documents and reports.

4 Abu Obeidah Street
Jerusalem 97200
Israel

Tel: +972 (2) 627 1698
mail@hamoked.org.il
http://www.hamoked.org.il

Contact: Dalia Kerstein, Executive Director

Number of staff: 37

Publications: Forbidden Families: Family Unification and Child Registration in East Jerusalem, 2004. *Families Torn Apart: Separation of Palestinian Families in The Occupied Territories,* 1999. *Captive Corpses,* 1999. Activity reports are posted on the website.

The Harry S. Truman Research Institute for the Advancement of Peace

RESEARCH
EDUCATION

The Harry S. Truman Research Institute for the Advancement of Peace, set up in 1965, is dedicated to fostering peace and advancing cooperation in the Middle East and around the world through research; the sponsorship of conferences, seminars, and colloquia; provision of fellowships for local and visiting scholars; and the maintenance of close relations with similar institutes abroad. In pursuit of these objectives, the Truman Institute's activities include studies on Middle Eastern issues, with an emphasis on Israeli-Palestinian relations, promoting and enhancing peace, cooperation, and welfare in the region as a whole. Joint Arab-Jewish research projects are particularly encouraged. There are six regional research units—Africa, Asia, the Balkans, Central Asia and the Caucasus, Latin America, and the Middle East—plus the Minerva Center for Human Rights. The Truman Institute maintains a small library and documentation center.

The Harry S. Truman Research Institute for the Advancement of Peace
The Hebrew University of Jerusalem
Mount Scopus
Jerusalem 91905
Israel

Tel: +972 (2) 588 2300
Fax: +972 (2) 582 8076
mstruman@mscc.huji.ac.il
http://truman.huji.ac.il

Contact: Professor Eyal Ben-Ari, Director

Number of staff: 21

Publications: Truman News (newsletter). *From Fahd to 'Abdallah: The Origins of the Saudi Peace Initiatives and Their Impact on the Arab System and Israel,* 2003. *Work, Land: The Story of a Palestinian Migrant Worker in the Age of Oslo,* 2003. *The Shebaa Farms: A Case Study of Border Dynamics in the Middle East,* 2002. *Social Identities of Young Jews, Arabs and Palestinians,* 2001.

House of Hope International Peace Center

The House of Hope International Peace Center is a Christian organization, which since 1978 works on an ecumenical, nonsectarian basis. The House of Hope provides a venue for Arab-Jewish dialogue and exchange, and hosts guest lecturers from around the world. It makes its facility available to local as well as international civic and social organizations. Each year is the Summer Peace Camp, offering a month-long program of recreational and peace-related activities for about 150 young people. House of Hope established the first Peace Kindergarten in Galilee and has an expanding peace library and international peace intern volunteer program. It has limited resources to distribute some aid to needy Christian and Muslim families in Shefa-Amr, Haifa, and the lower Galilee. Its long-term vision is to develop and operate a peace academy researching peace education in preschool through postsecondary settings.

P.O. Box 272
Shefar'am 20200
Israel

Tel: +972 (4) 986 8558
Fax: +972 (4) 986 1211
hoh@inter.net.il
http://www.hohpeacecenter.org

Contact: Rev. Thomas C. Cook, Jr., Project Minister for Israel

Number of staff:

Publications: Twice yearly newsletter. *Sulha: Palestinian Traditional Peacemaking Process,* 1993.

Interfaith Encounter Association

The Interfaith Encounter Association is dedicated to promoting peace in the Middle East through interfaith dialogue and cross-cultural study. It is based in the belief that religion can and should be a source of the solution for conflicts that exist in the region and beyond. Its projects and activities from 1994 onward include retreats and conference, interfaith encounters and general study sessions, women and youth interfaith encounters, Israeli-Palestinian dialogue, and cross-cultural study visits. Its Middle East Abrahamic Forum is an annual conference of Muslims, Jews, and Christians focused on coexistence and cooperation in and among their local communities.

17 Hameshoreret Rachel
Jerusalem 96348
P.O. Box 3814
Jerusalem 91037
Israel

Tel: +972 (2) 651 0520
Fax: +972 (2) 651 0557
msyuda@phys.huji.ac.il
http://www.interfaith-encounter.org/

Contact: Yehuda Stolov, Director

Number of staff: 33

Publications: Event and encounter reports.

EDUCATION
ACTION

Interns for Peace

Interns For Peace (IFP) was established in 1976 in Israel. IFP trains community development peace workers in Israel and in Palestine and Gaza/West Bank, Jordan, and Egypt. It is based on the principle that common action to achieve a shared task unites people to see each other's humanity and breaks down walls of suspicion, fear, distrust, and hatred. Over 200 Interns (community peace workers) engaged 80,000 Jews and Arabs in business, athletic, cultural, educational, women's, and community development projects. IFP is also developing pilot projects to improve ethnic relations worldwide.

Rehov Geula 35
P.O. Box 4796
Tel Aviv, 63304
Israel
_____

Tel: +972 (3) 517 6525
Fax: +972 (3) 517 7995

El Bahar St, Jassar Aga Bldg
Khan Yunis
Gaza
Palestine
_____

Tel/Fax: +972 (8) 206 8866
Office also in the United States.
ifpus@mindspring.com, ifppal@planet.com
http://www.internsforpeace.org/

Contact: Karen Walden and Bruce Cohen, International Directors

Number of staff:

Publications: Annual reports.

Interreligious Coordinating Council in Israel

ACTION

The Interreligious Coordinating Council in Israel (ICCI) is an umbrella organization of over seventy Jewish, Muslim, and Christian institutions actively working toward interreligious and intercultural understanding in Israel and the region. Founded in January 1991 by 23 Jews, Muslims, and Christians, the ICCI reaches thousands of people with programs that build confidence and trust, and shatter stereotypes, ignorance, and prejudice. The ICCI coordinates and sponsors intercultural and interreligious dialogues, public lecture series, and youth encounters, and publishes books, pamphlets, and articles on the these issues.

P.O. Box 8771
Jerusalem 91086
Israel

Tel: +972 (2) 561-1899
Fax: +972 (2) 563-4148
iccijeru@icci.org.il
http://www.icci.org.il

Contact: Ron Kronish, Director

Number of staff:

Publications: "Insight Israel," a series of articles written by various members of the ICCI staff addressing current interreligious and intercultural events in Israel and the world. *2001 Guide to Interreligious and Intercultural Activities in Israel: Common Values/Different Sources,* 1999. *Toward the Third Millennium: Trialogue in Jerusalem—Jews, Christians & Muslims,* 1999. *Christian Documents in Jewish-Christian Relations in The Contemporary Era,* 1996. *I am Joseph Your Brother,* a video film.

RESEARCH

Israel Democracy Institute

Israel Democracy Institute (IDI) is an independent, nonpartisan research institute. It was founded in 1991 as a center for policy studies with the purpose of strengthening Israel's democratic institutions and shaping its values. The Institute assists the Knesset and its committees, government ministries, and institutions; local authorities; and political parties by submitting research papers and proposals for changes and reforms in their areas of operation. In addition, the Israel Democracy Institute compiles comparative information on legislative topics and on ways of functioning in various democratic regimes. The IDI also publishes an annual index that provides a reliable and comprehensive picture of the quality and functioning of Israeli democracy, and the way it is perceived by the public.

4 Pinsker Street,
Jerusalem 92228
P.O. Box 4702
Jerusalem 91046
Israel

Tel: +972 (2) 530 0849
Fax: +972 (2) 530 0837
http://www.idi.org.il

Contact: Professor Arik Carmon, President

Number of staff: 90

Publications: Publishes material based on Institute fellows research. Summaries of Institute conferences and seminars, such as the Army-Society Forum, the Public Council, and the Annual Economic Conference.

Israeli Committee Against House Demolitions

EDUCATION
ACTION
ADVOCACY

The Israeli Committee Against House Demolitions (ICAHD) is a nonviolent, direct action, and advocacy organization opposing the demolition of Palestinian homes by Israeli authorities since 1996. It also works on other human rights violations by occupation forces as appropriate. Participants in its activities, which are closely coordinated with Palestinian groups, include members of a wide range of peace groups. While its focus is on resisting house demolition and rebuilding demolished houses, the ICAHD also organizes public awareness and education events including media work, youth workshops, exhibitions, and cultural activities; solidarity action in Israel and abroad including workcamps, tours of the occupied territories, and family and community twinning projects; and strategic practical support to Palestinian families and communities.

P.O. Box 2030
Jerusalem 91020
Israel

Tel: +972 (2) 624 5560
Fax: +972 (2) 622 1530
info@icahd.org
http://www.icahd.org/eng/

Contact: Jeff Halper, Director

Number of staff:

Publications: Article of the Week and Stories of the Month series posted on the website. *The Key to Peace: Dismantling the Matrix of Control.*

Israeli Council for
Israeli-Palestinian Peace

ADVOCACY

The Israeli Council for Israeli-Palestinian Peace (ICIPP) was formed in 1975 by a group of prominent Israeli Zionists as a private initiative in response to signs of moderation in the Palestinian national movement and the perceived lack of response from the Israeli government. The founders' manifesto describes the belief that Israel should challenge the PLO to make peace on the basis of Israeli withdrawal from the territories occupied in June 1967, the establishment of a Palestinian state in the West Bank and Gaza, and carefully negotiated agreements to guarantee the security of Israel. In addition, ICIPP calls for abolishing all discriminatory laws and practices toward Palestinian Israeli citizens. ICIPP's main activity is the publication of its quarterly newsletter, *The Other Israel,* providing coverage of the diverse struggles waged by the Israeli peace movement at large. It also contains commentaries on events in Israel and the Middle East from a perspective in which the interests of Israelis and Palestinians are ultimately reconcilable.

P.O. Box 2542
Holon 58125
Israel

Tel/Fax: +972 (3) 556 5804
AICIPP@igc.org; otherisr@actcom.co.il
http://otherisrael.home.igc.org/ICIPP.html

Contact: Adam Keller, *The Other Israel* Editor

Publications: The Other Israel, quarterly newsletter.

RESEARCH
EDUCATION
ACTION
ADVOCACY

Kav La'Oved

Kav La'Oved, founded in 1991, is dedicated to protecting the rights of migrant workers and low-paid Israelis and Palestinian workers. On an individual level, Kav La'Oved files Labor Court claims on behalf of workers and provides legal advice through the volunteer hotline. In the public sphere, Kav La'Oved exposes instances of exploitation that point to flaws in the Israeli labor system. The organization runs worker empowerment activities and promotes and initiates proposals for legislative change. Kav La'Oved conducts site tours, distributes multilingual rights information, publishes reports, publishes a weekly newspaper column answering readers' questions, participates in a weekly call-in radio program on worker's rights, initiates media exposure, and lobbies for improved policies. They also conduct education workshops for youth movements, students, lawyers, international groups, and workers.

17 Peretz Street
Tel-Aviv 66853
Israel
Local branch offices in
  Jerusalem, Be'er Sheba,
  and Haifa

Tel: +972 (3) 688 3766
Fax: +972 (3) 688 3537
email@kavlaoved.org.il
http://www.kavlaoved.org.il

Contact: Hanna Zohar, Executive Director

Number of staff: 15

Publications: Kav La'oved Newsletter, Systematic Violations with State Encouragement, December 2003; *Depriving Women Migrant Workers of Their Maternity Rights and Baby Benefits,* October 2003; *Civil Enforcement—For Better Standards,* February 2003. *Immigration Administration or Expulsion Unit?* May 2003. *Who Will Protect the Protective Legislation?* Monthly activity reports.

EDUCATION
ACTION
ADVOCACY

Kol HaIsha – Women's Center

Kol HaIsha was established in 1994 as a feminist grassroots organization for women of all backgrounds and political persuasions. The primary goals of Kol HaIsha are: to provide a space for the celebration of women's cultures and values; to reach out to women of Jerusalem and create programs that empower them and support them; to bring about social change in Jerusalem in keeping with the feminist vision; and to promote a vision and a model of true peace and tolerance. Its Resource and Referral Center provides information, referrals, and evaluation of women's social and legal services and legal rights. The Antea is its women's gallery, which runs educational programs using art as a tool for educating the public about women's issues. Its Community Outreach Project works with women from disadvantaged communities in an effort to help them establish support groups and other frameworks for empowering and bringing about social change. Kol HaIsha also is active in supporting and protecting battered women.

38 Ben Yehuda Street
P.O. Box 37157
Jerusalem
Israel
_____
Tel: +972 (2) 622 2591, 622 2455
Fax: +972 (2) 625 6187
Kolisha@netmedia.net.il

Contact: Yvonne Deutsch, Executive Director

Number of staff: 4

Publications: Newsletter published every two months advertising activities.

ACTION

Kvisa Shchora

Kvisa Shchora ("Black Laundry") is a direct action group of lesbians, gays, bisexuals, transgenders, and others, which was founded in 2001 against the occupation and for social justice. Kvisa Shchora tries to stress the connection between different forms of oppression.

Israel
_____
Tel: +972 55 300 385
kvisamail@yahoo.com
http://www.blacklaundry.org/

Publications: Online newsletter, distribution through self-registration.

EDUCATION
ACTION

Link to the Environment

Link to the Environment (LINK) is composed of a diverse group of Galilee residents, Arab and Jewish citizens of Israel, who have been uniting since 1996 across cultural and social boundaries to protect the shared environment of the north of Israel for their common future. LINK's goals are: to improve the quality of the environment in the Galilee, to encourage people to volunteer for the environment and for preservation of nature, and to advance cooperation between Arabs and Jews to improve the environment. Examples of LINK's activities include: engaging businesses, municipalities, and organizations in solid waste management, community-based planning in Nahal Tsalmon; encouraging environmental initiatives through a network of Arab and Jewish volunteers; a thrift center in Tivon called On Second Thought; and promoting the principles of sustainable development by using ecological building techniques in its Bustan Olami ("Golden Garden").

P.O. Box 272
Kaukab El Hija
20185
Israel

Tel: +972 (4) 980 3794
thelink@zahav.net.il
http://www.picus.org/link/

Contact: Marganit Ofir-Gutler, Director
Number of staff: 6
Publications: LINK to the Environment, quarterly newsletter

ACTION

Machsom Watch

Machsom Watch was founded in 2001 in response to repeated reports in the press about human rights abuses of Palestinians crossing army and border police checkpoints. Initiated by three women, Machsom Watch now has over 400 women members. The goals of the group are threefold: to monitor the behavior of soldiers and police at checkpoints, to ensure that the human and civil rights of Palestinians attempting to enter Israel are protected, and to record and publicly report the results of observations. Machsom Watch is open exclusively to women. All members are Israeli. The group is politically pluralistic within the context of opposition to the occupation and a commitment to human rights.

c/o Bat Shalom
P.O. Box 8083
Jerusalem 91080
Israel

Tel: +972 (55) 300 385 (messages only)
machsomwatch@hotmail.com
http://www.machsomwatch.org/

Number of staff: over 400 volunteers
Publications: Twice daily reports on checkpoints monitored and monthly summary reports.

ACTION

Middleway—Shivil Zahav

Middleway ("Shivil Zahav" in Hebrew) is an Israeli nonprofit dedicated to a spiritual approach to peacemaking. Its primary activity has been organizing silent and mindful peace walks across Israel and Palestine. Its future work is to support, promote, and extend such walks and humanitarian aid to specific villages in the occupied territories. Future walks will include dialogue and conflict resolution activities. Middleway plans to initiate programs to teach nonviolence in communication and social action to all kinds of groups and organizations including political and professional bodies. This organization stands for the middle ground of sane, and balanced action, to promote tikkun and healing, and the path of peace and reconciliation. It emphasizes that the way we do things is as important as our goals.

34 Kanfey Nesharim   *Contact:* Danny Belinson
Ramat Gan 52357
Israel

Tel: +972 (54) 451 2736
mail@middleway.org
http://www.middleway.org

RESEARCH
EDUCATION
ACTION
ADVOCACY

The New Israeli Fund

The New Israeli Fund (NIF) was established in 1979 as a philanthropic partnership of Israelis, North Americans, and Europeans with the purpose of promoting freedom, justice, and equality for all individuals and groups within Israel's borders. NIF is based on the belief that the long-run strength and survival of Israel depend as much on its moral as on its physical strength. NIF funds nongovernmental, grassroots organizations for their work in advocacy, litigation, education, policy analysis, community-organizing, leadership development, and the dissemination of information. All grant recipients are involved in social-change activities that strengthen citizen participation, involvement, and democratic processes. In 1982, NIF established its Shatil as a capacity- and coalition-building program to provide technical assistance to Israel's social change organizations. NIF allocates resources to Israel's Arab population as well, working to guarantee that community's equal access to education, health care, employment, and land.

P.O. Box 53410
Jerusalem 91534
Israel
Shatil Program Offices
   also located in Haifa
   and Be'er Sheva.
International NIF Offices in the
   United States, Canada, Great Britain
   and Switzerland.

Contact: Eliezer Ya'ari, Executive
Director, Israel
Number of staff: 20
Publications: NIF News newsletter.

Tel: +972 (2) 672 3095
Fax: +972 (2) 672 3099
nif@nif.org.il
http://www.nif.org.il, http://www.newisraelfund.org

New Profile—Movement for the Civilization of Israeli Society

EDUCATION
ACTION
ADVOCACY

New Profile is a feminist-based movement of concerned Israeli men and women working to demilitarize Israeli society since 1998. Its platform characterizes Israeli conscription law as discriminatory and nondemocratic, and calls for the recognition of the basic right of every person to refuse military service based on reasons of conscience and to express their social commitment by means of alternative civic service. New Profile volunteers work to change the Israeli educational system to provide a democratic civic education, which teaches the practice of peace and conflict resolution, and the repudiation of war.

P.O. Box 48005
Tel Aviv 61480
Israel

Tel: +972 (3) 516 0119
info@newprofile.org
http://www.newprofile.org/

Contact: Ruth Hiller and Sharon Galant

Number of staff: 8

Publications: Articles, reports and press releases.

Open House Center

EDUCATION
ACTION

Open House Center was founded in 1991 to further peace and coexistence among Israeli Arabs and Jews in Jerusalem, the mixed city of 65,000 residents. Open House has two interrelated goals: to provide educational and social opportunities to Arab children and their families through its Center for the Development of the Arab Child and to be a place of encounter and cooperation between Jews and Arabs in the Ramle-Lod area through its Center for Jewish-Arab Coexistence. Programs for Ramle Arabs include a day-care center for children aged two to three years, a tutorial program for elementary school pupils, computer classes, and a telecommunications training course for Arab women. Joint activities include an annual Summer Peace Camp, a Jewish-Arab Parents' Network, Coexistence Training Programs for teachers and other social service professionals, a youth Environmental Arts Program, facilitated encounters between 7th and 8th grade students, sports tournaments, and holiday celebrations for Jewish and Arab families.

1 Klausner Street, Ramle
P.O. Box 26187
Jerusalem 91261
Israel

Tel: +972 (8) 922 1874
Fax: +972 (8) 925 4340
contacts@openhouse.org.il
http://www.openhouse.org.il/

Contact: Rini Zini, Director

Number of staff: 9

Publications: Voices From Jerusalem: Jews and Christians Reflect on the Holy Land by David Burrell and Yehezkel Landau, testimonials, articles, and audiotapes.

Oz VeShalom—Netivot Shalom

Oz Veshalom–Netivot Shalom was founded in 1975 by a group of academics in order to present an alternative to the growing militant expression of religious Zionism. It is committed to promoting the ideals of tolerance, pluralism, and justice, concepts central to Jewish tradition and law. Its leaders publish opinion pieces in local newspapers and appear frequently on television and on the radio. Oz Veshalom-Netivot Shalom's programs include both educational and protest activities. Seminars, lectures, workshops, conferences, and weekend programs on a variety of topics are held for youth, students, educators, and families, while protest activities focus on issues of human rights, co-existence between Jews and Arabs, and responses to issues of particular religious relevance.

P.O. Box 4433
Jerusalem, 91043
Israel

Tel: +972 (2) 566 4218
ozshalom@netvision.net.il
http://www.netivot-shalom.org.il/

Publications: Weekly Torah flyer available online, media articles, and press releases on the dynamic political situation.

Peace Child Israel

Peace Child Israel was founded in 1988 to teach democratic values and coexistence using theater and the performing arts in an experiential environment. In the Du Drama program, Arab and Jewish high school students in Israel work to create original dramas about coexistence in both Arabic and Hebrew. Past program participants have the opportunity to become young leaders and role models in their communities by performing their original plays for 6th and 7th grade students in public schools. Peace Child's annual Facilitator Staff Training teaches staff to deal with the regional conflict, enhance facilitation skills, and learn drama methodology and experiential techniques in a retreat-environment seminar. Peace Child also works with the parents and teachers of participant teens. Through these efforts, Peace Child strives to facilitate greater understanding with regard to the two cultures and the historical narratives of each nationality.

P.O. Box 3669
Tel Aviv 61036
Israel

Tel: +972 (3) 730 0481
Fax: +972 (3) 730 0695
pci@netvision.net.il
http://www.mideastweb.org/peacechild

Contact: Melisse Lewine-Boskovich
Number of staff: 15
Publications: Bilingual theater scripts and a dialogue-process curriculum based on combining theater and group-facilitation skills.

Peace Now

Peace Now is the largest extraparliamentary movement in Israel with over 200,000 names on its contact list. The movement was founded in 1978 by a group of 348 reserve officers of the Israel Defense Forces. Peace Now's founding principle is that only a negotiated end to the conflict in the Middle East can bring true security to Israel. Peace Now calls for the creation of a Jewish Israeli state beside a Palestinian state within the 1967 borders, the condemnation on both sides of the use of violence and force, and the limiting of hardships and collective punishment measures used by Israel against the Palestinian people under occupation. Peace Now operates through media campaigns, petitions, distribution of educational materials, conferences and lectures, public surveys and opinion polls, dialogue groups, and demonstrations. Peace Now's Settlement Watch Program monitors the growth of settlements and their governmental budgetary support. They are also active in encouraging university-based student activism, calling for building Israel's Security Wall on the 1967 border, and working on Israeli-Palestinian relationship-building projects in Jerusalem.

P.O. Box 29828
Tel Aviv 61297
Israel
_____

Tel: +972 (3) 566 3291
Fax: +972 (3) 566 3286
info@peacenow.org.il
http://www.peacenow.org.il

Contact: Lee Wilson

Number of staff: 5

Publications: Speeches and articles, including, "Israeli Failure—Palestinian Mistake," "The Palestinian Elections and Hopes for Peace," and "Wanted: Minister for Re-engagement."

People's Voice/Ha-Mifkad Ha-Leumi

People's Voice/Ha-Mifkad He-Leumi (Mifkad, National Census) is a Israeli-Palestinian organization that since 2002 has been canvassing mass support for the Nusseibeh-Ayalon initiative for a final status settlement (see "People's Campaign for Peace and Democracy" for details). It is a membership organization composed of local committees. Its activities include grassroots lobbying, expert-led public forums on relevant topics held in supporters' homes, and international lobbying at the political and civil society levels.

3 Ha-Yetzira Street
Ramat Gan
Israel
_____

Tel: +972 (3) 753 8888
Fax: +972 (3) 753 8887
http://www.mifkad.org.il

The Peres Center for Peace

RESEARCH
EDUCATION
ACTION
ADVOCACY

Nobel Laureate Shimon Peres founded The Peres Center for Peace in 1996 with the aim of building the infrastructure for peace through socioeconomic cooperation and people-to-people activities. The Center's programs work to dispel negative images and stereotypes while simultaneously addressing real social or economic needs within the community. These activities are in the fields of economic cooperation, civil society cooperation, and global initiatives. A major programmatic area in the field of economic cooperation is joint agricultural projects—including activities related to water protection and utilization, integrated crop management, replanting of olive trees in the West Bank, and high-tech strategies—coordinated through the Center's Andreas Agricultural Development Trust. In the technology, business, and economy arenas, the Peres Center for Peace has assisted Palestinian, Jordanian, and Israeli companies, as well as international business partners, in establishing technology-oriented financial investment vehicles, training programs, and joint business ventures, which advance mutually beneficial trade and business relations, and peaceful cooperation and peacebuilding goals. In the civil society programmatic area, the Peres Center provides joint training and project work related to community development, culture and media, peace education, medicine and health, student forums, and youth. The global initiatives programmatic area is based on the Peres Center's partnership with the United Nations Office for Projects Services (UNOPS), established in 2000. The alliance synthesizes the Peres Center's expertise in creating new models of peacebuilding and UNOPS' experience in implementing development projects in conflict and postconflict areas, building collaborative efforts between the intergovernmental, nongovernmental, and private sectors.

2 Ha Shalom Road, 4th Floor
Tel Aviv 67892
Israel

Tel: +972 (3) 568 0680
Fax: +972 (3) 568 0681
info@peres-center.org
http://www.peres-center.org

Contact: Dr. Ron Pundak, Director General

Physicians for Human Rights—Israel

Physicians for Human Rights—Israel (PHR-Israel) was established in 1988 as a nonpartisan, nonprofit organization, dedicated to promoting and protecting the right to health care in Israel and in territories under Israel's effective control. PHR-Israel works to maintain human rights as they pertain to health as a necessary condition for social justice, as well as a legal obligation in accordance with international human rights law. They work on behalf of many marginalized groups, including migrant workers, Bedouin residents of the "unrecognized villages," socioeconomically disadvantaged Israeli communities, residents of the occupied territories, and Israeli and Palestinian prisoners and detainees. Activities include direct intervention and the provision of medical aid, advocacy, legal action, public outreach, community education, and campaigning. Much of their effort is concentrated upon the struggle to bring about policy changes and end systematic abuses of the right to health.

52 Golomb Street
Tel-Aviv 66171
Israel

Tel: +972 (3) 687 3718
Fax: +972 (3) 687 3029
mail@phr.org.il
http://www.phr.org.il/phr

Contact: Shabtai Gold, Public Outreach Coordinator

Number of staff: 19

Publications: Reports, including "The Delay, Abuse and Humiliation of Medical Personnel by the Israeli Security Forces," Joint report with B'tselem; "Comprehensive Report and Position Paper on Refugees and Asylum Seekers in Israel," among others.

Public Committee
Against Torture in Israel

RESEARCH
EDUCATION
ACTION
ADVOCACY

The Public Committee Against Torture in Israel (PCATI) is an independent human rights organization founded in 1990 to monitor the implementation of Israel's prohibition of the use of torture during interrogation in both Israel and the Palestinian Authority. PCTI works through legal means, support of relevant legislation, and through an information campaign aimed at raising public awareness of the subject. Activities include providing legal counsel and assistance to victims of torture and their attorneys; lobbying against legislation that allows torture during interrogation; documenting cases of torture, exploitation, and humiliation of detainees; and acting as a national and international resource center on torture and related human rights fields.

P.O. Box 4634
Jerusalem 91046
Israel

Tel: +972 (2) 642 9825
Fax: +972 (2) 643 2847
pcati@stoptorture.org.il
http://www.stoptorture.org.il

Contact: Orah Maggen, Lobbying Director

Number of staff: 14

Publications: Back to a Routine of Torture: Torture and Ill-treatment of Palestinian Detainees during Arrest, Detention and Interrogation, 2001– 2003. Expert Opinion on Whether Israel's Targeted Killings of Palestinian Terrorists Is Consonant with International Humanitarian Law, 2003. Comments on Issues Relating to Palestinian Detainees in the Third Periodic Report of the State of Israel Concerning the Implementation of the International Covenant on Civil and Political Rights, 2002.

Rabbis for Human Rights

Rabbis for Human Rights (RHR) was founded in 1988 during the first intifada to give voice to the Jewish tradition of human rights in the context of serious abuses by Israeli armed forces and the lack of a robust human rights–centered response from rabbinical authorities and the religiously identified population. Its members include ninety ordained rabbis as well as rabbinical students from Reform, Orthodox, Conservative, and Reconstructionist Judaism. Members participate in nonviolent direct action, demonstrations of solidarity with the victims of human rights abuses, ecumenical dialogue, and work for disadvantaged communities within Israel. RHR also promotes the Jewish tradition of human rights in yeshives and the Israeli education system as well as through the press and its own publications.

42 Gaza Road
Jerusalem 92384
Israel
US-based affiliate organization
(Rabbis for Human Rights North
America) in West Tisbury,
Massachusettes

Tel: +972 (2) 563 7731
Fax: +972 (2) 5662815
info@rhr.israel.net
http://www.rhr.israel.net

Contact: Rabbi Arik W. Ascherman,
Executive Director

Number of staff: 5

*Publications: Pencraft on Liturgy and
Philosophy.*

EDUCATION
ADVOCACY

Shemesh

Shemesh was started in 1986 by the people of the Arab village of Shaab and the Jewish community Shorashim as a grassroots good-neighbor organization and continues to be a center for coexistence and friendship between Jews and Arabs in the Galilee Region of Israel. Shemesh works to build trust, respect, and understanding between Jews and Arabs in the region through "people-to-people programs" that create friendships and impart skills for coexistence. Shemesh operates educational and cultural programs, summer camps, a joint program just for women, and establishes model programs for communities throughout Israel. Shemesh was one of the initiators of the bilingual Jewish-Arab School in the Misgav Region of the Galilee, sponsored by Hand in Hand and endorsed by the Israeli Ministry of Education.

Mata Misgav
D.N. Misgav 20179
Israel

Contact: Matti Picus, Director
Number of staff: 10

Tel: +972 (4) 980 0039.
Fax: +972 (4) 980 0389
shemesh@shemesh.org
http://www.shemesh.org/

EDUCATION
ACTION

Shministim—
Israeli Youth Refusal Movement

The Shministim (Hebrew for "high school") youth movement was founded by a group of young political activists who refuse to serve the Israeli occupation in the territories. The movement began in 2001 with a letter signed by 62 high school students to the Israeli prime minister condemning the 1967 occupation and Israeli war crimes and pointing to the connection between Israeli aggression and the increase in attacks on Israeli citizens by Palestinians. A subsequent letter in 2002 had 300 signatories. The youth movement aims to expand the circles of conscientious objectors and to promote awareness of this phenomenon, primarily in high schools and within youth movements. Activities include protests and vigils on behalf of those who refuse to serve. They also support refusers who face difficulties as a result, such as discrimination in the schools and at work.

P.O. Box 70094
Haifa 31700
Israel

Publications: Refusal letters to the prime minister of Israel, 2001, 2002.

Tel:
Fax:
shministim@hotmail.com
http://www.shministim.org/

Sikkuy: The Association for the Advancement of Civic Equality in Israel

RESEARCH
ACTION
ADVOCACY

Sikkuy (a "chance" or "opportunity" in Hebrew) is a nonpartisan, nonprofit, nongovernmental organization that develops and implements projects to advance civic equality between Palestinian Arab and Jewish citizens of Israel in government budgets, resource allocation, hiring policy, land usage, and other related contexts. Founded in 1991 as a Jewish-Arab advocacy organization, Sikkuy's programs include monitoring government actions regarding civic equality between Arab and Jewish citizens (*The Sikkuy Report*); developing local groups of Jewish citizens advocating for civic equality; advocating for equitable hiring practices; monitoring implementation of Or Commission recommendations (*Or Commission Watch*); promoting cooperation between Jewish and Arab municipalities (Jewish-Arab Mayor's Forum); and working to mainstream the core value of human dignity to Israeli governmental, educational, and public institutions (Human Dignity Initiative). Sikkuy's Information Center for Effective Advocacy provides data to facilitate civic action and advocacy advancing civic equality.

Jerusalem Office
17 Hameshoreret Rachel St.
96348 Jerusalem
Israel
_____

Haifa Office
P.O. Box 99650
Hatzionot 10
Haifa 31996
Israel
_____

Tel: +972 (2) 654 1225 (Jerusalem);
    +972 (4) 852 188 (Haifa)
Fax: +972 (2) 654 1108 (Jerusalem);
    +972 (4) 852 065 (Haifa)
jerusalem@sikkuy.org.il;
    haifa@sikkuy.org.il
http://www.sikkuy.org.il

Contact: Shalom (Shuli) Dichter,
Co-Director

Number of staff: 19

Publications: The Sikkuy Report, annual report.

The Tami Steinmetz Center for Peace Research

RESEARCH
EDUCATION
ACTION

The Tami Steinmetz Center for Peace Research (TSC) is a multidisciplinary academic framework shared by the faculties of the humanities, social sciences, and law at Tel Aviv University. The purpose of the Center, established in 1992, is to promote systematic research and thinking on issues connected with peacemaking processes and conflict resolution. The Center conducts periodic Israeli public opinion surveys; maintains a database on Israeli-Palestinian cooperation in particular and Israeli-Arab cooperation in general; sponsors conferences and workshops; encourages teaching, research projects, and authorship of graduate theses and dissertations on conflict-resolution themes; and fosters interrelations and cooperation with similarly focused institutions in Israel and abroad.

Tel-Aviv University
Naftali Building, 705
Ramat-Aviv
Tel-Aviv 69978
Israel

Tel: +972 (3) 642 4298
Fax: + 972 (3) 6407489
tscpeace@post.tau.ac.il
http://www.tau.ac.il/peace

Contact: Tamar Hermann, Director

Number of staff: 6

Publications: Peace In Brief academic reports on various topics based on Center research findings. Research Findings series. *The Palestinian Refugees Issue and the Right of Return: Proceedings of a Symposium Held on 29 December 2003. The Palestinian Health System: Proceedings of a Seminar Held on 5–6 September 2003. The Palestinian Education System: Proceedings of a Seminar Held on 13–14 June 2003. International Intervention in Protracted Conflicts: The Israeli-Palestinian Case,* 2003.

Movement of Democratic Women in Israel (Tandi) (MDWI)

EDUCATION
ACTION
ADVOCACY

The Movement of Democratic Women in Israel (Tandi) (MDWI) was formed when two separate groups, one Jewish and one Arab, both working within the Israel Communist Party, merged in 1951. Tandi is now affiliated with the Democratic Front for Equality and Peace. Its largest constituency is of Israeli Arab women. MDWI pursues four objectives: to advance the civil and social rights of all Israeli women and to eliminate all forms of discrimination against women; to promote child welfare and children's rights; to advance equal rights, budgets, and opportunities for Israeli Arabs; and to end the military occupation of the West Bank and the Gaza Strip and to negotiate with the PLO toward the establishment of an independent Palestinian state alongside the state of Israel. Tandi's 50 branches across the country, most of them in Arab towns and villages, sponsor courses, lectures, and literacy campaigns. MDWI sponsors 33 kindergartens in Arab villages, as well as summer day-camps for children. MDWI activists visit women's organizations on the West Bank every week and have organized a sweater-knitting campaign for Palestinian women prisoners. The Movement sponsors political demonstrations and annual International Children's Day and International Women's Day events.

P.O. Box 29501   *Number of staff:* 1
Tel Aviv
Israel
_____

Tel: +972 (3) 292 792

RESEARCH
EDUCATION

Van Leer Jerusalem Institute

The Van Leer Jerusalem Institute is an intellectual center for the interdisciplinary study and discussion of issues related to philosophy, society, culture, and education. Founded in 1959, the Institute and its mission are based on the founding Van Leer family's vision of Israel as both a homeland for the Jewish people and a democratic society, predicated on justice, fairness, and equality for all its residents. The Institute pursues its mandate by employing different methodologies: academic research, public policy analysis, advocacy, and civil society projects. Activities range from the sponsorship of domestic and international conferences, symposia, and workshops to the publication of periodicals, books, and monographs to the initiation of grassroots dialogue and major educational initiatives. Additionally, the Institute houses a unique, 25,000-volume library focused on the history of ideas.

43 Jabotinsky Street
P.O. Box 4070
Jerusalem 91040
Israel

Tel: +972 (2) 560 5222
Fax: +972 (2) 561 9293
vanleer@vanleer.org.il
http://www.vanleer.org.il/

Contact: Shimshon Zelniker, Director

Number of staff: 24

Publications: Publishes a wide range of books, anthologies, monographs, position papers, and periodicals by distinguished scholars and public figures affiliated with the Institute, mostly in English and Hebrew. *Maelstrom of Identities: A Critical Look at Religion and Secularity in Israel. Men and Women: Gender, Judaism and Democracy. Israeli Haredim: Integration Without Assimilation?*

Yakar's Center for Social Concern

Yakar's Center for Social Concern is a secular body working on an Orthodox Jewish base since 1992. Its founding principle is that a secure future depends on making contact and creating trust between peoples—Jews and Jews, Jews and Muslims, Jews and Christians, Israelis and Palestinians and other Arabs. The Center aims to stimulate and challenge Israelis to think afresh about problems. It brings together for discussion people of different views and backgrounds. The Center conducts lecture series and publishes reports based on Judaism and human rights.

Rechov HaLamed Heh 10
Jerusalem 93661
Israel

Tel: +972 (2) 561 2310
Fax: + 972 (2) 563 2917
info@yakar.org
http://www.yakar.org/center_for_
    social_concern/about_csc.htm

Contact: Benjamin Pogrund, Director

Number of staff: 13

Publications: Various web-based articles, including: "How the Holocaust Affects Israeli Attitudes Towards 'The Other,'" 2004. "Visits to Arab Villages: Two Reports," 2003. "Jews in Apartheid South Africa," 2003. "The Future of the Settlements: Evacuation or Expansion?" 2003. "Is the Media to Blame?" 2003.

Yesh Gvul

Founded in 1982, Yesh Gvul's activities primarily pertain to soldiers, both young Israelis subject to military conscription and reservists. Yesh Gvul operates in three main domains: personal support for each refusenik soldier refusing to serve in the occupied territories; activities for an end to the occupation; and a broad campaign of public education for social change. They organize many public vigils, including monthly vigils at the military prisons where refuseniks are incarcerated, as well as weekly vigils mounted by the Refuseniks Parents Forum at the home of the chief military prosecutor and outside the military court to protest persecution of young refuseniks. Their telephone hotline has operated continuously for over 20 years, offering help and counsel to soldiers, reservists, and youth awaiting induction. The family support fund, Keren Yesh Gvul, offers modest financial aid to dependents of jailed refuseniks. Direct action with other groups has included picking olives in groves to which Palestinian owners were denied access by the "Apartheid Wall" and working for Israeli court injunctions to prevent the demolition of Palestinian homes and to investigate deadly military operations in Palestinian civilian areas. Leaflets, books, and other publications focus on educating soldiers and young people about human rights and soldiers' legal, moral, and political responsibilities. The Adopt a Jailed Refusenik project has channeled international political and financial support to incarcerated refusers.

P.O. Box 6953
Jerusalem 91068
Israel
_____

Tel: +972 (2) 625 0271
Fax: +972 (2) 643 4171
info@yesh-gvul.org
http://www.yesh-gvul.org

Contact: Ishai Menuchin, Coordinator
Number of staff: 0
Publications: Weekly e-mail updates on activities to subscribers

EDUCATION
ADVOCACY

Arab Educational Institute (AEI)

The Arab Educational Institute (AEI) is a Palestinian organization dedicated to bringing hope to the community by stimulating young people to work for the public good and to spread a message of peace. AEI, which was founded in 1986, uses community education to contribute to the local capacity for peace. Their activities, for which they cooperate closely with other Palestinian NGOs in the Bethlehem, Ramallah, and Hebron areas of Palestine, aim to strengthen people's learning capacity to develop nonviolent alternatives, to stimulate the community to work together across social and religious borders, and to address and work with the international media and international organizations. Taught skills range from cultural expression and activity organization to English.

Paul VI Street
P.O. Box 681
Bethlehem
Palestine
_____
Tel: +972 (2) 274 4030
Fax: +972 (2) 277 7554
aei@p-ol.com
http://www.aeicenter.org

Contact: Fuad Giacaman, Director

Number of staff: 13

Publications: Bethlehem Community Book 2000/2001 (English and Arabic). *Palestinian Education Across Religious Borders,* 2000 (English). *When Abnormal Becomes Normal,* 2001 (English). *Discovering Palestine,* 2001 (Arabic). *Your Stories Are My Stories,* 2001 (English).

Association of Women's Action for Training and Rehabilitation

EDUCATION
ACTION
ADVOCACY

Association of Women's Action for Training and Rehabilitation (AOWA) is a women's development organization established in 1994 by a group of women activists from Palestine. The programs of the Association focus on civil education, educational unity, and social solidarity. Objectives of the Association are to promote women's initiatives, the national participation of women, leadership development, development of rural women's capacities, and to contribute to raise health, educational, and cultural awareness of Palestinian women.

Palestine-Ramallah
Malido Abo abed, Str. No. 3
P.O. Box 938
Ramallah

Tel: + 972- (2) 2961563
Fax: + 972- (2) 2961563
E-mail: Aowa2006@hotmail.com

Contact: Siham Barghouthi, Director

Number of staff: 7

Budget: $25,000

Publications: Newsletter, manual of training for women candidates for local and legislative elections.

Bethlehem Peace Center

EDUCATION

The Bethlehem Peace Center is a cultural center owned and operated by the Municipality of Bethlehem, although it has been functioning, since its inauguration in 2000, under a broader board. The Bethlehem Peace Center promotes peace, democracy, human rights, and tolerance for religious and cultural diversity from within the spirit and values of Palestinian culture. It tries not to affiliate itself with any religion, faith, or belief system, nor with any political party, faction, or ethnic group. It promotes its goals by organizing art exhibits, festivals, workshop, and courses, especially for women, youth, and children.

Manger Square
P.O. Box 1166
Bethlehem
Palestine

Tel: +972 (2) 276 6677
Fax: +972 (2) 274 1057
info@peacenter.org
http://www.peacenter.org

Contact: Fadia Saleh, Project Coordinator

Number of staff: 14

EDUCATION
ACTION

Civic Forum Institute

Civic Forum Institute (CFI) was initiated in 1995 as a grassroots civic education program of the National Democratic Institute for International Affairs (NDI). In 1998 it became an independent organization. CFI works to build and strengthen the foundations of democracy in Palestine and develop Palestinian civil society organizations from the local, Arab, and international spheres. CFI organizes workshops, civic education sessions, town hall meetings with citizens and decisionmakers, and trainings of volunteers in various skills. The Forum's activities aim to promote understanding of the practices, organizations, and institutions of democratic governance, and of the role and responsibilities of citizens and leaders in a democracy.

Al-Ansar Street No. 17
P.O. Box 54719
Shu'fat – Jerusalem 93600
Palestine

Tel: +972 (2) 532 6261
Fax: +972 (2) 540 0471

Abu-Khalaf Building – First Floor
Jerusalem – Ramallah Road
Daheiet Al-Barid
P.O. Box 54719
Jerusalem 91190
Palestine

Tel: +972 (2) 234 8020
Fax: +972 (2) 234 8022
cfip@cfip.org
http://www.cfip.org

Contact: Aref Jaffal, Executive Director
Number of staff: 37
Publications: Annual reports. *Al-Ufuq,* annual newsletters. "Reform: A Palestinian Perspective," research series.

Gaza Community Mental Health Programme

RESEARCH
EDUCATION
ACTION

The Gaza Community Mental Health Programme (GCMHP) is a nonprofit organization that was established in 1990 to offer comprehensive community mental health services to the population of the Gaza Strip. GCMHP began after the founders realized the urgent needs of the people resulting from the Israeli occupation. The organization offers therapy and rehabilitation and aims to raise the public awareness. Special focus is on traumatized children, female victims of violence, and survivors of torture and other human rights violations. It provides training and education for workers in the field. GCMHP does research and documentation on their area of interest and organizes conferences for local and international experts to exchange ideas and experiences.

Abu-Zahir El-Betar Bldg.
P.O. Box 1049
Gaza City
Palestine
_____
Tel: +972 (8) 282 5700
Fax. +972 (8) 282 4072
pr@gcmhp.net
http://www.gcmhp.net

Contact: Eyad As-Sarraj, General Director
Number of staff: 174
Publications: Press releases, research papers, and independent articles.

Holy Land Trust

EDUCATION
ACTION

The Holy Land Trust (HLT) is a nonprofit organization that was founded in 1998. The core aims of the organization are to promote nonviolent resistance to end the occupation and to build a democratic Palestine. The HLT looks to improve the lives of the children, families, youth, and nongovernmental organizations of Palestine by creating comprehensive community awareness programs, working on local and international advocacy initiatives, building local and international networks and partnerships, and creating an alternative media. Three of its main programs are Peace and Reconciliation, Travel and Encounter, and the Palestine News Network.

529 Manger Street
P.O. Box 127
Bethlehem
Palestine
_____
Tel: +972 (2) 276 5930
Fax: +972 (2) 276 5931
info@holylandtrust.org
http://www.holylandtrust.org

Contact: Sami Awad, Executive Director
Number of staff: 8
Publications: The Palestine News Network, web newsletter, training manuals on nonviolence.

International Peace and Cooperation Center

RESEARCH
EDUCATION
ACTION

The International Peace and Cooperation Center (IPCC) was established in 1998 as an independent Palestinian nongovernmental organization aiming to develop proactive initiatives to come to a peaceful, democratic, and prosperous future for the Palestinian people. They seek to place concepts on the public agenda that support political, social, and economic transforming processes, and to stimulate building capacities and empowerment to move the Palestinian society away from conflict and toward peace and democracy. To attain these goals IPCC organizes workshops, seminars, and conferences both for and with other local and international organizations, ranging from composing think tanks and scenario-building projects, creating youth forums and other networks, and setting up mediation and arbitration centers.

21 Skeikh Jarrah
P.O. Box 24162
Jerusalem
Palestine
──────────
Tel: +972 (2) 581 1992
Fax: +972 (2) 532 5084
info@ipcc-jerusalem.org
http://www.ipcc-jerusalem.org

Contact: Rami Nasrallah, Director
General
Number of staff: 6
Publications: The Jerusalem Urban Fabric, 2003. *Jerusalem on the Map,* 2003. *The Future of Jerusalem,* 2003. *Divided Cities in Transition,* 2003.

Issam Sartawi Center for the Advancement of Peace and Democracy

EDUCATION
ACTION
ADVOCACY

Issam Sartawi Center for the Advancement of Peace and Democracy (ISCAPD) is a specialized institute for peace studies hosted at the Al Quds University. The Center was founded in 1998 with the aim of the advancement of peace and democratic values and the improvement of civil discourse, understanding, and effectiveness in the young democracy of Palestine. Its main programs focus on assisting in the establishment of political parties and improving the overall political party accountability, on strengthening civic leadership in Palestine, on reducing community conflict, and on increasing regional leadership to solve regional problems. To reach these goals, ISCAPD organizes trainings, workshops, and meetings at different levels.

P.O. Box 51000
Jerusalem
Palestine
──────────
Tel: +972 (2) 656 7428
msdajani@art.alquds.edu
http://www.alquds.edu/centers_institutes/iscps

Contact: Munther S. Dajani, Director
Number of staff: 11
Publications: Articles and reports in national and international periodicals.

Ittijah—Union of the Arab Community Based Organisations

EDUCATION
ACTION
ADVOCACY

Ittijah is the network for Palestinian nongovernmental organizations in Israel. Established in 1995, Ittijah works to increase cooperation and institutional capacity among Palestinian Arab organizations that provide support structures and offer services not otherwise available due to discriminatory practices and policies of the Israeli state. Ittijah strives to strengthen and empower the Palestinian Arab citizens of Israel by promoting the development of Palestinian civil society and advocating for political, economic, and social change. Ittijah has three principal activity areas: local, regional, and international advocacy on behalf of Palestinian citizens of Israel; human, technical, financial, and educational resource provision for institutional capacity building; and networks of issue-specific organizations, such as for youth and women. Among the work Ittijah undertakes are regular ambassadorial study days, hosting of solidarity delegations, fact sheet publications, and conferences.

P.O. Box 9577
Haifa 31095
Israel

Tel: +972 (4) 850 7110
Fax: +972 (4) 850 7241
ittijah@ittijah.org
http://www.ittijah.org/

Contact: Ameer Makhoul, General Director
Number of staff: 6
Publications: Fact sheets on various topics pertaining to the status of Palestinian Arab citizens of Israel, 2000. *The Horizon of Palestinian Community Work: Collective Thoughts,* 2003. *Assessment Training Needs Report for Ittijah's Member Organizations,* 2003. *International Advocacy and Local Community Work: One Year after Durban,* 2002.

The Jerusalem Center for Women

EDUCATION
ACTION
ADVOCACY

The Jerusalem Center for Women (JCW) was established in 1994, parallel to its West Jerusalem sister organization the Israeli Women's Center, Bat Shalom. JCW and Bat Shalom carry out joint Palestinian-Israeli programs through the Jerusalem Link. JCW is an independent organization that looks to empower women in the community and, through political activism, to protect and advance women's rights and status, to involve women in realizing a regional peace based on justice, and to establish local and international networks that support JCW in achieving its goals. Its main activities evolve around conflict resolution development, human rights monitoring, and the organization of training and empowerment series.

East-Jerusalem, Beit Hanina
Dahiet Al-Barid, Al-Hirbawi Bldg.
P.O. Box 51630
East-Jerusalem, Beit Hanina
Palestine
_____

Tel: +972 (2) 234 7068
Fax: +972 (2) 234 7069
jcw@palnet.com
http://www.j-c-w.org

Contact: Amneh Badran, Executive Director

Number of staff: 8

Publications: Stop the Apartheid Wall, 2004. Justice and Freedom Are the Road to Peace: No for Settlements, 2001. Between the Lines: German, Israeli and Palestinian Women in Dialogue, 2000. Sharing Jerusalem: Two Capitals for Two States, 2000.

Library on Wheels for Non-Violence and Peace

EDUCATION
ACTION

The Library on Wheels for Non-Violence (LOWNP) is a humanitarian institution based in Jerusalem. LOWNP travels to over one hundred isolated villages in the West Bank providing Palestinian children with books and other educational material. Their overarching goal is to teach children about peace and nonviolence. They also reach the children through a touring puppet show and videos of educational cartoons and music. Additional activities include helping families that cannot afford school fees, tree planting campaigns, and reporting on the conditions in the area via publications.

P.O. Box 20961
Jerusalem 91202
Israel
_____

Tel: +972 (2) 583 5146
Fax: +972 (2) 583 5127
lownp@palnet.com
http://www.towardshumanity.org/towards/library.html

Contact: Nafez Essylieh, Director
Publications: Mubarak Awad: Non-Violence in Palestine (in Arabic).

Middle East Non-Violence and Democracy

**EDUCATION
ACTION
ADVOCACY**

Middle East Non-Violence and Democracy (MEND) is an initiative that was started in 1998, as a member of the International Fellowship of Reconciliation. Its main focus is on nonviolence and democracy, using training and innovative media techniques to reach individuals in Palestine to help them deal with the difficulties they confront in their daily lives. MEND offers an interactive website to provide space for discussions, sharing of information, and counseling. MEND offers education and training programs on nonviolence and democracy, along with psychodrama and creative projects, like a radio soap opera for youth. In cooperation with several international organizations, they are increasingly developing training programs for women.

P.O. Box 6658
Beit Hanina
East-Jerusalem
Palestine
_____
Tel: +972 (2) 656 7310
Fax. +972 (2) 656 7311
info@mend-pal.org
http://www.mend-pal.org

Contact: Lucy Nusseibeh, Director

Number of staff: 13

Publications: Training manuals on nonviolence. *IMPACT* newsletter.

Palestinian Center for
Conflict Resolution and Reconciliation

EDUCATION
ACTION
ADVOCACY

The Palestinian Center for Conflict Resolution and Reconciliation (CCRR) is a Palestinian interfaith center working toward attaining a just peace, which has been registered as an official nongovernmental organization at the Palestinian National Authority since September 2000. It is committed to changing the approach to conflict resolution within the Palestinian community, but also among people in the broader region. The Center aims to achieve a nonviolent society by empowering marginalized groups, by strengthening the democratic relations and understanding inside the Palestinian community, and by promoting values of reconciliation and forgiveness. In pursuit of this goal, they offer professional training programs and consultation to students, teachers, educators, religious leaders, journalists, and civil society at large.

P.O. Box 861
Bethlehem
Palestine
_____

Tel: +972 (2) 276 745
Tel/Fax: +972 (2) 274 5475
ccrr@palnet.com
http://www.mideastweb.org/ccrr,
    http://www.ipctnet.org/ccrr.htm

Contact: Noah Salameh, Director
Number of staff: 8
Publications: The Tree of Hope:
Palestine without Violence,
bimonthly magazine on nonviolence.
The Young Negotiators Project:
Manual on Conflict Resolution in
Palestinian Schools, 2001, 2003.

The Palestinian Center for Helping Resolve Community Disputes

EDUCATION
ACTION
ADVOCACY

The Palestinian Center for Helping Resolve Community Disputes (PCHRCD), a Palestinian nongovernmental organization established in 1990, has as its mission to strengthen civil society, to empower Palestinians, and to create a truly democratic, participatory, and nonviolent community. It seeks to establish long-term programs that will become permanent features of Palestinian society—peer mediation; a student parliament; the provision of human rights, tolerance, and conflict resolution curriculum material for middle schools; a student political party cooperation system; counseling and interventions for youths with domestic problems; conflict-resolution training for governmental and nongovernmental organizations; and capacity-building for Palestinian institutions.

35 A/116 Charles De Gaulle Street
P.O. Box 5316
Gaza City
Palestine

Tel/Fax: +972 (8) 284 7488
Pchrcd1@palnet.com
http://www.palnet.com/~pchrcd

Contact: Sa'ed Mqadmeh, Director
Number of staff: 15
Publications: Annual reports.

The Palestinian Center for Human Rights

RESEARCH
ACTION
ADVOCACY

The Palestinian Center for Human Rights (PCHR) is an independent legal body dedicated to promote human rights, the rule of law, and democratic principles in the occupied Palestinian territories. PCHR was established in 1995 by a group of Palestinian lawyers and human rights activists. It holds Special Consultative Status with the UN Economic and Social Council (ECOSOC) and is an affiliate of the International Commission of Jurists (ICJ), the Fédération Internationale des Ligues des Droits de l'Homme (FIDH), and the Euro-Mediterranean Human Rights Network. The Center's activities focus on the documentation and investigation of human rights violations, the provision of legal aid and counseling, preparation of various research articles within their area of interest, and comments on Palestinian Draft Laws, urging the adoption of legislation that incorporates international human rights standards and basic democratic principles.

29 Omar al-Mukhtar Street
P.O. Box 1328
Gaza City
Gaza Strip
Palestine

Tel/Fax. +972 (8) 282 4776/
    282 5893/282 3725
pchr@pchrgaza.org
http://www.pchrgaza.org

Contact: Raji Sourani, Director

Number of staff: 55

Publications: Fact sheets, weekly reports, press releases, studies, position papers.

The Palestinian Center for Peace and Democracy

EDUCATION
ACTION
ADVOCACY

The Palestinian Center for Peace and Democracy (PCPD) is a nonprofit organization established in 1992 as a forum for free and uncensored dialogue by a group of Palestinian intellectuals and professionals aiming to enhance the practice of democracy and promote a culture of peace within Palestinian society. The Center's goals are to contribute to ending the Israeli occupation and building an independent Palestinian state. Their projects aim to promote democracy, the political role of women and women's rights, the development of Palestinian civil society, and the positive advancement of the role of youth by promoting civil awareness, stimulating local governance, and organizing discussions, workshops, and trainings.

Al-Sahel Street
P.O. Box 2290
Ramallah
Palestine
_____
Tel: +972 (2) 296 5981/2
Fax. +972 (2) 296 5983
pcpd@palnet.com
http://www.pcpd.org

Contact: Naseef Mu'alim, Director
General

Number of staff: 22

Publications: Annual report and reports
in Arabic on globalization, youth, and
women.

The Palestinian Center for Policy and Survey Research

RESEARCH
EDUCATION

The Palestinian Center for Policy and Survey Research (PCPSR) is an independent, nonprofit research institute and think tank for policy analysis and academic research established in 2000. The organization was founded to advance scholarship and knowledge on contemporary issues of concern for the Palestinians, specifically in the areas of domestic politics and government, strategic analysis, and foreign policy. PCPS focuses its activities around academic and policy analysis studies; sociopolitical surveys; and public opinion polls on current Palestinian views on sociopolitical developments; study groups and task forces on critical subjects; and the organization of conferences, public lectures, and briefings on current political themes.

Off Isral Street
P.O. Box 76
Ramallah
Palestine
_____
Tel: +972 (2) 296 4933
Fax. +972 (2) 296 4934
Pcpsr@pcpsr.org
http://www.pcpsr.org/./index.html

Contact: Khalil Shikaki, Director

Number of staff: 17

Publications: Public opinion polls on
Palestinian, Israeli, and domestic
politics. Brainstorming session reports.
*The Third Draft Constitution for a
Palestinian State,* 2003. *PSR Public
Opinion Poll,* 2003

The Palestinian Center for Rapprochement between People

EDUCATION
ACTION
ADVOCACY

The Palestinian Center for Rapprochement between People (PCR) was established in 1990 as a nonprofit organization to promote grassroots dialogue and joint work between Palestinians and people of different nationalities. Its main aim is to break down existing prejudices and stereotypes to come closer to a peaceful solution of the Palestinian situation. Its areas of interest are community service, peace and reconciliation, action for peace and justice, advocacy, serving the youth of Palestine, and community-based networks. Activities that follow from these interests are dialogue sessions between Palestinians and Israelis, an annual Christmas procession, protest marches, and the establishment of a youth network.

64 Star Street
Beit Sahour
P.O. Box 24
Palestine

Tel/Fax. +972 (2) 277 2018
info@rapprochement.org
http://www.rapprochement.org

Contact: Ghassan Andoni, Director

Number of staff: 7

Publications: Advocacy materials on nonviolence.

Palestinian Center for Research and Cultural Dialogue

RESEARCH
EDUCATION
ACTION

The Palestinian Center for Research and Cultural Dialogue (PCRD) was established in 2003 by a group of Palestinian academics. The PCRD believes that dialogue between cultures and religions is a way to bridge the gap between nations. The Center aims to help initiate dialogue and from this create mutual acceptance between parties in conflict in the Middle East. Palestinian youngsters, aged 17–23 years, comprise the Center's main target group, which PCRD educates and trains to become the new, peaceful and democratic leaders of Palestine. Aside from promoting and doing research on cultural dialogue, the Center also carries out public opinion surveys on political, economical, cultural, and social issues, focusing mostly on the Palestinian population.

P.O. Box 396
Bethlehem
West Bank
Palestine

Tel: +972 (2) 277 4325
Fax: +972 (2) 277 4707
pcrd@p-ol.com
website is being constructed

Contact Person: Walid Shomaly, Executive Director

Number of staff: 5

Publication: Reports of the results of public opinion surveys. *Fluctuations of Palestinian Public Opinion in Response to Israeli Measures,* 2004.

The Palestinian Center for Dissemination of Democracy and Community Development (Panorama)

RESEARCH
EDUCATION
ACTION
ADVOCACY

The Palestinian Center for Dissemination of Democracy and Community Development (Panorama) was established in 1991 with the aim to raise the awareness of Palestinian people on the concepts of democracy and on issues related to civil society. Panorama has several offices that look to actively promote and disseminate information on issues related to democracy, human rights, participation in public life, and the various decisionmaking processes that are based on the concept of freedom of expression. To attain its goals the organization uses several tools, such as workshops and panels, conferences and seminars, training courses, informative booklets and newsletters, research studies, creative productions (such as theater, music, and video production), community intervention and coordination, and networking with other organizations and groups.

AlAhliyya College Street,
    Cairo Amman Bank Bldg. 3rd Floor
P.O. Box 2049
Ramallah
Palestine
_____

Tel: +972 (2) 295 9618
Fax: +972 (2) 298 1824
panorama@panoramacenter.org

Ibn Batuta Street, Kamal Bldg. 3rd Floor
P.O. Box 20510
Jerusalem
Palestine
_____

Tel: +972 (2) 628 1151
Fax: +972 (2) 628 3351
walid@panoramacenter.org
Tel/Fax: +972 (8) 283 9188 (Gaza Office)
panorama@panoramacenter.org
http://www.panoramacenter.org

Contact: Riad Malki, Director,
Walid Salem, Director Jerusalem
Office, and Iman Abu Ramadan,
Director Gaza Office

Number of staff: 21

Publications: Research documents
and a newsletter.

The Palestinian Center of Alternative Solutions

EDUCATION
ACTION
ADVOCACY

The Palestinian Center of Alternative Solutions (PCAS) is a nongovernmental organization that was founded in 2003 by a group of experienced peace activists. They are supported by a large network of people who believe that there are alternative solutions to the current status quo that will bring a peaceful settlement to the Israeli-Palestinian conflict. Working with both Palestinians and Israelis, the Center tries to break the existing stereotypes by offering formal and informal peace education kits and professional training for dialogue facilitators, and engaging in lobbying and advocacy campaigns. At the same time, it intends to inform and involve as many participants from both societies as possible in peacebuilding activities. Activities are carried out with the conviction that better knowledge and skills will lead to better understanding.

Masyyoun Suburb
Ramallah
Palestine

Contact: Nedal Jayousi, Director

Tel. +972 (2) 296 1558
nedal1@palnet.com
website is under construction

The Palestinian Human Rights Monitoring Group

ACTION
ADVOCACY

The Palestinian Human Rights Monitoring Group (PHRMG) was founded in 1996 in response to the deteriorating state of democracy and human rights in Palestine. PHRMG documents and monitors human rights violations committed against Palestinians in the West Bank, Gaza Strip, and East Jerusalem, regardless of who is responsible. Its principle strategy is to appeal to both Palestinian and international public opinion through its monitoring and outreach activities with the hope of stimulating positive change. However, PHRMG is also active in assisting in the building of Palestinian institutions and offering legal assistance to victims of human rights violations.

Ahmad Jaber House
Beit Hanina
P.O. Box 19918
East-Jerusalem 91198
Palestine

Tel: +972 (2) 583 8189
Fax: +972 (2) 583 7197
admin@phrmg.org
http://www.phrmg.org

Contact: Bassem Eid, Executive Director

Number of staff: 13

Publications: The Monitor of Human Rights Periodical Magazine (in Arabic). *Summary of Palestinian Fatalities,* 2004. *New "Nakba" in Gaza City,* 2004. *Press Freedom Day,* 2004

The Palestinian Initiative for the Promotion of Global Dialogue and Democracy

RESEARCH
ACTION
ADVOCACY

The Palestinian Initiative for the Promotion of Global Dialogue and Democracy–MIFTAH is an organization dedicated to promoting dialogue and democracy based on a free flow of information and ideas. Since its establishment in 1998, it has functioned as a Palestinian platform founded on the principles of democracy, human rights, gender equity, and participatory governance. Although its website features many of the information-flow and dialogue components of MIFTAH, to further realize their objectives, independent teams set out activities and programs along the three main themes of governance and democracy, media and information, and external relations.

Rimawi Building
Radio Street
Ramallah
Palestine
_____
Tel: +972 (2) 298 9490/1
Fax: +972 (2) 298 9492
P.O. Box 69647
Jerusalem 97800
Palestine
_____
Tel. +972 (2) 585 1842
Fax. +972 (2) 583 5184
info@miftah.org
http://www.miftah.org

Contact: Hanan Ashrawi, Secretary-General

Number of staff: 21

Publications: Press releases (both in Arabic and English), fact sheets, and other independent sources of information offered on the website.

The Palestinian Media and Development Institute

EDUCATION
ACTION

The Palestinian Media and Development Institute (PMDI) was established in 1994 as a nongovermental organization dedicated to the development and advancement of the Palestinian private sector. The organization's mission is to better the capabilities of the private sector through training and development and to promote business relationships among local and international stake-holders. Training is conducted based on the idea that it is a primary component of economic development and sustainability. Research is performed in order to better understand the needs of the business community. PMDI organizes local and regional conferences for the private sector, at which Palestinian experts are brought in from abroad to assist the local business community, and is also involved in tourism promotion.

Kaloti Building
18 Zahra Street
Jerusalem
Palestine
_____
Tel/Fax: +972 (2) 627 2791
info@pmdip.org
http://www.pmdip.org

Contact: Abed Al-Fatah Darwiesh, Director
Number of staff: 4
Publication: Annuals report.

The Palestinian Youth Association for Leadership and Rights Activation (PYALARA)

EDUCATION
ACTION
ADVOCACY

The Palestinian Youth Association for Leadership and Rights Activation (PYALARA) is a nongovernmental organization established for the youth of Palestine in 1992. It aims to prevent young Palestinians from becoming thoroughly frustrated as a result of the harsh conditions in which they live. PYALARA tries to encourage young Palestinians to express themselves through writing, talking, and other forms of communication. Its main programs are the Youth Media Program, including *The Youth Times* newsletter and a television program; the Program for the Well-Being of Youth, focusing on the psychological, physical, and sociopolitical well-being of young Palestinians; and an international youth perspective awareness campaign.

Flat 12, 4th Floor, Julani Building
Ar-Ram
P.O. Box 54065
Jersusalem
Palestine
_____
Tel: +972 (2) 234 3428/9
Fax: +972 (2) 234 3430
pyalara@pyalara.org
http://www.pyalara.org

Contact: Haniya Al-Bitar, Director
Number of staff: 14
Publications: The Youth Times, monthly newsletter.

The Palestinian Academic Society for the Study of International Affairs— PASSIA

RESEARCH
EDUCATION
ADVOCACY

The Palestinian Academic Society for the Study of International Affairs–PASSIA was founded in Jerusalem in 1987 and seeks to present the Palestinian question in its national Arab and international contexts through academic research, dialogue, documentation, and publication, with the aim of imparting an understanding of Palestinian issues, past and present—the land, the people, their rights, and their leadership—to interested audiences. PASSIA activities are guided by scholarly objectivity and the desire to provide a forum for free expression and analysis of a plurality of local and foreign perspectives. PASSIA works to achieve its goals through the implementation of the following programs: research and studies, roundtable meetings, interfaith dialogue, training and education in international affairs, training programs for civil society empowerment, and the question of Jerusalem. PASSIA is involved with and contributes to a variety of networks, cooperates with regional and international institutes, and participates regularly in local, regional, and international conferences.

18 Hatem Al-Ta'i Street – Wadi Al-Joz
P.O. Box 19545
Jerusalem – Al-Quds
Palestine
_____

Tel: +972 (2) 628 4426 / 628 6566
Fax: +972 (2) 628 2819
passia@palnet.com
http://www.passia.org

Contact: Deniz Altayli, Program Director

Number of staff: 9

Publications: Research studies, seminar reports, *PASSIA Diary,* information papers, annual reports, publications on Jerusalem, The Dialogue Series, The Religious Studies Series, bulletins, and the recent books *The Conflict over Jerusalem: Some Palestinian Responses to Concepts of Dispute Resolution* and *Security Sector Reform in the Occupied Territories.*

EDUCATION
ACTION

Peace and Democracy Forum

The Peace and Democracy Forum (PDF–Palestine) is a Palestinian non-governmental organization based in East Jerusalem. Officially registered in 2003, the organization aims to raise awareness of Palestinians regarding their economic and social environment and to enhance involvement in developing a sustainable society. They encourage Palestinians to make use of available legal, economic, and social means. PDF–Palestine tries to enhance democratic behavior and practices within Palestinian institutions and society, promoting openness, transparency, and accountability within public and civil society institutions. Highlighting nonviolent methods, the organization mobilizes public support for negotiations in the Palestinian-Israeli conflict. Their activities range from organizing workshops, lectures, discussions, and meetings with and for partner institutions, youth groups, and interested peace activists, including artists, journalists, students, and teachers.

19 Nablus Road   *Contact:* Saman Khoury, Founder
P.O. Box 19315
East-Jerusalem
Palestine

Tel/Fax: +972 (2) 627 6718
info@pdf-palestine.org
http://www.pdf-palestine.org

People's Campaign for Peace and Democracy

The People's Campaign for Peace and Democracy (HASHD) is a Palestinian organization promoting grassroots support for the People's Voice initiative of Ami Ayalon and Sari Nusseibeh since 2002. The initiative calls for a two-state final settlement based on, inter alia, the 1967 borders with agreed one-to-one territorial exchange, no return of Palestinian refugees to Israel, no Jewish settlement in the Palestinian state, and free access to the holy sites in Jerusalem, which would have special status. In the first year and a half of its existence, HASHD gained 160,000 Palestinian and 254,000 Israeli expressions of support. The organization also aims to develop democratic awareness and participation in Palestinian civil society. It is a membership organization composed of local committees.

The Old Chamber of Commerce
  Building, 5th Floor
Al-Rashid Street
East-Jerusalem
Palestine

P.O. Box 51000
Jerusalem
Palestine

Tel/Fax: +972 (2) 628 4742
hashdpls@yahoo.com
http://www.hashd.org

Contact: Dimitri Diliani, Member of the Executive Council

Number of staff: 42

The Regional Council of the Bedouin Palestinian Unrecognized Villages in the Negev

ACTION
ADVOCACY

The Regional Council of the Bedouin Palestinian Unrecognized Villages in the Negev was established in 1997 as a community-based nongovernmental organization for Palestinian Bedouin equality in the Negev. The Regional Council consists of 22 elected heads of village local committees who advocate for social change and economic justice for their communities. The Regional Council works to achieve its goals through the implementation of the following programs: political mobilization to represent unrecognized village needs on the Israeli political agenda, promotion of democracy through local elections and community development work, and training and skill development.

Hazmaout 47
P.O. Box 10002
Beer Sheva
Israel

Tel: +972 (8) 628 3043
Fax: +972 (8) 628 3315
qura@rcuv.org
http://www.rcuv.org

Contact: Maha Qupty, Human Resource Coordinator

Sabeel Ecumenical Liberation Theology Center

EDUCATION
ACTION

The Sabeel Ecumenical Liberation Theology Center is an grassroots ecumenical liberation movement of Palestinian Christians. It began as an ad hoc committee in 1989 and was established as a permanent institution in 1990. Realizing that it has become a necessity to think about justice and peace on a theological level, Sabeel strives to develop a spirituality based on justice, peace, nonviolence, liberation, and reconciliation for different nationalities and faith communities. It offers leadership training for committed, responsible members of society, especially women, youth, and clergy. It also organizes an international awareness campaign and a project that allows visitors to experience the reality of living under the occupation.

P.O. Box 49084
91491 Jerusalem
Palestine

Tel: +972 (2) 532 7136
Fax: +972 (2) 532 7137
sabeel@sabeel.org
http://www.sabeel.org

Contact: Rev. Naim Ateek, Director
Number of staff: 11
Publications: Cornerstone, quarterly newsletter. Document series, *A Christian Palestinian Life,* 2003; *The Jerusalem Sabeel Document: Principles for a Just Peace in Israel-Palestine,* 2004

Ta'awon

RESEARCH
EDUCATION
ACTION
ADVOCACY

Ta'awon is a Palestinian youth nongovernmental organization founded in 2002 on the belief that volunteerism, peace, and democracy can be part of a new Palestine. Working mostly with young people between 15 and 24 years old, they try to build a civic and democratic society, to expand the knowledge of conflict resolution, and to further the possibilities of a culture of peace and democracy among Palestinian youth. Toward this end, Ta'awon organizes training and assemblies for young people, while trying to influence both Palestinians and policymakers on youth issues, like gender inequalities, elections, and unemployment. Ta'awon also carries out research and coordinates community projects such as distributing school bags, winter necessities, or Ramadan breakfasts to Palestinian school children or students that suffer under the difficult circumstances of the occupation.

MBC Bldg. First Floor
Ramallah 00970
Palestine
_____
Tel/Fax: +972 (2) 96 7930
taawon@taawon4youth.org
http://www.taawon4youth.org

Contact: Khaled Salim, Director

Number of staff: 12

Publications: Member contributions on the website, brochures, newsletters, administration reports

Wi'am–Palestinian Conflict Resolution Center

EDUCATION
ACTION

Wi'am–Palestinian Conflict Resolution Center was founded in 1995 as a grassroots organization aimed at building a democratic and just society by addressing injustices instead of avoiding them, dignifying persons on both sides of the conflict, promoting human rights, and advocating for peace among all groups. General activities of Wi'am focus on *Sulha,* which looks to resolve interpersonal conflicts through traditional Palestinian techniques, trainings, and workshops on conflict related topics, and youth activities from entertainment to education and community outreach both in social and financial support and international projects. Recently initiated programs include trauma healing, domestic violence counseling, examining increased emigration, stress-related sicknesses, displaced frustration, violent responses, and drug usage.

P.O. Box 1039
Bethlehem, West Bank
Palestine
_____
Tel. +972 (2) 277 0513
Fax. +972 (2) 277 7333
alaslah@planet.edu
http://www.planet.edu/~
   alaslah/index.html

Contact: Zoughbi Zoughbi, Director

Number of staff: 6

Publications: Annual reports, articles on current issues in Palestine. *Sulha: Palestinian Traditional Peacemaking Process,* 1996. *Folded Pages from Local Palestinian History in the Twentieth Century. Your Stories Are My Stories.*

Alternative Information Center

The Alternative Information Center (AIC) is a joint Palestinian-Israeli organization, which was founded in 1984. Their primary work is to disseminate information, research, and political analysis on Palestinian and Israeli societies as well as the Israeli-Palestinian conflict. Their offices are located in Jerusalem and Bethlehem. The AIC tries to promote cooperation between Palestinians and Israelis based on the values of social justice, solidarity, and community involvement. They publish a magazine nine times a year called *News from Within*. They will be publishing editions in Arabic called *Rou'ya Oukhra* in the near future.

34 Ben Yehuda St
  (City Tower) Suite 512
P.O. Box 31417
Jerusalem 91313
Israel
_____
Tel: +972 (2) 624 1159
Fax: +972 (2) 625 3151

Al-Maraqa Bldg. Bab-el-zqaq
Bethlehem
Palestine
_____
Tel/Fax: +972 (2) 2777558/9
aic@alt-info.org
http://www.alternativenews.org

Contact: Michael Warschawsky, Director

Number of staff: 7

Publications: News from Within,
published nine times a year. Reports from the occupied territories and Israel. Fact sheets and annual reports from the organization.

RESEARCH
ADVOCACY

Coalition of Women for a Just Peace

Ten Israeli women's groups make up the Coalition of Women for a Just Peace, who organized themselves in 2000 to coordinate the worldwide Women In Black vigil on June 8, 2001. The Jewish and Palestinian women members of the coalition are all citizens of Israel, agreeing to coordinate and organize joint activities in order to work together for a just peace based on the following principles: an end to the occupation; the full involvement of women in negotiations for peace; establishment of the state of Palestine side by side with the state of Israel based on the 1967 borders; the recognition of Jerusalem as the shared capital of two states; Israeli recognition of its share of responsibility for the results of the 1948 War and cooperation in finding a just solution for the Palestinian refugees; equality, inclusion, and justice for Palestinian citizens of Israel; opposition to the militarism that permeates Israeli society; equal rights for women and all residents of Israel; and social and economic justice for Israel's citizens and their integration in the region. The Coalition of Women for a Just Peace is a mix of Jewish and Palestinian women (all citizens of Israel) who call upon Israel to end the occupation and negotiate a just solution. The Coalition has been engaged in protest, nonviolent direct action, and advocacy inside Israel and the occupied territories.

Tel: +972 53 334 986
info@coalitionofwomen4peace.org
http://www.coalitionofwomen4peace.org/

Contact: Gila Svirsky, Volunteer

Number of staff: 5

EDUCATION
ACTION

Crossing Borders

Crossing Borders (CB) is a project for Israeli (both Jewish and Arab), Palestinian, and Jordanian youth, founded in October 1999 on the idea that it is important to involve youth in the process of working for a better tomorrow in the Middle East. It provides young people with a dynamic forum for self-expression, creating in that way a network to make contact, share experiences, exchange ideas, and learn from each other. Further main activities of Crossing Borders are the publication of a bimonthly magazine, a two-week summer course in Denmark, and intensive training in basic journalism, conflict management, communication skills, and the role of the media.

P.O. Box 51458
Jerusalem 91514
Israel
_____
Tel. +972 (2) 647 6054/5/6
Fax. +972 (2) 647 6057
cb@crossingborder.org
http://www.crossingborder.org

Contact: Hanna Saniora

Number of staff: 8

Publications: Crossing Borders,
a bimonthly Mideast youth
magazine.

The Economic Cooperation Foundation

ACTION
ADVOCACY

The Economic Cooperation Foundation (ECF) based in Tel Aviv, was founded by former Israeli Justice Minister Dr. Yossi Beilin, Dr. Ron Pundak, and Dr. Yair Hirschfeld at the end of 1990 as a nonprofit nongovernmental organization that would build, maintain, and support Israeli-Palestinian and Israeli-Arab cooperation in the political, economic, and civil society spheres. The ECF acts as a facilitator, initiator, catalyst, and implementer in a number of health and social welfare related projects, bringing the partners together and assisting with proposal writing, fund raising, permit arrangement, and other technical matters. Contacts among Drs. Pundak and Hirschfeld and Palestinian academics led directly to the diplomatic negotiations that resulted in some elements of the Oslo Accords.

4 Hashalom Rd.
Tel Aviv 67892
Israel

Contact: Yair Hirschfeld, Director

Tel: +972 (3) 561 4422
Fax: +972 (3) 561 8040
ecf@ecf.org.il
http://www.ecf.org.il

The Families Forum— The Parents' Circle

EDUCATION
ADVOCACY

Members of The Families Forum (also known as Israeli-Palestinian Bereaved Families for Peace and The Parents' Circle) include hundreds of Israeli and Palestinian bereaved families who have lost, as a result of the Israeli-Arab conflict, an immediate family member and have accepted the principles and objectives of the Forum. It was founded in 1995, but officially established in 1998. The Families Forum acts to prevent further bereavement, which is threatening the peoples in the region as a result of the absence of peace. The Forum members believe in an end to occupation, termination of hostility, and achievement of a political settlement. To this end, they work to influence the public and policymakers to adopt moves toward mutual reconciliation and understanding. Members of the Forum partake in joint Israeli-Palestinian seminars and engage in educational activities in high schools as well as other venues to convey their message. The Families Forum attaches major importance to activities of support within the organization and among its members.

Hayasmin 1 Street
Ramat-Efal, 52960
Israel
_____

Tel: +972 (3) 535 5089
Fax: +972 (3) 635 8367

Ibn Battuta 14 Street
East Jerusalem
Israel
_____

Tel: +972 (2) 627 5022
Fax: +972 (2) 627 5018
parents@theparentscircle.com
http://www.theparentscircle.org/

Contact: Boaz Kitain, General Manager
Number of staff: 15
Publications: Tears of Peace, a film. Various brochures, presentations, documentary films, stickers, and information material.

RESEARCH
ACTION

Friends of the Earth Middle East

Friends of the Earth Middle East (FoEME, formerly EcoPeace) is the Middle East chapter of Friends of the Earth International. FoEME has been bringing together Jordanian, Palestinian, and Israeli environmentalists since 1994. Its primary objective is to promote cooperative efforts to protect the shared environmental heritage and in so doing to advance sustainable regional development and the creation of necessary conditions for peace. Projects focus on transboundary ecosystems such as the Dead Sea Basin, Gulf of Aqaba, Eastern Mediterranean, and other water resources. Projects also cover key environmental and social issues, such as trade and investment, with a focus on a Euro-Mediterranean partnership, renewable energy, and advocating a Middle East perspective in global environmental issues, international organizations, and programs.

Nehalat Benyamin 85,
Tel-Aviv, 66102
Israel

Tel: +972 (3) 560 5383
Fax: +972 (3) 560 4693
info@foeme.org

Friends of the Earth Middle East/WEDO
P.O. Box 421
Bethlehem, Palestine

Tel: +972 (2) 274 7948
Fax: +972 (2) 274 5968
wedo@p-ol.com
http://www.foeme.org/

Contact: Gidon Bromberg, Israeli Director; Nader Khateb, Palestinian Director

Number of staff: 15 (combined offices)

Publications: Environment Middle East Watch Quarterly Newsletter. Euro-Mediterranean Free Trade Zone: Implications for Sustainability: Case Studies, Assessments and Recommendations, 2000. Let the Dead Sea Live, 1999. A Solar Bridge for Peace Building, 1999.

The Friendship Village

The Friendship Village is a center for educating young Israelis and Palestinians to live in a multicultural environment. Through well-structured workshops, seminars, and more informal and spontaneous education methods, participants are taught to respect and learn about the "other" and to recognize and build on what is common between people of different backgrounds. Through cooperation projects and campaigns, the wider message for peace is supported. The Friendship Village grew out of Re'ut Sadaka, a youth movement, and was officially established in 1996. Although much work still needs to be done on the "village" itself, which will host a seminar center, the School for Coexistence, a study center, and living quarters, the educational program was launched in 1998.

P.O. Box 36686
Tel Aviv 61366
Israel

Tel: +972 (9) 898 2694
Fax: +972 (9) 894 1158
friendshipvillage_2001@yahoo.com
http://www.friendshipvillage.org.il

Contact: Jonathan Peled, General Director

Number of Staff: 12

Publications: Articles and documents on the Middle East conflicts, Israeli society, and Palestinian society. A series on *Voices of Peace from Palestine and the Arab World.*

Israeli/Palestinian Centre for Research and Information

RESEARCH
EDUCATION
ADVOCACY

The Israeli/Palestinian Centre for Research and Information (IPCRI), founded in Jerusalem in 1988, is a joint Israeli-Palestinian public policy think tank devoted to developing practical solutions for the Israeli-Palestinian conflict. It was originally launched to promote dialogue at various levels between the Israeli and Palestinian civil societies. Research and fieldwork is organized into five areas: Strategic Analysis Department dealing with final status proposals; Law and Development Department working on issues of civil society, commercial law reform, and economic relations; Environment and Water Department addressing environmental and land and water use issues; Pathways Into Reconciliation Department providing training in teaching skills in multinational peace education; and Joint Environmental Mediation Services focusing on techniques to resolve environmental disputes. Activities organized by IPCR include ongoing roundtable discussions, conferences, commissioned research, and library and database resources.

P.O. Box 9321
Jerusalem 91092
Israel

Tel: +972 (2) 676 9460
Fax: +972 (2) 676 8011
ipcri@ipcri.org
http://www.ipcri.org/

Contact: Gerson Baskin and Zakaria al Qaq, Co-Directors

Number of staff: 12

Publications: Creating a Culture of Peace, 1999. Trilateral Confederation: A New Political Vision for Peace—The Just Way to Peaceful Coexistence on Both Sides of the Jordan River, 1999. A Revaluation of the Border Industrial Estates Concept, 1998. Guidelines for Final Status Economic Negotiations Between Israel and Palestine. Various papers and articles on Jerusalem, settlements, economy and trade, refugee issues, and the peace process.

Israeli-Palestinian Peace Coalition

RESEARCH
EDUCATION
ACTION
ADVOCACY

The Israeli-Palestinian Peace Coalition (IPPC) was formed in 2002 by a group of leading politicians, academics, nongovernmental organization activists, and cultural figures. The common denominator for the founding members was concern over the absence of a formal peace process, the assertion of the existence of partners for peace on both sides, and the mutual belief in an alternative to terror and militarism. IPPC's platform calls for a two-state solution, a divided Jerusalem, and a resolution to the Palestinian refugee issue. Their joint Israeli-Palestinian activities include: demonstrations against violence and occupation, political statements, media campaigns, open forums and conferences, youth development workshops overseas, and local and international advocacy.

P.O. Box 29828
Tel Aviv 61297
Israel

Tel: +972 (3) 566 3291
Fax: +972 (3) 566 3286

Contact: Lee Wilson
Number of staff: 4

EDUCATION

MidEast Web for Coexistence

MidEast Web for Coexistence is a news and information website designed to provide balanced news reporting; to promote and publicize dialogue, and people-to-people and educational projects; and to make nonviolence, tolerance, and rapprochement key values throughout society. MidEast Web was founded informally by Jews, Arabs, and others in 1999 and formally the next year to promote dialogue, coexistence, and peace education in the Middle East. The major goals of MidEast Web are: popularizing humanitarian values and humanizing the "other," envisioning a common reality, building a human network of those working for peace and understanding, and amplifying peace efforts. Also available through the website is the MidEast Webdialog, an e-mail forum begun in 2001 to encourage dialogue.

Hanassi Harishon 29
Rehovot 76302
Israel

Tel/Fax: +972 (8) 947 3603
mew@mideastweb.org
http://www.mideastweb.org

Contact: Ami Isseroff

Publications: Various articles published on the website.

EDUCATION
ACTION
ADVOCACY

Neve Shalom—Wahat al-Salam

Neve Shalom—Wahat al-Salam is a village that was jointly founded by Jews and Palestinian Arabs of Israeli citizenship to demonstrate the possibility of coexistence by developing a community based on mutual acceptance, respect, and cooperation. Established in 1972, it has since started projects on educational work for peace, equality, and understanding between the two peoples. Neve Shalom—Wahat al-Salam offers a bilingual children's education, which is also attended by children from surrounding villages. It has set up an outreach program named School for Peace that tries to spread the messages on which the village was founded. The village also features a Pluralistic Spiritual Center and a hotel, which offers accommodation and several cultural and educational programs.

Doar Na Shimshon 99761
Israel

Tel: +972 (2) 991 5621
Fax: +972 (2) 991 1072
info@nswas.org
http://www.nswas.org

Contact: Abdessalam Najjar, Elected Secretary General

Number of staff: 50–60

Publications: News articles and special documents. *Oasis of Dreams—The School for Peace: Identities in Dialogue,* 2004. *Autobiography of Founder Bruno Hassar. Dealing with Conflict: A Citizen Project for 14 to 18 Year Old Students*

ACTION
ADVOCACY

One Voice

One Voice is a platform set up after the failure of Camp David II in 2000. It looks to empower the moderate majority on both the Israeli and the Palestinian sides. Initiated by the PeaceWorks Foundation, an organization that believes that the Israeli-Palestinian conflict has been greatly exacerbated by small groups of radicals, One Voice sprung from the discussions of more then two hundred Palestinian and Israeli representatives on finding a viable and acceptable path of coexistence, based on the assumption that a majority of the two communities are desiring a moderate discourse and that there are solutions for the conflict that would suit both sides. One Voice has chosen to formulate different documents and proclamations that are spread around both communities to get support before they are presented to the public and politicians. An interactive negotiation form and a multimedia campaign are used to promote dialogue and raise awareness on their activities.

P.O. Box 2401
Ramalah
Palestine

Tel: +972 (2) 296 3843
Fax: +972 (2) 296 3849

15 Rothschild
Tel-Aviv 66881
Israel

Tel: +972 (3) 5168 005
Fax: +972 (3) 5166 119
contact@silentnolonger.org, info@silentnolonger.org
http://www.silentnolonger.org

Contact: Daniel Lubetzky, Founder and President

Number of staff: 15

Publications: One Voice monthly newsletter, press releases, articles, and opinion polls.

Re'ut Sadaka

Re'ut Sadaka is a Jewish-Arab Youth Movement for Coexistence and Peace in Israel. Established in 1983, the movement was founded on the idea that building mutual trust requires the fostering of real relationships. Seminars, workshops, fieldtrips, training programs, volunteer cooperation projects, lectures, coexistence, and multicultural activities are organized, creating a process of dialogue, promoting respect and tolerance, and preparing the young leaders of Israel to look at each other differently. Increasingly, Re'ut Sadaka is asked to organize workshops for other groups, and from this rose the idea for the Friendship Village, a center that offers an ongoing educational program.

Michaelangelo 29/6
Jaffa, 68092
Israel
_____
Tel/Fax: +972 (3) 518 2336
sadaka@netvision.net.il
http://www.reutsadaka.org

Contact: Fadi Shbeita, General Manager
Number of staff: 25
Publications: Newsletters and reports.

Seeds of Peace Center for Coexistence

The Seeds of Peace Center for Coexistence has worked to support Israeli and Palestinian teens in becoming leaders for peaceful coexistence within and between their communities since 1999. The Center is the clearinghouse for the follow-up activities of the Seeds of Peace organization in the Middle East. The Center provides administrative and follow-up support to Jewish and Arab participants in Seeds of Peace summer camp programs and conducts four-day intensive seminars with Israeli, Palestinian, and Jordanian youth. The activities are designed to allow the youth to teach each other about their culture, family, and identity. In 2003, Seeds of Peace launched its Advanced Coexistence Program in which Israelis and Palestinians come together for weekly meetings in four different locations from dozens of cities all over Israel, both sides of Jerusalem, and the West Bank.

P.O. Box 25045
Jerusalem 97300
Israel
_____
Tel: +972 (2) 582 0222
Fax: +972 (2) 582 2221
info@seedsofpeace.org
http://www.seedsofpeace.org

Contact: Tim Wilson, Director; Jen Marlowe, Program Director
Number of staff: 10
Publications: The Olive Branch quarterly magazine.

Selected Bibliography

Al-Aref, Aref, *Detailed History of Jerusalem* (Jerusalem: Al-Andalus, 2000).

Bar-On, Mordechai, *In Pursuit of Peace: A History of the Israeli Peace Movement* (Washington DC: United States Institute of Peace, 1996).

Bercovitch, Jacob, and Jeffrey Z. Rubin, eds., *Mediation in International Relations: Multiple Approaches to Conflict Management* (New York: St. Martin's Press, 1992).

Carey, Roan, and Jonathan Shainin, eds., *The Other Israel Voices of Refusal and Dissent* (New York: The New Press, 2002).

Chazan, Naomi, "Negotiating the Non-Negotiable: Jerusalem in the Framework of an Israeli-Palestinian Settlement," *Occasional Papers of the American Academy of Arts and Sciences,* no. 7 (March 1991).

Davies, John, and Edward (Edy) Kaufman, eds., *Second Track/Citizens Diplomacy: Concepts and Techniques of Conflict Transformation* (Lanham, MD: Rowman & Littlefield, 2003).

Flapan, Simha, ed., *When Enemies Dare to Talk: An Israeli-Palestinian Debate* (London: New Outlook/Croom Helm, 1979).

Gidron, Benjamin, Stanley N. Katz, and Yeheskel Hasenfeld, eds., *Mobilizing for Peace: Conflict Resolution in Northern Ireland, Israel/Palestine and South Africa* (Oxford: Oxford University Press 2002).

Hadi, Mahdi Abdul, ed., *Documents on Palestine: Volume 1, From the Pre-Ottoman Period to the Prelude of the Madrid Middle East Peace Conference* (Jerusalem: PASSIA 1997).

Hastings, Tom, *Meek Ain't Weak: Nonviolent Power and People of Color* (New York: University Press of America, 2002).

Hussein, Agha, Shai Feldman, Ahmad Khalidi, and Zeev Schiff, *Track II Diplomacy- Lessons from the Middle East* (Cambridge, MA: MIT Press, 2003).

Kaufman, Edy, "The Intifadah and the Peace Camp in Israel," *Journal of Palestine Studies,* vol. 17, no. 4 (summer 1988), pp. 66–80.

Kaufman, Edy, Shukri B. Abed, and Robert L. Rothstein, eds., *Democracy, Peace, and the Israeli-Palestinian Conflict* (Boulder, CO: Lynne Rienner Publishers, 1993).

Khalleh, Kamal Mohmoud, *Palestine and the British Mandate (1922–1939)* (Bierut, PLO Research Center, 1982).

Klein, Menachem, *The Jerusalem Problem: The Struggle for Permanent Status* (Gainesville: University of Florida Press, 2003).

Kriesberg, Louis, and Stuart J. Thorson, eds., *Timing the De-escalation of International Conflict* (Syracuse NY: Syracuse University Press, 1991).

McDonald, John, and Diane Bendahmane, eds., *Conflict Resolution: Track Two Diplomacy* (Washington DC: Foreign Service Institute, Department of State, 1987).

Melman, Yossi, and Dan Raviv, *Behind the Uprising: Israelis, Jordanians, and Palestinians* (Westport, CT: Greenwood Publishing Group, 1989).

Sharp, Gene, *The Politics of Non-Violent Action.* 3 Vols. (Boston: P. Sargent, 1973).

Stern, Paul, Alexander George, and Daniel Druckman, eds., *International Conflict Resolution: Techniques and Evaluation* (Washington DC: National Academy Press, 2000).

Stohlman, Nancy, and Laurieann Aladin, eds., *Live from Palestine: International and Palestinain Direct Action Against the Israeli Occupation* (Cambridge, MA: South End Press, 2003).

Weiner, Eugene, ed., *The Handbook of Interethnic Coexistence* (New York: Continuum, 1998).

The Contributors

Khaled Abu-Asbah is a teacher, educator, and sociologist and co-chair of Sikkuy: The Association for the Advancement of Civic Equality. Sikkuy is a Jewish-Arab advocacy organization working to advance civic equality between Arab and Jewish citizens of Israel. Abu-Asbah is a widely published expert on Arab youth and Arab education in Israel. He is director of the Massar Institute for Research, Strategic Planning and Educational Policy and a lecturer at the Beit Berl College. Abu-Asbah is also a senior staff member at the Mandel School for Educational Leadership in Jerusalem from which he graduated in 1995.

Mohammed Abu-Nimer is associate professor at the American University's School of International Service in International Peace and Conflict Resolution in Washington, DC, and director of the Peacebuilding and Development Institute. He has conducted research on dialogue for peace between Palestinians and Israelis, conflict resolution models in Muslim communities, interfaith dialogue, and evaluation of conflict resolution programs. As a practitioner, he has been conducting conflict resolution training workshops in many conflict areas around the world. He has published numerous books on these issues, including his latest, *Peacebuilding and Nonviolence in Islamic Context: Theory and Practice.* Abu-Nimer is co-founder and co-editor of the new *Journal of Peacebuilding and Development.*

Gershon Baskin is the founder and co-CEO of the Israel/Palestine Center for Research and Information (IPCRI). IPCRI is an Israeli-Palestinian public policy think tank located in Jerusalem and founded in 1988. He has been involved in Israeli-Palestinian relations for the past 27 years and has filled executive positions in government and in the NGO world since 1978. Baskin's op-ed pieces regarding issues concerning peace in the Middle East appear frequently in various newspapers and journals.

Mohammed S. Dajani is a Jerusalem-born scholar and peace activist. At present, he is chairman, board of directors of IPCRI; delegation leader at Seeds of Peace; founder and director at the American Studies Institute, Al-Quds University; director and founder, Jerusalem Studies and Research Institute; and director and founder of the ISBN Palestine Agency, Ramallah. Dajani frequently participates in local, regional, and international conference and is author or co-author of numerous academic books and articles both in English and Arabic. His peace vision can be viewed at www.bigdreamsmall hope.com.

Shalom (Shuli) Dichter, a civil society activist in Israel, has served as the co-dxecutive director of Sikkuy: The Association for the Advancement of Civic Equality since 1998. Sikkuy, based in Jerusalem, is a Jewish-Arab advocacy organization working to advance civic equality between Arab and Jewish citizens of Israel. Dichter has published, in Israel and internationally, numerous op-ed articles and essays on issues as equality and relations between Jews and Arabs in Israel. In 2004 Dichter was invited to present expert testimony before the Or State Commission of Inquiry examining the status of Israel's Arab citizens.

Manuel Hassassian is professor of international politics and relations. He is currently executive vice president of Bethlehem University. He has published extensively on the Palestine Liberation Organization, the peace process, democracy and elections, refugees, and civil society in Palestine. Hassassian is a board members of the Center of Nonviolence in Palestine and a member of the Arab Association for Human Rights. He is also the head of the Jerusalem Task Force in the Negotiations Affairs Department.

Tamar Hermann is a political scientist specializing in grassroots politics. She is chair of the Democracy Studies MA program at the Open University of Israel and director of the Tami Steinmetz Center in Tel Aviv University. Her publications focus mainly on Israeli public opinion and national foreign and security policymaking as well as on protest movements and peace activism in the context of the Middle East conflict.

Edward (Edy) Kaufman has served as the executive director of the Harry S. Truman Research Institute for the Advancement of Peace at the Hebrew University of Jerusalem since 1983. He has also been, since 1991, senior research associate at the Centre for International Development & Conflict Management, University of Maryland, College Park, having served as the center's director from 1994–1996. Kaufman has dedicated a great part of his time to applied research, the teaching and training of conflict resolution, and human rights in Israel and worldwide.

Menachem Klein is senior lecturer in the Department of Political Science at Bar-Ilan University, Israel. In 2000 he was an external expert adviser for Jerusalem Affairs and Israel-PLO Final Status Talks to the Israeli delegation. Since 1996 he has been active in many unofficial negotiations with Palestinian counterparts. In October 2003 Klein signed, together with prominent Israeli and Palestinian negotiators, the Geneva Agreement—a detailed proposal for a comprehensive Israeli-Palestinian peace accord.

Riad Malki is a writer and researcher. He was professor at Birzeit University from 1981 to 1996 and founder and director of the Panorama Center for the Dissemination of Democracy and Community Development since 1991. He holds several positions, including vice president of the Palestinian Council of Justice and Peace; member of the Steering Committee of the World Movement for Democracy; board member of the Euro-Arab Network of NGOs on Development; founder of the Mediterranean Charter for Peace; steering committee member of the Orient House in Jerusalem; and core team member of Palestinian Second Track Diplomacy. He is the recipient of the Humanitate European Peace Award in 2000, the World Democracy Courage Award in 2004, and the Italian Peace Award in 2005.

Walid Salem was born in East Jerusalem in 1957. He is a writer and also a consultant, evaluator, and trainer for several public and private bodies and, since 1993, is the director of Jerusalem office of the Panorama Center for Democracy and Community Development, East Jerusalem. He is the representative of Panorama in the Arabic NGOs' Network, coordinator of Middle East Citizen Assembly, and coordinator of the Bringing Peace Together project. He lectures at international conferences and seminars about democracy, Jerusalem, refugees, and development in Palestine.

Juliette Verhoeven is senior staff member at the European Centre for Conflict Prevention and the International Secretariat of the Global Partnership for the Prevention of Armed Conflicts, where she coordinates the research program and the activities related to the Middle East. She has co-edited several publications on issues related to conflict prevention and peacebuilding, including *Searching for Peace in Europe and Eurasia* (2002) and *People Building Peace II: Successful Stories of Civil Society,* published in 2005.

Index

About the Book

In the midst of the continuing violence of the Israeli-Palestinian conflict, there are many who remain committed to moving forward on the road to peace. The Palestinian and Israeli contributors to this book, recognizing the great potential of civil society and NGOs for the peacebuilding process, focus on realistic opportunities for conflict transformation.

Drawing from the experiences of the post-Oslo period—seeking to learn from the mistakes that have been made—the authors concentrate on possibilities for just solutions that will enable both peoples to live in peace, safety, and prosperity. Their work is part of the Searching for Peace Series, a program of the European Centre for Conflict Prevention.

Edy Kaufman is senior research associate at the Harry S. Truman Research Institute for the Advancement of Peace, Hebrew University of Jerusalem. **Walid Salem** is director of the Jerusalem Office of Panorama, the Palestinian Center for the Dissemination of Democracy and Community Development. **Juliette Verhoeven** is research coordinator and Middle East and Central Asia coordinator at the European Centre for Conflict Prevention.

About the European Centre
for Conflict Prevention

The European Centre for Conflict Prevention is a nongovernmental organization, based in the Netherlands, that promotes effective conflict prevention and peacebuilding strategies, and actively supports and connects people working for peace worldwide. It currently holds the secretariat for the Global Partnership for the Prevention of Armed Conflict.

European Centre for Conflict Prevention
Laan van Meerdervoort 70
2517 AN Den Haag
the Netherlands

Tel.: + 31 70 3110970
Fax: + 31 70 3600194
info@conflict-prevention.net
www.conflict-prevention.net
www.gppac.net

Other European Centre for Conflict Prevention titles published by Lynne Rienner Publishers:

People Building Peace II: Successful Stories of Civil Society, eds., Paul van Tongeren, Malin Brenk, Marte Hellema, and Juliette Verhoeven, 2005

Searching for Peace in Asia Pacific: An Overview of Conflict Prevention and Peacebuilding Activities, eds., Annelies Heijmans, Nicola Simmonds, and Hans van de Veen, 2004

Searching for Peace in Central and South Asia: An Overview of Conflict Prevention and Peacebuilding Activities, eds., Monique Mekenkamp, Paul van Tongeren, and Hans van de Veen, 2002

Searching for Peace in Europe and Eurasia: An Overview of Conflict Prevention and Peacebuilding Activities, eds., Paul van Tongeren, Hans van de Veen, and Juliette Verhoeven, 2002